American Sunday-School Union, Edwin W. Rice

A Pictorial Commentary on the Gospel Accoding to Mark

American Sunday-School Union, Edwin W. Rice

A Pictorial Commentary on the Gospel Accoding to Mark

ISBN/EAN: 9783337887070

Printed in Europe, USA, Canada, Australia, Japan

Cover: Foto ©Lupo / pixelio.de

More available books at **www.hansebooks.com**

PICTORIAL COMMENTARY

ON THE

GOSPEL ACCORDING TO MARK.

WITH THE TEXT

OF THE

AUTHORIZED AND REVISED VERSIONS.

EDITED BY

Rev. EDWIN W. RICE.

PHILADELPHIA:
THE AMERICAN SUNDAY-SCHOOL UNION,
No. 1122 CHESTNUT STREET.

NEW YORK: 8 & 10 BIBLE HOUSE, ASTOR PLACE; CHICAGO: 73 RANDOLPH ST.

INTERNATIONAL LESSONS FOR 1882.

While this Commentary aims to present for permanent use the important interpretations and timely applications of the sacred text, as suggested or accepted by the most learned and devout of European and American scholars, it will also be found specially adapted to aid pastors, superintendents, teachers, and scholars in the study of the International Sunday School Lessons. These lessons for 1882 are all in this gospel alone, and this *Commentary*, by its simplicity of language, clear topical divisions, with practical teachings at the end of each, its terseness of statement and aptness of illustration, will prove particularly helpful to those who cannot find time to read long expositions and many works in preparing the Sabbath lesson. A careful selection of the best that has been written is here presented in a compact form. For list of lessons for 1882 see p. 24.

Entered according to act of Congress, in the year 1881, by
THE AMERICAN SUNDAY SCHOOL UNION,
In the office of the Librarian of Congress, Washington.

TO THE READER.

Whoever hopes to gain instruction without attention or study, had better lay this book down before reading another line. Knowledge worth having cannot be had without labor.

The value of this work can soon be tested by use. The *Revised Version* of the New Testament has greatly diminished the value of all commentaries based on the current "Authorized Version," and rendered some of them misleading and next to worthless. *The design* of this "Pictorial Commentary" is to furnish for the English reader a commentary on the *Revised* as well as the "Authorized" Version, and one representing the latest accepted results of Biblical scholarship in explanation of Mark's Gospel. The full texts of the Authorized and of the Revised versions, therefore, are presented in parallel columns, at the head of each page.

In preparing this work the aim has been:

(1) to make no comment on what needed none;

(2) to explain whatever called for explanation, and to point out some inferences which might be overlooked by the ordinary reader;

(3) not to pass any obscure or difficult passage without giving some solution which the best scholars have offered;

(4) to state important explanations in the language, when practicable, of some leading expositor, giving his name;

(5) yet not to quote half a dozen expositors holding contradictory views on the same point, and leave the reader buried under this mass of contradictions. Having only partial statements before him, he would be quite as likely to miss, as to apprehend, the view supported by the greatest weight of scholarship. It is the work of the true author to guide his readers to a correct conclusion, and this has been the sincere aim of the writer of this work;

(6) to glean from the best works of eminent Biblical scholars and critics, from the apostolic age to the present, especially those of Post-apostolic writers and of the latest Biblical critics;

(7) to give particular attention to the events connected with our Lord's last Passover, his arrest and trial, and resurrection. The principal charge in the accusation against him before the Council and Pilate is brought out with greater clearness, it is believed, than in other current commentaries;

(8) to impress some practical lessons suggested by eminent and devout men of God, at the end of each of the topical divisions;

(9) in the introduction, to present briefly the results of recent scholarship in respect to the authorship, style, character and contents of Mark's

Gospel, with a special note on the disputed portion, at the close of the Gospel;

(10) to introduce illustrations, not for ornament, but to bring in the aid of the eye in explaining and impressing Scriptural truth.

The chronology indicated in the notes is that of Robinson, modified by Andrews.

The maps of Palestine are from the latest productions of Messrs. W. & A. K. Johnston, Edinburgh. The chart of the journeys of our Lord is from Alford's "New Testament for English Readers."

Especial aid has been derived from the Cambridge Bible for Schools, by J. J. S. Perowne and G. F. Maclear; from the recent commentaries of Ellicott and Canon Cook, and from the works of Farrar, Andrews, and Geikie, on the Life of Christ. A list of other leading authorities consulted is elsewhere given.

The reader will find the careful comparison of the Revised text with that of the King James' Version of great value. It will frequently show why no comment is made on phrases noted in commentaries confined to the Authorized Version, the *Revision* having removed the obscurity from a large number of passages.

The immense progress in Biblical knowledge in the past few years, and especially the issue of the Revised New Testament, imperatively demand new Commentaries in order that the student of God's word may be "ready always to give answer to every man that asketh you a reason concerning the hope that is in you."—1 Pet. iii, 15, Revised Version.

Philadelphia, November, 1881.

LIST OF LEADING AUTHORITIES CITED.

A.

Abbot, Ezra.
Abbott, Lyman.
Addison, Joseph, 1719.
Alexander, Archibald, 1851.
Alexander, Joseph Addison.
Alford, Henry, 1871.
Ambrose, Isaac, 397 A. D.
Andrews, S. J.
Athanasius, The Great, 373 A. D
Augustine, Aurelius, 430 A. D.

B.

Barclay, J. T.
Barnes, Albert.
Barrow, Isaac, 1677.
Baur, F. C.
Baxter, Richard, 1691.
Beecher, Henry Ward.
Bellarmine, Robert, 1621
Bengel, J. A., 1752.
Bentley, Richard, 1742.
Beza, Theodore, 1605.
Bleek, W. H. I.
Bloomfield, S. T.
Boardman, Henry A.
Bochart, Samuel, 1667.
Bonar, Horatius.
Brentius, Brentz, 1570.
Brookes, Thomas, 1680.
Brown, David.
Bucer, Martin, 1551.
Buchanan, Claudius.
Burgon, J. W.
Burkitt, William.
Butler, Bish. Joseph, 1752.
Buxtorf, John, 1629.

C.

Calvin, John, 1564.
Campbell, George, 1796.
Chalmers, Thomas, 1847.
Chrysostom, John, 407.
Clark, George W.
Clarke, Adam, 1832.
Clement, of Rome, 2d Century.
Conant, Thomas J.
Cook, Canon F. C.
Cranmer, Thomas, 1556.
Cyprian, Thascius C., 258 A. D.
Cyril of Alexandria, 444 A. D.
Cyril of Jerusalem, 386 A. D.

D.

Da Costa, J. M.
Davidson, Samuel, 1851.
Davis, Samuel, 1761.
Derenbourg, M.
De Wette, W. M. L., 1849.
Doddridge, Philip, 1751.
Dupin, M.
Dwight, Timothy, 1817.

E.

Ebrard, J. H. A.
Edersheim, Alfred.
Edwards, Jonathan, 1758.
Ellicott, Charles J.
Emerson, Ralph Waldo.
Erasmus, D., 1536.
Eusebius, Pamphili, 340 A. D.
Evans, Christmas.
Ewald, G. H. A., 1875.

F.

Fairbairn, P.
Farrar, Frederic W.
Fuller, Andrew, 1815.

G.

Geikie, Cunningham.
Gerlach, Otto Von.
Gerhard, E.
Gill, John, 1771.
Godwin, John H.
Gray, J. Comper.
Greenleaf, Simon.
Greswell, Edward, 1837.
Grotius, Hugo, 1645.

H.

Hackett, Horatio B.
Hales, William, 1814.
Haley, John W.
Hall, John.
Hall, Bish. Joseph, 1556.
Halyburton, Thomas, 1712.
Hengstenberg, E. W.
Henry, Matthew, 1714.
Hermas, Shepherd of, 141 A. D.
Hickok, Laurens P.
Hitchcock, Edward, 186
Hooker, Richard, 1600.
Hooper, Bish. John, 1554.
Hort, F. J. A.
Howson, J. S.

I.

Ignatius, St., 115 A. D.
Irenæus, St., 202 A. D.

J.

Jacobus, M. W.
Jahn, Johann, 1816.
Jerome, St., 419.
Josephus, Flavius, 103 A. D.

K.

Kitto, John, 1854.
Krafft.
Kuinoel, Chr. G., 1841.

L.

Lange, John Peter.
Lewin, Thomas.
Lichtenstein, F. W. J.
Lightfoot, John, 1675.
Lightfoot, J. B.
Lowth, Robert, 1787.
Lücke, G. C. F., 1855.
Luthardt, Christian E.
Luther, Martin, 1546.

M.

Maclear, G. F.
McCheyne, Robert, 1843.
McCosh, James.
McGregor J. (Rob Roy).
McKnight, James.
Maldonatus, John, 1583.
Mansel, H. L., 1871.
Martyr, Justin, 164 A. D.
Melancthon, Philip, 1560.
Meyer, H. A. W.
Miller, Hugh.
Miller, Samuel, 1850.
Milton, John, 1674.
Mimpriss, Robert.
Moody, D. L.

N.

Newcome, William, 1800.
Nicodemus, Gospel of.
Norton, Andrews, 1846.

O.

Olshausen, Hermann.
Osiander, Andreas.
Owen, John J.

P.

Paley, William.
Patrick, Simon, 1707.
Payson, Edward.
Penn, Granville, 1844.
Perowne, J. J. S.
Petter, George, 1661.
Phelps, Austin.
Pliny, 79 A. D.
Plumptre, E. H.
Plutarch, 120 A. D.
Poole, Matthew, 1679.
Porteus, Beilby, 1808.
Post, George E.

Q.

Quesnel, Pasquier, 1719.

R.

Regginbach, C. J.
Reland, Hadr, 1718.
Riddle, Joseph Esmond.
Ripley, Henry J.
Robinson, Edward, 1863.
Romaine, William, 1795.
Rosenmüller, Ernst F. K., 1835.
Rutherford, Samuel, 1661.
Ryle, J. C.

S.

Salvador, Joseph.
Schaff, Philip.
Schauffler, W. G.
Schleiermacher. Fredk. E. D., 1834
Scott, Thomas, 1821.
Scrivener, F. H.
Shakespeare, William, 1616
Shedd, Wm. G. T.
Smith, J. Pye.
Smith, William.
Spurgeon, C. H.
Stanley, Arthur P.
Starke, Christopher, 1744.
Stier, Rudolph.
Stock, Eugene.
Strabo, Pontus, B. C. 25.
Strong, James.
Sumner, Arch. J. B., 1862.
Suetonius, Caius, A. D. 117.

T.

Tacitus, C. Cornelius, first century.
Taylor, Isaac.
Taylor, Jeremy, 1667.
Tertullian, Quintus, third century.
Theodoret, 393.
Tholuck, Fredk. A. G.
Thompson, William M.
Thomson, Archbishop
Tischendorf, L. F. C., 1874.
Tobler, Titus, 1877.
Townsend, George, 1827.
Trapp, John, 1669.
Tregelles, S. P., 1875.
Trench, Richard C.
Tristram, H. B.
Tyndale, William, 1536.

V.

Van Dyck, C. V. A.
Van Lennep, Henry J.
Vincent, John H.

W.

Walker, James B.
Weiss, John.
Wesley, John, 1791.
Wetstein, Johann Jacob, 1754.
Westcott, B. F.
Whateley, Richard, 1836.
Whedon, D. D.
Whiston, William.
Whitby, Daniel, 1726.
Wieseler, Karl.
Williams, George.
Winer, Geo. Benedict, 1858.
Wordsworth, Bish. Christopher.
Wyclif, John De, 1384.

Z.

Zwingle, Ulrich, 1531.

GOSPEL ACCORDING TO MARK.

INTRODUCTION.

A general history of the Kingdom of God, or of Redemption, includes a complete history of the human race, viewed in its religious character: *Biblical history* relates the founding and extension of that kingdom, as it has been recorded by inspired authors, in the two great divisions of the Bible: the Old Testament and the New Testament. There are two natural divisions of the New Testament narratives: (1) *the Gospel history;* (2) *the Apostolical history.* The Gospel history, in the time it covers, is one of the smallest divisions of sacred history; yet, as containing the centre and core of all history, it is by far the most important, and intrinsically the grandest of all. It is the inspired account of the life, labors, and instructions of Jesus, the Christ, the Son of God. This history has come to us in a fourfold form; four portraitures, four Gospel narratives, yet but *one* Gospel.* While there is surprising freedom and diversity of topics, arrangement, and expression, they all exhibit to us the same great subject and the same wonderful life of Christ, far more harmoniously than Xenophon and Plato have presented to us their teacher, Socrates.†

Origin of the Gospels. The four Gospels have been generally accepted as having been written by the four persons whose names they bear. Two of these were apostles, and two were associated with the apostles, as constant companions. All their narratives were written under special direction of the Holy Spirit, between the ascension of Christ and the fall of Jerusalem, A. D. 70. They were received by the early Christians as authentic accounts of the life, teachings, death, and resurrection of Jesus.

How Preserved. No autograph copy of a gospel written by the Evangelists, has been preserved. They are all lost, with little hope of discovery, as they were probably written on the brittle papyrus then in use. A few specimens only of this paper have been preserved, accidentally, in Egyptian tombs and mummies, and in the lava at Pompeii.‡ Other copies and versions were made in great numbers by those succeeding the Apostles, and some of these are still preserved. Constantine the Great ordered Eusebius (died in 340) to make fifty MS. copies of the Scriptures, and some, as Tischendorf, think it probable that the Sinaitic MS. is one of these fifty.

---

* See Ulhorn, *Life of Jesus,* Am. Ed. pp. 78–114.

† J. A. Alexander, on Mark, p. vi.

‡ See Westcott and Hort Greek Testament, Am. Ed., p. xii.

7

The present Greek text of the Gospels is derived from three sources: I. Greek MSS.; II. Ancient versions; III. Quotations by the Early Fathers.

I. GREEK MSS. The MS. copies of the N. T. now in existence are of two classes: (1) *The Uncials*, or those written in capital letters, which are the oldest, dating from the fourth to the tenth century. Dr. Scrivener gives the whole number of Uncials, including lectionaries (*i. e.*, Scripture lessons), as 158; even his list is not complete. Professor Abbot reckons the whole number of *distinct* Uncial MSS. of the N. T., not including lectionaries, at 83, of which 61 have the Gospels in whole or in fragments. The five most important of these MSS. are the Sinaitic, the Vatican, the Alexandrian, codex Ephraim, and codex Bezæ. Another Uncial, probably of the sixth century, was discovered, in 1879, at Rossano, in Calabria, and is called codex Rossanensis. It was discovered by two German scholars, Gebhart and Harnack, and is written on purple-colored parchment, in silver letters, richly ornamented with pictures. Only portions of it have yet been made available for the use of scholars. (2) *The Cursives*, or MSS. written in a running hand, and dating from the tenth to the fifteenth century. There are known to be 1605 MSS. of this class, 600 of which are of the Gospels. This class of MSS. has been only partially examined or collated by critical scholars.

II. ANCIENT VERSIONS are a second source of the Greek text of the Gospels, and have aided in preserving and securing it to us. They are next in value to the MSS., and some of them are older witnesses than any MSS. in existence. Among the most important of the ancient Versions are: (1) the Syriac, which includes the Peshito, dating, in its oldest form, from the middle of the second century; the Philoxenian, of A. D. 508; the Curetonian fragment and the Jerusalem Syriac; (2) the Latin, including the old Italic, and the Vulgate of Jerome, A. D. 405 (which was the first book printed (A. D. 1455), and known as the Mazarin Bible); (3) the Ethiopic; (4) the Coptic, in two dialects, the Memphitic and Thebaic; (5) the Gothic of Ulphilas, of the fourth century; and (6) the Armenian versions of the fifth century.

III. QUOTATIONS FROM THE CHRISTIAN FATHERS include (1) *the Greek*, as Clement of Rome, Polycarp, Ignatius, Barnabas, of the first and second centuries, Justin Martyr, Irenæus, Clement of Alexandria, Origen, Eusebius, and others in the third and fourth centuries; (2) *the Latin*, as Tertullian, Cyprian, Novatian, Lactantius, Hilary, Ambrose, Pelagius, Augustin, and Jerome. About one hundred of these authors have been examined and their citations collated by various critics.

PRINTED EDITIONS OF THE GREEK TEXT. The most important of the printed editions of the Greek Text of the Gospels and of the N. T. are those by Erasmus, 1516-1535; Stephens, 1546-1551; Beza, 1565-1588-9; Elzevirs, 1624-1641; the Complutensian, 1514-1522; by Wetstein, 1751-52; Griesbach, 1775-1806; Lachmann, 1831-1850; Tischendorf, 1864-1872; Tregel

Specimens of existing MSS. of the Scriptures.

ΤΟ ΤΗΣ ΕΥΣΕΒΕΙΑΣ ΜΥΣΤΗΡΙΟΝ ΟΣ Ε

4th Cent. Codex Sinaiticus.—1 Tim. iii. 16.
το της ευσεβειας | μυστηριον [θε late corr.] ος ε.

ΝΟΓΕΝΗΣ ΘΣ ΕΙΣ ΤΟΝ

4th Cent. Codex Sinaiticus.—John i. 18.
νογενης θ͞ε ο͞ς [ο ων corr.] εις τον.

ΣΤΑΣΙΣ ΚΑΙ ΟΥΔΕΝΙ ΟΥ ΔΕΝ ΕΙΠΟΝ ΕΦΟΒΟΥΝ ΤΟ ΓΑΡ: ΚΑΤΑ ΜΑΡΚΟΝ

4th Cent. Codex Vaticanus.—Mark xvi. 8.
στασις και ουδενι ου | δεν ειπον εφοβουν | το γαρ:

ΕΝ ΑΡΧΗ ΗΝ Ο ΛΟΓΟΣ ΚΑΙ Ο ΛΟΓΟΣ ΗΝ ΠΡΟΣ ΤΟΝ Θ͞Ν ΚΑΙ Θ͞Σ ΗΝ Ο ΛΟΓΟΣ

5th Cent. Codex Alexandrinus.—John i. 1.
Εν αρχη ην ο λογος και ο λογος ην | προς τον θ͞ε ο͞ς ν͞ και θ͞ε ο͞ς ς ην ο λογος.

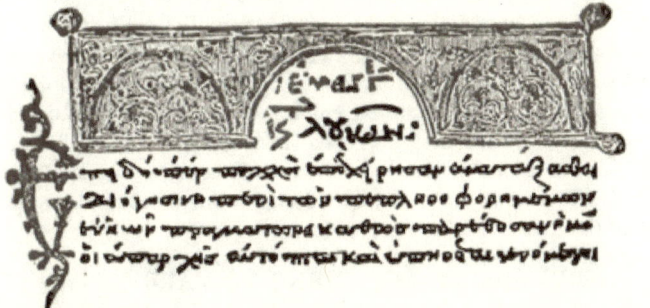

10th Cent. Codex Basiliensis, known to Erasmus, but little used by him.—Luke i. 1-2 nearly, as in all Greek Testaments.

GREEK MANUSCRIPTS OF THE N. T.

[From Schaff's Dictionary of the Bible.]

les, 1857-1879; Westcott and Hort, 1881. The English version of King James (1611) is based chiefly on the text of Beza and Stephens; the Revised version (1881) mainly on that of Westcott and Hort. The learned Richard Bentley, in 1720, proposed to issue an edition of the Greek Testament, by collating the oldest copies of the first five centuries, but his proposal led to a bitter controversy, which crushed the execution of his laudable scheme, set back Biblical criticism in England for more than a century, leaving it in the hands of German scholars, of some of whom it can justly be said, their devoutness was far less than their learning. The principles and plan which Bentley outlined, with rare critical discernment, have since been adopted as the only true or scientific method, and later scholars are reaping the rich results.

ENGLISH VERSIONS. The leading English versions are: Wiclif's or Wycliffe's, 1381; Tyndale's, 1525; Coverdale's, 1535; Matthew's or Rogers', 1537; Tavener's, 1539; the Great Bible, 1539; the Genevan, 1557 (this was the first that had the division into verses, following the Greek of Stephens, 1551); the Bishop's, 1568; the Rhemish, 1582; the King James' or so-called Authorized Version, 1611; the Revised Version, 1881.*

In this Commentary the Authorized and Revised versions are presented in parallel columns.

CHARACTERISTICS OF THE GOSPELS. The first three of the Gospel histories relate the birth, life, and chiefly the Galilean ministry of Jesus, and explain his dealings with men; the fourth presents more fully his Judæan ministry, and the deeper purposes and counsels of God, as revealed through His eternal Son. They are independent and distinct narratives, not one borrowed from another, but separate and trustworthy witnesses of the facts they record. Neither of them, however, intended to produce a *complete* history of the work and teachings of Jesus. Each account is designedly fragmentary, and all together, we may well believe, present but a small part of the teachings and transactions of the short but busy life of Christ on earth. Of the first readers for whom the Gospels were intended, it appears that Matthew wrote primarily for the Hebrews, Mark for the Gentiles, Luke for the learned heathen converts, John to exhibit Jesus as the Word made flesh, and as the Christ, the Son of God. See John i, 1; xx, 21. The early Christians assigned a special symbol for each Evangelist; to Matthew a bullock; to Mark a lion; Luke a man; John an eagle. The second and the briefest of the four Gospel narratives is

THE GOSPEL ACCORDING TO MARK.

The author has been universally believed to be Mark = *hammer*, and the same as John Mark, John, and Marcus. Acts xii, 12, 25; xiii, 5, 18; xv, 37, 39; Col. iv, 10; 2 Tim. iv, 11; Philem. 24. His mother's name

* See Schaff's *Dictionary of the Bible*, pp. 126-131.

was Mary, who resided at Jerusalem and was an aunt to Barnabas.* She was a person of repute, for the early Christians gathered at her house for prayer, and thither Peter repaired on his miraculous release from prison. Mark was probably converted to Christianity under the instructions of Peter (1 Pet. v, 13), and some conjecture that he was the young man that followed Jesus on the night of the betrayal. He became the companion of Paul and Barnabas, on their first missionary journey, about A.D. 48, but left them, for some unknown cause, at Perga, and returned to Jerusalem. This led to a sharp contention between Paul and Barnabas, causing them to separate, and Barnabas, with Mark, went to Cyprus. Mark, however, again became the companion of Paul, during the latter's imprisonment at Rome, and from the warm esteem with which he is mentioned, it is clear that the offence was explained, or forgiven by Paul. Whether Mark made his contemplated journey to Asia Minor, we are not informed (Col. iv, 10, 11). He was with Peter when the Apostle wrote his first Epistle (1 Pet. v, 13), and from the form of salutation there given, it is inferred that Mark spent some time in labors at Babylon, probably with Peter; he also appears at Ephesus with Timothy (2 Tim. iv, 11), and Paul then commends him highly, showing how completely his confidence in Mark had been restored. Tradition, according to Epiphanius, makes him one of the seventy; Eusebius and Clement, that he was Peter's interpreter or secretary, and sent on a mission to Egypt; and Jerome, that he founded the church of Alexandria, and suffered martyrdom there, A. D. 68, three years after the death of Peter and Paul. The "interpreter of Peter" may mean that Mark translated for the Apostle, or, as many understand, that he wrote his Gospel in conformity with the testimony and preaching of Peter.

DATE. This is uncertain, as the statements of ancient writers are indefinite, not to say confusing. Eusebius states that Papias, on the testimony of John, declared that Mark wrote down what he recollected as the interpreter of Peter; and that Irenæus said Mark wrote his Gospel in conformity to Peter's preaching, and after Peter and Paul were dead. Ancient authorities placed its composition as early as A. D. 43, but on no credible evidence now known. There are no statements in the N. T. to decide the date. The most reasonable inference is that it was not written earlier than A. D. 62, and not later than A. D. 68 or 70.

PLACE. Several ancient writers say it was written at Rome, as Clement, Eusebius, Jerome, Epiphanius. This is sometimes, though not necessarily, connected with the theory of its Petrine origin or character, and the assumption that Peter visited Rome, which is stoutly denied by many Protestant writers. Chrysostom mentions Alexandria, but his statement is not confirmed by other writers. The later theory, that Mark wrote at Antioch, is a mere assumption destitute of foundation.

* In the A.V. the original is translated "Marcus, sister's son to Barnabas," but ἀνεψιὸς does not necessarily mean "nephew," hence the R.V. reads "Mark, the cousin of Barnabas." So Ellicott, Lightfoot and Lange render it. Smith's *Bible Dictionary*; article, "Mary, mother of Mark," erroneously speaks of her as sister to Barnabas.

LANGUAGE. There has never been any reasonable doubt that Mark wrote his Gospel in Greek. Some Romanist writers started and defended the supposition of a Latin original, partly to maintain the authority of the Vulgate, and a pretended part of this original was shown in St. Mark's church, in Venice, but critics have detected it to be a part of an old Latin MS. of the *four* Gospels. We have not a single testimony to a Latin original of the Gospel. Had there been such a Latin original, it would have been familiar to many Christians, for the Latin was not like the Hebrew, little known, and though lost, it is almost incredible that every early writer should have omitted to mention it.* The later Romanist writers abandon the theory of a Latin original as utterly untenable. According to Milman, the church at Rome, if not all the churches of the West, for the first three centuries, were, so to speak, Greek colonies. Their language, their Scriptures, and their writers were Greek. All their Christian writings extant were originally Greek, as the works of Justin Martyr, the Shepherd of Hermas, and the Epistles of Clement. Hence, Mark writing even at Rome, would naturally do so in the Greek language.

FOR WHOM WRITTEN. Tradition asserts that this Gospel was primarily prepared for Gentile Christian readers. An examination of the Gospel confirms this view ; *e. g.* :

(1) The general omission of Old Testament quotations, except where they occur in the discourses of the Lord, and in Mark i, 2, 3; xv, 28.

(2) Omission of the genealogy of Jesus.

(3) The interpretation of Hebrew or Aramaic words for Gentile readers, as *Boanerges, Talitha cumi, Corban, Bartimæus, Abba, Eloi, lama sabachthani.*

(4) The explanation of Hebrew customs and usages, which would be familiar to the Jewish, but not to Gentile readers, as the Jews eat not unless they wash their hands oft (R.V., diligently; margin, "up to the elbow,"); the preparation was the day before the Sabbath; the Passover was killed (R.V., sacrificed, as in margin of A.V.) on the first day of unleavened bread.

(5) The use of Latinisms or Latin forms not in the other Gospels, as *speculator* = soldier of the guard ; *xestus* = sextarius ; *quadrantus* = a farthing ; *centurion.*

STYLE. "Of the first three Gospels," says Alford, "that of Mark is the most distinct and peculiar in style." I. It has those graphic touches which describe the look, gestures, and feelings of our Lord, the appearance of the persons whom he addressed, and minute particulars of time, place, persons, and number, which are unnoticed by other Evangelists ; *e. g.* :

(1) His peculiar *look* is noticed in Mark iii, 5, 32, 34; x, 23 ; xi, 11.

(2) His *acts* and *gestures* in receiving little children, ix, 36 ; x, 16 ; in rebuking Peter, viii, 33 ; in going before the Apostles, x, 32 ; in gathering the Twelve about him, ix, 35.

---

* See Alford, " N. T. for English Readers," p. 38.

(3) His *feelings* of indignation, sorrow, pity, hunger, wonder, see Mark iii, 5; viii, 12, 33; x, 14; vii, 34; viii, 12; x, 21; vi, 34; xi, 12; iv, 38.

(4) *Persons* about him: Simon and others, i, 29, 36; xiii, 3; of Pharisees, Herodians and Scribes, iii, 6, 22; the twelve and Peter, xi, 11, 21; xvi, 7; servants, xiv, 65; the Cyrenian, xv, 21.

(5) *Number*: two thousand, v, 13; two and two; by hundreds, and by fifties, vi, 7, 40; twice...thrice, xiv, 30.

(6) *Time* and *place*: great while before day, i, 35; at the rising of the sun, xvi, 2; when even was come, iv, 35; at eventide, xi, 11; the third hour, xv, 25; the sea and seaside, ii, 13; iii, 7; iv, 1; in Decapolis, v, 20; vii, 31; against the treasury, against the temple, xii, 41; xiii, 3; the porch, xiv, 68; right side, xvi, 5.

II. Mark's style is further characterized by abrupt transitions from one topic to another, executed with graphic power; *e. g.*, a favorite word is "εὐθέως," which occurs forty times, and is variously rendered in the A. V., by "straightway," "immediately," "forthwith," and "as soon as."

III. Another peculiarity of style is the frequent use of the historical *present*, instead of the *past* tense, imparting a lively and graphic effect to the narrative; *e. g.*, "came" ("cometh" in R.V.), and "come," i, 40; ii, 3; xiv, 43, 66; "saith" instead of "said," i, 41; ii, 10, 17, etc.

IV. Mark often uses the direct, instead of the indirect, form of expression, as "Peace, be still," "Come out of the man," "What is thy name?" "Send us into the swine." He also often gives the exact words used, as "Ephphatha," "Corban," "Talitha cumi," "Boanerges," "Abba," "Eloi."

GENERAL CHARACTER. The distinguishing features of Mark's Gospel are: (1) Its brevity; (2) Vividness and fullness in presenting particular historic events; (3) Brevity or omission of the discourses of the Lord. Of the thirty seven miracles of Jesus, including his ascension, Mark records nineteen; while of the thirty or thirty-one leading parables, he notices only eight. Two miracles are related by Mark only, the healing of the deaf and dumb man, and of the blind man of Bethsaida. Two parables, also (if the householder, Mark xiii, 34, be counted), are also given by Mark only, the principal one being the seed growing secretly, iv, 26; (4) The prominence given to Christ's power over evil spirits, in the miracles noted. Mark plainly aims to impress his Gentile readers with the kingly power of Jesus, as a spiritual conqueror and the wonder-working Son of God; (5) Rapid succession of periods of solitude, and of manifold and hurried labors.* Here Jesus, says Archbishop Thomson, "sweeps over his kingdom swiftly, meteor-like, and men are to wonder and adore. His course is sometimes represented as abrupt, mysterious, awful to the disciples; he leaves them at night, conceals himself from them on a journey; the disciples are amazed and afraid." "The Evangelist," observes Keim, "makes the histories more effective by the contrast

* This fact will be strikingly apparent by a glance at the analysis presented at the close of this introduction.

between the hurried progress...and the contemplative stillness in which he paints the scenery with a thousand touches—the house, the sea, the followers, the growing throng, the persons by name, the numbers of men, of beasts, of coins, the green grass, the pillow on the stern of the boat on Genessaret—all described with the ready use of softening diminutives, and with words of time that denote the present." In such a life of constant "pressure" from multitudes of pitiable cases of sickness, deformity, and sorest affliction; from disciples with crude beliefs, and ever recurring doubts; from a crowd of followers, full of hard problems and selfish ambitions, urging their claims upon his attention; from designing and crafty enemies, secretly striving to entrap him by their hypocritical manner and artful propositions; in this "restless" career, thus sketched by the vivid pen of Mark, must we not recognize a true history?

Its Relation to Peter. The great majority of ancient writers state or imply that Mark was the interpreter of Peter. This has been explained by some as meaning: (1) that Mark translated into Greek, or more probably into Latin, the discourses of the Apostle, and probably acted as his secretary also. Others adopt the view: (2) that Mark wrote a Gospel presenting more closely than others the facts and truths concerning Christ as Peter preached them, thus becoming Peter's interpreter to the church at large.*

Both views have been ingeniously, if not ably, defended, and there is nothing improbable in the supposition that Mark did act as interpreter for Peter, especially when preaching to Latin hearers, and that also in writing his Gospel, he presented the facts and teachings of Jesus as he had heard them from Peter's lips, during many years of companionship and labor with that Apostle.

Some, as Maclear and Perowne, understand the testimony of Jerome, Tertullian, and especially Justin Martyr, to declare that Mark wrote his Gospel as Peter dictated it to him, and, therefore, was accounted in reality, Peter's Gospel. Others, as Archbishop Thomson, dispute this view, and hold that Justin Martyr probably referred to the "memoirs" of Jesus and not of Peter. The writings of those early Fathers coming to us, are in a very fragmentary state, and the most that can be safely asserted is, that Peter's preaching and oral testimony in regard to the facts in the life of Jesus, had an important influence upon Mark in the preparation of this Gos-

* The testimony of John the Presbyter, as given by Papias and quoted by Eusebius, is: "This also [John] the Elder said: 'Mark, being the interpreter of Peter, wrote down exactly whatever thing he remembered, [or he (Peter) mentioned], but yet not in the order in which Christ either spoke or did them, for he was neither a hearer nor a follower of the Lord's, but he was afterwards, as I [Papias] said, a follower of Peter, who adapted his instructions to the needs [of his hearers], but not as designing to furnish a connected account of the Lord's oracles, so that Mark made no mistake while thus writing down some things, as he remembered them. For of one thing he took care, to omit nothing which he heard, and not to set down any false statement therein.'"

Irenæus says that, after the death of Peter and Paul, Mark, the disciple and interpreter of Peter, "gave us, in writing, what had been uttered by Peter in his preaching." Clement and Origen repeat a similar tradition.

pel, and that under the guidance of the Holy Spirit, Mark reproduced many of these facts from his recollection of them, as Peter had frequently related the same in his hearing. On the other hand, it must be concluded with Alford, Ellicott, and others, that this is Mark's, not Peter's, Gospel. It has been known as the Gospel according to Mark from the earliest time, and this ascription of it to him cannot be accounted for, except upon the ground that Mark was in fact the author.

GENUINENESS. That the second Gospel was written by Mark has been uniformly believed. It is attested by explicit testimony, and little disputed, even by German critics. The conjecture that Mark simply compiled his Gospel from the narratives of Matthew and Luke, is thoroughly exploded and has been abandoned by the best critics. On the other hand, its brevity and vivacity of style have led to the opposite supposition, that it was the primitive Gospel.

Authority and genuineness of the closing section.—The closing section of the Gospel, chapter xvi, 9-20, has given rise to critical difficulties. The brief marginal note of the Revised Version tends to arouse, rather than allay, the suspicions of the reader; hence the substance of the objections to, and of the arguments in favor of, retaining the passage will be stated. The objections are: (1) That the verses are wanting in two of the oldest MSS., and in some other MSS. of less importance: (2) That in Jerome's day (latter part of the fourth and early part of the fifth centuries) the passage was not in many Greek copies; (3) That there are many Greek words in these verses not before used in Mark's Gospel.

In reply to these objections, and in favor of retaining the passage, the arguments are: (1) It is found in all the important ancient Uncial MSS. except three (the Sinaitic, Vatican, and "L"). It is claimed that too much stress has been laid upon the Sinaitic MS. by Tischendorf and some other critics; for, according to Buttmann, Burgon, and others, that MS. is somewhat remarkable for its omissions, and for the evident carelessness of its transcribers. The Vatican MS. leaves a blank space of three lines and a whole column between Mark and the words "according to Mark," the usual phrase closing a book, while no such space is left in other N. T. books—a space sufficient to contain the omitted verses. Professor Abbot notes, however, a similar space in the MS. at the close of Nehemiah, and of the apocryphal book of Tobit; but it may be added, the MS. abruptly ends with Heb. ix, 14, the pastoral Epistles, Philemon and Revelation, being omitted. The MS. has never been accessible to scholars generally, the best edition being that of Tischendorf, issued after a partial inspection of it for only two weeks, and is by no means infallible. Its omission of the passage in Mark can be accounted for, as can also the omission in the MSS. of Jerome's day, as will presently be shown.

(2) The closing passage in Mark is sustained by witnesses older than our oldest MSS. Indeed, all the most ancient Versions (with two minor excep-

tions) recognize the passage; *e. g.*, the Syriac (including the Peshito, of the second century, the Philoxenian, in two revisions, and the older Curetonian fragment); the old Latin or Italic; the Coptic (including the Memphitic and Thebaic or Sahidic versions); the Vulgate; and the Gothic version of the fourth century. The Christian Fathers before Jerome's time also generally concur in accepting the passage; *e. g.*, the so called Epistle of Barnabas, written in the second century; the Shepherd of Hermas, Justin Martyr, and Irenæus. The testimony of the latter is clear and indisputable. It is also recognized by Cyril of Jerusalem, Ambrose, and Augustine.

(3) In reply to the objection of Greek words not before used in the Gospel, Canon Cook and others have ably shown that, applying a similar rule to any other passage peculiar to Mark, a larger proportion of unusual Greek words would be found than in the disputed passage, and hence those other passages would be thrown out, thus proving the objection untenable, if not absurd. This seems effectually to dispose of the linguistic objections of the critics.

The omission of the passage in the two MSS. above noticed is accounted for thus: The origin of the objections to the verses has been traced to Eusebius, who first made a supposition that the verses were omitted in order to answer an adversary, and subsequently changed the supposition into a stronger statement, out of which, it is conjectured by many, the objections have arisen. His original statements are characterized by Canon Cook, as "vague and inconsistent." Jerome simply reproduces the statements of Eusebius. The omission in the Sinaitic and Vatican MSS., which belong to about the same age, may be due to Eusebius. We know that he was ordered to prepare fifty MS. copies of the Bible, by Constantine the Great; and Tischendorf thinks it not improbable that the Sinaitic MS. is one of those fifty.

Many scholars retain the passage as authentic, who are not certain that it was written by Mark. Even Alford, who is more facile at finding difficulties and contradictions than harmonies, accepts it as authentic. It is received as undoubtedly a part of the second Gospel by such scholars as Scrivener, the foremost of textual critics, by Mill, Bengel, Matthæi, Eichorn, Kuinoel, Hug, Scholz, Guericke, Olshausen, Ebrard, Bleek, Wordsworth, Lachmann, Burgon, and Canon Cook. Tregelles, Alford, Westcott, and Hort retain it with some special mark, as brackets, or a space between it and the foregoing text, indicating thereby that they accept it as authentic, that is, an inspired record, but are in doubt respecting its genuineness, that is, they incline to the view that it may not be by Mark, but was penned by some other inspired person. Its right, therefore, to a place in the sacred canon may be regarded as sustained by a weight of testimony which places it beyond successful question.

ITS VALUE AS A SINGLE GOSPEL. If this Gospel by Mark were wanting we should be without a biography of Jesus calculated to enlist and carry the reader irresistibly along by the minuteness, vividness, and impetuous character of the narrative. Mark, as an intimate helper and companion, alike of Peter, Paul, and Barnabas, and laboring in each of the great centres of the Jewish and Roman world by turns, appears to have caught and preserved to us some of the grander features of the work and words of Jesus, as those great Apostles presented them to listening multitudes of every nation in the then known world. "By their simple force," observes Westcott, he was moved "to look beyond the varieties of doctrine in the vivid realization of the actions of the Son of God." And Wordsworth aptly says, "The brevity of this Gospel would commend it to the acceptance of the g eat body of the Roman people, especially of the middle classes engaged in practical business, legal affairs, commercial enterprise, and military campaigns, and migrating in frequent journeys from place to place." This purpose will account for the introduction of Latin words, and of a phraseology in accord with Roman usages. To conclude, in the thoughtful and judicious words of Canon Westcott: "In substance and style and treatment, the Gospel of St. Mark is essentially a transcript from life. The course and issue of facts are imaged in it with the clearest outline. If all other arguments against the mythic origin of the Evangelical narratives were wanting, this vivid and simple record, stamped with the most distinct impress of independence and originality, totally unconnected with the symbolism of the Old Dispensation, totally independent of the deeper reasonings of the New, would be sufficient to refute a theory subversive of all faith in history. The details which were addressed to the vigorous intelligence of Roman hearers are still pregnant with instruction for us. The teaching, which 'met their wants' in the first age, finds a corresponding field for its action now."

HARMONY WITH THE OTHER EVANGELISTS. While Mark's Gospel is thus independent of the other Gospel writers, it is not in contradiction with them, but in full harmony with their narratives. This is more fully shown in the notes upon various portions of the text, which relate matters in common with Matthew, Luke, or John. It was long ago noted by leading harmonists, that "Mark and John, who have little in common, follow, with few exceptions, the regular and true order of events and transactions recorded by them...Matthew and Luke manifestly have sometimes not so much regard to chronological order, as they have been guided by the principle of association, so that in them transactions having certain relations to each other are not seldom grouped together, though they may have happened at different times and various places." See Robinson's "Harmony," and Ellicott's "Lectures."

ANALYSIS OF MARK'S GOSPEL.*

A marked peculiarity of the Gospel is the succession of severe labors and conflicts, alternating with periods of withdrawal and rest. The ascension forms the final withdrawal, to be followed by a final victory at his second coming.

PART I.

Note in this part: (1) *the concise introduction;* (2) *omission of a genealogy of Jesus.*

I. Introduction:—i, 1–13.
    (1) Baptism and Preaching by John.......i, 1— 7.
    (2) Baptism of Jesus..............................i, 8—11.
    (3) The Temptation...............................i, 12—13.

PART II.

Note here: (1) *alternate periods of labor and rest;* (2) *opposition of Pharisees to his claim to forgive sins, to his eating with publicans, neglect of fasts, and breaking the sabbath;* (3) *selection of apostles;* (4) *mission of the twelve;* (5) *murder of Baptist;* (6) *feeding of five thousand.*

II. Ministry of Christ in Eastern Galilee:—i, 14—vii, 24.
  (A) Section (I)
    (1) Announcement of the Kingdom................ i, 14, 15.
    (2) Call of four disciples............................... i, 16—20.
    (3) Cure of the demoniac, at Capernaum......... i, 21—28.
    (4) Cure of Peter's wife's mother and others... i, 29—34.
        (i) *Retirement to a solitary place*........ i, 35.
    (5) Tour in Galilee...................................... i, 35—39.
    (6) Cleansing of a leper............................... i, 40—45.
        (ii) *Retirement to desert places*........... i, 45.
    (7) THE RULING POWERS COMPLAIN OF:
        (a) The cure of the paralytic................. ii, 1—12.
        (b) Call and feast of Matthew................ ii, 13—22.
        (c) The disciples pluck the ears of corn... ii, 23—28.
        (d) Cure of the withered hand and others.iii, 1—12.
        (iii) *Retirement to the lake*...................iii, 7—12.
  (B) Section (II)
    (1) Call of the Apostles................................iii, 13—19.
    (2) Conflict with Scribes from Jerusalem.......iii, 20—30.
    (3) His friends and true kindred....................iii, 31—35.
    (4) PARABLES OF THE KINGDOM:
        (a) The Sower....................................iv, 1— 9.
        (b) Explanation of the parable..............iv, 10—25.
        (c) The seed growing secretly...............iv, 26—29.
        (d) The mustard seed..........................iv, 30—34.
    (5) SIGNS OF THE KINGDOM:
        (a) The stilling of the storm..................iv, 35—41.
        (b) The Gadarene demoniac................. v, 1—20.
        (c) The woman with the issue of blood.....v, 25—34.
        (d) The daughter of Jairus................... v, 21—43.
    (6) Rejection at Nazareth.............................vi, 1— 6.
        (iv) *Retirement into the villages*..........vi, 6.

---

* In the preparation of this Analysis, aid has been derived from the scholarly Commentaries of Professors J. J. S. Perowne, G. F. Maclear, and J. P. Lange, Amer. Ed., by Professors Schaff and Shedd.

(C) *Section* (III).
 (1) Mission of the Apostles......................vi, 7—13.
 (2) The murder of the Baptist....................vi, 14—29.
 (3) Apostles return.................................vi, 30.
   (v) *Retirement to a desert place*..........vi, 31—32.
 (4) The feeding of the five thousand............vi, 33—44.
 (5) The walking on the sea.......................vi, 45—52.
 (6) Victories over disease in all its forms........vi, 53—56.
 (7) Renewed opposition of the Pharisaic party.vii, 1—23.
   (vi) *Retirement to the borders of Tyre and Sidon*..............................vii, 24.

Part III.

Note here: (1) *the renewed and deepening hostility of the rulers;* (2) *call for a sign;* (3) *hope for Gentiles in the answer to the Syro-Phœnician;* (4) *a crisis in Jesus' ministry;* (5) *the transfiguration;* (6) *foretelling his passion.*

III. Ministry of Christ in Upper Galilee :—vii, 24—ix, 37.

(A) *Section* (I)
 (1) Healing of the daughter of the Syro-Phœnician..vii, 24—30.
 (2) Gradual healing of the deaf and dumb.....vii, 31—37.
 (3) Feeding of the four thousand.................viii, 1— 9.
 (4) The Pharisees ask for a sign..................viii, 10—13.
 (5) Warning against the leaven of the Pharisees and of Herod...........................viii, 14—21.
 (6) Gradual cure of the blind man................viii, 22—26.
   (vii) *Retirement to the region of Cæsarea Philippi*..................................viii, 27.

(B) *Section* (II)
 (1) Jesus and Peter's great confession.........viii, 27—30.
 (2) *First Clear Prediction of his Passion, of the cross-bearing by disciples*............viii, 31—ix, 1.
   (viii) *Retirement to the mountain range of Hermon*...........................ix, 2.
 (3) The Transfiguration...............................ix, 2—13.
 (4) The lunatic child..................................ix, 14—27.
 (5) The secret source of strength.................ix, 28—29.
 (6) *Second Prediction of the Passion*...........ix, 31—32.
 (7) The Apostles taught (a) humility, (b) self-denial..ix, 33—50.

Part IV.

Note here: conflicts with the rulers.

IV. Conflicts and Victories in Peræa :—x, 1—45.

 (1) The question of marriage and divorce......x, 1—12.
 (2) The blessing of little children.................x, 13—16.
 (3) The rich young ruler............................x, 17—22.
 (4) The danger of riches............................x, 23—27.
 (5) The reward of self-sacrifice....................x, 28—31.
 (6) *Third Prediction of the Passion*..............x, 32—34.
 (7) The ambitious Apostles........................x, 35—45.

Part V.

Note here: (1) *the dullness of the Apostles as to the sufferings of the Messiah;* (2) *the triumphal entry;* (3) *the second cleansing of the temple;* (4) *the bitter hostility of the rulers;* (5) *Judas, a traitor;* (6) *the Lord's Supper;* (7) *how the narrative becomes full and minute towards the last.*

V. Conflicts and Victories in Judæa :—x, 46—xv, 47.

(A) *Section* (I)
  (1) Blind Bartimæus at Jericho..................x, 46—52.
  (2) The anointing at Bethany...................xiv, 3— 9.

(B) *Section* (II)
  (1) The triumphal entry........................... xi, 1—11.
     (ix) *Retirement to Bethany*................xi, 11.
  (2) The withering of the barren fig-tree.........xi, 12- 14.
  (3) The second cleansing of the temple..........xi, 15--18.
     (x) *Retirement to Bethany*.....................xi, 19.
  (4) Lesson of the withered fig-tree.................xi, 20—26.
  (5) The question of the deputation of the Sanhedrin and the counter question............xi, 27—33.
  (6) Parable of the wicked husbandmen..........xii, 1—12.
  (7) SUBTLE QUESTIONS:
     (a) Of the Pharisees; *the tribute-money*.xii, 13--17.
     (b) Of the Sadducees; *the resurrection*...xii, 18—27.
     (c) Of the Lawyer; *the importance of the Commandments*........................xii, 28—34.
  (8) The Lord's counter-question..................xii, 35—40.
  (9) The widow's two mites........................xii, 41—44.
  (10) Prediction of the destruction of Jerusalem and the end of the world....................xiii, 1—37.
     (xi) *Retirement at Bethany*......Comp. xiv, 12 and 16.
  (11) The Conspiracy..............................xiv, 1, 2, 10, 11.

(C) *Section* (III) THE PASSOVER, AGONY AND ARREST.
  (1) Directions respecting the passover.........xiv, 12—16.
  (2) The Passover meal and institution of the Lord's Supper...................................xiv, 17—26.
  (3) Peter's professions..............................xiv, 27—31.
  (4) The Agony in Gethsemane..................xiv, 32—42.
  (5) The Arrest......................................xiv, 43—50.
  (6) The Incident of the young man.............xiv, 51—52.

(D) *Section* (IV) THE TRIAL AND CRUCIFIXION.
  (1) The Jewish Trial..............................xiv, 53—65.
  (2) The denials by Peter..........................xiv, 66—72.
  (3) The Council...................................xv, 1.
  (4) The trial before Pilate........................xv, 1—15.
  (5) The Crucifixion...............................xv, 16—32.
  (6) The Death and Burial........................xv, 33—46.

Part VI.

Note here: (1) *the hesitation of the disciples to believe the resurrection of Jesus;* (2) *the final charge and distinct promise of miraculous power;* (3) *ascension as a final withdrawal;* (4) *the Lord's power in the growth of his church.*

VI. Christ's Resurrection and Ascension:—xvi, 1—20.

  (1) The rest of Christ in the tomb...xv, 47—xvi, 1.
  (2) The visit of the women........ ....xvi, 1— 3.
  (3) The Resurrection.............................xvi, 4— 8.

INTRODUCTION.

(4) THE APPEARANCES AFTER THE RESURRECTION:
   (a) Mary Magdalene..................................xvi, 9—11.
   (b) Two disciples....................................xvi, 12—13.
   (c) The Eleven......................................xvi, 14.
(5) The Last Charge...xvi, 15—18.
(6) The Ascension...xvi, 19.
(7) The Apostles preaching..................................xvi, 20.

MIRACLES AND PARABLES IN MARK.

The Miracles of our Lord recorded by Mark may be arranged as displaying His power over

(I) *Disease.*
  (1) Simon's wife's mother..............................i, 30—31.
  (2) The leper...i, 40—45.
  (3) The paralytic....................................ii, 3—12.
  (4) The woman with the issue of blood.................v, 25—34.
  (5) *The blind man at Bethsaida*....................viii, 22—26.
  (6) The lunatic boy..................................ix, 17—29.
  (7) Bartimæus..x, 46—52.

(II) *Nature.*
  (1) The stilling of the storm........................iv, 35—41.
  (2) The feeding of the five thousand.................vi, 32—44.
  (3) The walking on the lake..........................vi, 45—52.
  (4) The feeding of the four thousand...............viii, 1—9.
  (5) The withering of the fig-tree....................xi, 12—14.

(III) *The Spirit-world.*
  (1) The demon cast out in the synagogue..............i, 23—28.
  (2) The legion.......................................v, 1—20.
  (3) The daughter of the Syro-Phœnician woman.......vii, 24—30.
  (4) *The deaf and dumb man*.......................vii, 31—37.

(IV) *Death.*
  (1) The daughter of Jairus...........................v, 21—43.

(I) *Parables of the Early Group; to the Mission of the Seventy:*
  (1) The new cloth...................................ii, 21.
  (2) The new wine....................................ii, 22.
  (3) The sower......................................iv, 3—8.
  (4) *The seed growing secretly*....................iv, 26—29.
  (5) The mustard-seed...............................iv, 30—32.

(II) There are no *Parables of the Intermediate Group* related by Mark.

(III) *Parables of the Final Group:*
  (1) The wicked husbandmen..........................xii, 1—11.
  (2) The fig tree..................................xiii, 28.
  (3) *The Householder*............................xiii, 34.

* Recorded only by Mark.

CHRONOLOGICAL INDEX.

(From Andrews' "Life of Our Lord.")

Annunciation to Zacharias	Oct.,	6	B. C.
Elisabeth conceives a son, and lives in retirement	Oct.–March,	6–5	"
Annunciation to Mary	April,	5	"
Mary visits Elisabeth, and remains three months	April–June,	5	"
Birth of John the Baptist	June,	5	"
Joseph and Mary go to Bethlehem to be taxed	Dec.,	5	"
Jesus born at Bethlehem	Dec.,	5	"
The angel and the shepherds	Dec.,	5	"
Circumcision of Jesus	Jan.,	4	"
Presentation of Jesus	Feb.,	4	"
Coming of the Magi	Feb.,	4	"
Flight of Jesus into Egypt	Feb.,	4	"
Return to Nazareth, and sojourn there	May,	4	"
Jesus, at twelve years of age, attends the passover	April,	8	A.D.
John the Baptist begins his labors	Summer,	26	"
Baptism of Jesus	Jan.,	27	"
Jesus tempted in the wilderness	Jan.–Feb.,	27	"
Deputation of Priests and Levites to the Baptist	Feb.,	27	"
Jesus returns to Galilee	Feb.,	27	"
Wedding at Cana of Galilee	Feb.,	27	"
First Passover of Jesus' ministry; cleansing of temple	April,	27	"
Jesus begins to baptize	May,	27	"
Jesus departs into Galilee, through Samaria	Dec.,	27	"
A few weeks spent by Jesus in retirement	Jan.–April,	28	"
The Baptist imprisoned	March,	28	"
Second Passover; healing of impotent man	April,	28	"
Jesus begins His ministry in Galilee	April–May,	28	"
Calling of four disciples, and healings at Capernaum	April–May,	28	"
First circuit in Galilee; healing of the leper	May,	28	"
Return to Capernaum, and healing of the paralytic	Summer,	28	"
Plucking the corn, and healing the withered hand	Summer,	28	"
Choice of apostles, and Sermon on the Mount	Summer,	28	"
Healing of centurion's servant at Capernaum	Summer,	28	"
Journey to Nain, and raising of the widow's son	Summer,	28	"
Message to Jesus of the Baptist	Summer,	28	"
Jesus anointed by the woman; a sinner	Autumn,	28	"
Healing at Capernaum of the blind and dumb possessed; charge of the Pharisees that He casts out devils by Beelzebub	Autumn,	28	"
Teaching in parables; and stilling of the tempest	Autumn,	28	"
Healing of demoniacs in Gergesa, and return to Capernaum	Autumn,	28	"
Matthew's feast; healing of woman with issue of blood, and raising of Jairus' daughter	Autumn,	28	"
Healing of two blind men, and a dumb possessed; Pharisees blaspheme	Autumn,	28	"
Second visit to Nazareth; sending of the twelve	Winter,	29	"
Death of Baptist; Jesus returns to Capernaum	Winter,	29	"
Crossing of the sea, and feeding of the 5000; return to Capernaum	Spring,	29	"
Discourse at Capernaum respecting the bread of life	April,	29	"
Jesus visits the coasts of Tyre and Sidon; heals the daughter of Syro-Phœnician woman; visits the region of Decapolis; heals one with an impediment in his speech; feeds the 4000	Summer,	29	"
Jesus returns to Capernaum; is tempted by the Pharisees; reproves their hypocrisy; again crosses the sea; heals blind man at Bethsaida	Summer	29	"
Peter's confession that He is the Christ; He announces His death and resurrection; the transfiguration	Summer,	29	"
Healing of lunatic child	Summer,	29	"
Jesus journeys through Galilee, teaching the disciples; at Capernaum pays the tribute money, goes up to feast of Tabernacles	Autumn,	29	"

He teaches in the temple; efforts to arrest him.................................Oct., 29 A.D.
An adulteress is brought before him; attempt to stone him; healing of a man
  blind from birth; return to Galilee...Oct., 29 "
Final departure from Galilee; is rejected at Samaria; sending of the Seventy,
  whom he follows..Nov., 29 "
Jesus is attended by great multitudes; parable of the good Samaritan; He gives
  a form of prayer...Nov., 29 "
Healing of a dumb possessed man; renewed blasphemy of the Pharisees;
  dining with a Pharisee; Jesus rebukes hypocrisy; parable of the rich
  fool..Nov.-Dec., 29 "
Jesus is told of the murder of the Galileans by Pilate; parable of the fig tree;
  healing of a woman 18 years sick; is warned against Herod....Nov.-Dec., 29 "
Feast of Dedication, visit to Mary and Martha; the Jews at Jerusalem attempt
  to stone Him; He goes beyond Jordan...Dec., 29 "
Jesus dines with a Pharisee, and heals a man with dropsy; parables of the
  great supper, of the lost sheep, of the lost piece of silver, of the unjust
  steward, of the rich man and Lazarus..Dec., 29 "
Resurrection of Lazarus; counsel of the Jews to put Him to death; He retires
  to Ephraim...Jan.-Feb., 30 "
Sojourn in Ephraim till Passover at hand; journeys on the border of Samaria
  and Galilee; healing of ten lepers; parable of the unjust judge, and of
  Pharisee and publican; teaching respecting divorce; blessing of children;
  the young ruler, and parable of laborers in the vineyard.....Feb.-March, 30 "
Jesus again announces His death; ambition of James and John...........March, 30 "
Healing of blind men at Jericho; Zaccheus; parable of the pounds; departure
  to Bethany...March, 30 "
Supper at Bethany, and anointing of Jesus by Mary.............Sat., April 1, 30 "
Entry into Jerusalem; visit to the temple, and return to Bethany......
                                                        Sunday, April 2, 30 "
Cursing of the fig tree; second purification of the temple; return to Bethany
                                                        Monday, April 3, 30 "
Teaching in the temple; parable of the two sons, of the wicked husbandmen,
  of the king's son; attempts of his enemies to entangle Him; the poor
  widow; the Greeks who desire to see Him; a voice heard from Heaven;
  departure from the temple to the Mount of Olives; discourse respecting the
  end of the world; return to Bethany; agreement of Judas with the priests
  to betray Him..Tuesday, April 4, 30 "
Jesus seeks retirement at Bethany.....................Wednesday, April 5, 30 "
Sending of Peter and John to prepare the Passover, the paschal supper....
                                                        Thursday, April 6, 30 "
Events at paschal supper...............................Thursday eve., April 6, 30 "
After supper Jesus foretells the denials of Peter; speaks of the coming of the
  Comforter, and ends with prayer......................Thursday eve., April 6, 30 "
Jesus in the garden of Gethsemane....................Thursday eve., April 6, 30 "
Jesus is given into the hands of Judas..............Thursday, midnight, April 6, 30 "
Jesus is led to the house of Annas, and thence to the palace of Caiaphas; is
  condemned for blasphemy.............................Friday, 1-5 A.M., April 7, 30 "
Mockeries of His enemies; He is brought the second time before the council,
  and thence taken before Pilate.......................Friday, 5-6 A.M., April 7, 30 "
Charge of sedition; Pilate finds no fault with Him, and attempts to release
  Him, but is forced to scourge Him, and gives Him up to be crucified......
                                                  Friday, 6-9 A.M., April 7, 30 "
Jesus is crucified at Golgotha.........................Friday, 9-12 A.M., April 7, 30 "
Upon the cross is reviled by his enemies; commends His mother to John; dark-
  ness covers the land; He dies; the earth shakes, and rocks are rent......
                                                  Friday, 12 A.M.-3 P.M., April 7, 30 "
His body taken down and given to Joseph, and laid in his sepulchre.......
                                                        Friday, 3-6 P.M., April 7, 30 "
Resurrection of Jesus, and appearance to Mary Magdalene...................
                                                        Sunday, A.M., April 9, 30 "
Appearance to the two disciples at Emmaus; to Peter and to the eleven at
  Jerusalem..Sunday, P.M., April 9, 30 "
Appearance to the apostles and Thomas................Sunday, April 16, 30 "
Appearance to seven disciples at sea of Tiberias, and to 500 at mountain in Galilee,
                                                        April-May, 30 "
Final appearance to the disciples at Jerusalem, and ascension to heaven,
                                                        Thursday, May 18, 30 "

LESSONS AND GOLDEN TEXTS FOR 1882.

FIRST QUARTER.

1. Jan. 1.—THE BEGINNING OF THE GOSPEL. Mark 1: 1-13. *Commit vs. 9-11.* GOLDEN TEXT—Mal. 3: 1.
2. Jan. 8.—JESUS IN GALILEE. Mark 1: 14-28. *Commit vs. 27, 28.* GOLDEN TEXT.—Isa. 9: 2.
3. Jan. 15.—POWER TO HEAL. Mark 1: 29-45. *Commit vs. 40-42.* GOLDEN TEXT.—Exod. 15: 26.
4. Jan. 22.—POWER TO FORGIVE. Mark 2: 1-17. *Commit vs. 8-12.* GOLDEN TEXT.—Isa. 43: 25.
5. Jan. 29.—THE PHARISEES ANSWERED. Mark 2: 18-28, and 3: 1-5. *Commit vs. 3: 1-5.* GOLDEN TEXT—Exod. 20: 8.
6. Feb. 5.—CHRIST AND HIS DISCIPLES. MARK 3: 6-19. *Commit vs. 13-15.* GOLDEN TEXT.—John 15: 16.
7. Feb. 12.—CHRIST'S FOES AND FRIENDS. Mark 3: 20-35. *Commit vs. 31-35.* GOLDEN TEXT.—Matt 12: 30.
8. Feb. 19.—PARABLE OF THE SOWER. Mark 4: 1-20. *Commit vs. 3-8.* GOLDEN TEXT.—Rev. 2: 29.
9. Feb. 26.—THE GROWTH OF THE KINGDOM. Mark 4: 21-34. *Commit vs. 30-32.* GOLDEN TEXT.—Ps. 72: 16.
10. March 5.—CHRIST STILLING THE TEMPEST. Mark 4: 35-41. *Commit vs. 37-41.* GOLDEN TEXT.—Ps. 107: 29.
11. March 12.—POWER OVER EVIL SPIRITS. Mark 5: 1-20. *Commit vs. 18-20.* GOLDEN TEXT.—1 John 3: 8.
12. March 19.—POWER OVER DISEASE AND DEATH. Mark 5: 21-43. *Commit vs. 21-23.* GOLDEN TEXT.—Verse 36.
13. March 26.—REVIEW, or selected Lesson.

SECOND QUARTER.

1. April 2.—THE MISSION OF THE TWELVE. Mark 6: 1-13. *Commit vs. 10-12.* GOLDEN TEXT.—Matt. 10: 40.
2. April 9.—DEATH OF JOHN THE BAPTIST. Mark 6: 14-29. *Commit vs. 14-16.* GOLDEN TEXT.—Ps. 37: 12.
3. April 16.—THE FIVE THOUSAND FED. Mark 6: 30-44. *Commit vs. 41-44.* GOLDEN TEXT—Ps. 132: 15.
4. April 23.—CHRIST WALKING ON THE SEA. Mark 6: 45-56. *Commit vs. 47-50.* GOLDEN TEXT.—Isa. 43: 2.
5. April 30.—THE TRADITIONS OF MEN. Mark 7: 1-24. *Commit vs. 9-13.* GOLDEN TEXT.—v. 7.
6. May 7.—SUFFERERS BROUGHT TO CHRIST. Mark 7: 24-37. *Commit vs. 26-30.* GOLDEN TEXT.—Ps. 145: 9.
7. May 14.—THE LEAVEN OF THE PHARISEES. Mark 8: 1-21. *Commit vs. 14-17.* GOLDEN TEXT.—Luke 12: 1.
8. May 21.—SEEING AND CONFESSING CHRIST. Mark 8: 22-33. *Commit vs. 27-29.* GOLDEN TEXT.—Matt 16: 16.
9. May 28.—FOLLOWING CHRIST. Mark 8: 34-38; 9: 1. *Commit vs. 34-37.* GOLDEN TEXT.—v. 34.
10. June 4.—THE TRANSFIGURATION. Mark 9: 2-13. *Commit vs. 5-8.* GOLDEN TEXT.—Matt. 3: 17.
11. June 11.—THE AFFLICTED CHILD. Mark 9: 14-32. *Commit vs. 21-24.* GOLDEN TEXT.—v. 23.
12. June 18.—THE CHILDLIKE BELIEVER. Mark 9: 33-50. *Commit vs. 35-37.* GOLDEN TEXT.—Isa 57: 15.
13. June 25.—REVIEW, or selected Lesson.

THIRD QUARTER.

1. July 2.—A LESSON ON HOME. Mark 10: 1-16. *Commit vs. 13-16.* GOLDEN TEXT.—Ps. 101: 2.
2. July 9.—THE RICH YOUNG MAN. Mark 10: 17-31. *Commit vs. 21-24.* GOLDEN TEXT.—v. 21.
3. July 16.—SUFFERING AND SERVICE. Mark 10: 32-45. *Commit vs. 42-45.* GOLDEN TEXT.—v. 45.
4. July 23.—BLIND BARTIMEUS. Mark 10: 46-52. *Commit vs. 46-52.* GOLDEN TEXT.—Isa. 35: 5.
5. July 30.—THE TRIUMPHAL ENTRY. Mark 11: 1-11. *Commit vs. 7-10.* GOLDEN TEXT.—Zech 9: 9.
6. Aug. 6.—THE FRUITLESS TREE. Mark 11: 12-23. *Commit vs. 12-14.* GOLDEN TEXT.—John 15: 8.
7. Aug. 13.—PRAYER AND FORGIVENESS. Mark 11: 24-33. *Commit vs. 24-26.* GOLDEN TEXT.—Matt. 6: 12
8. Aug. 20.—THE WICKED HUSBANDMEN. Mark 12: 1-12. *Commit vs. 9-11.* GOLDEN TEXT.—Ps. 118: 22.
9. Aug. 27.—PHARISEES AND SADDUCEES SILENCED. Mark 12: 13-27. *Commit vs. 14-17.* GOLDEN TEXT.—1 Tim. 4: 8.
10. Sept. 3.—LOVE TO GOD AND MEN. Mark 12: 28-44. *Commit vs. 29-31.* GOLDEN TEXT.—Deut. 6: 5.
11. Sept 10.—CALAMITIES FORETOLD. Mark 13: 1-20. *Commit vs. 9-11.* GOLDEN TEXT.—Prov. 22: 3.
12. Sept. 17.—WATCHFULNESS ENJOINED Mark 13: 21-37. *Commit vs. 35-37.* GOLDEN TEXT.—1 Thess. 5: 6.
13. Sept. 24.—REVIEW, or selected Lesson.

FOURTH QUARTER.

1. Oct. 1.—THE ANOINTING AT BETHANY. Mark 14: 1-11. *Commit vs. 6-9.* GOLDEN TEXT.—v. 8.
2. Oct. 8.—THE PASSOVER. Mark 14: 12-21. *Commit vs. 17-21.* GOLDEN TEXT.—Ex. 12: 27.
3. Oct. 15.—THE LORD'S SUPPER. Mark 14: 22-31. *Commit vs. 22-26.* GOLDEN TEXT.—1 Cor. 11: 26.
4. Oct. 22.—THE AGONY IN THE GARDEN. Mark 14: 32-42. *Commit vs. 33-36.* GOLDEN TEXT.—Isa. 53: 4.
5. Oct. 29.—JESUS BETRAYED AND TAKEN. Mark 14: 43-54. *Commit vs. 43-46.* GOLDEN TEXT.—Mark 14: 41.
6. Nov. 5.—JESUS BEFORE THE COUNCIL. Mark 14: 55-72. *Commit vs. 61-64.* GOLDEN TEXT.—Isa. 53: 7.
7. Nov. 12.—JESUS BEFORE PILATE. Mark 15: 1-15. *Commit vs. 12-15.* GOLDEN TEXT.—Isa. 53: 3.
8. Nov 19.—JESUS MOCKED AND CRUCIFIED. Mark 15: 16-26. *Commit vs. 22-26.* GOLDEN TEXT.—Ps. 22: 16.
9. Nov. 26.—HIS DEATH ON THE CROSS. Mark 15: 27-37. *Commit vs. 33-37.* GOLDEN TEXT.—1 Peter 2: 24.
10. Dec. 3.—AFTER HIS DEATH. Mark 15: 38-47. *Commit vs. 43-46.* GOLDEN TEXT.—v. 39.
11. Dec. 10.—HIS RESURRECTION. Mark 16: 1-8. *Commit vs. 6-8.* GOLDEN TEXT.—1 Cor. 15: 20.
12. Dec. 17.—AFTER HIS RESURRECTION. Mark 16: 9-20 *Commit vs. 15-20.* GOLDEN TEXT.—v. 15.
13. Dec. 24.—Lesson selected by the School.
14. Dec. 31.—REVIEW, or selected Lesson.

A PICTORIAL COMMENTARY

ON

THE GOSPEL ACCORDING TO MARK.

AUTHORIZED VERSION.

CHAP. I.—The beginning of the gospel of Jesus Christ, the Son of God.
2 As it is written in the prophets, Behold, I send my messenger before thy face, which shall prepare thy way before thee.
3 The voice of one crying in the wilderness, Prepare ye the way of the Lord, make his paths straight.
4 John did baptize in the wilderness, and

REVISED VERSION.

THE beginning of the gospel of Jesus Christ, ¹the Son of God.
2 Even as it is written ²in Isaiah the prophet, Behold, I send my messenger before thy face,
Who shall prepare thy way;
3 The voice of one crying in the wilderness, Make ye ready the way of the Lord, Make his paths straight;
4 John came, who baptized in the wilderness

¹ Some ancient authorities omit *the Son of God*. ² Some ancient authorities read *in the prophets*.

1-9. BAPTISM AND PREACHING BY JOHN, A. D. 26, 27.

1. *The beginning*] " Here is *the beginning of* " or " *here begins the gospel*," etc. This is either a title to the book, or, as Schaff suggests, to the first section. "Some connect it with the next verse, the beginning of the gospel (was) as it is written in the prophets ; others with verse 4, the beginning of the gospel was, John baptizing. But these constructions are too artificial. The verse describes the whole book as 'the gospel of Jesus Christ, the Son of God.'"—*J. A. Alexander.* Mark begins abruptly and concisely, not with a genealogy of Jesus, as Matthew, nor with the infancy of Jesus, as Luke, nor with the Eternal Word, as John ; but he sets forth Jesus Christ in his acts, and as the Messiah and Saviour of men.

gospel] The noun occurs 75 times in the New Testament and the verb 25 times. Gospel is from Saxon, *god* = good and *spel* = speech or news. The meaning, in Greek and in English, is glad tidings, good news. This gospel is singularly full of precious facts about the Lord Jesus, narrated in a simple, terse, pithy, and condensed style.

the Son of God] Jesus as the Son of God, is the *subject* of the book. Contrast this with Matt. i, 1, "*the Son of David, the Son of Abraham.*" Matthew writes for Jews ; Mark for Gentiles.

2. *in the prophets*] The citation is from (1) Mal. iii, 1, and (2) Isa. xl, 3. The reading of the A.V. is in closest accord with the citations. "The subordinate relation of the later to the earlier prophecy would account for the reading, in *Isaiah the prophet*, regarded as the true text by the latest critics."—*Alexander.*

my messenger] The Greek word usually rendered *angel* is here used in its primary and wider sense. Mark makes only two Old Testament quotations of his own—here, and in xv, 28 (?), but notes several which Jesus made in his discourses.

3. *Lord*] that is, Jehovah. "As this verse refers to Christ it is proof of his deity."—*Beza.*

4. *the wilderness*] The region extending from the gates of Hebron to the shores of the Dead Sea. "It is a dreary waste of rocky valleys ; in some

AUTHORIZED VERSION.	REVISED VERSION.
preach the baptism of repentance for the remission of sins. 5 And there went out unto him all the land of Judæa, and they of Jerusalem, and were all baptized of him in the river of Jordan, confessing their sins. 6 And John was clothed with camel's hair,	and preached the baptism of repentance unto 5 remission of sins. And there went out unto him all the country of Judæa, and all they of Jerusalem; and they were baptized of him in 6 the river Jordan, confessing their sins. And John was clothed with camel's hair, and had a

parts stern and terrible, the rocks cleft and shattered by earthquakes and convulsions into rifts and gorges, sometimes a thousand feet in depth, though only thirty or forty in width. The whole district is, in fact, the slope of the midland chalk and limestone hills, from their highest point of nearly 3000 feet near Hebron, to 1000 or 1500 feet at the valley of the Dead Sea. The Hebrews fitly call it Jeshimon (1 Sam. xxiii, 19, 24), 'the appalling desolation,' or 'horror.'"—*Geikie.*

baptism of repentance] "A ceremonial washing, which denoted a profession of repentance, or a thorough change of mind,...with respect to sin."—*Alexander.* "It was a mere emblem of the purification required in the life and heart, and needed an after baptism by the Holy Spirit."—*Geikie.*

for the remission] or *unto the remission*, as in the Revised Version. Comp. Matt. xxvi, 28; Luke i, 77. Remission means a loosing, leaving, letting go unpunished. It was to be received through the Messiah. John required of *all* a change of mind and life with a view to pardon from Christ. Thus his baptism was preparatory to that of Christ. "Water baptism is an...emblem of that which must be received from the Holy Ghost."—*A. Clarke.*

GIRDLES.

5. *all the land*] The crowds that flocked to his baptism included representatives of every class, Pharisees and Sadducees (Matt. iii, 7), tax-gatherers (Luke iii, 12), soldiers (Luke iii, 14), rich and poor (Luke iii, 10). "How little dependence is to be placed on what is called 'popularity.' If ever there was a popular minister for a season, John the Baptist was that man. Yet, of all the crowds who came to his baptism and heard his preaching, how few, it may be feared, were converted. Some, we may hope, like Andrew, were guided to Christ, but the vast majority, in all probability, died in their sins."—*Ryle.*

confessing their sins] "The Greek verb being an intensive compound, denotes the act of free and full confession."—*Alexander.* "He was a good man, and commanded the Jews to exercise virtue, both as to righteousness towards one another, and piety toward God, and so to come to baptism."—*Josephus.* For further note on Baptism, see Chapter xvi, 16.

6. *was clothed*] "The Evangelist draws attention to three points in reference to the Baptist: (*a*) *His appearance.* He recalled the asceticism of the Essene. His raiment was of the coarsest texture (camel's hair), such as was worn by Elijah (2 Kings i, 8) and the prophets generally (Zech. xiii, 4). His girdle, an ornament often of the greatest richness in Oriental costume, and of the finest linen (Jer. xiii, 1; Ez. xvi, 10) or cotton, or embroidered with silver and gold (Dan. x, 5; Rev. i, 13; xv, 6), was of untanned leather (2 Kings i, 8), like that worn by the Bedouin of the present day. (*b*) *His diet* was the plainest and simplest. Locusts were permitted as an article of food (Lev. xi, 21, 22). Sometimes they were ground and pounded, and then mixed with flour and water and made into cakes; sometimes they were salted and then eaten. For *wild honey* comp. the story of

AUTHORIZED VERSION.	REVISED VERSION.
and with a girdle of a skin about his loins; and he did eat locusts and wild honey;	leathern girdle about his loins, and did eat 7 locusts and wild honey. And he preached,
7 And preached, saying, There cometh one mightier than I after me, the latchet of whose shoes I am not worthy to stoop down and unloose.	saying, There cometh after me he that is mightier than I, the latchet of whose shoes I am n t ³worthy to stoop down and unloose.
8 I indeed have baptized you with water: but he shall baptize you with the Holy Ghost.	8 I baptized you ⁴with water; but he shall baptize you ⁴with the ⁵Holy Ghost.
9 And it came to pass in those days, that Jesus came from Nazareth of Galilee, and was baptized of John in Jordan.	9 And it came to pass in those days, that Jesus came from Nazareth of Galilee, and was bap-10 tized of John ⁶in the Jordan. And straight-

³ Gr. *sufficient.* ⁴ Or, *in* ⁵ Or, *Holy Spirit:* and so throughout this book. ⁶ Gr. *into.*

Jonathan, 1 Sam. xiv, 25-27. (c) *His message.* (1) That the members of the Hebrew Nation were *all* morally unclean, and *all* needed moral and spiritual regeneration; (2) that One mightier than he was coming; (3) that he would baptize with the Holy Ghost."—*Camb. Bible.* "It would be well for the church and the world if there were more ministers like John."—*Ryle.*

7. *cometh*] present tense. The Baptist sees Christ as already come and in their midst.

latchet] diminutive of *latch*, like the Fr. *lacet*, dim. of *lacs*, comes from the Latin *laqueus* = a "noose," and means anything that catches. We now only apply la'ch to the catch of a door or gate. We speak of a "shoe-*lace*," and "lace" is radically the same word. It was the thong or strap by which the sandal was fastened to the foot; comp. Gen. xiv, 23; Isa. v, 27. To unloose the shoe was the work of the meanest slave. The idea of disparity in position between John and the coming one could not have been more forcibly expressed to an Eastern audience.

PRACTICAL LESSONS :—"The last messenger of the Old Covenant points to the first of the New. The New Testament looks back to the Old."—*Starke.* "Jesus is Christ, Son of God, and therefore divine." "The Gospel is an anthem from the harps of heaven; the music of the river of life, washing its shores on high and pouring in cascades on the earth."—*Hoge.* "The gospels are a garden enclosed, with its blossomed mounts and blazing parterres, and every several path leading up to that Tree of Life."—*J. Hamilton.* How little dependence can be placed on popularity. Crowds came to hear John; how few really followed God. "A preacher should be only a messenger who proclaims the coming of the Lord."—*Gossner.* The true preacher sinks his own identity, and exhibits Jesus only; 1 Cor. ii, 2.

9-13. THE BAPTISM AND TEMPTATION OF JESUS, A. D. 27.

9. *in those days*] Jesus was then thirty years of age (Luke iii, 23), the age appointed for the Levite's entrance on "the service of the ministry" (Num. iv, 3). It was, therefore, about A. D. 26.

came from Nazareth] his home and where he had grown up in peaceful seclusion, "increasing...in favor with God and man" (Luke ii, 52). The town Nazareth, unknown and unnamed in the Old Testament, was situated among the hills which form the southern ridges of Lebanon, just before they sink down into the Plain of Esdraelon.

baptized...in Jordan] Either at the ancient ford near Succoth, which some have identified with the Bethabara or rather, Bethany (as in revised version) of John i, 28; or at a more southern ford not far from Jericho. Conder thinks the place identical with *Abârah*, a leading ford of the Jordan, on the road to Gilead. "Without sins of his own to be confessed, repented of or pardoned, he identified himself, by this act, with his people whom he came to save from sin."—*Alexander.* " Mark's account of John's baptism has many phrases in common with both Matthew and Luke: but

AUTHORIZED VERSION.	REVISED VERSION.
10 And straightway coming up out of the water, he saw the heavens opened, and the Spirit like a dove descending upon him: 11 And there came a voice from heaven, *saying*, Thou art my beloved Son, in whom I am well pleased. 12 And immediately the Spirit driveth him into the wilderness.	way coming up out of the water, he saw the heavens rent asunder, and the Spirit as a 11 dove descending upon him: and a voice came out of the heavens, Thou art my beloved Son, in thee I am well pleased. 12 And straightway the pirit driveth him

from the additional prophecy quoted in verse 2, is certainly independent and distinct."—*Alford*.

10. *straightway*] This is Mark's favorite connecting word, and constantly recurs: the Greek word is sometimes rendered "immediately" in the A. V.; comp. i, 12, 28; iv, 5, 15; viii, 10; ix, 15; xi, 3, and other places.

he saw] We learn from Luke iii, 21, that Jesus was engaged in prayer. We find solemn prayer preceding (1) our Lord's baptism, (2) his choice of the twelve (Luke vi, 12), (3) his transfiguration (Luke ix, 29), (4) his agony in the garden (Matt. xxvi, 39).

heavens] a plural Hebrew form which has no singular, and means simply the sky.

opened] or *rent asunder* a graphic touch of Mark. Wiclif renders it "cleft." The same word in the Greek is used in Luke v, 36 (the new piece in the old garment); xxiii, 45 (rending the veil of the temple); Matt. xxvii, 51 (rending the rocks); John xxi, 11, (breaking or rending of the net).

a dove] This visible emblem of the Spirit may refer to its gentleness, and to that quality in Christ's ministry, to the brooding of the Spirit at creation, Gen. i, 2; or to the use of the bird in sacrifice, Lev. i, 14. Its descent taught the union of the Son and the Spirit.

11. *a voice*] The first of the three heavenly voices heard during his ministry at: (1) his baptism; (2) his transfiguration (Mark ix, 7); (3) in the courts of the temple during holy week (John xii, 28).

He was thus by baptism and the unction of the Holy Ghost which followed (Matt. iii, 16; comp. Ex. xxix, 4-37; Lev. viii, 1-30), solemnly consecrated to his office as Redeemer. He gave to his church for all time a striking revelation of the divine nature, the Son submitting in all lowliness to every requirement of the law, the Father approving by a voice from heaven, the Spirit descending and abiding upon the Son. "*Iad Jordanem, et videbis Trinitatem.*"= Go to Jordan and thou shalt see the Trinity.—*Maclear*.

12. *immediately*] or *straightway* "One main design (of the temptation) was to prefigure and exemplify that bitter and protracted warfare...between the seed of the serpent and the seed of the woman."—*Alexander*. The object of the Saviour was "to destroy the works of the devil" (1 John iii, 8). His very first work, therefore, was to enter on a conflict with the great enemy of mankind. The temptation was threefold in character: (1) through the appetites; (2) from presumption; (3) from ambition. See Matt. iv, 1-11.

AUTHORIZED VERSION.	REVISED VERSION.
13 And he was there in the wilderness forty days, tempted of Satan; and was with the wild beasts; and the angels ministered unto him.	13 forth into the wilderness. And he was in the wilderness forty days, tempted of Satan; and he was with the wild beasts; and the angels ministered unto him.

Tradition locates the scene of the temptation in Mt. Küründül or Qurantana, a few miles northwest of Jericho. He was tempted that he might sympathize with and succour those who are tempted. (Heb. iv, 15).

driveth him] Literally expels him, Wiclif says, putted forth. It is a stronger word than that used by Matthew, *led up* (Matt. iv, 1), or by Luke, *was led* (Luke iv, 1). The word here used is in Matt. ix, 38, "*send forth* labourers into his harvest;" and in John x, 4, "*putteth forth* his own." *The Spirit*, does not mean his own mind, nor Satan, but the Holy Spirit; not tempting him, James i, 13, but simply bringing him to the scene of temptation. The Spirit constrained him to go forth to the encounter with Satan, and the word *driveth* hints at rapid translation, such as caught and carried prophets and evangelists to a distance (1 Kings xviii, 12; 2 Kings ii, 16; Acts viii, 39).

13. *tempted of Satan*] The temptation lasted during the whole period of forty days, as the words in Mark and Luke naturally imply, or at the close of the period, as suggested by the language of Matthew (iv, 2). "Both statements may be true; he may have been assailed...during the whole period, but in a more palpable form at its conclusion."—*Alexander*. The Vulgate, Arabic and Ethiopic versions add "forty nights" to the "forty days." In Matt. iv, 1 and Luke iv, 2, he is said to have been tempted by the Devil, *i. e.*, the "Slanderer," who slanders God to man (Gen. iii, 1-5) and man to God (Job i, 9-11; Rev. xii, 10). Mark, who never uses this word, says he was tempted by *Satan*, *i. e.*, "the Enemy" of God and man alike.

the wild beasts] This intimates that he was beyond the reach of human help, and excludes the idea of even scattered human habitations.

the angels] Probably bringing him food. Matthew records the ministry of angels at the close, as to a Heavenly Prince (Matt. iv, 11). Mark records a ministry of the same celestial visitants apparently *throughout the trial*.

PRACTICAL SUGGESTIONS.—"*Baptism, without faith, saves no one*; let a man be baptized by immersion or sprinkling, in his infancy or in his adult age: if he be not led to put his trust in Jesus Christ—if he remaineth an unbeliever, then this terrible doom is pronounced upon him: 'He that believeth not shall be damned.'"—*Spurgeon*. Christ baptizes his people with the Holy Spirit. Great spiritual enjoyments are often followed by great trials. Angels are interested in the trials and sorrows of the Saints. "But then I sigh: and, with a piece of scripture, tell them that God bids us do good for evil."—*Shakspeare*. "Thou shalt be sure to be assaulted by Satan when thou hast received the greatest enlargements from heaven...This arch-pirate lets the empty ships pass, but lays wait for them when they return richest laden."—*Achb. Leighton*.

AUTHORIZED VERSION.	REVISED VERSION.
14 Now after that John was put in prison, Jesus came into Galilee, preaching the gospel of the kingdom of God, 15 And saying, The time is fulfilled, and the kingdom of God is at hand: repent ye and believe the gospel. 16 Now as he walked by the sea of Galilee, he	14 Now after that John was delivered up, Jesus came into Galilee, preaching the gospel 15 of God, and saying, The time is fulfilled, and the kingdom of God is at hand repent ye, and believe in the gospel. 16 And passing along by the sea of Galilee,

14–20. JESUS BEGINS HIS MINISTRY AND CALLS FOUR DISCIPLES.

Between the events just described and those on which the Evangelist now enters, came several recorded chiefly by John; viz., (1) The testimony of the Baptist to Christ (John i, 19-34); (2) the following of Andrew, John, Simon, Philip and Nathanael (John i, 35-51); (3) the marriage at Cana (John ii, 1-11); (4) the first visit to Jerusalem, first cleansing of the Temple and visit of Nicodemus (John ii, 13-21; iii, 1-21); (5) the ministry with the Baptist (John iii, 22-36); (6) the imprisonment of the Baptist (Luke iii, 19, 20); (7) the return of Jesus to Galilee through Samaria, the discourse with the woman at the well (John iv, 3-42); (8) cure of the nobleman's son at Cana (John iv, 43-54).

14. *put in prison*] or *delivered up* The imprisonment of the Baptist is more fully related by the Evangelist, chapter vi. 17-20.

came into Galilee] Galilee was the most northern and the most populous of the three provinces into which the Romans had divided Palestine. It was small in extent, about twenty-seven miles from east to west, and twenty-five miles from north to south; but rich in products of wheat, wine and oil, and teeming with a busy population engaged in agriculture, woolen manufactures, dyeing, weaving linen, and in producing earthenware famous for its character. The Rabbis, in their Oriental language, say that one waded in oil in Galilee.

15. *the time*] The appointed time of the Messiah. "However much the Jews misunderstood many other prophecies, the *time* and *place* of Christ's appearance seem to have been well apprehended."—*Campbell*.

the kingdom of God] Or, as it is called in Matthew iii, 2, *the Kingdom of heaven* (comp. Dan. ii, 44; vii, 13, 14, 27), is *the Kingdom of grace*.

repent...believe] To repent includes sorrow for sin, renouncing it and seeking forgiveness. Wiclif renders, *do penance;* Tyndale, *repent;* Genevan version, *amend your lives;* Rhemish, *be penitent;* Coverdale, *amend yourselves.* The word implies a radical change of heart—a complete change of mind. Believe, or rely upon the gospel as the way of salvation.

16. *as he walked*] Jesus had *come down* (Luke iv, 31; John iv, 47, 51) from the high country of Galilee to Capernaum, "his own city" (Matt. iv, 13; Luke iv, 31).

the sea of Galilee] Called (1) "the sea of Chinnereth" or "Cinneroth" (Num. xxxiv, 11; Josh. xii, 3), from a town of that name on or near its shore (Josh. xix, 35); (2) "the sea of Galilee," from the province which bordered on its western side (Matt. iv, 18; Mark vii, 31); (3) "the Lake of Gennesaret" (Luke v, 1); (4) "the Sea of Tiberias" (John xxi, 1), and sometimes (5) simply "the Sea" (Matt. iv, 15). It was pear-shaped, six and three-quarters by twelve miles in extent, 600 feet below the Mediterranean, and, in Christ's day, its western shore was thickly dotted with villages, and the hills and plains were covered with oaks, cypresses, figs, cedars, citrons, olives, myrtles and balsams. The landscape, now barren, was then a splendid garden. See Josephus, *Bell. Jud.* iii, 10. The eastern shore had towns at every opening in the basaltic hills. The lake, depressed below the

SYNAGOGUE AT MEIRON. (After Photograph, Palestine Fund.)

SEA OF GALILEE, FROM TIBERIAS. (After Original Photograph.)

32 A PICTORIAL COMMENTARY [Mark I, 16-19.

AUTHORIZED VERSION.
saw Simon and Andrew his brother casting a net into the sea; for they were fishers.
17 And Jesus said unto them, Come ye after me, and I will make you to become fishers of men.
18 And straightway they forsook their nets, and followed him.
19 And when he had gone a little further thence, he saw James the son of Zebedee, and

REVISED VERSION.
he saw Simon and Andrew the brother of Simon casting a net in the sea: for they were
17 fishers. And Jesus said unto them, Come ye after me, and I will make you to become
18 fishers of men. And straightway they left
19 the nets, and followed him. And going on a little further, he saw James the son of Zebedee, and John his brother, who also were in

sea level, and surrounded by high hills, cut by deep ravines, was subject to sudden and dangerous storms, as it is to this day. It still abounds in fish.

SKETCH MAP OF THE SEA OF GALILEE.—*Palestine Exploration Fund.*

he saw Simon] Greek form of Simeon, a Hebrew name. Jesus had before met Simon (John i, 40-42). The recent cure of the son of the officer in Herod's court had roused much interest at Capernaum, and many pressed upon the Saviour (Luke v, 1). Four of the number afterward known as "the Twelve" were now called to become "fishers of men."

The words of Jesus have a peculiar fitness, when he has just shown them (Luke v. 6) what successful fishers of the sea he could make them.

a net] An expressive phrase in Greek, *throwing around.* The net here and in Matt. iv, 18, was a *casting-net*, circular in shape, "like the top of a tent;" in Latin, *funda* or *jaculum.* The net in Matt. xiii, 47, 48, is the *drag-net* or *hauling-net*, the English seine or *sean*, sometimes half a mile in length; that in Luke v, 4-9 is the *bag-net* or *basket-net*, so constructed and worked as to enclose the fish out in deep water.

18. *forsook their nets*] Instantaneous obedience; leaving their vocation and entering upon the new one for life. A test of true discipleship.

19. *James...of Zebedee and John*] Two pairs of brothers were called at the same time. "James and John were the sons of one Zobdai, and we know, from a comparison of texts, that their mother was Salome, so honorably mentioned in the gospels."—*Geikie.* The word rendered ship or boat means any small craft or vessel, moved by sails and oars, such as fishing

AUTHORIZED VERSION.	REVISED VERSION.
John his brother, who also were in the ship mending their nets.	20 the boat mending the nets. And straightway he called them: and they left their father Zebedee in the boat with the hired servants, and went after him
20 And straightway he called them: and they left their father Zebedee in the ship with the hired servants, and went after him.	21 And they go into Capernaum; and straightway on the sabbath day he entered into the
21 And they went into Capernaum; and straightway on the sabbath day he entered into the synagogue, and taught.	22 synagogue and taught. And they were astonished at his teaching: for he taught them as having authority, and not as the scribes.
22 And they were astonished at his doctrine: for he taught them as one that had authority, and not as the scribes.	

smacks. Tyndale introduced the translation *ship*; Wiclif has the more correct term *boat*. The casual expression " mending their nets" is explained by Luke, who tells us of the miraculous draught of fishes which had broken them. "This is one of the undesigned coincidences which show the truth at the bottom of both narratives."—*Whedon.*

the hired servants] The mention of these, and of the two vessels employed (Luke v. 7), indicate that Zebedee, if not a wealthy man, was, at any rate, of some position at Capernaum. He was not dependent on his sons, and could spare them for a more important work.

went after him] They went away after him. For the miraculous draught of fishes which accompanied or followed this incident see Luke v, 2-11. *Gradually* the four had been called to their new work ; (1) they were disciples of the Baptist (John i, 35); (2) they were directed by him to *the Lamb of God* (John i, 36) ; (3) they were invited by our Lord to see where he dwelt (John i, 39) ; (4) they became witnesses of his first miracle (John ii, 2); (5) now they are enrolled among his attached followers. The more formal call was yet to come.

PRACTICAL THOUGHTS.—" Jesus, in the silent conflicts of the wilderness, prepares for the open conflicts of life."—*Lange.* Repenting and believing in Christ must go together. "The Lord's fishermen actually catch the fish ; the world's fishermen swim with the fish."—*Gossner.* Follow Jesus at any cost, and do it promptly. True repentance and faith are necessary to enter the kingdom of God. "Don't fight the devil on his own ground ; choose the ground of Christ's righteousness and atonement, and then fight him."—*A. Alexander.*

21-28. THE CURE OF THE DEMONIAC AT CAPERNAUM, A. D. 28.

21. *Capernaum*] Not mentioned in the Old Testament or the Apocrypha. It was situated on the northwest shore of the Lake, in "the land of Gennesaret" (Matt. xiv, 34 ; John vi, 17, 24), and was called " a city " (Matt. ix. 1). It had a customs station (Matt. ix, 9 ; Luke v, 27), and a detachment of Roman soldiers (Matt. viii, 8 ; Luke vii, 1, 8). It was noted as the scene of many remarkable events. At Capernaum the Lord wrought the miracle on the centurion's servant (Matt. viii, 5); healed Simon's wife's mother (Matt. viii, 14) ; cured the paralytic (Matt. ix, 2); called Levi from the toll house (Matt. ix, 9) ; taught his Apostles the lesson of humility (Mark ix, 35-37), and delivered the wonderful discourse on the " Bread of Life " (John vi, 59). The site of Capernaum is yet undetermined, strikingly illustrating the prediction of Jesus. Some locate the city at Tell Hum, about five miles southwest from the Jordan, and where the ruins of a synagogue have been discovered ; perhaps the one built by the centurion, and in which Jesus preached. Others place it at Khan Minyeh, two or three miles southwest of Tell Hum. See Schaff's *Dict. of the Bible.*

the synagogue] "The synagogue," implying that it was the only one, see v. 23 " their synagogue;" it was built for the Jews by the centurion (Luke vii. 5).

22. *not as the scribes*] The Scribes, *Sopherim*, first came into promi-

AUTHORIZED VERSION.	REVISED VERSION.
23 And there was in their synagogue a man with an unclean spirit; and he cried out, 24 Saying, Let us alone; what have we to do with thee, thou Jesus of Nazareth? art thou come to destroy us? I know thee who thou art, the Holy One of God. 25 And Jesus rebuked him, saying, Hold thy peace, and come out of him.	23 And straightway there was in their synagogue a man with an unclean spirit; and he cried out, saying, What have we to do with thee, thou Jesus of Nazareth? art thou come to destroy us? I know thee who thou art, the Holy One of God. And Jesus rebuked ¹him, saying. Hold thy peace, and come out of him. And the unclean spirit,

¹ Or, *it*.

nence in the time of Ezra (Ezra, vii, 11, 12). Their duty was to copy, read, study, explain, and "fence round" the law with "the tradition of the elders" (Matt. xv. 2). The Scribes proper only lasted till the death of Simon "the Just," B. C. 300. In the New Testament they are sometimes called "lawyers" (Matt. xxii, 35), or "doctors (*i.e. teachers*) of the law" Luke v, 17). Their teaching was preëminently second hand. They simply repeated the decisions of previous Rabbis. But our Lord's teaching was absolute and independent. His formula was not "It hath been said," but "*I say unto you.*"—*Maclear.* This does not mean that Jesus taught in a dogmatic manner, nor "powerfully," as Luther explains it, but with an authority belonging to the law-maker. "The distinction is not merely between traditional and textual instruction, but between two methods of the latter."—*Alexander.* "They [Rabbis] delivered, painfully, what they had learned like children, over-laying every address with citations in fear of saying a word of their own; but the teaching of Christ was the free expression of his own thoughts and feelings, and this, with the weight of the teaching itself, gave him power over the hearts of his audience."—*Geikie.*

23. *with an unclean spirit*] Wiclif renders it "in an unclean spirit," that is, in his power, under his influence. Luke describes him as having a "spirit of an unclean devil" (Luke iv, 33). *He cried out*, thus indicating the presence of a foreign influence or agent; and that this was a real agent, and not a mere disease.

24. *saying*] Many MSS. omit the Greek word translated "let us alone." Even if genuine, it appears to be rather an exclamation of horror = the Latin *vah! heu!* It is not the man who cries out, so much as the Evil Spirit which had usurped dominion over him.—*Maclear.*

Jesus of Nazareth] The evil spirits instantly recognize him, but with cries of despair. "Demoniacs knew what madmen, insane persons, epileptics could not know. that Jesus was the Son of God."—*Jahn.*

"It is a solemn and sorrowful thought, that...some professing Christians have even less faith than the devil....It is one thing to say, 'Christ is a Saviour;' it is quite another to say, 'He is my Saviour and my Lord.' The devil can say the first. The true Christian alone can say the second."—*Ryle.*

destroy us] "Not the demon and the man together, for the latter was to be set free by the expulsion of the former, but 'us,' the seed of the serpent ...the devil and his angels."—*Alexander.* "Dost thou think it enough to know and believe that Christ lived and died for sinners? The devil and his angels believe as much. Labor to outstrip them and to get a better faith."—*Petter*, 1661.

the Holy One of God] "The unholy, which is resolved to be unholy still, understands well that its death knell has sounded when the Holy One of God (Comp. Ps. xvi, 10, where this title first appears) has come to make war against it.—*Trench.*

25. *Hold thy peace*] Lit. *Be muzzled.* The same word is used by our Lord in rebuking the storm on the Lake, "Peace, *be still*" (Mark iv, 39).

AUTHORIZED VERSION.	REVISED VERSION.
26 And when the unclean spirit had torn him, and cried with a loud voice, he came out of him. 27 And they were all amazed, insomuch that they questioned among themselves, saying, What thing is this? what new doctrine is this? for with authority commandeth he even the unclean spirits, and they do obey him. 28 And immediately his fame spread abroad throughout all the region round about Galilee. 29 And forthwith, when they were come out of the synagogue, they entered into the house of Simon and Andrew, with James and John. 30 But Simon's wife's mother lay sick of a fever, and anon they tell him of her.	27 tearing him and crying with a loud voice, came out of him. And they were all amazed, insomuch that they questioned among themselves, saying, What is this? a new teaching! with authority he commandeth even the unclean spirits, and they 28 obey him. And the report of him went out straightway everywhere into all the region of Galilee round about. 29 And straightway, ²when they were come out of the synagogue, they came into the house of Simon and Andrew, with James 30 and John. Now, Simon's wife's mother lay sick of a fever; and straightway they

¹Or, *convulsing.* ² Some ancient authorities read *when he was come out of the synagogue, he came.*

Wiclif translates it "wexe doumbe." "Christ will not be named and praised by devils....Oh, that ministers would so reply when devils offer them flattering testimony!"—*Steir.*

26. *had torn him*] or, *tearing him,* as in R. V. A strong expression for convulsions, so the Syriac, Persian and Ethiopic versions imply. According to Luke's account, *he was thrown in the midst* (Luke iv, 35), comp. Mark ix, 26. The first miracle recorded by Matt. is the healing of a leper by a touch (Matt. viii. 1-4); the first miracle which John records is the changing water into wine (John ii, 1-11); the first miracle recorded by Mark and Luke (iv, 33-37) is this casting out of a demon in the synagogue of Capernaum.

27. *new doctrine*] The people connected the teaching with the power over evil spirits; the latter attesting the truth of the former.

PRACTICAL THOUGHTS.—Mark the contrast between the state of fallen men and fallen angels. "The great truth, Jesus is the Son of God, was not spoiled because once again proclaimed by devils."—*Pres. Edwards.* "He who would fight the devil with his own weapon, must not wonder if he finds him an overmatch."—*South.* "Fame is like a river, that beareth up things light and swollen, and drowns things weighty and solid."—*Bacon.* "If the devil must give way, yet he rages fearfully."—*Osiander.*

29-34. THE CURE OF PETER'S WIFE'S MOTHER AND OTHERS, A. D. 28.

29. *they*] See marginal reading R. V. The reading "they" refers to the Lord and the four disciples, whom he had already called, and the sense is nearly the same. It was a sabbath day, and he probably went to Peter's house to eat bread. Comp. Luke xiv, 1. "In his house Jesus henceforth found a home, as, perhaps, he had done on his former short stay."—*Geikie.*

30. *Simon's wife's mother*] We thus learn incidentally that Peter was married. For Paul's allusion to him and the other apostles as *married men* see 1 Cor. ix. 5. It is hard to reconcile these texts with the celibacy of the clergy required by the Romish church. To an ordinary reader it seems plain that forbidding ministers to marry is utterly opposed to the scripture. Clement of Alexandria, asserts positively that Peter had children, and describes the martyrdom of Peter's wife.

sick of a fever] A "great" or "violent fever" according to the physician Luke. Intermittent fever and dysentery are ordinary Syrian diseases.

tell him] "The days of darkness in a man's life are many...It needs no prophet's eye to foresee that we shall shed many a tear, and feel many a heart wrench, before we die. Let us know what to do when sickness, or bereavement, or cross, or loss, or disappointment, break in upon us like an armed man....Let us at once 'tell Jesus.'"—*Ryle.*

Authorized Version.	Revised Version.
31 And he came and took her by the hand, and lifted her up; and immediately the fever left her and she ministered unto them. 32 And at even, when the sun did set, they brought unto him all that were diseased, and them that were possessed with devils. 33 And all the city was gathered together at the door. 34 And he healed many that were sick of divers diseases, and cast out many devils; and suffered not the devils to speak, because they knew him. 35 And in the morning, rising up a great while before day, he went out, and departed into a solitary place, and there prayed.	31 tell him of her: and he came and took her by the hand, and raised her up; and the fever left her, and she ministered unto them. 32 And at even, when the sun did set, they brought unto him all that were sick, and 33 them that were ¹possessed with devils. And all the city was gathered together at the 34 door. And he healed many that were sick with divers diseases, and cast out many ²devils; and he suffered not the ²devils to speak, because they knew him³. 35 And in the morning, a great while before day, he rose up and went out, and departed 36 into a desert place, and there prayed. And

¹ *Or, demoniacs.*   ² Gr. *demons.*   ³ Many ancient authorities add *to be Christ.* See Luke iv, 41.

31. *he came*] Notice the graphic touches: the Lord (1) *went to* the sufferer, (2) *took her by the hand*, (3) *lifted her up*, and (4) *rebuked the fever* (Luke iv, 39), it *left her*, and (5) she *ministered unto them*.

32. *when the sun did set*] The sabbath ended at sunset. All three Evangelists carefully record that it was not till then that these sick were brought to Jesus. The reason of this probably was (1) either that they waited till the mid-day heat was passed, and the cool of the evening was come, or (2) the day being the sabbath (Mark i. 29–32), they were unwilling to violate the sacred rest of the day, and so waited till it was ended It is a great but common error to suppose that Jesus performed only a few miracles. After giving two particular cases the Evangelist then adds a statement (verse 34), which implies that a large number were miraculously healed on the same day.

33. *at the door*] of Peter's house. "Forthwith began to gather from every street, and from thickly sown towns and villages round, the strangest assemblage. The child led its blind father as near the enclosure of Simon's house as the throng permitted; the father came carrying the sick child; men bore the helpless in swinging hammocks; all that had any sick brought them....Fevers, convulsions, asthma, consumption, swelling dropsy, shaking palsy, the deaf, the dumb, the brain-affected, and 'possessed with devils,' that last and worst symptom of despairing misery and dark confusion of the times."—*Geikie*.

34. *devils to speak*' "It is not the office of the devil to preach the gospel, otherwise Christ might seem to have something in common with Satan; who is never more to be feared by us than when he transforms himself into an angel of light."—*Beza*.

35–39. Solitary Prayer. Tour in Galilee, A. D. 28.

35. It is often recorded of Jesus that he prayed, as at his baptism, his transfiguration, choosing his disciples, when the people would have made him king, John vi, 15, Matt. xiv, 33, and in Gethsemane. A praying master should have no prayerless servants. Ministers and teachers should be much in prayer. "They used to reckon how many hours they spent in reading and study. It were far better if more time were spent in prayer. Luther spending three hours daily in secret prayer, and Bradford studying on his knees, and other instances, are talked of rather than imitated."—*Traill*, 1696.

solitary place] "A remarkable feature of the Lake of Gennesaret was that it was closely surrounded with desert solitudes. These 'desert places' thus close at hand on the table lands or in the ravines of the eastern and western ranges, gave opportunities of retirement for rest or prayer. Rising up early in the morning, while it was yet dark, or passing over to the other side in a

AUTHORIZED VERSION.	REVISED VERSION.
36 And Simon and they that were with him followed after him.	Simon and they that were with him followed after him; and they found him, and say unto
37 And when they had found him, they said unto him, All men seek for thee.	37 him, All are seeking thee. And he saith unto them, Let us go elsewhere into the next
38 And he said unto them, Let us go into the next towns, that I may preach there also; for therefore came I forth.	towns, that I may preach there also; for to 39 this end came I forth. And he went into their synagogues throughout all Galilee,
39 And he preached in their synagogues throughout all Galilee, and cast out devils.	preaching and casting out ¹devils.
40 And there came a leper to him, beseeching	40 And there cometh to him a leper, beseech-

¹Gr. *demons.*

boat, he sought these solitudes, sometimes alone, sometimes with his disciples."—*Stanley.*

36. *Simon*] In whose house Jesus lodged; Simon missed him, and, doubtless, informed the others.

followed after him] hunted him. The Greek word is very expressive, and only occurs here. It denotes (1) *to follow hard upon,* (2) *to pursue closely, to track out.* It is used by Xenophon to describe the pursuit of an enemy in war. It occurs in a good sense in the LXX rendering of Ps. xxiii, 6, "Thy mercy shall *follow* me."

38. *towns*] Rather *village-towns* or *country-towns.* "The original distinguishes between villages which had a synagogue, those which had none, and walled towns."—*Lightfoot.* He was not to be confined to Capernaum. Dalmanutha, Magdala, Bethsaida, Chorazin, were all near at hand. For this he came, not from Simon's house, as some explain the last clause of v. 38, but into the world.

39. *all Galilee*] This was the first of a series of circuits which were made for the purpose of preaching. This circuit was begun when the harvest was ripening, and the heat at noon oppressive, making traveling comfortable mornings and evenings only. See Map of Journeyings.

PRACTICAL SUGGESTIONS.—"Satan and Satan's emissaries can speak the truth when it will serve an evil end."—*Schaff.* "The dwelling of a poor fisherman pleases Christ more than a great palace. There are always wretched ones in this vale of tears, who stand in need of the help of the most High."—*Quesnel.* "Christ should be our first resort in times of trouble." —*Clarke.* "Prayer with him seems to have been not only intimate communion with his Father, but a necessary preparation for his ministry. How much more needful for us!"—*Schaff.*

40-45. CLEANSING OF A LEPER, A. D. 28.

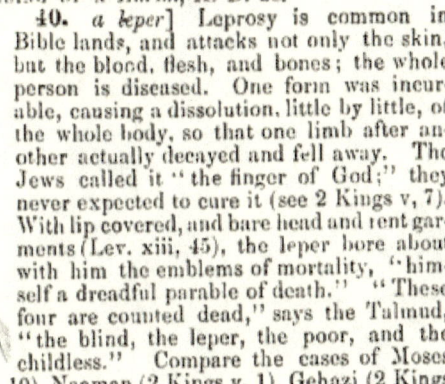

40. *a leper*] Leprosy is common in Bible lands, and attacks not only the skin, but the blood, flesh, and bones; the whole person is diseased. One form was incurable, causing a dissolution, little by little, of the whole body, so that one limb after another actually decayed and fell away. The Jews called it "the finger of God;" they never expected to cure it (see 2 Kings v, 7). With lip covered, and bare head and rent garments (Lev. xiii, 45), the leper bore about with him the emblems of mortality, "himself a dreadful parable of death." "These four are counted dead," says the Talmud, "the blind, the leper, the poor, and the childless." Compare the cases of Moses (Ex. iv, 6), Miriam (Num. xii, 10), Naaman (2 Kings v, 1), Gehazi (2 Kings

AUTHORIZED VERSION.	REVISED VERSION.
him, and kneeling down to him, and saying unto him, If thou wilt, thou canst make me clean.	ing him, ¹and kneeling down to him, and saying unto him, If thou wilt, thou canst make me clean.
41 And Jesus, moved with compassion, put forth *his* hand, and touched him, and saith unto him, I will; be thou clean.	41 And being moved with compassion, he stretched forth his hand, and touched him, and saith unto him, I will; be thou made clean.
42 And as soon as he had spoken, immediately the leprosy departed from him, and he was cleansed.	42 And straightway the leprosy departed from him, and he was made clean.
43 And he straitly charged him, and forthwith sent him away;	43 And he ²strictly charged him, and straightway sent him out, and saith unto him, See thou say nothing to any man: but go thy way, shew thyself to the priest, and offer for thy cleansing the things which Moses commanded, for a testimony unto them.
44 And saith unto him, See thou say nothing to any man; but go thy way, shew thyself to the priest, and offer for thy cleansing those things which Moses commanded, for a testimony unto them.	
45 But he went out, and began to publish *it* much, and to blaze abroad the matter, insomuch	45 them. But he went out and began to publish it much, and to spread abroad the ³matter,

¹ Some ancient authorities omit *and kneeling down to him*. ² Or, *sternly* ³ Gr. *word*.

v. 27). It is used as a type of sin, the leprosy of the soul, from which no man is free, until made whole by the blood of Christ.

kneeling down to him] Not as an act of worship, but of entreaty. Mark alone describes this (see marginal note on these words in R. V.) as also the look of compassion from the Lord, spoken of in the next verse.

41. *I will*] The words have point and brevity not brought out by either the A. V. or the R. V. "If thou wilt....I will. Thou canst cleanse me....Be thou cleansed." The Revised Version is correct in sense, but fails to show the verbal beauty given in the Greek.

43. *And he straitly charged him*] The word thus rendered occurs in four other places; (1) Matt. ix, 30, "Jesus *straitly charged* them," (2) Mark xiv, 5, "And they *murmured against* her," (3) John xi, 33, 38, "He *groaned* in the spirit." It signifies (1) strong grief or indignation, (2) to command with sternness. Comp. Gen. xliii, 7, "The man asked us *straitly* of our state;" Josh. vi, 1, "Now Jericho was *straitly* shut up." Comp. also Shakspeare, *Richard III*, I, 1, 85, 86,

"His majesty hath *straitly* given in charge
That no man shall have private conference."

44. *shew thyself to the priest*] This was the object of sending him away, that the priest might attest the reality of his cure (Lev. xiv. 3).

which Moses commanded] viz. (1) two birds, "alive *and* clean," (2) cedar wood, (3) scarlet, and (4) hyssop (Lev. xiv, 4–7). On the eighth day further offerings were to be made: (1) two he lambs without blemish, (2) one ewe lamb without blemish, (3) three tenth deals of fine flour, (4) one log of oil (Lev. xiv, 10). If the leper was poor, he was permitted to offer one lamb and two turtle-doves or two young pigeons, with one tenth deal of fine flour (Lev. xiv, 21, 22).

for a testimony unto them] Some render this "for a testimony against them;" that is, against the priests, for not accepting Jesus as the Messiah; others take the meaning to be "as proof to them that I comply with the law." It is more natural to regard the words as referring to the fact of the cleansing, which could only be publicly accepted after it was attested by the priest.

45. *began to publish*] Others in similar circumstances did not keep silence; (1) the blind men, Matt. ix, 30, 31; (2) the man with an impediment of speech, Mark vii, 36.

AUTHORIZED VERSION.	REVISED VERSION.
that Jesus could no more openly enter into the city, but was without in desert places: and they came to him from every quarter.	insomuch that ¹Jesus could no more openly enter into ²a city, but was without in desert places: and they came to him from every quarter.
CHAP. II.—And again he entered into Capernaum after some days; and it was noised that he was in the house.	2 And when he entered again into Capernaum after some days, it was noised that he was in ³the house. And many were gathered together, so that there was no longer room for them, no, not even about the door: and he spake the word unto them. And they come, bringing unto him a man sick of the palsy, borne of four. And when they could not ⁴come nigh unto him for the crowd, they uncovered the roof where he was: and when they had broken it up, they let down the bed
2 And straightway many were gathered together, insomuch that there was no room to receive them, no, not so much as about the door: and he preached the word unto them.	
3 And they came unto him, bringing one sick of the palsy, which was borne of four.	
4 And when they could not come nigh unto him for the press, they uncovered the roof where he was: and when they had broken it up, they let down the bed wherein the sick of the palsy lay.	

¹Gr. *he.* ²Or, *the city.* ³Or, *at home.* ⁴ Many ancient authorities read *bring him unto him.*

could no more openly enter into the city] This shows why the Lord enjoined silence on the leper. We may be silent in respect to the truth: "1. When the uttering of it may bring hurt to the truth itself. 2. When we are in the company of persons more likely to cavil and scoff at the truth than to make good use of it. 3. When in company of malicious enemies of the truth."—*Petter*, 1661. "Unquestionably the majority of Christians are far more inclined to be silent about their glorious Master, than to confess him....There are good men who have more zeal than discretion, and help the enemy of truth by unseasonable acts and words."—*Ryle.*

desert places] "The deserts mentioned in the Bible are uncultivated tracts of earth of two kinds: some *mountainous,* but not destitute of water; others *plains* covered with sterile *sands,* in which fountains are very rare. The mountainous deserts are not of so dreary and unproductive a character." —*Jahn.*

CH. II. 1–12. THE PARALYTIC AND THE POWER TO FORGIVE SINS.

1. *the house*] Some suppose this was his own house, as implied in the margin of the R. V., or that of his friends, Mark iii, 21 but it is more consistent to suppose that he made Peter's house his home. *Comp.* his reply to Herod's messengers.

2. *about the door*] The Greek phrase implies that all the avenues of approach to the house were blocked up, and the courtyard or vestibule was filled.

3. *borne of four*] Notice the pictorial definiteness of the Evangelist.

4. *they uncovered the roof*] The Greek word implies "digging through" the tiles, as Luke says, and perhaps the earth or plaster often placed above them. It was not the simple removal of a parapet or awning, as some suggest. They appear (1) to have ascended to the flat roof, probably by a flight of steps outside (Luke v, 19); (2) to have broken through earth and the tiling or thin stone slabs; (3) to have lowered the paralytic upon his bed through the opening. Bedsteads were not in use in Syria, and the explanation given in the *Comprehensive Commentary* is

ASIATIC BEDS.
(From Fellows' Asia Minor.)

AUTHORIZED VERSION.	REVISED VERSION.
5 When Jesus saw their faith, he said unto the sick of the palsy, Son, thy sins be forgiven thee. 6 But there were certain of the scribes sitting there, and reasoning in their hearts, 7 Why doth this *man* thus speak blasphemies? who can forgive sins but God only? 8 And immediately, when Jesus perceived in his spirit that they so reasoned within themselves, he said unto them, Why reason ye these things in your hearts? ¹ Gr. *Child*.	5 whereon the sick of the palsy lay. And Jesus seeing their faith saith unto the sick of the palsy, ¹Son, thy sins are forgiven. But there were certain of the scribes sitting there, and 7 reasoning in their hearts, Why doth this man thus speak? he blasphemeth: who can forgive sins but one, *even* God? And straightway Jesus, perceiving in his spirit that they so reasoned wi hin themselves, saith unto them, Why reason ye these things in your

absurd. The room was either the court or, more probably, an upper chamber, which often extended over the whole area of the house. Comp. Acts i, 13; ix. 37; xx, 8.

AN EASTERN HOUSE TOP.

5. *their faith*] The faith of the paralytic himself and those that bore him. Jesus did not reject this "charitable work" of theirs in bringing before him the palsied man.

Son] Or "child," for the Greek word is neuter, and used for persons of both sexes. Luke v. 20, gives the words thus: "Man, thy sins are forgiven thee." Mark has preserved to us the tenderer word, as Matthew does in the case of the woman with the issue of blood (Matt. ix. 22).

thy sins] Comp. the words of the Saviour to the man who had an infirmity thirty and eight years: "sin no more, lest a worse thing come unto thee," John v. 14. So this man's consciousness of sin was such that it was necessary to speak to his soul before healing his body. See Luke vii, 48. But Jesus did elsewhere condemn the Jewish notion that all suffering was caused by some special sin. See John ix, 3; Luke xiii. 2-5.

forgiven] "The Greek verb is ambiguous, and may be either a command or an affirmation, 'be forgiven.' 'are forgiven.' or, 'have been forgiven.' The revisers adopt the second rendering. "How many in every age can testify that this palsied man's experience has been their own? They have learned wisdom by affliction. Bereavements have proved mercies. Losses have proved real gains. Sicknesses have led them to the Great Physician of souls."—*Ryle.*

6. *certain of the scribes*] Some from Galilee and Judea, who had come to watch Jesus.

7. *blaspheme*] Forgiveness was the direct act of God; no human lips dared pronounce it...None would venture to declare it, except in the name of Jehovah, and by his authority. "The lofty words of Jesus....sounded new, and to be new was to be dangerous."—*Geikie.*

8. *perceived*] The knowledge "was supernatural, as is most carefully and precisely here signified."—*Alford.*

in his spirit] This refers to his mind; either his divine or his human

AUTHORIZED VERSION.	REVISED VERSION.
9 Whether is it easier to say to the sick of the palsy, Thy sins be forgiven thee; or to say, Arise, and take up thy bed, and walk? 10 But that ye may know that the Son of man hath power on earth to forgive sins (he saith to the sick of the palsy). 11 I say unto thee, Arise, and take up thy bed, and go thy way into thine house. 12 And immediately he arose, took up the bed, and went forth before them all; in-omuch that they were all amazed, and glorified God, saying, We never saw it on this fashion. 13 And he went forth again by the sea side; and all the multitude resorted unto him, and he taught them.	9 hearts? Whether is easier, to say to the sick of the palsy, Thy sins are forgiven; or to say, Arise, and take up thy bed, and walk? But that ye may know that the Son of man hath 'power on earth to forgive sins (he saith to 11 the sick of the palsy), I say unto thee, Arise, take up thy bed, and go unto thy house. 12 And he arose, and straightway took up the bed, and went forth before them all; insomuch that they were all amazed, and glorified God, saying, We never saw it on this fashion. 13 And he went forth again by the sea side; and all the multitude resorted unto him, and

¹ Or, *authority*.

nature. He perceived their thoughts "thoroughly," as the Greek implies.

9. *Whether is it easier*] A striking instance of the consummate wisdom of Jesus in refuting his enemies. Notice what is here contrasted. Not, " Which is easier to do?" but, " Which is easier to *claim*, this power or that; *to say*, Thy sins be forgiven thee, or *to say*, Arise and walk?"

10. *that ye may know*] " By doing that which is capable of being put to the proof, I will vindicate my right and power to do that which, in its very nature, is incapable of being proved." If there was imposture it would be easier to detect it in respect to the healing than in respect to the forgiveness; so Jesus would prove that his power was real in both cases. He had power, not delegated, but his own, as Messiah. Alexander states: " A mere declaratory absolution they could utter...but he spoke with authority and not as the scribes."

Son of man] This is the first time this title occurs in Mark, where we find it 14 times. This title is never applied by the writers of the Gospels themselves to the Eternal Son of God. Whenever it occurs, it is so applied by our Lord. There are only three exceptions to this rule; (1) where the title is used by Stephen (Acts vii, 56), and (2) by John (Rev. i, 13; xiv, 14). (See also Dan. vii, 13.)

on earth] This power is not exercised, as ye think, only in heaven, by God, but also by the Son of Man on earth.

11. *thy bed*] The original word thus rendered means a portable pallet (so the American revisers render it here, and in verses 4, 9 and 12), and was little more than a mat, used for mid-day sleep and the service of the sick. It was of the commonest kind, and used by the poorest. (See Illustration p. 39.)

12. *before them all*] Now yielding before him and no longer blocking up his path. " He not only rises, but shows that he is fully restored, by taking up his couch."—*Clarke*. The miracle was an attestation of the divine authority of Jesus.

PRACTICAL SUGGESTIONS.—We, like the city of Capernaum, may have great spiritual privileges, and make no use of them. Bodily afflictions may prove a blessing to the soul. " Christian love demands that we should serve and help the sick."—*Starke*. " Great faith discovers and adopts wonderful plans."—*Lange*. " Christ, by his visible miracles, taught men to understand his invisible miracles."—*Quesnel*. We may bear our friends to Christ now, in the arms of faith and prayer. Has Jesus said to you, " Son, child, thy sins are forgiven?"

13-22. CALL OF LEVI; THE DISCOURSE AT HIS HOUSE, A.D., 28.

13. *he went forth*] *i. e.*, from the town of Capernaum to the shore of the lake, probably through a suburb of fishers' huts and custom-houses.

AUTHORIZED VERSION.	REVISED VERSION.
14 And as he passed by, he saw Levi the son of Alphæus sitting at the receipt of custom, and said unto him, Follow me. And he arose and followed him. 15 And it came to pass, that, as Jesus sat at meat in his house, many publicans and sinners sat also together with Jesus and his disciples: for there were many, and they followed him.	14 he taught them. And as he passed by, he saw Levi the son of Alphæus sitting at the place of toll, and he saith unto him, Follow me. 15 And he arose and followed him. And it came to pass, that he was sitting at meat in his house, and many [1]publicans and sinners sat down with Jesus and his disciples: for there were many, and they followed him.

[1] See marginal note on Matt. v, 46; which is, "That is, *collectors or renters of Roman taxes.*"

14. *Levi*] The three gospel narratives clearly relate the same circumstances in respect to Levi and Matthew, and hence the two names are generally believed to refer to one person. He may have been first known by the name of Levi, then as Matthew, or Mattathias, a favorite name amongst the Jews after the Captivity, and meaning the same as *Theodore*, "Gift of God."

son of Alphæus] Some have identified this Alphæus with Alphæus the father of James the Less. But in the lists of the apostles the two are never named together, like other pairs of brothers in the apostolic body.

sitting...receipt of custom] In Syria the people sit at all kinds of work. "The carpenter saws, planes and hews with his adze, sitting on the ground or plank he is planing. The washerwoman sits by her tub....Shopkeepers always sit; and Levi sitting is the exact way to state the case."—*Thomson*. Situated, as Capernaum was, at the nucleus of roads which diverged to Tyre, Damascus, Jerusalem, and Sepphoris, it was a busy centre of merchandise, and a natural place for the collection of tribute and taxes. The collector may have been in a toll-booth, as Wiclif renders the word.

Follow me] Though he belonged to a class above all others hated and despised by the Jews, yet the Lord did not hesitate to invite him to become one of the Twelve. And Levi did not hesitate to obey the call, though it was a great change in his life work, as in his opinions. "No liberal man would impute a charge of unsteadiness to another for having changed his opinions."—*Cicero*.

ROMAN TRICLINIUM, ILLUSTRATING JEWISH METHOD OF EATING.

15. *sat at meat*] Or "reclined" according to the Roman custom. Luke says that Matthew made "a great feast" in honor of his new Master, not in the "Lord's house," as Meyer interprets it, but in Levi's house. To it, perhaps by way of farewell, he invited many of his old associates. This shows that he had made large sacrifices in order to follow Christ; see Neander's *Life of Christ*.

publicans and sinners] The publicans or tax gatherers under the Roman government were of two classes: (1) Persons who farmed the Roman taxes, and in later times were usually Roman knights and men of wealth and position, of whom Cicero thus wrote: "Publicani homines et honestissimi et ornatissimi." (2) Subordinate collectors, each of whom was required to pay a certain sum to his superior, with the privilege of raising as much more as he could for his own profit. These inferior collectors were natives of the

AUTHORIZED VERSION.	REVISED VERSION.
16 And when the scribes and Pharisees saw him eat with publicans and sinners, they said unto his disciples, How is it that he eateth and drinketh with publicans and sinners?	16 And the scribes ¹of the Pharisees, when they saw that he was eating with the sinners and publicans, said unto his disciples, ²He eateth ³ and drinketh with publicans and sinners.
17 When Jesus heard it, he saith unto them, They that are whole have no need of the physician, but they that are sick : I came not to call the righteous, but sinners to repentance.	17 And when Jesus heard it, he saith unto them, They that are ⁴ whole have no need of a physician, but they that are sick : I came not to call the righteous, but sinners.
18 And the disciples of John and of the Pharisees used to fast : and they come and say unto him, Why do the disciples of John and of the Pharisees fast, but thy disciples fast not?	18 And John's disciples and the Pharisees were fasting: and they come and say unto him, Why do John's disciples and the disciples of the Pharisees fast, but thy disciples fast not?

¹ Some ancient authorities read *and the Pharisees.* ² Or, how is it *that he eateth....sinners?* ³ Some ancient authorities omit *and drinketh.* ⁴ Gr. *strong.*

province where the taxes were collected, and were properly called *portitores* or *exactores*. So notorious were they for rapacity and dishonesty that Suetonius (*Vit. Vesp.* 1.) tells us how several cities erected statues to Sabinius, "the honest publican;" and Theocritus, in answer to the question, which were the worst kind of wild beasts, said, "On the mountains, bears and lions; in cities, publicans and pettifoggers." The Jews included them in the same category with harlots and sinners ; see Matt. xvii, 17 ; xxi, 31, 32. "They were nothing less than renegades and traitors, who, for filthy lucre's sake, had sided with the enemy, and now collected for a profane heathen treasury that tribute which was the evident sign of the subjection of God's people to a Gentile yoke. This scorn and hate found utterance in a thousand ways; no alms might be received from their money chest; it was not even lawful to change money there; their testimony was not received in courts of justice; they were as the heathen (to keep which in mind adds an emphasis to Luke xix, 9), and in some sort worse than the heathen "—*Trench*. "Matthew alone styles *himself*, in the list of the Apostles, as ' the publican.'"

16. *said unto his disciples*] Overawed by the miracles he had wrought and the overthrow they had lately experienced at the healing of the paralytic, and not as yet venturing on any open rupture with him, they vent their displeasure on his disciples. It is not likely that the Pharisees were present at the feast, or they would have involved themselves in the same blame. Probably they looked in while it was in progress, and afterwards came forward to the disciples coming out.—*Maclear.*

17. *not to call the righteous.*] That is, the self-righteous, as the Pharisees were, or the sinless, or those complying fully with the law, as the Pharisees claimed they did. "I came not to call men, as unfallen, sinless beings, to repentance"....The distinction he draws is not between two classes of men, but between two characters or conditions of the whole race."—*Alexander.*

18. *the disciples of John*] The contrast between their Master in prison and Jesus at the feast could not fail to be felt.

used to fast] Moses enjoined only one fast, that of the great day of atonement (Lev. xvi, 29). Others were added later, as, those in the fourth, fifth, tenth and twelfth months (Jer. lii, 6, 7, 12, 13 ; xli, 1, 2 ; lii, 4 ; Esth. ix, 31. See also, Zech. vii, 5 ; viii, 19). The number of annual fasts have been increased in the present Jewish calendar to twenty-eight. The Jews were wont to fast on Thursday, because on that day Moses was said to have re-ascended Mount Sinai ; on Monday, because on that day he returned. The Pharisee said (Luke xviii, 12), "I fast twice in the week." Perhaps this feast took place on one of their weekly fasts. Fasting is of very early origin. "Abstinence which seemed imposed by Providence, if not in expiation for guilt, yet as an accompaniment of sorrow, easily became to be regarded as a religious duty "—*Kitto*. It was likewise, as we have seen, commanded by Jehovah in certain cases.

AUTHORIZED VERSION.	REVISED VERSION.
19 And Jesus said unto them, Can the children of the bridechamber fast, while the bridegroom is with them? as long as they have the bridegroom with them, they cannot fast. 20 But the days will come, when the bridegroom shall be taken away from them, and then shall they fast in those days. 21 No man also seweth a piece of new cloth on an old garment: else the new piece that filled it up taketh away from the old, and the rent is made worse. 22 And no man putteth new wine into old bottles: else the new wine doth burst the bottles, and the wine is spilled, and the bottles will be marred: but new wine must be put into new bottles.	19 And Jesus said unto them, Can the sons of the bridechamber fast, while the bridegroom is with them? as long as they have the bridegroom with them, they cannot fast. But the days will come, when the bridegroom shall be taken away from them, and then will they fast in that day. 21 No man seweth a piece of undressed cloth on an old garment: else that which should fill it up taketh from it, the new from the old, and a worse rent is made. 22 And no man putteth new wine into old ¹wine-skins: else the wine will burst the skins, and the wine perisheth, and the skins: but *they put* new wine into fresh wine-skins.

¹ That is, *skins used as bottles*.

19. *children of the bridechamber*] i. e., the friends and companions of the bridegroom, who accompanied him to the house of the bride for the marriage. Comp. Judges xiv, 11. The marriage feast lasted seven days.

the bridegroom] He reminds the disciples of John of the image under which their Master had spoken of him as the bridegroom (John iii, 29).

20. *the days will come*] at his death ; a dim hint of the same kind he had already given, when he said to the Jewish rulers, " Destroy this temple, and in three days I will raise it up" (John ii, 19), and in his conversation with Nicodemus (John iii, 14). The passage should read, " *But days will come.*"

taken away] The same word is used in three of the gospels, and implies a violent termination of his life. The word occurs nowhere else in the New Testament.

22. *new*] " In religion, no less than in secular affairs, new emergencies require new means to meet them."—*Alexander*. Men don't pour new, or unfermented, wine into old and worn wine-skins. " My disciples," our Lord seems to say, " are not yet strong. They have not yet been baptized into the Spirit. They need tenderness and consideration. They could no more endure severe new doctrine, than an old robe could the insertion of a piece of new cloth, which had never passed through the hands of the fuller." Besides, " New teaching like his must be put into new bottles; the forms and rites that had served until now were of no more use....New forms were needed for the new religious life he came to introduce."—*Geikie*.

bottles] " The manufacture of these skin bottles is very simple. The animal is skinned from the neck by simply cutting off the head and legs, and them drawing the skin back without making any slit in the belly. The skins in this state, with the hair on, are then steeped in tannin, and filled with a decoction of bark for a few weeks....They are then sewn up at the neck, the sutures being carefully pitched. They are then exposed to the sun, on the ground, for a few days, covered with a strong decoction of tannin and water, pumped on them from time to time, to keep them on the stretch till sufficiently saturated. Dry bottles crack. The hair on the skins preserves them from friction in traveling. An old skin is not able to bear the distention of new wine in the process of fermentation, and would burst with it."—*Tristram*.

SKIN-BOTTLES (Ayre).

PRACTICAL SUGGESTIONS —Christ can and will call men from the world into his service. Christ's chief work is to call sinners. His calls should be

AUTHORIZED VERSION.	REVISED VERSION.
23 And it came to pass, that he went through the corn fields on the sabbath day; and his disciples began, as they went, to pluck the ears of corn.	23 And it came to pass, that he was going on the sabbath day through the cornfields; and his disciples ¹began, as they went, to pluck
24 And the Pharisees said unto him, Behold, why do they on the sabbath day that which is not lawful?	24 the ears of corn. And the Pharisees said unto him, Behold, why do they on the sabbath day that which is not lawful? And he
25 And he said unto them, Have ye never read what David did, when he had need, and was an hungred, he, and they that were with him?	said unto them, Did ye never read what David did, when he had need, and was an hungred, he, and they that were with him?

¹ Gr. *began to make their way plucking.*

obeyed at once. He is to be preferred to all others. Opposition may be helpful. "Kites rise *against*, not with the wind."—*Neal.* "Grace draws Matthew from love of gold, and makes of him an apostle; the love of gold drew Judas away from Christ and his apostleship." In our social life we should have spiritual things in view. "Fasting is good; but to make a merit of it, or even to burden the conscience with it, is opposed to Christian freedom."—*Cramer.*

23-28. THE DISCIPLES PLUCK THE EARS OF CORN, A.D., 28.

23. *on the sabbath day*] A fourth charge against Jesus was that he broke the sabbath. Luke tells us that this was on the "*second sabbath after the first*" i. e., either (1) the first Sabbath after the second day of unleavened bread; or (2) the first Sabbath in the second year of a Sabbatical cycle; or (3) the first Sabbath of the second month (Luke vi, 1). See Wieseler's *Chronol. Synop.*, p. 353 et seq. "Probably about a month intervened between this and the last event."—*Clarke.*

to pluck the ears of corn] Not to "make a way," as some interpret it, for that was not necessary. Matthew says that they were "an hungred"(Matt. xii, 1). The act described marks the season of the year. The wheat was ripe, for they would not have rubbed barley in their hands (Luke vi, 1). We may conclude, therefore, the time was a week or two after the Passover, when the first ripe sheaf was offered as the first fruits of the harvest. Thomson says: "I have often seen my muleteers, as we passed along the wheat fields, pluck off ears, rub them in their hands, and eat the grains unroasted, just as the apostles are said to have done."

24. *that which is not lawful*] They did not accuse them of theft, for the Law allowed what they were doing (Deut. xxiii, 25), but of profaning the Sabbath. The Law, of course, forbade reaping and threshing on that day, but the Rabbis had decided that even to pluck corn was to be construed as reaping, and to rub it as threshing. They even forbade walking on grass as a species of threshing, and would not allow so much as a fruit to be plucked from a tree on that day. See Lightfoot, *Hor. Heb.*, in Matt. xii. 2.

TABLE OF SHEW BREAD.

25. *ye never read*] With a gentle irony he adopts one of the favorite formulas of their own Rabbis, and inquires if they had never read what David, their favorite hero, had done when flying from Saul. He came to the high priest at Nob, and entered the Tabernacle, and ate of the hallowed bread (1 Sam. xxi, 1-9), of the "twelve cakes of fine flour," which no stranger might eat. If David is justified in relaxing some of the strictness of God's laws, in case of necessity, much more may Christ, the head of the Church, do so in regard to the sabbath.

AUTHORIZED VERSION.	REVISED VERSION.
26 How he went into the house of God in the days of Abiathar the high priest, and did eat the shewbread, which is not lawful to eat but for the priests, and gave also to them which were with him? 27 And he said unto them, The sabbath was made for man, and not man for the sabbath: 28 Therefore the Son of man is Lord also of the sabbath. CHAP. III.—And he entered again into the synagogue; and there was a man there which had a withered hand.	26 How he entered into the house of God ¹when Abiathar was high priest, and did eat the shewbread, which is not lawful to eat save for the priests, and gave also to them that 27 were with him? And he said unto them, The sabbath was made for man, and not man 28 for the sabbath: so that the Son of man is lord even of the sabbath. 3 And he entered again into the synagogue; and there was a man there which had his hand 2 withered. And they watched him, whether

¹ *Some ancient authorities read* in the days of Abiathar the high priest.

26. *Abiathar*] In 2 Sam. viii, 17, and the parallel passage, 1 Chron. xviii, 16, we find *Ahimelech* or *Abimelech* substituted for Abiathar; while in 2 Sam. xx, 25, and in every other passage of the O. T., Abiathar is named as priest with Zadok in David's reign, and that he was the son of Ahimelech. Several explanations of this difficulty have been suggested: 1. A clerical error in the text; 2 That father and son had both names; 3. That the son acted as High Priest at the same time with his father. The Persian version reads Ahimelech, instead of Abiathar.

27. *the sabbath*] "According to Rabbinical authorities, it was forbidden to travel more than 2000 cubits on the sabbath, to kill the most offensive kinds of vermin, to write two letters of the alphabet, to use a wooden leg or a crutch, to carry a purse. or, for a woman, to carry a seal ring or a smelling bottle, to wear a high head dress or a false tooth. Amongst other restraints laid upon animals the fat-tailed sheep was not allowed to use the little truck on which the tail was borne, to save the animal from suffering. These are a portion of 39 prohibitions of the same kind."—*Bible Com.* Jesus opposed such traditionalism and fanaticism when he said, "*The sabbath was made for man, and not man for the sabbath*"—a great principle, says Schaff, "which must regulate the whole sabbath question, and settles both the permanent necessity of the sabbath for the temporal and eternal welfare of man, and the true Christian freedom in its observance."

28. *the Son of man is Lord*] "As being himself the *divine Rest* and the *divine Celebration*; he is both the principle and the object of the sabbath. He rests in God and God in him; hence he is the mediator of proper sabbath observance, and the interpreter of the sabbath law."—*Lange.* Jesus is Lord of the sabbath, "to *own* it, to *interpret* it, to *preside over* it and to *ennoble* it, by merging it in 'the Lord's day.'"

PRACTICAL SUGGESTIONS.—"When Jesus thus, with his disciples, suffered them to be poor, we may learn that poverty is not disgraceful."—*Barnes.* The law of the sabbath is always to be construed in this light, as providing for man's highest welfare."—*Jacobus.* "The sabbath is an institution meant for human benefit," but Jesus "says not a word to justify the notion that Christians need not remember the day to keep it holy." "National prosperity and personal growth in grace are intimately bound up in the maintenance of the holy Sabbath."—*Ryle.* We are "to observe the sabbath in such a way that our temporal and spiritual welfare is thereby furthered." —*Schaff.*

CH. III. **1-12.** THE WITHERED HAND, AND WITHDRAWAL OF JESUS.

1. *And he entered*] Mark is peculiarly vivid and pictorial. The incident occurred at Capernaum, and probably on the next sabbath after plucking the ears of grain. See Luke vi, 6.

hand withered] Luke says his "right hand." Withered or "dried up," as

AUTHORIZED VERSION.	REVISED VERSION.
2 And they watched him, whether he would heal him on the sabbath day; that they might accuse him. 3 And he saith unto the man which had the withered hand, Stand forth. 4 And he saith unto them, Is it lawful to do good on the sabbath days, or to do evil? to save life, or to kill? But they held their peace. 5 And when he had looked round about on them with anger, being grieved for the hardness of their hearts, he saith unto the man, Stretch forth thine hand. And he stretched it out: and his hand was restored whole as the other. 6 And the Pharisees went forth, and straight-	he would heal him on the sabbath day; that 3 they might accuse him. And he saith unto the man that had his hand withered, ¹Stand 4 forth. And he saith unto them, Is it lawful on the sabbath day to do good, or to do harm? to save a life, or to kill? But they held their 5 peace. And when he had looked round about on them with anger, being grieved at the hardening of their heart, he saith unto the 6 man, Stretch forth thy hand. And he stretched it forth: and his hand was restored. And the Pharisees went out, and straightway with the

¹ Gr. *Arise into the midst.*

the original implies, and the effect of disease or a wound. Such cases were incurable. Comp. 1 Kings xiii, 4, for the case of Jeroboam.

2. *they watched him*] The original word for "watched" signifies stratagem and hostility; comp. Luke xx. 20, "And they watched *him* and sent forth spies;" Acts ix, 24, "And they watched the gates day and night to kill him." They intended to accuse Jesus before the Jewish rulers.

4. *he saith*] It would seem that the Pharisees first asked him, "Is it lawful to heal on the sabbath days?" (Matt. xii, 10). This question he answered, as was his wont (Matt. xxi, 24), by a counter-question: I also will ask you one thing. Is it lawful to do good on the Sabbath days, or to do evil? to save life, or to destroy it? "One of their own most approved maxims was, that he who neglected to preserve life, when it was in his power, was a murderer."—*A. Clarke.*

But they held their peace] Mark alone mentions this striking circumstance, as also what we read in the next verse.

5. *with anger*] He "*looked round*" upon them, surveyed each face with grief and anger. "By this word anger and grieved, it is signified that Christ was offended at their wickedness; yet, so that he also pitied their misery." —*Beza.* We owe to Mark this passing shadow over the countenance of our Lord, with whom grief for the sinner ever accompanied anger against the sin.

hardness] The word thus rendered denotes (1) *the process by which the extremities of fractured bones are reunited by a callus*; then (2) *callousness, hardness.* Paul uses the word in Rom. xi, 25, which there reads "blindness."

restored whole as the other] Without the employment of any external means. This miracle forms one of seven wrought on the Sabbath day. The other six were, (1) The demoniac at Capernaum (Mark i, 21); (2) Simon's wife's mother (Mark 1, 29); (3) the impotent man at the pool of Bethesda (John v, 9); (4) the woman with a spirit of infirmity (Luke xiii, 14); (5) the man who had the dropsy (Luke xiv, 1); (6) the man born blind (John ix, 14).—*Camb. Bible.* "Jesus chose to do many of his miracles on the Sabbath, that he might do the work of abrogation and institution both at once.—*Jeremy Taylor.*

6. *And the Pharisees went forth*] The Scribes and Pharisees were "*filled with madness,*" and held a consultation, *i. e.*, a formal assembly. The Saviour had not merely broken their traditions, but had put them to silence before all the people. In their blind hate they joined the Herodians, the court party, and their political opponents, in taking counsel how they might put him to death.

AUTHORIZED VERSION.	REVISED VERSION.
way took counsel with the Herodians against him, how they might destroy him. 7 But Jesus withdrew himself with his disciples to the sea: and a great multitude from Galilee followed him, and from Judæa, 8 And from Jerusalem, and from Idumæa, and from beyond Jordan; and they about Tyre and	Herodians took counsel against him, how they might destroy him. 7 And Jesus with his disciples withdrew to the sea: and a great multitude from Galilee followed: and from Judæa, and from Jerusalem, and from Idumæa, and beyond Jordan,

the Herodians] As the partisans of Marius were called "Mariani," of Pompeius "Pompeiani," of Otho "Othoniani," so the partisans of Herod and who "were such Jews as favored Herod Antipas, and thus, outwardly at least, were friends of Rome, whose vassal Antipas was," were called "Herodiani." The sect was rather a political than a religious body; its object being to gain for Antipas, as a son of Herod, the kingdom of Judea and Samaria, which had been made a Roman procuratorship. Accordingly there was enmity between him and his family on the one hand, against the procurators on the other, Luke xxiii, 12. As the annexation to Rome had disappointed the hopes of many, they looked with fear on the Herodian family, who were Idumæans, who again regarded Jesus as their enemy, because his mission was to set up, as they thought, a temporal kingdom. This alliance between the Pharisees and the Herodians against Jesus was the first step to the union between them in their anti-Roman schemes, though the latter held Sadducean opinions, and believed that the hopes of the Jewish nation rested on the Herods, against Roman ambition, and almost looked to them for a fulfillment of the prophecies respecting the advent of the Messiah. "Between lie and lie there are always points of contact, so that they can act together for a while; it is only between a lie and the truth that there is absolute opposition, and no compromise possible."

7. *a great multitude*] These multitudes were from (1) Tyre and Sidon and Galilee; (2) Judæa and Jerusalem in the centre; (3) Peræa "beyond Jordan" on the East, (4) Idumæa in the extreme South. Tyre, meaning *rock*, and Sidon, meaning fishery (see illustrations, pp. 49, 54): such were the two "mother" cities of Phœnicia, on the Mediterranean Sea. They were probably the oldest cities in that region, and are still represented by the modern towns of *Sur* and *Saida*. Sidon or Saida is about 20 miles north of Tyre.

8. *Iaumæa*] A Greek name for Edom, which lay southeast of Palestine,

THE APPROACH TO EDOM FROM THE EAST (After a Photograph by Frith).

Modern Tyre. (After a Photograph.)

AUTHORIZED VERSION.	REVISED VERSION.
Sidon, a great multitude, when they had heard what great things he did, came unto him. 9 And he spake to his disciples, that a small ship should wait on him because of the multitude, lest they should throng him. 10 For he had healed many; insomuch that they pressed upon him for to touch him, as many as had plagues. 11 And unclean spirits, when they saw him, fell down before him, and cried, saying, Thou art the Son of God. 12 And he straitly charged them that they should not make him known. 13 And he goeth up into a mountain, and calleth *unto him* whom he would: and they came unto him.	and about Tyre and Sidon, a great multitude, hearing [1] what great things he did, came unto 9 him. And he spake to his disciples, that a little boat should wait on him because of the 10 crowd, lest they should throng him: for he had healed many; insomuch that as many as had [2]plagues [3]pressed upon him that they 11 might touch him. And the unclean spirits, whensoever they beheld him, fell down before him, and cried, saying, Thou art the Son 12 of God. And he charged them much that they should not make him known. 13 And he goeth up into the mountain, and calleth unto him whom he himself would:

[1] Or, *all the things that he did* [2] Gr. *scourges.* [3] Gr. *fell.*

on the eastern side of the Valley of Akabah. The country was about 125 miles long by thirty miles wide. It was inhabited by the children of Edom, who were subdued by David, 2 Sam. viii, 14; and again conquered by John Hyrcanus, a Maccabean ruler, B. C. 125. It was the birth place of Antipas, father of Herod the Great. Idumæa is not elsewhere named in the N. T. "This is the fullest statement to be found in any of the Gospels as to the extent of our Lord's personal influence, and the composition of the multitudes who followed him."—*Alexander.*

9. *multitude*] or "crowd." The Greek word is not the same as that in v. 7, but implies a confused and tumultuous company.

10. *pressed*] or "fell upon him," as a crowd would.

plagues] The word thus rendered denotes (1) *a whip* or *scourge*, and is used in this sense in Acts xxii, 24; Heb. xi, 36; (2) a *plague* or *disease of the body.* Comp. Mark v, 29, 34; Luke vii, 21.

11. *Thou art the Son of God*] In the synagogue of Capernaum they had called him the "Holy One of God" (Mark i, 24), they now acknowledge him as the "Son of God" (comp. Luke iv, 41). The force of the imperfect tense in the original here is very striking, "whenever the demons saw him. they kept falling down before him and saying."

PRACTICAL SUGGESTIONS.—"The ability to do good imposes the obligation to do it."—*C. Mather.* "What an obligation rests on the rich to do good!" —*Barnes.* Christ's people "are marked men." Their dress, expenditures, use of time, conduct, spirit, are rigidly scanned, and the world watches to see them fall into error. It is lawful to do good works of necessity and mercy on the sabbath. Christians are not to stop doing good because of opposition. One field of usefulness may be left for another, to avoid unnecessary conflict. "We fear man so much because we fear God so little."

13-19. CALLING TWELVE APOSTLES, A. D. 28.

13. *calleth*] "We have...in the process of preparing men to organize the church: (1) The personal call of at least seven persons into Christ's society, as friends and pupils; (2) a second call to constant personal attendance; (3) The more formal designation of twelve persons to the apostolic office." —*Alexander.* They would have "for their high commission, the organization of the new kingdom of God, first in Israel, then throughout the world."— *Geikie.* "The general opinion is, that they (Apostles) were men taken from the humblest classes, and were, with the exception of Paul, wholly illiterate. What powers they exhibited in preaching, in argument, and in writing, are commonly supposed to have been the result of supernatural gifts

AUTHORIZED VERSION.	REVISED VERSION.
14 And he ordained twelve, that they should be with him, and that he might send them forth to preach:	14 and they went unto him. And he appointed twelve,[1] that they might be with him, and that he might send them forth to preach,
15 And to have power to heal sicknesses, and to cast out devils:	15 and to have authority to cast out [2] devils:
16 And Simon he surnamed Peter;	16 [3] and Simon he surnamed Peter; and James
17 And James, the son of Zebedee, and John	17 the son of Zebedee, and John the brother of

[1] Some ancient authorities add whom also he named apostles. See Luke vi. 13. [2] Gr. demons.
[3] Some ancient authorities insert and he appointed twelve.

and graces.. An investigation would show that they were not taken from the humblest classes, and that in intellectual training they far excelled those haughty Scribes and Pharisees who sneered at them."—*Kitto.*

The scene of his retirement was, in all probability, the singular elevation now known as the Kurn Hattin, or "Horns of Hattin, singularly adapted by its conformation, both to form a place for short retirement and a rendezvous for gathering multitudes." A tradition of the fifteenth century identifies this hill with that on which the sermon on the mount was delivered; it is also said to be the place where the Lord's Prayer was first given to the disciples.

14. *ordained twelve*] or "appointed, nominated;" "ordained" is too strong a term. Hitherto they had been his friends and disciples; now he formally called them, and joined them in a united band. This company was formed for three special objects: (1) As companions of Jesus; (2) as gospel preachers; (3) to cast out demons. "To heal sicknesses, and" is omitted in R. V., because not in the best authorities. Mark gives special prominence "to the power of casting out demons." Four lists of the *Twelve* are recorded, one by Matthew (x, 2-4), this by Mark, and two by Luke (vi, 14-16; Acts i, 13). Bengel noticed that they were divided into three groups of four each, the leaders in each group being always the same, viz., Peter, Philip, and James the son of Alphæus.

(i) 1 Peter.   (ii) 5 Philip.   (iii) 9 James the Less
    2 James.   6 Bartholomew.   10 Thaddæus.
    3 John.   7 Matthew.   11 Simon the Canaanite.
    4 Andrew.   8 Thomas.   12 Judas Iscariot.

Simon] Or Simeon (Acts xv. 14)," hearer," the son of Jona or Jonas (John i, 42; xxi, 16), whom our Lord surnamed Peter or Cephas, *the Rock-man*, stands first in all the four lists. He was brought up in his father's occupation, as a fisherman on the Galilean Lake, and lived originally at Bethsaida, and afterwards in a house at Capernaum (Mark i, 21, 29). His earliest call came to him through his brother Andrew (John i, 42). His second call took place on the lake near Capernaum, where he and the other three in his group were fishing. He is specially prominent among the Apostles. Sometimes he *speaks in their name* (Matt. xix, 27; Luke xii, 41); sometimes *answers when all are addressed* (Matt. xvi, 16; Mark viii, 29); sometimes he is addressed as *principal,* even among the favored three, by our Lord himself (Matt. xxvi, 40; Luke xxii, 31); sometimes he is appealed to by others as *representing the rest* (Matt. xvii, 24; Acts ii, 37). After the ascension he assumes a position of special prominence (Acts i, 15; ii, 14; iv, 8; v, 29)..

he surnamed Peter] "It is not asserted that this name was first given on this occasion. Still, the words of our Lord at his first meeting with Simon (John i. 42) were prophetic, and Mark seems to have mentioned the name for the first time here, because it was the Apostolic name."—*Schaff.*

17. *James the son of Zebedee* and Salome (Matt. xxvii, 56; Mark xv, 40); a native of Bethsaida, commonly known as James "the Great;" the

AUTHORIZED VERSION.	REVISED VERSION.
the brother of James; and he surnamed them Boanerges, which is, The sons of thunder: 18 And Andrew, and Philip, and Bartholomew, and Matthew, and Thomas, and James the son	James; and them he surnamed Boanerges, 18 which is, Sons of thunder: and Andrew, and Philip, and Bartholomew, and Matthew, and Thomas, and James the son of Alphaeus, and

first of the Apostolic body to suffer martyrdom, and the only one of the twelve whose death is actually recorded in the New Testament.

John] the brother of James, who never in his Gospel calls himself by this name, but sometimes *the disciple* "*whom Jesus loved*" (John xiii, 23; xix, 26), sometimes "*the other disciple*" (John xviii, 15; xx, 2, 3). To him Christ committed the care of his mother. These brothers were surnamed *Boanerges, i. e.,* "*sons of thunder,*" an Aramaic word transferred into the Greek, and used in allusion, possibly, to the fiery, intrepid zeal (some say eloquence) which marked their character. Of this we have traces in Luke ix, 54; Mark ix, 38; x, 37. "John was not, as he is often portrayed, of a soft and almost effeminate disposition." "With the ancients, thunder was the symbol for profound and solemn utterances." What more profound than John's gospel! What more solemn than the book of Revelation!

18. *Andrew*] a brother of Peter (Matt. iv, 18), and a native of Bethsaida, and a former disciple of the Baptist (John i, 40). There are three notices of him in the Gospels. (1) On the occasion of the feeding of the five thousand, it is he who points out the little lad with the five barley loaves and two fishes (John vi, 8); (2) when certain Greeks desired to see Jesus, Andrew, with Philip, introduced them to the Lord (John xii, 22); (3) together with Peter, James and John he inquired of our Lord's future coming (Mark xiii. 3). Andrew and Philip are old Greek names.

Philip] also a native of Bethsaida, and one of the earliest disciples (John i, 43). He brought Bartholomew (John i, 45), and of him the question was asked "*Whence shall we buy bread, that these may eat?*" (John vi, 5-9). Together with his friend and fellow townsman, Andrew, he brought the inquiring Greeks to the Saviour (John xii, 20–22); it was he who said, "*Lord, shew us the Father, and it sufficeth us*" (John xiv, 8).

Bartholomew] *i. e.,* Bar-Tolmai, the "*Son of Tholmai,*" and probably identical with Nathanael, = "*gift of God.*" For (1) John twice mentions Nathanael, never Bartholomew (John i, 45; xxi, 2); (2) the other Evangelists all speak of Bartholomew, never of Nathanael; (3) Philip first brought Nathanael to Jesus, and Bartholomew is mentioned by each of the Synoptic Evangelists immediately after Philip; (4) John couples Philip with Nathanael precisely in the same way that Simon is coupled with his brother Andrew. Respecting him, under the name of Nathanael, we learn from the Gospels little more than (*a*) his birth place, Cana of Galilee (John xxi, 2); (*b*) his simple, guileless character (John i, 47); and (*c*) that he was one of the seven to whom our Lord showed himself by the lake of Gennesaret after his resurrection (John xxi, 2).—*Camb. Bible.*

Matthew] or *Levi,* whose call has just been described. See above, on ii, 14, page 42.

Thomas] or Didymus = *a twin* (John xi, 16; xxi, 2), was marked by a deep attachment to his Master and a readiness even to die with him (John xi. 16), but at the same time, by a tendency to despondency, which made him ever ready to distrust other evidence than that of his senses (John xiv, 5; xx, 25). He is named eight times in John's Gospel.

James] or "James the Less," the son of Alphæus (not, it is thought, the same Alphæus who was the father of Matthew). He was called "the Less," to distinguish him from James, the son of Zebedee. He is probably a distinct person from James, the Lord's brother (Gal. i, 19), who was author of the Epistle which bears his name.

AUTHORIZED VERSION.	REVISED VERSION.
of Alphæus, and Thaddæus, and Simon the Canaanite,	19 Thaddæus, and Simon the ¹Cananæan, and Judas Iscariot, which also betrayed him.
19 And Judas Iscariot, which also betrayed him: and they went into an house.	20 And he cometh ²into a house. And the multitude cometh together again, so that
20 And the multitude cometh together again, so that they could not so much as eat bread.	21 they could not so much as eat bread. And when his friends heard it, they went out to
21 And when his friends heard *of it*, they went out to lay hold on him: for they said, He is beside himself.	lay hold on him: for they said, He is beside 22 himself. And the scribes which came down from Jerusalem said, He hath Beelzebub,
22 ¶ And the scribes which came down from Jerusalem said, He hath Beelzebub and by the prince of the devils casteth he out devils.	and, ³By the prince of the ⁴devils casteth he

¹ Or, *Zealot*. See Luke vi, 15; Acts i, 13. ² Or, *home* ³ Or, *In* ⁴ Gr. *demons*.

Thaddæus] *i. e., Judas*, a brother, or possibly a son of James (Luke vi, 16; Acts i. 13; Jude i). He was surnamed *Thaddæus* and *Lebbæus* (Matt. x, 3), which some interpret as " a man of energy and courage." He is the author of the Epistle which bears his name (Jude). Once only in the Gospels do we find any act or saying of his recorded, John xiv, 22.

Simon] *the Cananæan* (Matt. x, 4), in Greek *Zelotes* or Zealot (Luke vi, 15; Acts i, 13). The word does not signify a native of Canaan, or of Cana, but comes from a Chaldee or Syriac word, *Kanean* or *Kaneniah*, by which the Jewish sect or faction of " the Zealots," who acted as reprovers of open and public sin, was designated. To this sect Simon had probably belonged before his call.

19. *Judas Iscariot*] sometimes called *the son of Simon* (John vi, 71; xiii, 2, 26), more generally *Iscariot, i. e.*, probably "*a native of Kerioth*," a little village in the tribe of Judah (Josh. xv, 25).

into an house] Wiclif's and the margin of the R. V. read, "came home," *i. e.*, to Capernaum, which throws light on the preaching tours of Christ through Galilee. The sentence strictly belongs to the next section.

PRACTICAL LESSONS.—God calls into his service every variety of talent. There was a Judas among the Apostles; so hypocrites and unworthy professors are to be expected now. "Different types of men meet different types of the community; some famous, some unknown, but all useful. Is every twelfth man a 'devil?'"—*J. Parker*. Christ's messengers are to be heard. When his congregation became inattentive, Bishop Aylmer recited some verses from the Hebrew Bible. His audience would stare in astonishment; then he would remind them of the folly of listening to an unknown tongue and neglecting a message in words easily understood.

20-35. THE BOLDNESS OF JESUS, A. D., 28.

"At this point we find the largest gap in Mark's narrative. Shortly after the choice of the twelve the sermon on the mount was delivered.—*Schaff*.

21. *when his friends*] literally, " those from him," or " belonging to him," in which sense the phrase is used by Xenophon. The exact meaning is doubtful, but it is usually understood to refer, not to the apostles, but his relatives, including " his brethren and his mother," who are noticed here as going forth, and a few verses later on as having arrived at the house where our Lord was (Mark iii, 31), or the place where the crowds were thronging him.

He is beside himself.] The phrase is designedly ambiguous, and may be used in a good sense, or in a bad sense, *i. e.*, insane. They deemed him in a sort of ecstacy or religious enthusiasm, which made him no longer master of himself. Paul uses the word in this sense in 2 Cor. v, 13. "For whether we be beside ourselves, *it is* to God." Comp the words of Festus to Paul (Acts xxvi, 24). Many earnest preachers are still regarded as beside themselves.

22. *He hath Beelzebub*] Matthew connects this blasphemy with the cure of a man not only possessed with a demon, but also blind and dumb (Matt.

Zidon. (After Casas.)

Authorized Version.	Revised Version.
23 And he called them *unto him*, and said unto them in parables, How can Satan cast out Satan? 24 And if a kingdom be divided against itself, that kingdom cannot stand. 25 And if a house be divided against itself, that house cannot stand. 26 And if Satan rise up against himself, and be divided, he cannot stand, but hath an end. 27 No man can enter into a strong man's house, and spoil his goods, except he will first bind the strong man; and then he will spoil his house. 28 Verily I say unto you, All sins shall be forgiven unto the sons of men, and blasphemies wherewith soever they shall blaspheme: 29 But he that shall blaspheme against the Holy Ghost hath never forgiveness, but is in danger of eternal damnation:	23 out the ¹devils. And he called them unto him, and said unto them in parables, How can Satan cast out Satan? And if a kingdom be divided against itself, that kingdom cannot stand. And if a house be divided against itself, that house will not be able to stand. 26 And if Satan hath risen up against himself, and is divided, he cannot stand, but hath an end. But no one can enter into the house of the strong *man*, and spoil his goods, except he first bind the strong *man*; and then he will spoil his house. Verily I say unto you, All their sins shall be forgiven unto the sons of men, and their blasphemies wherewith soever they shall blaspheme: but whosoever shall blaspheme against the Holy Spirit hath never forgiveness, but is guilty

¹Gr. *demons*.

xii, 22). Beelzebub or rather Beelzebu-*l* was the title of a heathen deity. (*a*) Some would connect the name with *zebûl* = habitation, so making it = *the Lord of the dwelling* (Matt. x, 25), in his character of "prince of the power of the air" (Eph. ii, 2), or of the lower world, or as occupying a mansion in the seventh heavens. (*b*) Others would connect it with *zebel* = *dung*, and so make it = *the lord of dung* or *the dung-hill*, a term of derision amongst the Jews for the Philistine Fly-God. This fearful blasphemy was repeated more than once. See Luke xi, 17, et seq.

said unto them in parables] See after, on Mark iv, 2. p. 57.

23. *How can Satan cast out Satan?*] Using this irresistible form of argument, he shows them the absurdity of supposing that Satan could be his own enemy. If neither a kingdom, nor city (Matt xii, 25), nor house could stand, when divided against itself, much less could the empire of the Evil one. Satan, says Romaine, has an old grudge against Christ, and will not scruple to tell any lies of him. The devils won't aid Christ, even by fighting among themselves.

26. *but hath an end*] *i. e.*, ceases to be what he is. The theory which the enemies of Christ advanced would put Satan out of existence.

27. *No man...strong man*] Calvin maintains that the "strong man" represents Satan, and the "man" who binds him means Christ.

28. *be forgiven*] *i. e.*, "is pardonable;" not that every such sin shall be actually pardoned, unless repented of.

29. *shall blaspheme*] "The sin against which these words are a terrible but merciful warning is not so much an *act*, as a *state* of sin, on the part of one who, in defiance of light and knowledge, *of set purpose* rejects, and not only rejects, but *perseveres* in rejecting, the warnings of conscience, and the grace of the Holy Spirit: who, blinded by religious bigotry, rather than ascribe a good work to the spirit of good, prefer to ascribe it to the spirit of evil.—*Camb. Bible.* Lightfoot suggests the Jews had hope that every sin would be atoned for by death, in their case, but Christ shows that violent or willful contempt of the Holy Spirit would never be forgiven.

eternal damnation] or "eternal sin," according to the best MSS., and as in R. V. This implies far more than the reading of the A. V., for, while it signifies that the unpardonable sin may begin in one act of blasphemy, it results in a state of sinful activity which is endless

PRACTICAL SUGGESTIONS.—In regard to the power of Satan over men, even in sleep, the elder Alexander says: We should (1) avoid evil thoughts and such pampering of the body as has a tendency to pollute our dreams; (2) pray

AUTHORIZED VERSION.	REVISED VERSION.
30 Because they said, He hath an unclean spirit.	30 of an eternal sin: because they said, He hath an unclean spirit.
31 ¶ There came then his brethren and his mother, and, standing without, sent unto him, calling him	31 And there come his mother and his brethren; and, standing without, they sent
32 And the multitude sat about him, and they said unto him, Behold, thy mother and thy brethren without seek for thee.	32 unto him, calling him. And a multitude was sitting about him; and they say unto him, Behold, thy mother and thy brethren
33 And he answered them, saying, Who is my mother, or my brethren?	33 without seek for thee. And he answereth them, and saith, Who is my mother and my
34 And he looked round about on them which sat about him, and said, Behold my mother and my brethren!	34 brethren? And looking round on them which sat round about him, he saith, Behold
35 For whosoever shall do the will of God, the same is my brother, and my sister, and mother.	35 my mother and my brethren! For whosoever shall do the will of God, the same is my brother, and sister, and mother

God to preserve us from evil thoughts, even in, sleep....I am inclined to believe that, somehow or other, both good and evil spirits have access to our minds in sleep. They actually seem to hold conversation with us, and suggest things of which we had never thought before.' St. Bernard says of evil thoughts: 'They pass and repass; I would fain remove them but cannot.' So Paul also declared, see Rom. vii. This arch fiend is deeply versed in the physiology of human nature....On uninstructed minds the effect is often to induce the belief that they have sinned the sin unto death, by blaspheming the Holy Ghost."—*A. Alexander.* The poet Cowper, in a fit of insanity, was under the hallucination that he believed he had been commanded to kill himself, and for not having done so,, had forfeited paradise. There is a limit to divine mercy and forgiveness. "There is such a thing as a sin which is never forgiven. But those who are troubled about it are most unlikely to have committed it."—*Ryle.*

31-35. HIS MOTHER AND HIS BRETHREN COME TO HIM.

31. *his brethren*] their names, James, Joses, Simon, Judas, are given in Matt. xiii, 55; and Mark vi. 3. Some understand them to have been his literal "brethren," others think they were the sons of Cleophas and Mary, the sister and namesake of Mary the mother of Jesus. See on ch. vi, 3.

his mother] hence Theophylact taxes her...of vain glory and of guilt, in endeavoring to draw him...from teaching the word. Tertullian pronounceth her guilty of incredulity: Chrysostom of vain glory, infirmity and madness, for this very thing."—*Whitby.* Mariolatry has little support or sympathy from these early Christian fathers. Some authorities add "and thy sisters" to "thy mother and thy brethren."

without] either outside the house, although it is not certain he was in a house, but certainly outside of the crowd (Luke viii. 19).

33. *Who is*] it is thought that the "brethren" also wished to share in his fame, and to prove to the people their connection with him, and their influence over him. But "the most sacred of earthly ties lost its greatness, before the grandeur of spiritual kinship in the new, deathless communion he (Christ) was founding."—*Geikie.*

34. *looked round*] another graphic touch peculiar to Mark. "The look was probably one of friendly recognition."—*Riddle.* Luke states the saying here recorded in another form, Luke viii, 21.

do the will of God] the parallel words by Matthew (xii, 50) are "the will of my Father which is in heaven." The sinner unrenewed does the works of his father, the devil but "whosoever is born of God doth not commit sin." Thus the will of God is "your sanctification."

PRACTICAL SUGGESTIONS.—"True courage is unassuming; true piety serious and humble."—*R. Hall.* "The qualities of your friends will be those of your enemies—cold friends, cold enemies; half friends, half enemies;

ON THE GOSPEL OF MARK.

AUTHORIZED VERSION.

CHAP. IV.—And he began again to teach by the sea side: and there was gathered unto him a great multitude, so that he entered into a ship, and sat in the sea; and the whole multitude was by the sea on the land.
2 And he taught them many things by parables, and said unto them in his doctrine,

REVISED VERSION.

4 And again he began to teach by the sea side. And there is gathered unto him a very great multitude, so that he entered into a boat, and sat in the sea; and all the multitude were by the sea on the land. And he taught them many things in parables, and

fervid enemies, warm friends."—*Lavater.* True disciples are Christ's nearest relatives. Divisions in any organization tend to destruction; churches and families are no exception to this rule.

CH. IV. 1-25. PARABLE OF THE SOWER, A. D. 28.

1. *began again to teach*] the scenery round the lake doubtless suggested many of the details of the parables. (1) The vast multitude "out of every city" (Luke viii, 4); (2) from the fishing-boat; (3) patches of corn fields with the *trodden pathway* running through them, the *rocky ground* protruding here and there, the *thorn* growing in the midst of the waving wheat, the *rich soil;* (4) the mustard tree; (5) the fishermen plying amidst its marvelous shoals of fish, the *drag net* or *hawling net* (Matt. xiii, 47, 48), the *casting net* (Matt. iv, 18; Mark i, 16), the *bag net* and *basket net* (Luke v, 4-9); (6) the women and children employed in picking out from the wheat the tall, green stalks, called by the Arabs, *zuriwân*, the *tares* of our version; (7) the countless flocks of birds, aquatic fowls by the lake-side, partridges and pigeons hovering over the rich plain. Consult Stanley's *Sinai and Palestine;* Thomson's *Land and the Book;* Tristram's *Land of Israel.* Prior to this occasion, Mark mentions other three, when Jesus was beside the sea (Mark i, 16; ii, 13; iii, 7).

in the sea] Christ's position was in a boat on the water, the audience being slightly elevated above him. "This is the best way of arranging an audience, but the world seems to have discovered it quicker than the church."—*Schaff.* Music halls and theatres are constructed on a similar principle, but few churches have adopted it.

2. *by parables*] "The Greek word thus rendered denotes (a) *a placing beside,* (b) *a comparing, a comparison.* In Hellenistic Greek it became coextensive with the Hebrew *mâshâl* = similitude. In this sense it is applied (1) *In the Old Testament,* to—(a) *The shortest proverbs:* as 1 Sam. x, 12; xxiv, 13; 2 Chron. vii, 20; (b) *Dark prophetic utterances;* as Num. xxiii, 7; Ezek. xx, 49; (c) *Enigmatic maxims:* as Ps. lxxviii, 2; Prov. i, 6; (2) *In the Gospels,* to (a) *Short sayings:* as Luke iv, 23; (b) *A comparison without a narrative:* as Mark xiii, 28."—*Camb. Bible.* The parables of Christ differ from (1) proverbs, by presenting truth in new and fuller forms; from (2) fables, by their higher spiritual aim, and the intrinsic probability of their incidents; from (3) allegories, by not being always self-interpreting, the difference between them being rather in the form than in the aim. "I am the true vine," etc., Jno. xv, 1-8, is an allegory; "the kingdom of heaven is like a grain of mustard seed," is a parable. They differ from apologues by being drawn from events which may actually take place, while an apologue is founded on supposed actions of brutes and inanimate things. Æsop's fables are apologues, not parables. "There is good reason to believe that all the parables of Christ are founded in fact if not entirely composed of real incidents.— *Alexander.* Parables have always been popular in the East They were commonly used by the Rabbis in their teaching, and Trench gives some of the most striking of those presented in the Talmud. The object of Jesus in teaching by parables was twofold: (1) to *reveal* and (2) to *conceal* truth: reveal it to those who sincerely sought it; to conceal it from those who did not wish such knowledge.

AUTHORIZED VERSION.	REVISED VERSION.
3 Hearken; Behold, there went out a sower to sow: 4 And it came to pass, as he sowed, some fell by the way side, and the fowls of the air came and devoured it up. 5 And some fell on stony ground, where it had not much earth; and immediately it sprang up, because it had no depth of earth: 6 But when the sun was up, it was scorched; and because it had no root, it withered away. 7 And some fell among thorns, and the thorns grew up, and choked it, and it yielded no fruit. 8 And other fell on good ground, and did yield fruit that sprang up and increased; and brought forth, some thirty, and some sixty, and some an hundred.	3 said unto them in his teaching, Hearken: 4 Behold, the sower went forth to sow; and it came to pass, as he sowed, some seed fell by the way side, and the birds came and devoured it. 5 And other fell on the rocky ground, where it had not much earth; and straightway it sprang up, because it had no deepness of 6 earth: and when the sun was risen, it was scorched; and because it had no root it withered away. And other fell among the thorns, 7 and the thorns grew up, and choked it, and it 8 yielded no fruit. And others fell into the good ground, and yielded fruit, growing up and increasing; and brought forth, thirtyfold, 9 and sixtyfold, and a hundredfold. And he

3. *went out*] The expression implies that the sower did not sow near his own house, or in a garden fenced or walled, but went forth into the open country.

4. *by the way side*] *i. e.* on the hard footpath, or road, passing through the cultivated land. *Fowls*, or rather "birds," as in the R. V., such as the lark, sparrow and raven.

5. *stony ground*] or "rocky ground." This must be compared with "the rock" mentioned by Luke (viii. 6). What is meant is not a soil mingled with stones, but a thin coating of mould covering the surface of a rock.

PALESTINE THORN (*Zizyphus Spina Christi*.)

7. *thorns*] the "nâbk" or "bellan" of the Arabs, which grows abundantly in Syria and Palestine. Of some of these varieties the crown of thorns was probably woven. "The travele finds them [thorns] in his path, go where he may. Many of them are small, but grow as high as a man's head."—*Hackett.*

and choked it] or as Wyclif translates it, "thornes stieded up, and *strangliden* it." The seed and the thorns grew together, but the thorns gradually out-topped it. Stanley and Thomson saw regions exhibiting all these four kinds of soil at one view. In the open country there are no fences, the path passes through cultivated ground, where thorns grow and the rocks peep out in places through the scanty soil, and near by are fertile patches. "Here we have the whole four within a dozen rods of us. Our horses are actually tramping down the seeds which have fallen by the wayside, and larks and sparrows are busy picking them up. That man with his mattock is digging about places where the rock is too near the surface for the plow, and much that is sown there will wither away. And not a few seeds have fallen among this *bellan*, and will be effectually choked by this most entangled of thorn-bushes. But a large portion falls into really good ground, and four months hence will exhibit every variety of crop up to the richest and heaviest that ever rejoices the heart even of an American farmer."—*Thomson.*

8. *on good ground*] rather "into" good ground, as in R. V. The reading in the R. V. of the verse gives the best sense of the original.

some thirty] Matthew says "some an hundred-fold, some sixty-fold, some thirty-fold." Isaac sowed and "received in the same year an hundred fold" (Gen. xxvi. 12). Herodotus tells us that two hundred-fold was a common return in the plain of Babylon, while a kind of white maize often in Pales-

AUTHORIZED VERSION.	REVISED VERSION.
9 And he said unto them, He that hath ears to hear, let him hear.	said, Who hath ears to hear, let him hear.
10 And when he was alone, they that were about him with the twelve asked of him the parable.	10 And when he was alone, they that were about him with the twelve asked of him the
11 And he said unto them, Unto you it is given to know the mystery of the kingdom of God: but unto them that are without, all these things are done in parables:	11 parables. And he said unto them, Unto you is given the mystery of the kingdom of God; but unto them that are without, all things
12 That seeing they may see, and not perceive; and hearing they may hear, and not understand; lest at any time they should be converted, and their sins should be forgiven them.	12 are done in parables: that seeing they may see, and not perceive; and hearing they may hear, and not understand; lest haply they should turn again, and it should be forgiven
13 And he said unto them, Know ye not this parable? and how then will ye know all parables?	13 them. And he saith unto them, Know ye not this parable? and how shall ye know all
14 ¶ The sower soweth the word.	14 the parables? The sower soweth the word.

tine returns several hundred-fold. Professor Post states that a similar yield is now obtained on the plains of Bashan There are three causes of unfruitfulness; three *degrees* of fruitfulness, but only one *cause* of fruitfulness.

9. *hath ears to hear*] "Now, now, if ever, he who can hear must hear, or incur the penalty of inattention."—*Alexander*.

10. *And when he was alone*] with his disciples only. Mark states what took place after the Saviour had "sent the multitudes away" and "gone into the house" (Matt. xiii, 36). But the Syriac, Persic, and Ethiopic versions read, "when they were alone." The scene described is much the same by either reading. See Gill. "The parables" is the reading of most MSS., and so in the R. V.

11. *the mystery*] the word "mystery," denotes (*a*) *a religious mystery* like those of Eleusis, into which men were initiated; (*b*) *a secret* (as in 1 Cor. xv, 51); and is applied (1) *to the Gospel itself* (as here and in 1 Cor. ii, 7; Rom. xvi, 25; Eph. i, 9); (2) *to the various parts and truths of the Gospel* (Matt. xiii, 11; Luke viii, 10; 1 Cor. iv, 1); (3) *to a symbolic representation* or *emblem* (Rev. xvii, 5, 7).—*Camb. Bible*. Here it means "the secret" things. Notice the revised version, "Unto you is given the mystery, etc." "The mysteries concerning the kingdom of heaven are mysteries to the natural man, whose mind is darkened by sin. The Jews failed to perceive its *spirituality* as well as its *universality*" (Eph. iii, 4; Rom. xvi, 25).—*Lange*.

them that are without] comp. 1 Cor. v, 12, 13; Col. iv. 5; 1 Thess. iv, 12; 1 Tim. iii, 7. "Here, where a separation between Christ's followers and those without is first plainly marked, the point of discrimination is *spiritual knowledge*. This shows the importance of Christian truth, which implies *doctrine*."—*Schaff*.

12. *that seeing they may see, and not perceive*] to see and not see, hear and not hear. was a paradoxical Greek proverb, used by Demosthenes and Æschylus to express an act of the senses, without mental or moral conviction. When Christ's direct teaching was met with scorn, unbelief and hardness, he taught in "parables," and so was fulfilled the prophecy of Isaiah (vi, 9, 10), which is quoted by Matthew in the parallel passage (Matt. xiii 14, 15). See article on *Parables* in Schaff's *Bible Dict*.

13. *Know ye not this parable?*] For it was the simplest type of a parable. "The question suggests.....an ever-growing insight ....But if they were such slow scholars in this early stage, how was that insight to be imparted? The question is followed by the answer."—*Ellicott*.

14. *The sower*] this is applicable to (1) Christ; (2) his apostles; (3) all who go forth in his name, and with his authority. Comp. 1 Pet. i, 23; 1 John iii, 9.

AUTHORIZED VERSION.	REVISED VERSION.
15 And these are they by the way side, where the word is sown; but when they have heard, Satan cometh immediately, and taketh away the word that was sown in their hearts. 16 And these are they likewise which are sown on stony ground; who, when they have heard the word, immediately receive it with gladness. 17 And have no root in themselves, and so endure but for a time: afterward, when affliction or persecution ariseth for the word's sake, immediately they are offended. 18 And these are they which are sown among thorns; such as hear the word, 19 And the cares of this world, and the deceitfulness of riches, and the lusts of other things entering in, choke the word, and it becometh unfruitful. 20 And these are they which are sown on good ground; such as hear the word, and receive *it*, and bring forth fruit, some thirtyfold, some sixty, and some an hundred. 21 ¶ And he said unto them, Is a candle brought to be put under a bushel, or under a bed? and not to be set on a candlestick?	15 And these are they by the way side, where the word is sown; and when they have heard, straightway cometh Satan, and taketh away the word which hath been sown in them. 16 And these in like manner are they that are sown upon the rocky *places*, who, when they have heard the word, straightway 17 receive it with joy; and they have no root in themselves, but endure for a while; then, when tribulation or persecution ariseth because of the word, straightway they stumble. 18 And others are they that are sown among the thorns; these are they that have heard 19 the word, and the cares of the ¹ world, and the deceitfulness of riches, and the lusts of other things entering in, choke the word, 20 and it becometh unfruitful. And those are they that were sown upon the good ground; such as hear the word, and accept it, and bear fruit, thirtyfold, and sixtyfold, and a hundredfold. 21 And he said unto them, Is the lamp brought to be put under the bushel, or under the bed,

¹ Or, *age*.

15. *these are they*] there were four kinds of soil, and four kinds of hearers; only one kind produced fruit. "Not that one hearer only out of four, or ten out of forty, embrace the doctrine and yield fruit; for Christ did not intend here to fix an exact number....the produce is not always alike, but is sometimes more abundant, at other times more scanty."—*John Calvin.*

17. *affliction*] the word thus translated denotes (1) *pressure*; then (2) the *distress* arising therefrom. The word *tribulation* rests upon this image, coming from *tribulum = the threshing-roller.*

offended] in the old English sense of stumbling or causing to stumble; see R. V.

18. *these are they*] or "these are others which," or as in R. V.

19. *the cares of the world*] the word rendered "cares" denotes in the original "distracting anxieties," which, as it were, "cut a man in sunder." See Hos. x, 2; Jas. i, 8.

lusts of other things] "certainly by the 'other things' are to be understood gluttony, drunkenness, and intemperance, and sensuality of every kind."—*Bloomfield.*

it becometh unfruitful] or, as Luke has it, "they bring no fruit to perfection;" a word not elsewhere in the N. T., and used with reference to a woman bringing a child to the birth, or a tree to its full maturity. The mere hearer of the word has at first a "name to live," but the life of godliness has no abiding root, and it dies.

20. *such as hear the word, and receive it*] mark the contrast; what a glorious harvest. Luke leaves out the two least returns.

21. *Is a candle brought*] The simple and indispensable furniture in every Jewish household. The original word means not a *candle*, but a *lamp*, as in R. V.

to be put under the bushel] the original word *modius* denotes a dry measure containing 16 sextarii, or about a peck, though Canon Cook regards it as only six pints. The English equivalent is greatly in excess of the Latin.

a candlestick] or *the lamp-stand*. "Do not suppose that what I now commit to you

MEASURES OF CAPACITY.

AUTHORIZED VERSION.	REVISED VERSION.
22 For there is nothing hid, which shall not be manifested; neither was any thing kept secret, but that it should come abroad.	22 and not to be put on the stand? For there is nothing hid, save that it should be manifested; neither was *anything* made secret, but
23 If any man have ears to hear, let him hear.	23 that it should come to light. If any man
24 And he said unto them, Take heed what ye hear; with what measure ye mete, it shall be measured to you: and unto you that hear shall more be given.	24 hath ears to hear, let him hear. And he said unto them, Take heed what ye hear; with what measure ye mete it shall be measured unto you; and more shall be given
25 For he that hath, to him shall be given: and he that hath not, from him shall be taken even that which he hath.	25 unto you. For he that hath, to him shall be given; and he that hath not, from him shall be taken away even that which he hath.
26 ¶ And he said, So is the kingdom of God, as if a man should cast seed into the ground;	26 And he said, So is the kingdom of God, as if a man should cast seed upon the earth;
27 And should sleep, and rise night and day, and the seed should spring and grow up, he	27 and should sleep and rise night and day, and the seed should spring up and grow, he know-

in secret I would have concealed forever; the light is kindled by me in you, that by your ministry it may disperse the darkness of the whole world."—*Erasmus.*

22. *nothing hid....secret*] the Greek word for "secret" is the same as we have in our word "apocrypha," *i. e.*, "books having a spurious sacredness." Some render as in R. V., "save that it should be manifested;" others, as Tregelles, "except it be manifested."

ASSYRIAN TERRA COTTA LAMPS.

manifested...come abroad] verses 21, 22, refer to teaching in parables. Thus, when the Spirit came and brought all things to the remembrance of the apostles, "he filled all the outlines of truth which they before possessed with its substance, quickened all its forms with the power and spirit of life."

24. *with what measure ye mete*] "according to the measure of your ability and diligence as hearers, ye shall receive instruction, and be enabled to preach to others."—*Maclear.*

what ye hear] we are not to hear everything—not to run after some new thing, like the Athenians, for, as Bunyan warns us, "Satan enters at eargate."

25. *he that hath*] or "seemeth to have." Comp. Matt. xiii, 12; xxv, 29; Luke viii. 18; xix. 26.

PRACTICAL SUGGESTIONS.—"Earthly things must remind us of heavenly. We must translate the book of nature into the book of grace."—*Thos. Taylor*, 1634. On the rocky ground hearers, read Edwards' work on *The Affections*. "Never preach a sermon from which an unenlightened hearer might not learn the plan of salvation."—*Legh Richmond*. "Small draughts of knowledge lead men to atheism; but larger bring men back to God."—*Bacon*. The parable of the sower is a beautiful picture of the rise and progress of religion in the soul, which has been expanded and illustrated in Doddridge's wonderful book. There were four kinds of soil, representing four classes of hearers: (1) wayside; (2) rocky ground; (3) thorny ground; (4) good ground; *i. e.*, (1) the hard-hearted hearers; (2) the faint-hearted; (3) the half-hearted; (4) the true-hearted.

26–34. THE SEED AND THE MUSTARD SEED, A. D. 28.

26. *cast seed*] This is *one of the two parables peculiar to Mark*, and seems to take the place of "the leaven (Matt. xiii, 33), but it is different from "the leaven." That declares the *intensive*, this the *extensive* development of the Gospel.

27. *The seed*] In this parable it is not the soil, nor the sower, but the seed, which is prominent. "I believe the parable one taken simply from

AUTHORIZED VERSION.	REVISED VERSION.
knoweth not how. 28 For the earth bringeth forth fruit of herself; first the blade, then the ear, after that the full corn in the ear. 29 But when the fruit is brought forth, immediately he putteth in the sickle, because the harvest is come. 30 ¶ And he said, Whereunto shall we liken the kingdom of God? or with what comparison shall we compare it? 31 It is like a grain of mustard seed, which,	eth not how. The earth [1] beareth fruit of herself; first the blade, then the ear, then 29 the full corn in the ear. But when the fruit [2] is ripe, straightway he [3] putteth forth the sickle, because the harvest is come. 30 And he said, How shall we liken the kingdom of God? or in what parable shall 31 we set it forth? [4] It is like a grain of mustard seed, which, when it is sown upon the

[1] Or, *yieldeth*. [2] Or, *alloweth*. [3] Or, *sendeth forth*. [4] Gr., *As unto*.

human things—the sower being quite in the background, and the whole stress being on the seed, its power and development."—*Alford.*

knoweth not how] it is a mistaken notion to be taking up the seed to see whether it is growing. "He who sows does not know how that takes place." He sleeps and rises, *i. e.*, goes about his ordinary duties, without being anxious as to its growth, and not, as Wesley explains it, "has it continually in his thoughts." See Alford. It rather illustrates the confidence the Christian teacher should have in the growth of the seed he has sown.

28. *of herself*] = *of its own accord*, spontaneously. It is used of the gate of Peter's prison *opening of its own accord*, in Acts xii, 10.

first the blade] there is a law of orderly development in natural growth; so also is it in reference to spiritual growth; comp. 1 John ii, 12-14. "By such insensible degrees shall the Gospel gain ground in the world and ripen into a harvest of glory."—*Doddridge.*

29. *the sickle*] The sickle is only mentioned in the N. T. here, and in Rev. xiv, 14, 15. For the entire parable comp. 1 Pet i, 23-25.

30. *Whereunto shall we liken*] This method of asking a question before beginning a discourse was known to the Rabbis. The parables of the Sower and the Tares (Matt. xiii, 24-30 and 36-43) had been discouraging to the disciples, and now, lest they should be tempted to lose heart and to despair, the two parables (the Mustard Seed and the Leaven) are spoken for their encouragement. "My kingdom," the Lord would say, " shall survive these losses and surmount these hindrances, until, small as its first beginnings may appear, it shall, like a mighty tree, fill the earth with its branches; like leaven, diffuse its influence through all the world."

31. *a grain of mustard seed*] the growth of a worldly kingdom had been already set forth under the image of a tree. and that of the kingdom of God also had been similarly compared. (See Dan. iv, 10-12; Ezek. xvii, 22. 24: xxxi. 3-9). Christ himself sows the seed, which attains a corresponding spiritual growth.

MUSTARD (*Sinapis Nigra*, after Dr. Carruthers).

AUTHORIZED VERSION.	REVISED VERSION.
when it is sown in the earth, is less than all the seeds that be in the earth: 32 But when it is sown, it groweth up, and becometh greater than all herbs, and shooteth out great branches; so that the fowls of the air may lodge under the shadow of it. 33 And with many such parables spake he the word unto them, as they were able to hear it. 34 But without a parable spake he not unto them: and when they were alone, he expounded all things to his disciples.	earth, though it be less than all the seeds 32 that are upon the earth, yet when it is sown, groweth up, and becometh greater than all the herbs, and putteth out great branches; so that the birds of the heaven can lodge under the shadow thereof. 33 And with many such parables spake he the word unto them, as they were able to hear it: and without a parable spake he not unto them: but privately to his own disciples he expounded all things.

in the earth] in Matt. xiii. 31, a man is represented as taking and sowing it "*in his field*," while Luke, xiii, 19, says "*into his garden*." As to the sowing and its purpose, see John xii, 24.

less than all the seeds] "small as a grain of mustard seed" was a proverbial expression among the Jews for something exceedingly minute. The mustard seed is not the least of all seeds *in the world*, but of all which the husbandman was accustomed to *sow*, and the "tree," when full grown, was larger than the other herbs in his garden.—*Camb. Bible.* "Doubtless this is chosen [to represent the kingdom] not with reference to greatness which it obtains in the end, for in this many trees surpass it, but to the proportion between the smallness of the seed and the greatness of the tree which unfolds itself therefrom."—*Trench.* Then it possessed medicinal qualities best brought out by being bruised. See Ezek. xlvii, 12; Rev. xxii, 2.

32. *great branches*] in hot countries, as in Judea, the mustard tree attains a great size. Thomson saw it on the rich plain of Akkâr as tall as the horse and his rider. Hackett saw plants of mustard from seven to nine feet high, and the birds lighting on their branches. Whitby quotes Rabbi Calipha as saying, "A stalk of mustard seed was in my field, into which I was used to climb, as men do into a fig tree."

lodge under the shadow of it] "Christ's kingdom shall attract multitudes by the shelter and protection which it offers; shelter, as it has often proved, from worldly oppression, shelter from the great power of the devil."

33. *many such parables*] it is obvious that Mark did not write all he knew; so with John. See John xxi, 25.

as they were able] "This does not refer to their worthiness, as Grotius suggests, but to their ability to apprehend. It includes, however, their being able to bear without being offended."—*Lange.*

34. *But without a parable*] "But," better "*and*," as in R. V. "This cannot mean that he never taught them in any other form, which would be contradicted by the whole course of the history, but only that whatever he did teach in parables he did not also teach in other forms."—*Alexander.* Or, a better explanation is, that on this occasion he taught them only by parables.

expounded] the Greek word primarily means "to untie a knot"; hence to unfold, make plain or clear.

PRACTICAL LESSONS.—"We know as little of the growing above ground as of the growing under ground."—*Stier.* "God's workmen die, but his work goes on."—*From the monument to the Wesleys, in Westminster Abbey.* "He who sows the Master's seed, with an upright heart, shall come again rejoicing, bringing his sheaves with him."—*A. Clarke.* "Only when the seed comes forth of itself does it spring up, and only this it is which proves it to be a seed."—*Stier.* Ryle maintains that the parable of the mustard seed indicates the growth of the visible church; most interpreters hold that it is intended to show the growth of grace in the individual believer.

[MARK IV, 35-39.

AUTHORIZED VERSION.	REVISED VERSION.
35 And the same day, when the even was come, he saith unto them, Let us pass over unto the other side. 36 And when they had sent away the multitude, they took him even as he was in the ship. And there were also with him other little ships. 37 And there arose a great storm of wind, and the waves beat into the ship, so that it was now full. 38 And he was in the hinder part of the ship, asleep on a pillow: and they awake him, and say unto him, Master, carest thou not that we perish? 39 And he arose, and rebuked the wind, and said unto the sea, Peace, be still. And the wind ceased, and there was a great calm.	35 And on that day, when even was come, he saith unto them, Let us go over unto the other side. And leaving the multitude, they take him with them, even as he was, in the 36 boat. And other boats were with him. And 37 there ariseth a great storm of wind, and the waves beat into the boat, insomuch that the 38 boat was now filling. And he himself was in the stern, asleep on the cushion: and they awake him, and say unto him,[1] Master, carest thou not that we perish? And he awoke, and 39 rebuked the wind, and said unto the sea, Peace, be still. And the wind ceased, and

[1] Or, *Teacher*.

35-41. STILLING THE STORM, A. D., 29.

35. *the same day*] how busy Jesus had been—he had healed a demoniac (Matt. xii, 22); encountered the opposition of his friends (Mark iii, 20, 21); of his foes (Matt. xii, 24-45); and probably preached several sermons (Matt. xiii; Mark iv; Luke xi, 37-xii. 59); and met several would-be followers (Matt. viii, 19-22). No wonder he was weary.

he saith unto them] the three Evangelists agree in the time and in the chief incidents of this storm.

the other side] after a long and exhausting day he needed retirement, and repose could nowhere be more readily obtained than in the solitude of the eastern shore. So Farrar and others. But Canon Cook thinks repose is not intimated as the object in crossing the lake, and points to the usual course of our Lord, after teaching in one place, to pass to another to teach others. It was a night voyage.

36. *as he was*] without any preparation for the voyage. So Thucydides (III, 30) and Xenophon use the phrase.

37. *a great storm*] the same word is found in Luke viii, 23. Properly, it means a hurricane. It was one of those sudden and violent squalls to which the Lake of Gennesaret was notoriously exposed, lying as it does fully six hundred feet lower than the sea and surrounded by mountain gorges, which act "like gigantic funnels to draw down the cold winds from the mountains." These winds are not only violent, but they come down suddenly, and often when the sky is perfectly clear. One half of the lake may be in perfect rest. while the other half is in a wild confusion and a sheet of foam. The words are remarkable: Mark and Luke speak of a "*hurricane of wind*"; Matthew refers to the effect *on the sea*. See Thomson's *Land and the Book*; Wilson's *Recovery of Jerusalem*.

beat] rather, *kept beating*. Comp. Matt. viii, 24.

38. *a pillow*] the word only occurs here. It was probably the leathern cushion of the steersman. These details we learn only from Mark. So Van Lennep describes a low bench in the stern, where the steersman sits, and the captain sometimes rests his head when he sleeps, as is his custom, on the quarter-deck. "The high stern made a safe and sloping place, where our Saviour slept in the storm."—*Macgregor*.

Master] The "*Master, master*," of Luke (viii, 24), imply haste and dread. which is fully exhibited in the rebuke and apprehensive complaint recorded by Mark in the words, "*carest thou not that we perish!*"

39. *rebuked the wind*] all three Evangelists record that he *rebuked* the wind (comp. Ps. cvi, 9). Mark alone gives his words to the storm.

the wind ceased] lit. *grew tired*. We have the same word in Matt. xiv, 32, and again in Mark vi, 51. After a storm the waves continue to heave

AUTHORIZED VERSION.	REVISED VERSION.
40 And he said unto them, Why are ye so fearful? how is it that ye have no faith? 41 And they feared exceedingly, and said one to another, What manner of man is this, that even the wind and the sea obey him?	40 there was a great calm. And he said unto them, Why are ye fearful? have ye not yet 41 faith? And they feared exceedingly, and said one to another, Who then is this, that even the wind and the sea obey him?

and swell for hours, but here there was a "great calm." "He here shows how perfect harmony and peace, even in natural elements, can be restored by him."—*Jacobus.* "This term [rebuked] has given countenance to a conjecture sanctioned by many eminent critics, that our Saviour had in view, not merely the storm, but the evil spirits by whose agency it had been stirred up."—*Boardman.* Alexander also favors this view. Compare the destruction of Job's children by a hurricane, raised through Satan's agency. Job i, 18, 19. Lange suggests that nature has acquired a wild independence and anarchy since man became unfaithful to his destiny.

40. *Why are ye so fearful*] rather, why are ye so apprehensive. They were not actually terror-stricken. Some of them, as fishermen, had doubtless been on the lake in severe storms, although perhaps not in so wild a one as this; and we cannot suppose Peter, or John, or James, to be cowards, but they were apprehensive. Neither had they literally "no faith" in Jesus, for, if it had been wanting altogether, they would not have called to him for help. Their faith was "little" (Matt. viii, 26), and Jesus inquired, "have ye not yet faith," as in R. V., rather than "no faith," as in A. V., or, according to Luke, "where is your faith?" (Luke viii, 25). Matthew records the rebuke by Jesus prior to, while Mark and Luke place it after the stilling of the tempest.

41.. *they feared exceedingly*] they were awed at the exhibition of almighty power, so that one thought and one question was put by each to the other, "What manner of man is this?" or rather as in the R. V., "Who then is this?" At such a moment the disciples must have regarded Jesus with the holy awe which is due to God only, an awe which would doubtless be felt by the mariners who were in the other "little ships" (v. 36), and who, though not among the avowed followers of Jesus, were sharers of the peace which now pervaded the bosom of the lake; so, many who are outside the church participate in the peaceful blessings which it brings.

PRACTICAL SUGGESTIONS.— 'The heathen poet makes the god force the winds, with his trident, into their cave; there is a greater and simpler grandeur in Mark's narrative....Jonah slept in a storm, weary, but with a guilty conscience; Jesus slept, weary also, but with a conscience undefiled. Jonah was running away from duty; Jesus was hastening to do it."—*John Hall.* "Storms may indeed assail us, and our fears may be great...when he awakes for our help he will speak every tempest into a calm, and turn our terrors into adoring love."—*Scott.* "As certainly as he could not sink with his disciples on that day, he will not suffer his disciples to sink on this."—*Schleiermacher.* "When there is storm in the soul, thou knowest what it is for and whither to fly. What calmness in the soul when the Lord arises and utters his voice!"—*Gossner.* "The Lord rises, confronting the storm, speaks as the Master of the elements that are raging about him, and the result is immediate...He is Master of the Universe; all things must serve him."—*Hanson.* "The miracles of Jesus, as attestations that the elements of nature were plastic in his hands, are really a new key to the grandest scientific principle in the universe, which is that God lives, and moves, and acts in all nature, every instant, and that the whole creation is formed and guided in the interest of the spiritual man."—*F. D. Huntingdon.*

AUTHORIZED VERSION.	REVISED VERSION.
CHAP. V.—And they came over unto the other side of the sea, into the country of the Gadarenes. 2 And when he was come out of the ship, immediately there met him out of the tombs a man with an unclean spirit. 3 Who had his dwelling among the tombs; and no man could bind him, no, not with chains:	5 And they came to the other side of the sea, 2 into the country of the Gerasenes. And when he was come out of the boat, straightway there met him out of the tombs, a man 3 with an unclean spirit, who had his dwelling in the tombs: and no man could any more

Ch. V. 1—10. The Healing of the Gadarene Demoniac.

This chapter brings to our consciousness, in the most vivid manner, the depth of the evil filling this fallen world. The mind is often oppressed with the inquiry. Why are all these terrible trials and sorrows in any system of created things? The question must remain without a complete answer until man reaches another state of intelligence; but it may be partially answered here: (1) evil is an incident to any moral system; (2) natural evils are in keeping with fallen man; (3) pain is a safeguard, warning man against serious danger; (4) evil may be made subservient to greater good in a race fallen as we are. Consult Hitchcock, *Relig. of Geology*, pp. 179-251; Butler's *Anology*, Leibnitz, etc.

1. *the Gadarenes*] on the eastern side of the lake. The records of this miracle vary in their readings between (1) *Gadarenes*, (2) *Gergesenes*, and (3) *Gerasenes*. Most authorities give *Gerasenes*, as in R. V. Alford reads, *Gergesenes*. (*a*) *Gadara*, the capital of Peræa, lay S. E. of the southern extremity of Gennesaret, at a distance of about seven miles from Tiberias, its country being called Gadaritis; (*b*) *Gerasa* lay on the extreme eastern limit of Peræa, and was too far from the lake to meet the requirements of the narrative; (*c*) *Gergesa* was a little town nearly opposite Capernaum, the ruined site of which is still called *Kerza* or *Gersa*. Origen tells us that the exact site of the miracle was here pointed out in his day. Mark and Luke indicate *generally* the scene of the miracle. Gadara being a place of importance and acknowledged as the capital of a district, while Gerasa may refer to some district. See Schaff's *Dict. of the Bible*.

2. *out of the tombs*] the Hebrews used natural caves, and also recesses hewn by art out of the rock, for tombs. They were often so large as to be supported with columns, and had cells upon their sides for the reception of the dead. Such places were regarded as unclean (Num. xix, 11, 16; Matt. xxiii, 37). These rock caves are frequently used for shelter, and the Arabs sometimes dwell in them during the winter. Many such caves or tombs can still be traced in the ravines on the Eastern side of the lake.

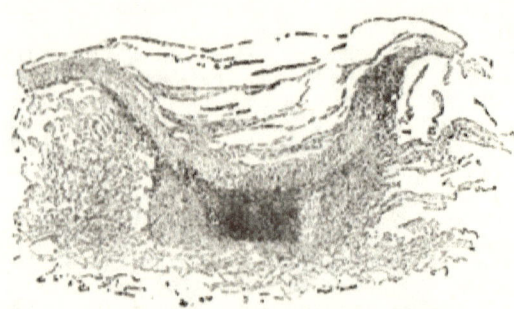

The above illustration of a rock-cut tomb is from the "Memoirs of the Survey of Western Palestine," and is one of great antiquity. Many such tombs exist near the village of Meron, supposed to be identical with Meroth, mentioned by Josephus, and in upper Galilee.

a man] Matthew (viii. 28) mentions two demoniacs, Luke (viii, 27) and Mark only one. Probably one was so much fiercer, that the other was hardly

AUTHORIZED VERSION.

4 Because that he had been often bound with fetters and chains, and the chains had been plucked asunder by him, and the fetters broken in pieces: neither could any *man* tame him.
5 And always, night and day, he was in the mountains, and in the tombs, crying, and cutting himself with stones.
6 But when he saw Jesus afar off, he ran and worshipped him,
7 And cried with a loud voice, and said, What have I to do with thee, Jesus, *thou* Son of the most high God? I adjure thee by God, that thou torment me not.
8 For he said unto him, Come out of the man, *thou* unclean spirit.
9 And he asked him, What *is* thy name? And he answered, saying, My name *is* Legion: for we are many.

REVISED VERSION.

4 bind him, no, not with a chain; because that he had been often bound with fetters and chains, and the chains had been rent asunder by him, and the fetters broken in pieces: 5 and no man had strength to tame him. And always, night and day, in the tombs and in the mountains, he was crying out, and cutting himself with stones. And when he saw Jesus from afar, he ran and worshipped him: 7 and crying out with a loud voice, he saith, What have I to do with thee, Jesus, thou Son of the Most High God? I adjure thee 8 by God, torment me not. For he said unto him, Come forth, thou unclean spirit, out of 9 the man. And he asked him, What is thy name? And he saith unto him, My name is

noticed. "Amid all the boasted civilization of antiquity, there existed no hospitals, no penitentiaries, no asylums; and unfortunates of this class, being too dangerous and desperate for human intercourse, could only be driven forth from among their fellow-men, and restrained from mischief by measures at once inadequate and cruel."—*Farrar.*

an unclean spirit] *i. e.*, an evil spirit; a demon.

no, not with chains] comp. R. V. It is a general expression for any bonds confining the hands or feet. Comp. Acts xxi, 33; Eph. vi, 20; Rev. xx, 1; *fetters* were restricted to the feet. "These were not necessarily of metal. The two processes of snapping the chains by one convulsive movement, and wearing away (not breaking) the latter [fetters] by friction, rather suggests the idea of ropes or cords, as in the case of Samson (Judg. xv, 13)." —*Plumptre.*

4. *he had been often*] each Evangelist adds something to complete the picture; Matthew says he made the way impassable for travellers (viii, 28); Luke says he was without clothing (viii, 27); Mark that he cried night and day and cut himself with stones (v, 5).

broken in pieces] for another instance of the extraordinary muscular strength which maniacs put forth, see Acts xix. 16.

6. *worshipped him*] the Greek word signifies primarily, "kissing," as in salutation. The English word "worship" has a wider meaning among old writers than that of adoring God, which is now attached to it. Luke says "he fell down before him."

7. *What have I to do with thee?*] literally, *What is there between thee and me?* What have we in common? Why interferest thou with us?

most high] "The old Hebrew word *Elion* found a ready equivalent in the Greek 'ὕψιστος,' which had already been used by Pindar as a divine name." —*Ellicott.* "These men [demoniacs] must have made their remarkable confessions by a preternatural influence common to them all, which controlled their minds and shaped their utterance."—*S. Hopkins.* Their public recognition of Jesus as the Son of God was in advance of the *popular* opinion, and, indeed, generally quite contrary to it. Public feeling, therefore, did not influence them to make this confession.

9. *My name is Legion*] Why Jesus asked this question is not clear. It may have been addressed to the man and answered by the demon; or it may have been intended to call forth this answer, to show the desperate nature of the case. "He had seen the thick and serried ranks of a Roman legion, that fearful instrument of oppression, that sign of terror and fear to the conquered nations." The legion originally consisted of about 3000 soldiers, but

AUTHORIZED VERSION.	REVISED VERSION.
10 And he besought him much that he would not send them away out of the country.	10 Legion; for we are many. And he besought him much that he would not send them away
11 Now there was there nigh unto the mountains a great herd of swine feeding.	11 out of the country. Now there was there on the mountain side a great herd of swine
12 And all the devils besought him, saying, Send us into the swine, that we may enter into them.	12 feeding. And they besought him, saying, Send us into the swine, that we may enter
13 And forthwith Jesus gave them leave. And the unclean spirits went out, and entered into the swine: and the herd ran violently down a steep place into the sea, (they were about two thousand;) and were choked in the sea.	13 into them. And he gave them leave. And the unclean spirits came out, and entered into the swine: and the herd rushed down the steep into the sea, in number about two thousand; and they were choked in the sea.
14 And they that fed the swine fled, and told it in the city, and in the country. And they went out to see what it was that was done.	14 And they that fed them fled, and told it in the city, and in the country. And they came to see what it was that had come to
15 And they come to Jesus, and see him that was possessed with the devil, and had the legion, sitting, and clothed, and in his right mind: and they were afraid.	15 pass. And they come to Jesus, and behold ¹ him that was possessed with devils sitting, clothed and in his right mind, even him that
	16 had the legion: and they were afraid. And

¹ Or, *the demoniac*.

at that time comprised 6000 footmen and 600 cavalry. It is a phrase for any indefinitely large number. Compare (1) the "seven demons" by whom Mary Magdalene was possessed (Luke viii, 2); (2) the "seven other spirits" "worse than the first" taking up their abode in a man (Matt. xii, 45).

10. *he besought*] the Alexandrian MS. reads "they besought."
out of the country] Luke says into "the deep," *i. e.*, ' the abyss " of hell (viii, 31).

11. *a great herd of swine*] in that region Jews lived mingled with Gentiles. If their owners were only in part Jews, who merely trafficked in these animals, still they were not justified before the law. The wâdy Semak in this region is still ploughed up by wild hogs, in search of roots, upon which they live. "A modern physician suggests that the newly-discovered disease, *trichina spiralis*, [Trichinosis?] found in the muscles of hogs, is a scientific endorsement of the wisdom of the Levitical enactments."—*Vincent*.

12. *send us into the swine*] "From this we should infer," says Whedon: "(1) That the infernals preferred a human residence to a bestial one; (2) but they preferred a bestial one to their own infernal home."

13. *gave them leave*] clearly an inaccurate translation. It should read, "suffered them." In Luke (viii, 32), the same word is rendered "suffered." The R. V. reads, "gave leave," in both passages, though in six of the other seven passages in the Gospels it renders the same word "suffer"; See Matt. viii, 21, 31; xix, 8; Mark x, 4; Luke ix, 59, 61; the exception is John xix, 38. "Even Weiss, who will not be accused of extreme orthodoxy, admits that the narrative does not imply that Jesus gave the demons leave to enter the swine....There is a great difference between ' suffering,' that is, ' not prohibiting,' and ' giving leave.' Quoted by *A. Edersheim*.

went out] "it was a magnificent display of the power of Christ, that by his voice, not one devil, but a great multitude of devils, were suddenly driven out."—*John Calvin*.

down a steep place] At *Kerza* or *Gersa*, "where there is no precipice running sheer to the sea, but a narrow belt of beach, the bluff behind is so steep, and the shore so narrow, that a herd of swine rushing frantically down, must certainly have been overwhelmed in the sea before they could recover themselves."—*Tristram*.

and were choked] what an interposition to the inhabitants of the district. If the swine, naturally wild, had been allowed to roam at large possessed by the untameable devils, they would have been a hundredfold worse and more dreadful than the poor man had been whom they had made terrible to all.

15. *clothed*] Luke informs us (viii, 27), that the wretched man *wore no*

AUTHORIZED VERSION.	REVISED VERSION.
16 And they that saw *it* told them how it befell to him that was possessed with the devil, and also concerning the swine.	they that saw it declared unto them how it befell [1] him that was possessed with devils,
17 And they began to pray him to depart out of their coasts.	17 and concerning the swine. And they began to beseech him to depart from their borders.
18 And when he was come into the ship, he that had been possessed with the devil prayed him that he might be with him.	18 And as he was entering into the boat, he that had been possessed with [2] devils besought him that he might be with him. And he
19 Howbeit Jesus suffered him not, but saith unto him, Go home to thy friends, and tell them how great things the Lord hath done for thee, and hath had compassion on thee.	19 suffered him not, but saith unto him, Go to thy house unto thy friends, and tell them how great things the Lord hath done for
20 And he departed, and began to publish in Decapolis how great things Jesus had done for him: and all men did marvel.	20 thee, and how he had mercy on thee. And he went his way, and began to publish in Decapolis how great things Jesus had done for him: and all men did marvel.

[1] Or, *the demoniac*.   [2] Gr. *demons*.

clothes. "On descending from the heights of Lebanon, I found myself," writes Warburton, "in a cemetery....The silence of the night was now broken by fierce yells and howlings, which I discovered proceeded from a naked maniac, who was fighting with some wild dogs for a bone." Seeing the demonized one sane and sound, they "were afraid," terrified, awe-struck, not from fear of further loss or bodily danger, but filled with religious terror.

17. *to depart out of their coasts*] many were doubtless annoyed at the losses they had already sustained, and feared greater losses might follow. "And their prayer was heard: he did depart; he took them at their word; and let them alone," (cf. Exod. x, 28, 29).—*Trench*.

18. *And when he was...*] or, *when he was stepping into the boat*.
that he might be with him] either (1) in a spirit of the deepest gratitude, longing to be with his benefactor; or, (2) fearing lest the many enemies, from whom he had been delivered, shou'd return. Comp. Matt. xii, 44, 45.

19. *and tell them*] he requires the man to declare his cure and the power of Jesus in Decapolis, since the people would not bear the presence of Jesus himself. On others (comp. Matt. viii, 4 ; Luke viii, 56) after shewing forth towards them his miraculous power, he enjoined silence.

20. *Decapolis*] When the Romans conquered Syria, B. C. 65, they rebuilt, partially colonized, and endowed with certain privileges "ten cities," the region being called Decapolis, and which had been originally colonized by the veterans of Alexander the Great. All the cities lay, with the exception of Scythopolis, east of the Jordan, and to the east and southeast of the Sea of Galilee. They were (but there is some variation in the lists), 1 Scythopolis (the largest); 2. Hippos ; 3, Gadara ; 4. Pella (to which the Christians fled when Jerusalem was destroyed by Titus); 5, Philadelphia ; 6, Gerasa ; 7, Dion ; 8, Canatha ; 9. Raphana ; 10, Damascus. The name occurs three times in the Scriptures : (*a*) here ; (*b*) Matt. iv. 25 ; and (*c*) Mark vii, 31. It denoted a large district on both sides of the Jordan.

PRACTICAL SUGGESTIONS.—"That evil spirits exist is as certain as the existence of angels. They are in sympathy with Satan, their head, who is god of this world, in a limited sense, and at war with Christ's kingdom."—*John Hall*. Go to Jesus to be delivered from any form of evil. "Satan, as a master, is bad ; his work much worse ; and his wages worst of all. If Satan doth fetter us, it is indifferent to him whether it be by a cable or a hair : nay, perhaps the smallest sins are his greatest stratagems."—*Fuller*. "Many fly from this history as though the devils had entered into them and plunged them into a sea of unbelief."—*Stier*. "The greatest demoniac becomes a preacher of salvation to ten cities. In the dark land of Gadara Christ leaves for a while a representative, since they cannot bear his personal presence." —*Lange*. "I doubt whether men who have been suddenly converted to

AUTHORIZED VERSION.	REVISED VERSION.
21 And when Jesus was passed over again by ship unto the other side, much people gathered unto him: and he was nigh unto the sea.	21 And when Jesus had crossed over again in the boat unto the other side, a great multitude was gathered unto him: and he was by the sea.
22 And, behold, there cometh one of the rulers of the synagogue, Jairus by name; and when he saw him, he fell at his feet,	22 And there cometh one of the rulers of the synagogue, Jairus by name; and seeing him, he falleth at his feet,
23 And besought him greatly, saying, My little daughter lieth at the point of death: *I pray thee*, come and lay thy hands on her, that she may be healed; and she shall live.	23 and beseecheth him much, saying, My little daughter is at the point of death: *I pray thee*, that thou come and lay thy hands on her, that she may be¹ made whole, and live.
24 And *Jesus* went with him; and much people followed him, and thronged him.	24 And he went with him; and a great multitude followed him, and they thronged him.
25 And a certain woman, which had an issue of blood twelve years,	25 And a woman, which had an issue of blood twelve years, and had suffered many things
26 And had suffered many things of many physicians, and had spent all that she had, and was nothing bettered, but rather grew worse,	of many physicians, and had spent all that she had, and was nothing bettered, but rather grew worse,
27 When she had heard of Jesus, came in the press behind, and touched his garment.	27 having heard the things concerning Jesus, came in the crowd behind,

¹ Or, *saved*

God in the army, the navy, the law, or the merchant's office, do not forsake their professions with undue precipitation, in order to become clergymen."—*Ryle*. The demoniac was not allowed to be with Jesus, but sent to his home. A converted man wherever he is, should be a missionary to his fellow-men. "Though we are not tortured by the devil, yet he holds us as his slaves, till the Son of God delivers us from his tyranny. Naked, torn and disfigured, we wander about, till he restores us to soundness of mind. It remains that, in magnifying his grace, we testify our gratitude."—*John Calvin*.

21—43. JAIRUS'S DAUGHTER AND THE WOMAN WITH AN ISSUE OF BLOOD.

21. *unto the other side*] i. e., the western side of the lake, near Capernaum.

22. *the rulers of the synagogue*] "The Jews had three courts: (1) The great Sanhedrin at Jerusalem; (2) in cities having 120 men to bear office, the smaller council or Sanhedrin of 23 judges; (3) in the smallest towns, a court of 3 judges. A synagogue was formed in places where there were 10 students of the law; and of these ten, three usually served as magistrates." See Lightfoot, Greswell, and Edersheim. Each synagogue had a kind of chapter or college of elders, presided over by *a ruler*, who superintended the services, and possessed the power of excommunication. From this, as well as Acts xiii, 15, it would appear that some synagogues had several rulers.

Jairus by name] a Greek form of Jair (Judg. x, 3), with a Latin termination.

23. *My little daughter*] His "*only daughter*." Luke viii. 42. The use of diminutives is characteristic of Mark. Here we have "little daughter;" in v. 41, "Damsel," or "*little maid;*" in vii. 27, "dogs = little dogs," "*whelps;*" in viii. 7, *a few* "*small fishes;*" in xiv. 47, *his ear.* literally "*a little ear.*" She was about twelve years of age, Luke viii. 42. Of the three persons who are mentioned as having been raised from the dead by Christ, one was the only son of a widow, one the only daughter of Jairus, and the third the only brother of the two sisters, Mary and Martha.

at the point of death] the original word is one of the frequent Latinisms of Mark. She lay a dying (Luke viii. 42), and all but gone when he left her. life ebbing out so fast, that he could even say of her that she was "dead" (Matt. ix, 18), at one moment expressing himself in one language, at the next in another.

25. *a certain woman*] "such overflowing grace is in him, the Prince of life, that as he is hastening to the accomplishing of one work of his power, he accomplishes another, as by the way."—*Trench*.

an issue of blood] her malady (Lev. xv, 19–27), not only unfitted her for all

Authorized Version.	Revised Version.
28 For she said, If I may touch but his clothes, I shall be whole. 29 And straightway the fountain of her blood was dried up; and she felt in her body that she was healed of that plague. 30 And Jesus, immediately knowing in himself that virtue had gone out of him, turned him about in the press, and said, Who touched my clothes? 31 And his disciples said unto him, Thou seest the multitude thronging thee, and sayest thou, Who touched me? 32 And he looked round about to see her that had done this thing. 33 But the woman fearing and trembling,	28 and touched his garment. For she said, If I touch but his garments, I shall be ¹ made 29 whole. And straightway the fountain of her blood was dried up; and she felt in her body 30 that she was healed of her ² plague. And straightway Jesus, perceiving in himself that the power proceeding from him had gone forth, turned him about in the crowd, and 31 said, Who touched my garments? And his disciples said unto him, Thou seest the multitude thronging thee, and sayest thou, Who 32 touched me? And he looked round about 33 to see her that had done this thing. But the

¹ Or, *saved*. ² Gr. *scourge*.

the relationships of life, but was popularly regarded as the direct consequence of sinful habits.

28. *his garment*] the law of Moses commanded every Jew to wear at each corner of his *tallîth* a fringe or tassel of blue, to remind them that they were God's people (Num. xv. 37-40; Deut. xxii. 12). "Two of these fringes usually hung down at the bottom of the robe, while one hung over the shoulder where the robe was fastened round the person." Those who wished to be esteemed eminently religious were wont to make broad, or "enlarge, the borders of their garments" (Matt. xxiii. 5).

29. *of that plague*] or, scourge; see chap. iii. 10. She "said," or literally, "was saying" this. "It is important, though difficult to realize the situation of this woman, once possessed of health and wealth, and no doubt moving in respectable society, now beggared and diseased, without hope of human help, and secretly believing in the power of Christ to heal her."—*Alexander*. "Her case was such that she could not in modesty tell him publicly, as others did their grievances, and, therefore, she wished for a private cure, and her faith was suited to her case."—*M. Henry*.

30. *Who touched my clothes?*] "He meant to bring the woman to open avowal, for her highest good."—*S. N. World*. "Many throng him, but only one touches him." "Caro premit, fides tangit," says Augustine.

31. *he looked round*] another proof of Mark's graphic power. The tense in the original is still more expressive. It denotes that he *kept on looking all round*, that his eyes *wandered over* one after the

Eastern Fringed Garment (from Farrar's Life of Christ).

other of the faces before him, till they fell on her who had done this thing.

33. *fearing and trembling*] she may have dreaded his anger, for, according to the law (Lev. xv. 19). the touch of one afflicted as she was caused ceremonial defilement until the evening.

AUTHORIZED VERSION.	REVISED VERSION.
knowing what was done in her, came and fell down before him, and told him all the truth.	woman fearing and trembling, knowing what had been done to her, came and fell down
34 And he said unto her, Daughter, thy faith hath made thee whole; go in peace, and be whole of thy plague.	34 before him, and told him all the truth. And he said unto her, Daughter, thy faith hath ¹ made thee whole; go in peace, and be whole of thy ² plague.
35 While he yet spake, there came from the ruler of the synagogue's *house certain* which said, Thy daughter is dead; why troublest thou the Master any further?	35 While he yet spake, they come from the ruler of the synagogue's *house*, saying, Thy daughter is dead: why troublest thou the
36 As soon as Jesus heard the word that was spoken, he saith unto the ruler of the synagogue, Be not afraid, only believe.	36 ³ Master any further? But Jesus,⁴ not heeding the word spoken, saith unto the ruler of
37 And he suffered no man to follow him, save Peter, and James, and John the brother of James.	37 the synagogue, Fear not, only believe. And he suffered no man to follow with him, save Peter, and James, and John the brother of
38 And he cometh to the house of the ruler of the synagogue, and seeth the tumult, and them that wept and wailed greatly.	38 James. And they come to the house of the ruler of the synagogue; and he beholdeth a tumult, and *many* weeping and wailing
39 And when he was come in, he saith unto them, Why make ye this ado, and weep? the damsel is not dead, but sleepeth.	39 greatly. And when he was entered in, he saith unto them, Why make ye a tumult, and weep? the child is not dead, but sleepeth.

¹ Or, *saved thee* ²Gr. *scourge.* ³ Or, *Teacher* ⁴ Or, *overhearing.*

told him] probably all the particulars in regard to her long affliction and fruitless employment of physicians (Luke viii, 47). "This woman would have borne away a maimed blessing, hardly a blessing at all, had she been suffered to bear it away in secret and unacknowledged."

34. *Daughter*] Our Lord is recorded to have addressed no other woman by this title. He sometimes addressed men as "Son." It calmed all her doubts and fears.

go in peace] not merely "go with a blessing." but *abi in pacem* = enter into peace. "as the future element in which thy life shall move," and *be whole of thy plague.* "After a long sorrow a lasting blessing."—*Bengel.* "Without the legend of the later church, that she set up a brazen statue of Christ before her dwelling, in memory of this deed, we may well believe that she trusted Christ for all."—*John Hall.*

35. *why troublest thou the Master?*] the meaning is, Jesus might have helped you; he cannot raise her from the dead. Luke says (viii, 49), "trouble not the Master." The word translated "trouble," one which is used here, and here alone, by Mark and Luke (except Luke vii. 6), denotes properly (1) *to flay*; then (2) *to fatigue* or *to worry*, often with a more particular allusion to fatiguing with the length of a journey.

36. *heard*] or "*not heeding*," is in R. V., or, according to another authority, "overhearing," as in margin of R. V. The very instant the Lord heard the message, he hastens to reassure the ruler with a word of confidence and encouragement.

37. *save Peter, and James, and John*] this is the first time we hear of this selection of the three. "That which he was about to do was so great and holy that those three only, the flower and crown of the apostolic band, were its fitting witnesses." The other occasions when we read of such a selection are: (1) the transfiguration (Matt. xvii, 2); and (2) the agony in the garden of Gethsemane (Matt. xxvi. 37).

38. *them that wept and wailed*] a verb from *alala.* the ancient war-cry, and used by Euripides and Xenophon, in the sense of crying out, sometimes with pain. They were the hired mourners. chiefly women, whose business it was to beat their breasts (Luke viii, 52), and to make loud lamentations at funerals; comp. 2 Chron. xxxv. 25; Jer. ix, 17, 18; Amos v, 16. The Rabbinic rule provided for the poorest Israelite at least two flute players and one mourning woman.

39. *but sleepeth*] comp. his words in reference to Lazarus (John xi, 11).

AUTHORIZED VERSION.	REVISED VERSION.
40 And they laughed him to scorn. But when he had put them all out, he taketh the father and the mother of the damsel, and them that were with him, and entereth in where the damsel was lying.	40 And they laughed him to scorn. But he, having put them all forth, taketh the father of the child and her mother and them that were with him, and goeth in where the child
41 And he took the damsel by the hand, and said unto her, Talitha cumi; which is, being interpreted, Damsel, I say unto thee, arise.	41 was. And taking the child by the hand, he saith unto her, Talitha cumi; which is, being interpreted, Damsel, I say unto thee, Arise.
42 And straightway the damsel arose, and walked; for she was *of the age* of twelve years. And they were astonished with a great astonishment.	42 And straightway the damsel rose up, and walked; for she was twelve years old. And they were amazed straightway with a great
43 And he charged them straitly that no man should know it; and commanded that something should be given her to eat.	43 amazement. And he charged them much that no man should know this; and he commanded that *something* should be given her to eat.
CHAP. VI.—And he went out from thence, and came into his own country; and his disciples follow him.	6 And he went out from thence; and he cometh into his own country; and his disciples
2 And when the sabbath day was come, he began to teach in the synagogue: and many hearing *him* were astonished, saying, From whence hath this *man* these things? and what wisdom *is* this which is given unto him, that	2 follow him. And when the sabbath was come, he began to teach in the synagogue: and ¹many hearing him were astonished, saying, Whence hath this man these things?

¹ Some ancient authorities insert *the*.

41. *Talitha cumi*] Westcott and Hort read "ταλειθά κουμ." "'Talei-tha Kum' is not only the better reading, but the only one which corresponds to the Aramaic original... In the Talmud the same command, spoken to a woman, reads not 'kumi,' but 'kum,' and occurs in that form not less than seven times in one page (Shab. 110b)."—*Edersheim*. So also Tischendorf: But Canon Cook still insists on *cumi*, not *cum*, as the true reading. "The words express endearment; 'Little maiden, rise.'" Other Aramaic words given by Mark are: "Boanerges" (iii, 17); "Ephphatha" (vii, 34); "Abba" (xiv, 63).

42. *And straightway the damsel arose*] Luke says her spirit came again (viii, 55). There is no struggle, no effort, no crying "unto the Lord," or stretching "himself upon the child three times," as in the case of Elijah at Sarepta (1 Kings xvii, 21). He speaks but a word and instantly the dead is alive again.

a great astonishment] the word thus rendered denotes sometimes (1) *a trance*, as in Acts x, 10, "but while they made ready, he [Peter] fell into a trance"; and Acts xxii, 17, "while I prayed in the temple, I was in a trance," with which comp. 2 Cor. xii, 2; (2) *amazement, awe*, as in Luke v, 26, "and amazement seized all"; Mark xvi, 8, "trembling and amazement seized them"; Acts iii, 10, "and they were filled with wonder and amazement." Here it points to the very extremity of astonishment.

43. *something should be given her to eat*] to strengthen the life thus wonderfully restored, and to prove that she was not a spirit.

PRACTICAL LESSONS.—"We should act with as much energy as those who expect everything from themselves; and we should pray with as much earnestness as those who expect everything from God."—*Colton*. "Keep up a confidence in Christ and he will do what is best."—*Henry*. See what Jesus can do for dead souls! "One touch of real faith can do more for the soul than a hundred self-imposed austerities."—*Ryle*.

CH. VI. 1–6. REJECTED AT NAZARETH. A. D. 29.

1. *his own country*] i. e., in the sense of his family home, from Capernaum to the region of Nazareth.

2. *to teach in the synagogue*] This was the second rejection at Nazareth. See Matt xiii, 54. For his first visit see Luke iv, 16, etc. Jacobus describes the building now shown to travellers as this synagogue, which consists of a

AUTHORIZED VERSION.	REVISED VERSION.
even such mighty works are wrought by his hands?	and, What is the wisdom that is given unto this man and *what mean* such ¹ mighty
3 Is not this the carpenter, the son of Mary, the brother of James, and Joses, and of Juda, and Simon? and are not his sisters here with us? And they were offended at him.	3 works wrought by his hands? Is not this the carpenter, the son of Mary, and brother of James, and Joses, and Judas, and Simon? and are not his sisters here with us? And they were ² offended in him. And Jesus
4 But Jesus said unto them, A prophet is not without honour, but in his own country, and among his own kin, and in his own house.	4 said unto them, A prophet is not without honour, save in his own country, and among
5 And he could there do no mighty work,	5 his own kin, and in his own house. And he

¹ Gr. *powers*. ² Gr. *caused to stumble*.

plain room 28x35 feet, with vaulted roof and two windows with arched heads on one side. It can scarcely be the synagogue of Christ's day.

mighty works] or "powers," as in R. V. Some render, "and whence are such mighty works wrought." Others, as in R. V., "*what mean* such mighty works." This is one of the four names given by the Evangelists to the miracles: (1) "*Wonders*," a term never used alone, but always in conjunction with other names. (2) "*Signs*," as being tokens and indications of the near presence and working of God, the seals and credentials of a higher power. (3) "*Powers*," that is, of God, coming into and working in this world of ours. (4) "*Works*." This is a significant term very frequently used by John. Comp. John vi, 28; vii, 21; x, 25, 32 38.

3. *Is not this the carpenter?*] The Greek word signifies any worker in wood, iron, or stone, but without the adjective it means, in Scripture, a worker in wood. Jesus is not elsewhere called the carpenter, but by Matthew (xiii, 55,) the carpenter's son. According to the custom of the Jews, even the Rabbis learned some handicraft. One of their proverbs was that "he who taught not his son a trade, taught him to be a thief." Paul was a tent-maker; the famous Hillel a hewer of wood; Rabbi Isaac was a blacksmith; Rabbi Juda a tailor; Rabbi Jochanan a shoemaker. Maimonides says that the holy place needed repairs, and great care should be taken that the carpenter or workman be a right priest. "In the cities the carpenters would be Greeks and skilled workmen; the carpenter of a provincial village could only have held a very humble position and secured a very moderate competence."—*Farrar*.

brother of James and Joses] (or "Joseph," as the Sinaitic MS. reads) There are three theories about the degree of relationship of these brothers (and also sisters): (1) That they were full brothers of Jesus, or younger children of Joseph and Mary. This is the simplest and most natural explanation. Comp. Matt. i, 25; xii, 55. But reverence for the "Virgin Mary," and the feeling that shrinks from regarding her as the mother of other children, has led the Greek and other churches and some Protestant writers to propose, (2) that they were half brothers. *i. e.*, children of Joseph by a former marriage: held by the Greek Church and lately defended by Bishop Lightfoot; or (3) That they were children of Clopas (or Alphaeus) and Mary, a supposed sister of the "Virgin Mary," and hence *cousins* of Jesus, as held by Jerome and the Romish Church. But this latter view does violence to the word "brother," and assumes that there were two sisters of the same name. A word for "cousin" is used by N. T. writers, and it is fair to presume they would have used it here, had they meant this instead of "brothers." See Renan *Les Evangiles*, pp. 537–549, and Canon Cook's note in *Bib. Com'y*, p. 73.

4. *A prophet is not without honor*] so we have a similar proverb, "familiarity breeds contempt." He repeats almost the same proverb which he before uttered in their hearing, and from the same place (Luke iv, 24).

5. *no mighty work*] literally, *no power*. "His power was not changed."

AUTHORIZED VERSION.	REVISED VERSION.
save that he laid his hands upon a few sick folk, and healed them.	could there do no ¹ mighty work, save that he laid his hands upon a few sick folk, and
6 And he marvelled because of their unbelief. And he went round about the villages, teaching.	6 healed them. And he marvelled because of their unbelief.
7 ¶ And he called unto him the twelve, and began to send them forth by two and two; and gave them power over unclean spirits;	And he went round about the villages teaching.
8 And commanded them that they should take nothing for *their* journey, save a staff only;	7 And he called unto him the twelve, and began to send them forth by two and two; and he gave them authority over the unclean 8 spirits; and he charged them that they should take nothing for *their* journey, save a

¹ Gr. *power*.

His miracles were not feats of magic, but pre-supposed belief and opportunity. If none believed, none would come to him; hence he could do no mighty work. "Not because he was powerless, but they were faithless."— *Theophylact*. Bentley says because it was not fit and reasonable that he should. Le Clerc, that he could not consistently with his rules perform miracles. He performed some miracles, but not what he would have done. It teaches that faith is a condition of receiving help from Christ, for soul or body.

few sick...healed] "What an amazing contest, that while we are endeavoring by every possible method to hinder the grace of God from coming to us, it rises victorious and displays its efficacy in spite of all our exertions." —*John Calvin*.

6. *he marvelled*] he marvels at faith in the centurion, and at unbelief in the face of numerous manifestations of divine power. He seems to have forsaken Nazareth from this time.

went round] The unbelief of the Nazarenes, though his life-long acquaintances, did not stop the activity of Jesus. He began another circuit (probably the third) in Galilee.

PRACTICAL LESSONS.—Men are apt to think little of things with which they are familiar. How great is our unbelief! Jesus, as a carpenter and carpenter's son, put great honor upon mechanics. "Unbelief and contempt of Christ stop the current of his favors."—*M. Henry*. "The unbelief of those who have the means of grace is most amazing." "I would rather dwell in the dim fog of superstition," says Ichter, "than in air rarified to nothing by the air-pump of unbelief." "Jesus Christ professed to give a universal spiritual religion...to bless by its influence the whole family of man: and faith he set forth as the great motive power of the whole plan." —*Walker Phil. of Plan of Salvation*.

7-13. MISSION OF THE TWELVE. A. D. 29.

7. *he called*] or, *he calleth unto him*.

two and two] Matthew and Luke note the sending of the twelve. Mark says they were sent "by two and two," that they might support and encourage each other.

power over, etc.] "The man who is afraid, who holds down his head like a bulrush, is not the worker whom God will bless; but God gives courage to him whom he means to use."—*Moody*.

8. *and commanded them*] or "charged," as in R.V. Matthew gives the directions at greater length. Mark records a summary only of the commands.

save a staff] Matthew x. 10 says, "nor yet staves," or "staff," as the margin and R.V. read. They were not to seek or procure a "staff" for this journey, for the meaning there depends on "provide," in verse 9. If one has a staff, let him take it, but let him not provide one specially. This explanation is strictly grammatical, and removes any apparent contradiction in the narratives.

AUTHORIZED VERSION.	REVISED VERSION.
no scrip, no bread, no money in *their* purse: 9 But *be* shod with sandals; and not put on two coats. 10 And he said unto them, In what place soever ye enter into a house, there abide till ye depart from that place. 11 And whosoever shall not receive you, nor hear you, when ye depart thence, shake off the	staff only; no bread, no wallet, no [1] money 9 in their [2] purse; but *to go* shod with sandals: 10 and, *said he*, put not on two coats. And he said unto them, Wheresoever ye enter into a house, there abide till ye depart thence. And whatsoever place shall not receive you, and they hear you not, as ye go forth thence,

[1] Gr. *brass*. [2] Gr. *girdle*.

no scrip] or "wallet." Scrip, from Sw. *skreppa*, denotes a "wallet" or "small bag." Comp. 1 Sam. xvii, 40. The scrip of the Galilean peasants was of leather, "the skins of kids stripped off whole, and tanned by a very simple process," used especially to carry their food on a journey, and slung over their shoulders.

no money] the word signifies a piece of brass or bronze worth about a farthing, but is probably used here for any kind of money. "There was no departure from the simple manners of the country in this. At this day the farmer sets out on excursions quite as extensive, without a *para* in his purse, and a modern Moslem prophet of Tarshisha thus sends forth his apostles over this identical region. No traveller in the East would hesitate to throw himself on the hospitality of any villager."—*Thomson.*

9. *with sandals*] not shoes, which would look like luxury, but the sandals of the common people. "A shoe was of softer, a sandal of harder

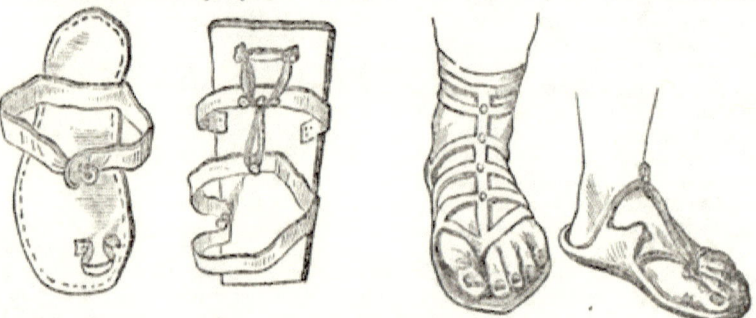

SANDALS (see *Chap. I*).

leather."—*Talmud.* "The Galilean peasants now wear a coarse shoe, answering to the sandal of the ancients, but never take two pair with them."

two coats] tunics, or under garments having sleeves, and reaching to the knees. They were not to encumber themselves with changes of raiment. Canon Cook observes that persons of distinction usually wore two tunics, the under one of fine linen.

10. *there abide*] "When a stranger arrives in a village or an encampment, the neighbors, one after another, must invite him to eat with them. There is a strict etiquette about it, involving much ostentation and hypocrisy: and a failure in the due observance of this system of hospitality is violently resented, and often leads to alienation and feuds among neighbors...The Evangelists...were sent, not to be honored and feasted, but to call men to repentance, prepare the way of the Lord, and proclaim that the kingdom of heaven was at hand. They were, therefore, first to seek a becoming habitation to lodge in, and there abide until their work in that city was accomplished."—*Thomson.*

11. *whosoever*] or, "whatsoever place," as in R. V.

AUTHORIZED VERSION.	REVISED VERSION.
dust under your feet for a testimony against them. Verily I say unto you, It shall be more tolerable for Sodom and Gomorrah in the day of judgment, than for that city. 12 And they went out, and preached that men should repent. 13 And they cast out many devils, and anointed with oil many that were sick, and healed them. 14 And king Herod heard of him; (for his name was spread abroad:) and he said, That John the Baptist was risen from the dead, and therefore mighty works do shew forth themselves in him. 15 Others said, That it is Elias. And others said, That it is a prophet, or as one of the prophets. 16 But when Herod heard thereof, he said, It is John, whom I beheaded: he is risen from the dead.	shake off the dust that is under your feet for 12 a testimony unto them. And they went out, 13 and preached that men should repent. And they cast out many ¹ devils, and anointed with oil many that were sick, and healed them. 14 And king Herod heard thereof; for his name had become known: and ² he said, John ³ the Baptist is risen from the dead, and 15 therefore do these powers work in him. But others said, It is Elijah. And others said, It 16 is a prophet, even as one of the prophets. But Herod, when he heard thereof, said, John,

¹ Gr. demons. ² Some ancient authorities read they. ³ Gr. the Baptizer.

the dust under your feet] for instances of the carrying out of this command, compare the conduct of Paul at Antioch, in Pisidia, Acts xiii. 51, and at Corinth, Acts xviii, 6. The action must be regarded as symbolical of a complete cessation of all fellowship, and a renunciation of all further responsibility. The words, "Verily I say," etc., to the end of verse 11, are not found in four of the oldest MSS. See R. V., which omits them without any note.

13. *anointed with oil*] Mark alone mentions this anointing as the method whereby the healing of the sick was effected. Though not expressly ordered, it was doubtless implied in the injunction to "heal the sick" (Matt x. 8). For the uses of oil for medicinal purposes, see Isa. i. 6; Jas. v. 14. This passage is cited by the Romish writers in favor of their pretended sacrament of extreme unction. The sick were not anointed because "in articulo mortis," but that they might be healed. The text gives no support to the Romish doctrine. Anointing with oil is a common practice of eastern physicians now. Calvin admits this, but thinks the anointing "was a visible token of spiritual grace ..for under the law oil was employed to represent the grace of the Spirit."

PRACTICAL SUGGESTIONS.—They preached repentance. Have we repented? This, after all, is the great question. Christ would teach his ministers to unite and associate in doing his work. The work should be done for Christ.

14-29. THE MURDER OF JOHN THE BAPTIST. A. D. 29.

14. *And king Herod heard*] that is, Herod Antipas, one of the three sons of Herod the Great, and who was tetrarch of Ituræa and Peræa. He is here called "king," or "prince," in the ancient and wide sense of the word. Matt. (xiv, 1) and Luke (ix. 7) style him more exactly "the tetrarch." Antipas was banished to Gaul, A.D. 39, whither Herodias is said to have followed him, and both died in exile.

his name] It is peculiar to Mark that he connects the watching of Herod Antipas with the work of Christ as extended by the preaching and miracles of his apostles. "A palace is late in hearing spiritual news."—*Bengel.*

risen from the dead] The best authorities sustain the reading "he said"; "they said" is given by a few of lesser weight only. Herod's guilty conscience triumphed over his Sadducean profession of belief that there is no resurrection. Comp. Matt. xvi. 6; Mark viii, 15.

16. *It is John*] The words in the original, according to the best MSS., are very striking. *John whom I* (= *I myself*; the pronoun "has the emphasis of a guilty conscience") *beheaded—this is he—he is risen.* See R.

AUTHORIZED VERSION.	REVISED VERSION.
17 For Herod himself had sent forth and laid hold upon John, and bound him in prison for Herodias' sake, his brother Philip's wife: for he had married her.	17 whom I beheaded, he is risen. For Herod himself had sent forth and laid hold upon John, and bound him in prison for the sake of Herodias, his brother Philip's wife: for he had married her.
18 For John had said unto Herod, It is not lawful for thee to have thy brother's wife.	18 For John said unto Herod, It is not lawful for thee to have thy brother's wife.
19 Therefore Herodias had a quarrel against him, and would have killed him; but she could not:	19 And Herodias set herself against him, and desired to kill him; and she could
20 For Herod feared John, knowing that he was a just man and a holy, and observed him; and when he heard him, he did many things, and heard him gladly.	20 not; for Herod feared John, knowing that he was a righteous man and a holy, and kept him safe. And when he heard him, he [1] was much perplexed; and he heard him gladly.
21 And when a convenient day was come, that	21 And when a convenient day was come, that

[1] Many ancient authorities read, *did many things*.

V., which gives the same thought as the A. V. John was beheaded, probably in the winter of A. D. 28, or the spring of 29. Josephus confirms the account of these forebodings when he tells us that after the utter defeat of Herod Antipas by Aretas, the people regarded it as a righteous retribution for the murder of John (Jos. *Ant.* xviii, 5, 1. 2).

17. *for Herodias' sake*] Herod himself had long been married to the daughter of Aretas, Emir of Arabia Petræa, but this did not prevent him from courting an adulterous alliance with Herodias, the wife of his brother Philip (not the tetrarch of Ituræa, but another Philip, living in private life). Herodias consented to become his wife, on condition that the daughter of the Arabian prince was divorced. But the latter, suspecting her husband's guilty passion, did not wait to be divorced, and indignantly fled to the castle of Machærus, and thence to her father's rocky fortress at Petra, who forthwith assembled an army to avenge her wrongs, and defeated Herod, as already stated.

18. *For John had said*] John boldly denounced the royal crimes (Luke iii, 19), and declared the marriage unlawful (Matt. xiv, 4). For this outspoken faithfulness he was flung into prison, probably in the castle of Machærus or "the Black Fortress" (though some say, in a fortress near Tiberias; but Josephus is more likely to be correct). This castle had been built by Herod's father, in one of the most abrupt wâdys to the east of the Dead Sea, to overawe the wild Arab tribes of the neighborhood. Though originally in the possession of Aretas, Herod had probably seized the fortress after the departure of his first wife to her father's stronghold at Petra (Jos. *Ant.* xviii, 5, 2).

19. *had a quarrel*] or "*had an inward grudge*" against him. See also R. V. In Tyndale's and Cranmer's Versions it is rendered "laid waite for him"; in the Rhemish, "sought all occasions against him."

would have killed] The word in the original is much stronger, and denotes that she *had a settled wish* to kill him. Some Versions read "*she sought*," or "*kept seeking*" means to kill him.

20. *observed him*] rather "kept him safe" from Herodias for a time; not "esteemed him," or "observed him."

when he heard him] The Greek is still more emphatic; "he *used to do many things*, and *used to listen to him gladly*." But see R. V., for a different reading; this indicates the trouble arising from a guilty conscience.

21. *a convenient day*] a suitable day for her fell purposes. "She doubtless felt like another woman of her time, Fulvia, who forced her needle through the tongue of dead Cicero, as Agrippina did to the head of her rival, Lollia Paulina."—*John Hall.*

AUTHORIZED VERSION.	REVISED VERSION.
Herod on his birthday made a supper to his lords, high captains, and chief *estates* of Galilee; ²² And when the daughter of the said Herodias came in, and danced, and pleased Herod and them that sat with him, the king said unto the damsel, Ask of me whatsoever thou wilt, and I will give *it* thee.	Herod on his birthday made a supper to his lords, and the ¹ high captains, and the chief men of Galilee; ²² and when ² the daughter of Herodias herself came in and danced, ³ she pleased Herod and them that sat at meat with him; and the king said unto the damsel, Ask of me whatsoever thou wilt, and I

¹ Or, *military tribunes.* Gr., *chiliarchs.* ² Some ancient authorities read, *his daughter Herodias.* ³ Or, *it*

on his birthday] in imitation of the Roman emperors, the Herodian princes kept their birthdays with feasting and revelry and magnificent banquets. Wieseler, however, thinks the word denotes a feast celebrating Herod's accession, but this is more than doubtful.

made a supper] probably at the castle of Machærus, near the Dead Sea, where Josephus says John was imprisoned. The Roman poet, Persius, (A. D. 62) is supposed to refer to this occasion:

" But when the feast of Herod's birthday comes,
* * * * * and in fear
Thou keepest the sabbath of the circumcised,
And then there rise dark spectres of the dead."

lords] literally, great men: *high captains* were properly tribunes, *chiliarchs* (see note R. V.), or captains of thousands, though, strictly speaking, Herod had no *chiliarchs.* It is supposed that, at this time, Herod was collecting his forces to meet Aretas; *chief estates* were men of first rank generally.

22. *the daughter of Herodias*] her name was Salome; she afterwards married (1) Philip, the tetrarch, and then (2) Aristobulus, the king of Chalcis. " A luxurious feast of the period was not regarded as complete unless it closed with some gross pantomimic representation; and doubtless Herod had adopted the evil fashion of his day. But he had not anticipated for his guests the rare luxury of seeing a princess—his own niece, a granddaughter of Herod the Great and of Mariamne, a descendant, therefore, of Simon the High Priest, and the great line of Maccabæan princes—a princess who afterwards became the wife of a tetrarch, and the mother of a king—honoring them by degrading herself into a scenic dancer."— *Farrar.* Of the oriental dance Thomson says, " They (the dancing girls) move forward and backward, and sidewise, now slowly, then rapidly, throwing their arms and heads about at random, and rolling the eye, and wriggling the body into various preposterous attitudes, languishing, lascivious, and sometimes indecent, and this is repeated over and over...The different sexes do not interming'e in these indecorous sports."

"A DANCING GIRL."

AUTHORIZED VERSION.	REVISED VERSION.
23 And he sware unto her, Whatsoever thou shalt ask of me, I will give it thee, unto the half of my kingdom. 24 And she went forth, and said unto her mother, What shall I ask? And she said, The head of John the Baptist. 25 And she came in straightway with haste unto the king, and asked, saying, I will that thou give me by and by in a charger the head of John the Baptist. 26 And the king was exceeding sorry; yet for his oath's sake, and for their sakes which sat with him, he would not reject her. 27 And immediately the king sent an executioner, and commanded his head to be brought:	23 will give it thee. And he sware unto her, Whatsoever thou shalt ask of me, I will give it thee, unto the half of my kingdom. And 24 she went out, and said unto her mother, What shall I ask? And she said, The head of John ¹ the Baptist. And she came in 25 straightway with haste unto the king, and asked, saying, I will that thou forthwith give me in a charger the head of John ¹ the Baptist. And the king was exceeding sorry; but 26 for the sake of his oaths, and of them that sat at meat, he would not reject her. And 27 straightway the king sent forth a soldier of his guard, and commanded to bring his head:

¹ Gr. *the Baptizer*.

23. *unto the half of my kingdom*] compare the words of Ahasuerus to Esther: "what is thy request? and it shall be performed, *even to the half of the kingdom*" (Esther v, 3; vii, 2). "A shameful example truly, that a drunken king not only permits himself to behold with approbation a spectacle which was disgraceful to his family, but holds out such promise of reward. Let us, therefore, be careful in anticipating and resisting the devil, lest he entangle us in such snares."—*John Calvin.*

24. *The head of John the Baptist*] the daughter retired to the women's apartment, which was separate from the men's. John's fidelity marred the pleasures of Herodias, and she saw that her hour was come. No jewelled trinket, no royal palace, no splendid robe, should be the reward of her daughter's feat—"Ask for the head of John." It was customary for princes to require the head of those they ordered to be executed brought to them, that they might be assured of their deaths.

25. *straightway with haste*] observe the ready alacrity with which she proved herself a true daughter of her mother. The "by and by" is used in the sense of "forthwith," as in R. V., "immediately." See A. V. in Luke xviii, 8; xxi, 9; Matt. xiii, 21, and compare with R. V.

a charger] old English for a "large dish," or platter. Fuller speaks of a silver charger of Oswald, King of Northumberland. The Greek word first meant a board, then a wooden dish, and later a platter of any kind.

26. *exceeding sorry*] "as if," tersely says Calvin, "it were more dishonorable to retract a rash and foolish promise than to persist in a heinous crime." The Greek word is very strong, and denotes very great grief and sorrow. It is used of the rich young ruler (Luke xviii, 23), and of Jesus (Matt. xxvi, 38). It was an ill omen among the Romans to take away life on one's birthday. "The devil is remorseless to his servants." Herod is horrified, but his oath had been witnessed by his generals and boon companions; the code of honor must be obeyed.

27. *an executioner*], *a soldier of the guard.* The Greek word σπεκουλάτωρα denotes (1) *a looker-out, a spy, scout*; (2) *a special adjutant, soldier of the guard.* These scouts formed a special division in each legion; but under the emperors a body bearing this name was specially appointed to guard the emperor and execute his commands (Tac. *Hist.* I, 24, 25; II, 11; Suet. *Claud.* xxxv.). Hence, they were often employed as special messengers in seeking out those who were proscribed or sentenced to death (Seneca, *de Ira* I, 16). In the earlier English Versions the word is rendered "hangman," but this term describes a mere accident of his office. The use of a military term, compared with Luke iii, 14, is in accordance with the fact that Herod was at this time making war on Aretas (Jos *Antiq.* xviii, 5, 1).

AUTHORIZED VERSION.	REVISED VERSION.
and he went and beheaded him in the prison, 28 And brought his head in a charger, and gave it to the damsel: and the damsel gave it to her mother. 29 And when his disciples heard *of it*, they came and took up his corpse, and laid it in a tomb. 30 And the apostles gathered themselves together unto Jesus, and told him all things, both what they had done, and what they had taught. 31 And he said unto them, Come ye yourselves apart into a desert place, and rest awhile: for there were many coming and going, and they had no leisure so much as to eat. 32 And they departed into a desert place by ship privately. 33 And the people saw them departing, and many knew him, and ran afoot thither out of all cities, and outwent them, and came together unto him. 34 And Jesus, when he came out, saw much people, and was moved with compassion toward them, because they were as sheep not having	and he went and beheaded him in the prison, and brought his head in a charger, and gave 28 it to the damsel; and the damsel gave it to 29 her mother. And when his disciples heard *thereof*, they came and took up his corpse and laid it in a tomb. 30 And the apostles gather themselves together unto Jesus; and they told him all things, whatsoever they had done, and whatsoever they had taught. And he saith unto 31 them, Come ye yourselves apart into a desert place, and rest a while. For there were many coming and going, and they had no 32 leisure so much as to eat. And they went away in the boat to a desert place apart. 33 And ¹*the people* saw them going, and many knew *them*, and they ran there together ¹on foot from all the cities, and outwent them. 34 And he came forth and saw a great multitude, and he had compassion on them, because they were as sheep not having a shepherd: and 35 he began to teach them many things. And

¹ Or, *by land*

beheaded him] this implies that the prison was near and the execution done promptly.

29. *laid it in a tomb*] and then *"went and told Jesus"* (Matt. xiv, 12). Herod, no doubt, gave the body to John's disciples, for this would accord with his feelings toward the intrepid preacher. There is no ground for the tradition noticed by Jerome, that Herod flung the headless body over the prison walls. At Samaria, in the crypt of a ruined church, the pretended tomb of the Baptist is shown to credulous travellers.

PRACTICAL SUGGESTIONS.—What amazing power has truth over the conscience of even wicked men! Men may hear, yet not heed the truth. Evil men are haunted by the thoughts of their evil deeds. Bad men may reverence good men. Christians who would be faithful to God must not fear the face of man. A wicked daughter readily obeys the desires of a wicked mother.

30-44. RETURN OF THE TWELVE. FIVE THOUSAND FED. A. D. 29.

30. *gathered themselves together*] Here, for the first time, the text of all the four Gospels runs parallel.

31. *there were many coming and going*] the passover was now nigh (John vi, 4), and the pilgrim companies would be moving towards the Holy City.

32. *into a desert place*] it was not safe for Jesus to remain openly in the territory of Antipas. They crossed the Lake of Gennesaret (John vi, 1) and proceeded in the direction of Bethsaida, at its northeastern corner (Luke ix, 10). just above the entrance of the Jordan into it. Bethsaida was enlarged by Herod Philip, not long after the birth of Christ. He raised it to the dignity of a town, and called it *Julias*, after Julia, the daughter of Augustus. Philip occasionally resided there, and there died and was buried in a costly tomb (Jos. *Antiq.* xviii, 4, 6).

33. *the people saw them*] comp. the R. V. Some authorities read, "many saw them departing, and understood it," as Alford. Lachmann, and Tregelles; others read the last clause, "and knew them," as Tischendorf. There is close similarity of thought in all these readings.

34. *he came out*] either from the boat, or from his place of retirement, as implied in John vi, 3. He went up a hill, and then saw the crowd. John gives an important item of information; the passover was nigh, and hence the crowds thronging about Jesus.

AUTHORIZED VERSION.	REVISED VERSION.
a shepherd: and he began to teach them many things. 35 And when the day was now far spent, his disciples came unto him, and said, This is a desert place, and now the time *is* far passed: 36 Send them away, that they may go into the country round about, and into the villages, and buy themselves bread: for they have nothing to eat. 37 He answered and said unto them, Give ye them to eat. And they say unto him, Shall we go and buy two hundred pennyworth of bread, and give them to eat? 38 He saith unto them, How many loaves have ye? go and see. And when they knew, they say, Five, and two fishes. 39 And he commanded them to make all sit down by companies upon the green grass.	35 he began to teach them many things. And when the day was now far spent, his disciples came unto him, and said, The place is 36 desert, and the day is now far spent: send them away, that they may go into the country and villages round about, and buy themselves somewhat to eat. But he answered 37 and said unto them, Give ye them to eat. And they say unto him, Shall we go and buy two hundred [1] pennyworth of bread, and give 38 them to eat? And he saith unto them, How many loaves have ye? go and see. And when they knew, they say, Five, and two fishes. 39 And he commanded them that all should [2] sit down by companies upon the green

[1] See marginal note on Matt. xviii. 28; which reads "The word in the Greek denotes a coin worth about eight pence halfpenny," that is about 17 cents. [2] Gr. *recline.*

many things] *i. e.,* "he spent a long time in preaching, that they might reap some lasting advantage."—*Calvin.*

35. *desert place*] the locality was probably part of the rich but uninhabited plain below where the Jordan enters the sea of Galilee.

37. *Shall we go and buy*] with one voice they seem to have reiterated what Philip had said earlier in the day. See R. V. in John vi, 5-7. The question of bread for the hungry, how often it is asked in this land of plenty! "It is the echo of a deeper question from starving souls...And both puzzle disciples to this day. How shall we deal with pauperism, and how with ignorance? Let disciples learn at once their own impotence, the wisdom of doing all they can and leaving the rest to the Master."—*John Hall.*

DENARIUS.

two hundred pennyworth] the specifying of this sum is peculiar to Mark and John. The word translated *penny* is the *denarius,* a silver coin of the value originally of 10 and afterwards of 16 ases. The denarius was first coined in B. C. 269, or four years before the first Punic war, and originally was of the value of 16 or 17 cents of our money; later, it = 15 cents. It was the day wages of a laborer in Palestine (Matt. xx, 2, 9, 13). "It so happens that in almost every case where the word *denarius* occurs in the N. T., it is connected with the idea of a liberal or large amount; and yet, in these passages, the English rendering names a sum which is absurdly small."—*Lightfoot.*

38. *go and see*] this does not imply that Jesus was ignorant of what was in their possession, but rather that he wished to try their faith. They found a lad who had *five barley loaves, and two small fishes,* which they could secure. They were only *barley loaves* (John vi, 9), the food even then, for the most part, of the poor and the unfortunate. Comp. 2 Kings vii, 1.

39. *by companies*] literally, *drinking parties.* The word alludes to an orderly social grouping. The words are repeated by a Hebraism in the original, like the "two and two" of ver. 7.

upon the green grass] this fact aids in fixing the season of the year when the miracle was performed. Andrews assigns it to the month of April. A. D. 29. Mark alone mentions *the green grass,* "still fresh in the spring of the year, before it had faded away in the summer sun." It was near the

AUTHORIZED VERSION.	REVISED VERSION.
40 And they sat down in ranks, by hundreds, and by fifties. 41 And when he had taken the five loaves and the two fishes, he looked up to heaven, and blessed, and brake the loaves, and gave *them* to his disciples to set before them; and the two fishes divided he among them all. 42 And they did all eat, and were filled. 43 And they took up twelve baskets full of the fragments, and of the fishes.	40 grass. And they sat down in ranks, by hundreds, and by fifties. And he took the five loaves and the two fishes, and looking up to heaven, he blessed, and brake the loaves; and he gave to the disciples to set before them; And the two fishes divided he among them 42 all. And they did all eat, and were filled. 43 And they took up broken pieces, twelve baskets

passover, corresponding to our March or April, hence there was "*much grass in the place;*" comp. John vi, 10.

40. *in ranks*] literally, *in beds* (as of a garden) or *in rows, i. e., they reclined in parterres (areolatim)*. "Our English '*in ranks*' does not reproduce the picture to the eye, giving rather the notion of continuous lines. Wyclif was better, 'by parties;' perhaps *in groups* would be as near as we could get to it in English."—*Trench*. Mark doubtless reproduces the description of the scene by Peter himself.

by hundreds, and by fifties] "Two long rows of one hundred, a shorter one of fifty persons. The fourth side remained, after the manner of the tables of the ancients, empty and open."—*Gerlach*. Rabbi Eliezer is said to have arranged his hearers or disciples in a similar manner.

41. *blessed*] probably the customary grace said before meals by the Jews. The Greek verb primarily means to speak well of, but is applied to the asking for divine favors upon others; praising God for such favors; and to the act of God in granting favors to men.

and brake the loaves, and gave them to his disciples] in the East bread is always spoken of as broken, never as having been cut. The first of these words implies an *instantaneous*, the second a *continuous* act. The multiplication of the loaves and fishes *was continuous* in the hands of Christ between the acts of breaking and distributing the bread. Comp. 2 Kings iv. 42-44.

43. *baskets*] There were twelve baskets full of fragments, or one for each of the disciples. All the Evangelists use κόφινος for the small, common *wicker-baskets*, in which these fragments were collected, at the feeding of the five thousand, and the word σπυρίς = or large *rope-basket*, when they describe the feeding of the four thousand. Watson and Mimpriss have strangely mistaken the "spurides" for the smaller hand-baskets," and the other for the larger basket sometimes used to rest upon, while, according to the best authorities, the reverse was the fact. The wicker baskets were the common possession of the Jews, in which to carry their food, in order to avoid pollution with heathens; "*Judæis, quorum*

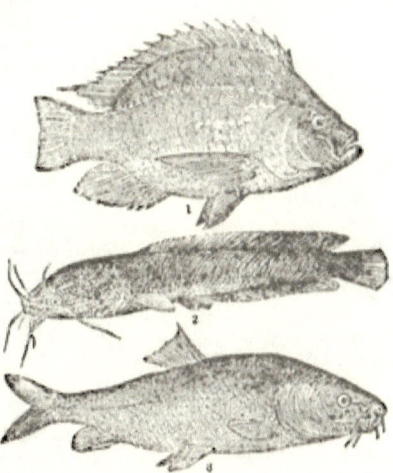

FISHES OF THE SEA OF GALILEE. (*After Tristram*)
1 Chromis Nilotica.
2 Clarias Macracanthus.
3 Labiobarbus Canis.

AUTHORIZED VERSION.	REVISED VERSION.
44 And they that did eat of the loaves were about five thousand men.	44 ketfuls, and also of the fishes. And they that ate the loaves were five thousand men.
45 And straightway he constrained his disciples to get into the ship, and to go to the other side before unto Bethsaida, while he sent away the people.	45 And straightway he constrained his disciples to enter into the boat, and to go before him unto the other side to Bethsaida, while
46 And when he had sent them away, he departed into a mountain to pray.	46 he himself sendeth the multitude away. And after he had taken leave of them, he departed into the mountain to pray. And when even
47 And when even was come, the ship was in the midst of the sea, and he alone on the land.	47 was come, the boat was in the midst of the

cophinus fœnumque supellex." Juv. *Sat.* III, 14. The same distinction is made by our Lord when he alludes to both miracles (Mark viii. 19, 20; Matt. xvi. 9, 10).

44. *five thousand men*] Observe the R. V. omits "about." Mark uses a word which excludes women and children, and Matthew states *beside women and children* (xiv. 21), who would not sit down with the men, but sit or stand apart. "The women and children would probably be few, not, as sometimes fancied, 5000 more." The Latin, Syriac, Arabic, Persic, and Ethiopic versions omit "about," and read "five thousand" definitely.

PRACTICAL SUGGESTIONS.—Go and tell Jesus our trouble. Come and rest awhile. So Christ knows the fears of some, and the toils of others of his disciples. He gives refuge for the terrified and rest for the tired. A desert place—but the presence of Christ will change a desert into a paradise. Jesus praying—we have little because we ask for little. "Let us not fear to lose earthly in search of heavenly comfort."—*John Hall.*

45-52. WALKING ON THE WATER. A.D. 29.

45. *And straightway*] This miracle made a deep impression on the people. It was the popular expectation that the Messiah would repeat the miracles of Moses, and this "bread of wonder," of which they had just partaken, recalled to the multitudes the manna. They would have *taken Jesus by force and made him a king* (John vi. 14, 15). To defeat this intention the Saviour bade his apostles take a boat and cross over the Lake.

unto Bethsaida] Bethsaida, the town of Philip, Andrew, and Peter (John i, 44). Macgregor, after careful examination, holds to the theory that there were two Bethsaidas, and that this voyage was from the Plain of Batihah near Bethsaida Julius to Khan Minyeh, near the other supposed Bethsaida. Thomson believes the miracle was on this plain, but disputes the theory of two Bethsaidas, a theory advocated if not invented by Reland and adopted by some others, but not really required by the Gospel narrative, and not sufficiently supported by historical and topographical facts. If there were *two* Bethsaidas, upon which of them was the woe pronounced? But Jesus gives no intimation in his work of two Bethsaidas. Andrews places the scene of this miracle four or five miles southeast of the Jordan, and therefore, only seven or eight miles from Capernaum. The boat in returning would then go across the northeast corner of the Lake to Bethsaida.

46. *a mountain to pray*] or, "the mountain," one well known and frequented. How often Jesus is thus said to have retired for prayer! What an example to disciples in this busy commercial age! What mountain it was, is unknown.

47. *in the midst of the sea*] *i. e.*, out at sea, it does not imply that they were in the middle or centre of the lake. Toiling the entire night, they had not, in consequence of contrary winds (John vi. 18), gone more than three or four miles (see John vi. 19), something more than half of their way, when one of

AUTHORIZED VERSION.	REVISED VERSION.
48 And he saw them toiling in rowing; for the wind was contrary unto them: and about the fourth watch of the night he cometh unto them, walking upon the sea, and would have passed by them.	48 sea, and he alone on the land. And seeing them distressed in rowing, for the wind was contrary unto them, about the fourth watch of the night he cometh unto them, walking on the sea; and he would have passed by
49 But when they saw him walking upon the sea, they supposed it had been a spirit, and cried out:	49 them: but they, when they saw him walking on the sea, supposed that it was an appari-
50 For they all saw him, and were troubled. And immediately he talked with them, and saith unto them, Be of good cheer: it is I; be not afraid.	50 tion, and cried out: for they all saw him, and were troubled. But he straightway spake with them, and saith unto them, Be of good
51 And he went up unto them into the ship; and the wind ceased: and they were sore amazed in themselves beyond measure, and wondered.	51 cheer: it is I; be not afraid. And he went up unto them into the boat; and the wind ceased: and they were sore amazed in them-

the sudden storms, to which the Lake is subject, rushed down from the mountains. See above, iv. 37.

48. *he saw them toiling in rowing*] the word translated "toiling," "distressed," in R. V. occurs in Matt. xiv, 24, and is a striking expression. It denotes (1) *to test metals*, (2) *to rack, torture*, (3) *to torment* as in Matt. viii, 6, 29. Here it seems to imply that they were *tortured, baffled*, by the waves, which were boisterous by reason of the strong wind that blew (John vi, 18). Wyclif translates it *"travailing in rowing;"* Tyndale and Cranmer, "*troubled in rowing.*"

the fourth watch] the proper Jewish reckoning recognized only three watches: (1) from sunset to 10 P.M (Lam. ii, 19), (2) *the middle watch*, from 10 P.M. to 2 A.M. (Judges vii, 19), and (3) *the morning watch*, from 2 A.M. to sunrise (Ex xiv, 24; 1 Sam. xi, 11). After the Roman supremacy the number of watches was increased to *four*, sometimes described by their numerical order, as here and in Mark xiii, 35; Matt. xiv, 25: sometimes by the terms. *even, midnight, cock-crowing, morning*. In eight or nine hours' rowing they had made only three or four miles.

walking upon the sea] not upon the shore by the sea, as some rationalists would interpret it, but *on the sea*, as the context unmistakably implies.

would have passed by them] Jesus came quite near their vessel on the storm-tost waves, and as if to go by them or to lead the way before them to the western shore. Comp. Luke xxiv, 28. 29. "*Cried out*" is the same word used to express the cries of persons possessed of evil spirits.

49. *a spirit*] so they thought on the eve of the resurrection. See Luke xxiv, 36, 37. Wyclif translates it "they gessiden him for to be a fantum;" Tyndale and Cranmer "a sprete;" the Rhemish "a ghost."

50. *be not afraid*] is connected with "Be of good courage." The latter is represented by a single Greek word, used in Homer, and requires a more expressive rendering. "Take courage," or "Cheer up." indicates the graphic style of the Greek. Mark does not record Peter's attempt to go to his Lord upon the Lake, which is narrated only by Matthew, xiv. 28-30.

51. *they were sore amazed*] a strong expression. The A. V. adds "and wondered," and "at him," the Ethiopic version further adds. These are omitted, however, in the R. V. The Greek does not imply that they were "grievously" or "sorely" amazed *i. e.*, not the quality but the extent of their amazement is meant, and agrees with the English "much amazed," more than they had any good reason to be; as the next verse states. Matthew, xiv, 33, says that a similar impression was made on those who were with them in the boat, *i. e.*, probably the crew. Not only did they approach him with an outward unforbidden gesture of worship, "but they avowed for the first time collectively what one of them had long since separately declared him to be, *the Son of God*" (Matt. xiv, 33: comp. John i, 41).—*Ellicott.*

AUTHORIZED VERSION.	REVISED VERSION.
52 For they considered not *the miracle* of the loaves; for their heart was hardened.	52 selves; for they understood not concerning the loaves, but their heart was hardened.
53 And when they had passed over, they came into the land of Gennesaret, and drew to the shore.	53 And when they had ¹ crossed over, they came to the land unto Gennesaret, and moored
54 And when they were come out of the ship, straightway they knew him,	54 to the shore. And when they were come out of the boat, straightway *the people* knew him,
55 And ran through that whole region round about, and began to carry about in beds those that were sick, where they heard he was.	55 and ran round about that whole region, and began to carry about on their beds those that were sick, where they heard he was. And
56 And whithersoever he entered, into villages, or cities, or country, they laid the sick in the streets, and besought him that they might touch if it were but the border of his garment: and as many as touched him were made whole.	56 wheresoever he entered, into villages, or into cities, or into the country, they laid the sick in the marketplaces, and besought him that they might touch if it were but the border of his garment: and as many as touched ² him were made whole.
CHAP. VII.—Then came together unto him the Pharisees, and certain of the scribes, which came from Jerusalem.	7 And there are gathered together unto him the Pharisees, and certain of the scribes,

¹ *Or, crossed over to the land, they came unto Gennesaret*   ² *Or, it*

52. *hardened*] this rather implies dullness of apprehension than spiritual and wilful hardness of heart. See note above, iii, 5. Peter's attempt to walk on the sea is omitted by Mark.

PRACTICAL SUGGESTIONS.—Sometimes when believers most need Christ's presence they are most affrighted if he really comes to them. We of en know not Christ until he is pleased to reveal himself to us. How often are we frightened by creatures of our imagination! Christ's presence gives confidence, though storms and darkness are about us on the sea of life.

53–56. MIRACLES IN GENNESARET. A.D. 29.

53. *the land of Gennesaret*] Gennesaret is only mentioned here and in Matt. xiv, 34. It is the same as the modern *el-Ghuweir*, a fertile, crescent-shaped plain, on the northwestern shore of the Lake of Gennesaret, about three miles in length and one in width. From its sheltered situation and especially from its depression of more than 500 feet below the level of the ocean, its climate is almost of a tropical character. Josephus speaks of it as if it were an earthly paradise, in which every kind of useful plant grew and flourished. Jos. *B. J.* III, 10, 8. See Schaff's *Bible Dict.*

drew to the shore] "Moored," or, as Tyndale and Cranmer translate it, "drew up into the haven." It is a nautical term not elsewhere used in the New Testament.

54. *knew him*] the people, not the disciples, for the latter had recognized him before. The A. V. is misleading, see R. V.

55. *in beds*] a sort of mat, mattress, or common rug. See Schaff's *Bible Dict.*

56. *but the border of his garment*] the numbers that pressed upon him seemed almost too large to be healed singly, therefore many begged that they might be allowed to touch *if it were but the border of his garment.* (For cut of garment see p. 71). Comp. v. 27. Soon after followed the ever memorable discourse in the synagogue of Capernaum respecting the *Bread of Life* (John vi. 22–65). The "streets," more accurately, are "market places," as in R. V.

CH. VII. 1—23. THE PHARISEES AND TRADITIONS OF EATING. A D. 29.

1. *Then came together*] Assigning this event to the time of the passover or near it, *i. e.*, April, A.D. 29, then, with Andrews, Schaff, and some others, it may be regarded as coming at the beginning of the history of the last year of our Lord's ministry. Alexander notes that "this incident naturally brings to view the constant and intrusive surveillance to which our Lord and his disciples were subjected."

AUTHORIZED VERSION.	REVISED VERSION.
2 And when they saw some of his disciples eat bread with defiled, that is to say, with unwashen, hands, they found fault.	2 which had come from Jerusalem, and had seen that some of his disciples ate their bread with [1] defiled, that is, unwashen,
3 For the Pharisees, and all the Jews, except they wash their hands oft, eat not, holding the tradition of the elders.	3 hands. For the Pharisees, and all the Jews, except they wash their hands [2] diligently, eat not, holding the tradition of the elders;
4 And when they come from the market, except they wash, they eat not. And many other things there be, which they have received to hold, as the washing of cups, and pots, brazen vessels, and of tables.	4 and when they come from the marketplace, except they [3] wash themselves, they eat not; and many other things there be, which they have received to hold, [4] washings of cups,

[1] Or, *common* [2] Or, *up to the elbow* Gr. *with the fist*. [3] Gr. *baptize* Some ancient authorities read *sprinkle themselves* [4] Gr. *baptizings*.

2. *with defiled, that is to say, unwashen hands*] thus Mark explains for his Roman readers, and then more fully sets forth certain Jewish usages. The words, "they found fault," are omitted by the best authorities, and the reading in them is given in the R. V., which see.

3. *except they wash their hands oft*] *oft*, literally, *with their fist*, instead of the open hand, lest washing one hand with the other *open* hand would render it unclean, or, (2) up to the wrist to insure ceremonial cleanliness, or, (3) it may be "diligently" or "thoroughly," as in the Revised Version. The second is the most probable meaning. "When they washed their hands, they washed *the fist unto the jointing of the arm.* The hands are polluted, and made clean *unto the jointing of the arm.*"—*Lightfoot*. When water was poured on the hands, they had to be lifted, yet so that the water should neither run up above the wrist, nor back again upon the hand. "Unwashed," not dirty hands, but ceremonially unclean.

WASHING HANDS.

eat not] "the Jews of later times related with intense admiration how the Rabbi Akiba, when imprisoned and furnished with only sufficient water to maintain life, preferred to die of starvation rather than eat without the proper washings." *Buxtorf*; quoted by *Farrar and Geikie*.

the tradition of the elders] the Rabbinical rules about ablutions occupy a large portion of one section of the Talmud. The oral law or traditions, the Jews pretended were handed down through Moses and Joshua. The Talmud is composed of two, or properly of three portions: (1) the Mishna, compiled by Rabbi Jehudan, in the second century. To this two commentaries were added, as (2) the Gemara of Jerusalem, completed in the fourth century, and (3) the Gemara of Babylon, completed about A.D. 500.

4. *except they wash*] "wash," or literally, "baptize themselves," in contrast with washing only the hands, in v. 3. The American revisers preferred to read "bathe," instead of "wash," and Meyer interprets it, "to take a bath." "Market," or "market place," is not to be restricted to the place where food is sold; it includes the place of public meeting, like the Latin *forum*. See R. V.

pots] the original word is regarded as one of Mark's Latinisms, and a corruption of the Latin *sextarius*, a Roman measure both for liquids and dry things, and holding about a pint. In Tyndale's and Cranmer's Versions it is translated "*cruses*." Earthen vessels were broken; those of metal and wood scoured and rinsed with water. See Lev. xv. 12.

tables] "and of tables" is omitted in several MSS.; see R. V. The bet-

AUTHORIZED VERSION.	REVISED VERSION.
5 Then the Pharisees and scribes asked him, Why walk not thy disciples according to the tradition of the elders, but eat bread with unwashen hands?	5 and pots, and brasen vessels [1]. And the Pharisees and the scribes ask him, Why walk not thy disciples according to the tradition of the elders, but eat their bread with [2] defiled
6 He answered and said unto them, Well hath Esaias prophesied of you hypocrites, as it is written, This people honoureth me with *their* lips, but their heart is far from me.	6 hands? And he said unto them, Well did Isaiah prophesy of you hypocrites, as it is written, This people honoureth me with their lips, But their heart is far from me.
7 Howbeit in vain do they worship me, teaching *for* doctrines the commandments of men.	7 But in vain do they worship me, Teaching *as their* doctrines the precepts of men.
8 For laying aside the commandment of God, ye hold the tradition of men, *as* the washing of pots and cups: and many other such like things ye do.	8 Ye leave the commandment of God, and hold 9 fast the tradition of men. And he said unto them, Full well do ye reject the commandment of God, that ye may keep your tradi-
9 And he said unto them, Full well ye reject the commandment of God, that ye may keep your own tradition.	10 tion. For Moses said, Honour thy father and thy mother; and, He that speaketh evil of father or mother, let him [3] die the death:
10 For Moses said, Honour thy father and thy mother; and, Whoso curseth father or mother, let him die the death:	11 but ye say, If a man shall say to his father or his mother, That wherewith thou mightest have been profited by me is Corban, that is
11 But ye say, If a man shall say to his father or mother, *It is* Corban, that is to say, a gift, by whatsoever thou mightest be profited by me; *he* shall be free.	12 to say, Given *to God*, ye no longer suffer him to do aught for his father or his mother;
12 And ye suffer him no more to do ought for his father or his mother;	13 making void the word of God by your tradition, which ye have delivered: and many
13 Making the word of God of none effect through your tradition, which ye have delivered: and many such like things do ye.	14 such like things ye do. And he called to him the multitude again, and said unto them,
14 ¶ And when he had called all the people *unto him*, he said unto them, Hearken unto me every one *of you*, and understand:	

[1] Many ancient authorities add, *and couches*. [2] Or, *common* [3] Or, *surely die*

ter translation is "couches," the wide, low benches which were placed near the tables and on which the guests reclined. These couches had to be carefully washed, for a heathen might have lain on them and defiled them.

6. *Well hath Esaias*] or *full well did Isaiah prophesy of you*. ' *Well* " is said in irony. This expression recurs in v. 9, "Full well ye reject" = "*finely* do ye set at naught and obliterate."

This people honoureth me] The words are found in Isaiah xxix, 13.

8. *tradition of men*] God's commands in contrast with the rules of men. Lange suggests that, underlying the rigorous enforcement of tradition, there was a half conscious repugnance to God's law. The best MSS. omit the rest of verse 8. See Revised Version.

9. *keep your own*] This implies watching, guarding their traditions, while in verses 3, 4, and 8, "hold" implies an obstinate clinging to custom or opinion.

10. *Honour thy father*] The words are quoted partly from Ex. xx. 12, and partly from Ex. xxi, 17. The thought is quoted with precision, but not the form, though the verbal variation is slight.

11. *If a man shall say*] See the Revised Version. Corban is a Hebrew word peculiar to Mark, though often used in Leviticus and Numbers. where it is rendered "offering," and "oblation." Lev. ii. 1, 5; Num. vii, 3, 5. Alexander remarks, "that such things were permitted and applauded, may be proved by certain dicta of the Talmud."

13. *your tradition*] The Jews venerated tradition, as shown by this assertion current among them; "The law is like salt, the Mishna like pepper, the Gemara like balmy spice."—*Buxtorf.*

14. *all the people*] or "called the multitude again." Wyclif has it in his Version, "and he eftsone clepinge to the cumpanye of pepie." Tyndale renders it as in the A. V. See R. V.

ON THE GOSPEL OF MARK.

AUTHORIZED VERSION.

15 There is nothing from without a man, that entering into him can defile him: but the things which come out of him, those are they that defile the man.
16 If any man have ears to hear, let him hear.
17 And when he was entered into the house from the people, his disciples asked him concerning the parable.
18 And he saith unto them, Are ye so without understanding also? Do ye not perceive, that whatsoever thing from without entereth into the man, it cannot defile him;
19 Because it entereth not into his heart, but into the belly, and goeth out into the draught, purging all meats?
20 And he said, That which cometh out of the man, that defileth the man.
21 For from within, out of the heart of men, proceed evil thoughts, adulteries, fornications, murders,
22 Thefts, covetousness, wickedness, deceit, lasciviousness,

REVISED VERSION.

15 Hear me all of you, and understand: there is nothing from without the man, that going into him can defile him: but the things which proceed out of the man are those that defile the man.[1] And when he was entered
17 into the house from the multitude, his disci-
18 ples asked of him the parable. And he saith unto them, Are ye so without understanding also? Perceive ye not, that whatsoever from without goeth into the man, it cannot defile
19 him; because it goeth not into his heart, but into his belly, and goeth out into the draught?
20 This he said, making all meats clean. And he said, That which proceedeth out of the
21 man, that defileth the man. For from within, out of the heart of men, [2]evil thoughts pro-
22 ceed, fornications, thefts, murders, adulteries, covetings, wickednesses, deceit, lascivious-

[1] Many ancient authorities insert ver. 16, *If any man hath ears to hear, let him hear.* [2] Gr. *thoughts that are evil.*

15. *defile*] make common, or profane, is the meaning in Greek: here it signifies, to make ceremonially unclean; or, more accurately, morally unclean; see vs. 2 and 23. Verse 16 is omitted by many MSS. and authorities, as in R. V.

17. *his disciples*] From Matthew we learn that the questioner was Peter (Matt. xv. 15). As in the walking on the water, so here, Mark omits the name of the person, perhaps, in deference to Peter's feelings.

the parable] So they regarded the words uttered in the hearing of the multitude, and which deeply offended the Pharisees (Matt. xv, 12).

19. *into the draught*] Comp. 2 Kings x. 27, "And they...brake down the house of Baal, and made it a *draught house* unto this day." Alford explains it as "sewer."

purging all meats] This phrase is difficult, if not obscure. Alford, Meyer, Weiss, and others, connect it with draught, and make it refer to the purifying or removal of the useless portion of the food from the body. But there is a grammatical difficulty in this view. The revisers, following an old explanation, add: "*This he saith,* making all meats clean." Chrysostom early suggested this interpretation, and it is accepted by Scrivener, Field, Bauer, Canon Cook, Ellicott, and Plumptre.

21. *evil thoughts*] not merely bad thoughts, but evil designs. Thirteen forms of evil are here noticed as proceeding from the heart. The first seven, in the plural number, are *predominant actions,* the plural possibly indicating either the multitude of them, or the variety of forms under which each sin is committed. The latter six, in the singular, are *dispositions.* The change to singular may be for euphony: there seems to be nothing in the nature of the sins calling for it. Comp. the blending of the singular and plural in Paul's enumeration of the works of the flesh. Gal. v, 19-21.

adulteries] violations of the marriage vow; *fornications,* violations of chastity by unmarried persons.

22. *covetousness*] The original word denotes more than the mere *love of money,* it is "the drawing and snatching to himself, on the sinner's part, of the creature in every form and kind, as it lies out of and beyond himself." Hence, we find it joined not only with "thefts" and with "extortion" in 1 Cor. v, 10, but also with sins of the flesh, as in 1 Cor. v, 11 : Eph. v, 3, 5; Col. iii, 5. "Impurity and covetousness may be said to divide between them nearly the whole domain of human selfishness and vice." See Canon Lightfoot on Col. iii, 5.

AUTHORIZED VERSION.	REVISED VERSION.
ciousness, an evil eye, blasphemy, pride, foolishness: 23 All these evil things come from within, and defile the man. 24 ¶ And from thence he arose, and went into the borders of Tyre and Sidon, and entered into	23 ness, an evil eye, railing, pride, foolishness: all these evil things proceed from within, and defile the man. 24 And from thence he arose, and went away into the borders of Tyre [1] and Sidon. And

[1] Some ancient authorities omit *and Sidon*.

wickedness] or *wickednesses*. It denotes the active working of evil, or, as Jeremy Taylor explains it, an "aptness to do shrewd turns, to delight in mischief and tragedies; a love to trouble our neighbour and to do him ill offices; crossness, perverseness, and peevishness of action in our intercourse."—*Trench*.

lasciviousness] The word, in classic Greek, denotes all excess and extravagance, and in later writers, lust. In the N. T. it is generally translated "*lasciviousness*," as here and 2 Cor. xii, 21; Gal. v, 19; Eph. iv, 19; 1 Pet. iv, 3; 2 Pet. ii, 18; sometimes (2) "*wantonness*," as in Rom. xiii, 13. The Vulgate renders it now "impudicitia," now "lascivia." "Wantonness" seems the better rendering.

an evil eye, blasphemy] Of these the first denotes *concealed, i. e.,* the inward disposition; the second, proud, spiteful anger. *The evil eye* is notorious in the East; it may here include the outward envious look. In both cases the outward expression is used to signify the inward feeling or disposition, for it is to the inward corruptions, not their outward manifestations, that Jesus primarily refers.

pride] The word thus translated only occurs here in the N. T., its adjective occurs in Luke i, 51; Rom. i, 30, "*proud*, boasters;" 2 Tim. iii, 2, "*proud*, blasphemers;" James iv, 6; 1 Pet. v, 5, "God resisteth the *proud*."

foolishness] only occurs here in the Gospels, and three times in the Epistles of Paul, 2 Cor. xi, 1, 17, 21. Matthew Henry wisely observes: "*Ill-thinking* is put first, as that which is the spring of all our commissions, and *unthinking* put last, as that which is the spring of all our omissions."

23. *from within*] "The common arguments against public school education," says Ryle, "appear to me to be based on a forgetfulness of our Lord's teaching about the heart. Unquestionably there are many evils in public schools...But there are great dangers in private education, and dangers in their kind quite as formidable as any which beset a boy at public school...Without a change of heart, a boy may be kept at home and yet learn all manner of sin."

PRACTICAL SUGGESTIONS.—We are to serve God in his way, not according to men's traditions or customs. Inward purity is what God desires. The heart is the chief source of impurity. "Every man has within him the root of every sin." "What can we say to the exaggerated attention paid by many to ceremonies, ornaments, gestures, and postures in the worship of God... What is it all but pharisaism over again?"—*Ryle*. "Our care must be to wash our hearts from wickedness."—*M. Henry*.

24–30. THE SYROPHŒNICIAN WOMAN. A. D. 29.

24. *from thence he arose*] *i. e.*, from the region of Capernaum or Gennesaret. See vi, 53-56. The Pharisaic party in Galilee were deeply offended (Matt. xv, 12); Herod Antipas was inquiring concerning him (Luke ix, 9), and his inquiries boded only ill. He therefore now leaves for a while western Galilee, avoids publicity and gains rest, and makes his way northeast, through the mountains of upper Galilee into the border-land of Phœnicia.

the borders of Tyre and Sidon] Not merely to, but "into," the borders

AUTHORIZED VERSION.	REVISED VERSION.
a house, and would have no man know it: but he could not be hid. 25 For a certain woman, whose young daughter had an unclean spirit, heard of him, and came and fell at his feet: 26 The woman was a Greek, a Syrophenician by nation; and she besought him that he would cast forth the devil out of her daughter. 27 But Jesus said unto her, Let the children first be filled: for it is not meet to take the	he entered into a house, and would have no man know it: and he could not be hid. 25 but straightway a woman, whose little daughter had an unclean spirit, having heard of 26 him, came and fell down at his feet. Now the woman was a ¹Greek, a Syrophœnician by race. And she besought him that he would cast forth the ²devil out of her daughter. 27 ter. And he said unto her, Let the children first be filled: for it is not meet to take the

¹ Or, Gentile   ² Gr. demon.

of Tyre and Sidon, and hence beyond the limits of Galilee. So Alford, Bleek, De Wette, Farrar, Cook, Ellicott, and others; though some think he only went unto the border. The former view is the more probable. So in ancient times Elijah traveled out of his own land into Phœnicia (1 Kings xvii, 10-24).

Tyre] A celebrated commercial city of antiquity, in Phœnicia. The Hebrew name "Tzôr" signifies "a rock," and well agrees with the site of *Sûr* a modern town on a rocky peninsula, which was formerly an island, and twenty miles distant from Sidon. Hiram, King of Tyre, sent cedar wood and workmen to David and afterwards to Solomon (2 Sam. v, 11; 1 Kings ix, 11-14; x, 22). Ahab married a daughter of Ithobal, King of Tyre (1 Kings xvi, 31). It was besieged by Nebuchadnezzar; captured by Alexander the Great, after seven months' siege, but became again a populous and thriving city in the time of Christ. Strabo gives an account of it at this period, and speaks of the great wealth which it derived from the production of the celebrated Tyrian purple. The old town is in ruins now, but the modern city has a population of about five thousand. See Schaff's *Bible Dict.*

Sidon] The Greek form of the Phœnician name *Zidon*, an ancient and wealthy city of Phœnicia, on the narrow plain between the Lebanon and the Sea. Its Hebrew name *Tsidôn* signifies "Fishing" or "Fishery." Its modern name is *Saida*. It is mentioned in the Old Testament (Gen. x, 19; Josh. xi, 8; Judg. i, 31), and in ancient times was more influential even than Tyre, though from the time of Solomon it appears to have been subordinate to it. Homer has many allusions to the skill of the Sidonians, and Herodotus speaks of its kings and ships. The city was captured by Alexander the Great, B. C. 333. The ruins of the ancient city are extensive and remarkable; the population of the modern city is about ten thousand.

would have no man know it] desiring seclusion, and perhaps greater freedom to instruct his disciples.

25. *heard of him*] Of his miracles and his arrival; for his fame had reached even to these old Phœnician cities, from whence had come "a great multitude." Comp. Mark iii, 8; Matt. iv, 24.

26. *a Greek*] *i. e.*, in the broad sense of Gentile, as "Frank" is now applied to all Europeans in the East. Matthew describes her as a "*woman of Canaan*" (Matt. xv. 22); Mark calls her *a Greek, a Syrophœnician.* The first term describes her religion, that she was a Gentile; the second, the stock of which she came. Juvenal uses the same term, as Justin Martyr and Tertullian mention. She is called a *Syro-phœnician*, as distinguished from the *Liby phœnicians*, the Phœnicians of Africa, that is, Carthage. Phœnicia belonged at this time to the province of Syria. The Emperor Adrian divided Syria into three parts: Syria proper, Syro-Phœnicia, and Syro-Palestina; and we may well believe that this official distinction rested on a pre existing nomenclature. See Ellicott.

27. *said unto her*] Mark passes more briefly over the interview than

AUTHORIZED VERSION.	REVISED VERSION.
children's bread, and to cast it unto the dogs. 28 And she answered and said unto him, Yes, Lord: yet the dogs under the table eat of the children's crumbs.	children's [1] bread and cast it to the dogs. 28 But she answered and saith unto him, Yea, Lord: even the dogs under the table eat of

[1] Or, *loaf.*

Matthew. The latter Evangelist points out three stages of this woman's trial: (i) Silence; "*He answered her not a word*" (Matt. xv, 23); (ii) Refusal; "*I was not sent but unto the lost sheep of the house of Israel*" (Matt. xv, 24); (iii) Reproach; "*It is not meet to take the children's bread and cast it to the dogs*" (Matt. xv, 26). But in spite of all she persevered and finally conquered.

the dogs] In the original the diminutive is used = "*little dogs.*" "Little whelps," *Wyclif;* "the whelps," *Tyndale, Cranmer.* The Jews, *the children of the kingdom* (Matt. viii, 12), were wont to designate the heathen as "*dogs,*" the noble characteristics of which animal are seldom brought out in Scripture (comp. Deut. xxiii, 18; Job xxx, 1; 2 Kings viii, 13; Phil. iii, 2; Rev. xxii, 15. The Syrian dog is a howling scavenger, and not the companion of man, as the dog is among us. Here, however, the term is somewhat softened. Alexander thinks the heathen are compared to the small dogs in the house, not to the great wild dogs infesting Eastern towns; but the dog was an unclean animal to the Jews and not kept as with us. If he was in heathen territory, as inferred above, the expression would still more naturally refer to the Jewish designation of heathen, and, therefore, not convey the "revolting harshness" which Alexander supposes. In the East now the Mohammedans apply this name to Christians.

SYRIAN DOG.

28. *yet the dogs*] *Yea, Lord, for even the little dogs under the table eat of the children's crumbs.* So it is rightly translated in Wyclif's and Cranmer's Versions, following the Vulgate. "*Truth it is Maister, for indeed the whelpes eat under the table, of the childerns crommes.*"—Geneva version, 1557. She accepts the declaration of Christ, and in that very declaration, she affirms, is involved the granting of her petition. "Saidst Thou dogs? It is well; I accept the title and the place; for the dogs have a portion of the meat—not the first, not the children's portion, but a portion still—the crumbs which fall from the table." Her words speak to us even now, across the centuries. The Episcopal Church adopts her words in a prayer to be used at the celebration of the Lord's Supper.—*Camb. Bible.*

crumbs] "From the very word dog, which seemed to make most against her, with the ready wit of faith, she drew an argument in her own favor."— *Trench.* "Was not that a master-stroke! She snares Christ in his own words."—*Luther.* "The twelve had learned at last that even heathen 'dogs' were not to be sent, unheard, away."—*Geikie.*

AUTHORIZED VERSION.	REVISED VERSION.
29 And he said unto her, For this saying go thy way; the devil is gone out of thy daughter. 30 And when she was come to her house, she found the devil gone out, and her daughter laid upon the bed. 31 ¶ And again, departing from the coasts of Tyre and Sidon, he came unto the sea of Galilee, through the midst of the coasts of Decapolis. 32 And they bring unto him one that was deaf, and had an impediment in his speech; and they beseech him to put his hand upon him. 33 And he took him aside from the multitude,	29 the children's crumbs. And he said unto her, for this saying go thy way; the ¹ devil is gone out of thy daughter. And she went away unto her house, and found the child laid upon the bed, and the ¹ devil gone out. 31 And again he went out from the borders of Tyre, and came through Sidon unto the sea of Galilee, through the midst of the borders of Decapolis. And they bring unto him one that was deaf, and had an impediment in his speech; and they beseech him to lay 33 his hand upon him. And he took him aside

¹ Gr. *demon*.

29. *go thy way*] There were two notable examples of faith found in heathen persons and commended by Jesus: this woman and the centurion.

30. *devil gone out*] This is an instance of a cure effected *at a distance*: other instances are, (1) the nobleman's son at Capernaum (John iv. 46); (2) the centurion's servant (Luke vii. 6). "Devil" here, as elsewhere, when relating to persons possessed, means "demons."

PRACTICAL SUGGESTIONS.—"Mothers, widows, sisters, with sick, sinful, wayward relatives, go and tell Jesus."—*John Hall.* "The first act of salvation in the Gentile world."—*Bauer.* "It is a great consolation to a Christian mother when God converts, in answer to prayer, a daughter possessed by a worldly spirit. But how little prayer is urged for that blessing!"—*Quesnel.*

31—37. HEALING THE DEAF AND DUMB, A. D. 29.

31. *the coasts*] a misleading archaism. No allusion is made in the original word to the seaboard. Compare verse 24 "From the borders of Tyre, and came through Sidon unto the Sea of Galilee," is the reading of nearly all important MSS., though Scrivener adheres to the common text. See R. V.

Sidon] or "through Sidon," which is the preferable reading, supported by several MSS., and found in several ancient versions. See R. V. If he made a visit to this city of Baal and Astarte, no further account of it is given. It would be a long, circuitous journey, and must have been full of incidents. The silence of the Evangelists throws some doubt on the genuineness of the revised reading, unless we interpret it (as Schaff does) to mean a district of Sidon and not the city. A *district* of Sidon is not elsewhere noticed, hence Canon Cook holds that Jesus went through the city of Sidon.

unto the sea of Galilee] The journey appears to have been northward through Sidon and towards Lebanon, then through the deep gorge of the Leontes to the Jordan, thence along its eastern bank into Decapolis.

32. *one that was deaf*] The healing of this man, on the east side of the Jordan, is related only by Mark.

and had an impediment] The Greek implies that the man could scarcely articulate. As Canon Cook aptly says, "such a condition is an ordinary result of long-continued deafness," and leads us to infer that the man having lost his hearing from some cause, had gradually been losing his power of speech.

they beseech him] This is one of the few instances where the friends of the sufferer brought the sick man to Christ. So the paralytic was borne of four (Mark ii. 3–5); the blind man of Bethsaida was also led to Jesus (Mark viii. 22–26).

33. *aside from the multitude*] Comp. Mark viii. 23. Why? (1) Some think it was to avoid all show and ostentation; (2) others, to prevent a publicity which might bring together the Gentiles in crowds; (3) others, that the few might be convinced that he was not bound to any one mode of healing. Geikie suggests, that these simpler forms were intended to awaken

AUTHORIZED VERSION.	REVISED VERSION.
and put his fingers into his ears, and he spit, and touched his tongue;	from the multitude privately, and put his fingers into his ears, and he spat, and touched
34 And looking up to heaven, he sighed, and saith unto him, Ephphatha, that is, Be opened.	34 his tongue; and looking up to heaven, he sighed, and saith unto him, Ephphatha, that
35 And straightway his ears were opened, and the string of his tongue was loosed, and he spake plain.	35 is, Be opened. And his ears were opened, and the bond of his tongue was loosed, and
36 And he charged them that they should tell no man: but the more he charged them, so much the more a great deal they published it;	36 he spake plain. And he charged them that they should tell no man: but the more he charged them, so much the more a great deal
37 And were beyond measure astonished, saying, He hath done all things well: he maketh both the deaf to hear, and the dumb to speak.	37 they published it. And they were beyond measure astonished, saying, He hath done all things well: he maketh even the deaf to hear, and the dumb to speak.
CHAP. VIII.—In those days the multitude being very great, and having nothing to eat, Jesus called his disciples unto him, and saith unto them,	8 In those days, when there was again a great multitude, and they had nothing to eat, he called unto him his disciples, and saith

faith in one who could hear no words. for without a fi'ting spirit the miracle would not have been wrought. So also Trench supposes these acts were suited to stir up a lively expectation of a blessing, and these seem more probable than the first three reasons.

put his fingers into his ears] His cure was (1) gradual, and (2) effected by visible signs.

34. *looking up to heaven*] This upturned look, expressive of an act of prayer. occurs also (1) in the blessing of the five loaves and two fishes (Matt. xiv. 19; Mark vi. 41); (2) at the raising of Lazarus (John xi, 41); and (3) before the great high-priestly prayer for the apostles (John xvii, 1).

he sighed] or "groaned," as in the Rhemish Version. It was a natural expression of distress (Rom. viii, 23), and also implied intense desire and supplication. Comp. John xi, 33. Luther says: "This sigh was not drawn from Christ on account of the single tongue and ear of this poor man, but it is a common sigh over all tongues and ears, yea over all hearts, bodies and souls."

Ephphatha] The actual Aramaic word used by our Lord, like the "Talitha cum" or "cumi" of Mark v, 41.

36. *he charged them*] *i. e*, the friends of the afflicted man, who had accompanied or followed him. "Everything in God's way and in his word is glorious and honorable, and like himself. He needs none of our testimonies, but it is the least we can do to signify our wishes to have his praises celebrated."—*Thos. Halyburton.*

37. *astonished*] The original word for "beyond measure" occurs nowhere else in the New Testament. Alexander observes: "The effect of this great miracle on those who witnessed it was so extraordinary that the writer has to coin a Greek word to express the boundlessness of this amazement."

PRACTICAL SUGGESTIONS.—"Most people can both hear and speak; but how great and how common is spiritual deafness and dumbness!"—*Zeisius.* "Scarcely is the power of speech given him, but he is ordered to be silent, that he might learn, or we through him, that the right use of the unbound tongue shall consist in a free will binding of it to obedience."—*Stier.* Many Christians have a spiritual impediment; they seldom speak, but only stammer in praise of God. He hath done all things well; how great a mercy we did not have things our way!

CH. VIII. 1—9. FEEDING THE FOUR THOUSAND, A. D. 29.

1. *the multitude being very great*] Jesus had returned from the region of Tyre to the east side of the Sea of Galilee. The effect of his miraculous cures on the inhabitants of the half pagan district of Decapolis was very

AUTHORIZED VERSION.	REVISED VERSION.
2 I have compassion on the multitude, because they have now been with me three days, and have nothing to eat:	2 unto them, I have compassion on the multitude, because they continue with me now three days, and have nothing to eat: and if
3 And if I send them away fasting to their own houses, they will faint by the way: for divers of them came from far.	3 I send them away fasting to their home, they will faint in the way; and some of them are come from far. And his disciples answered
4 And his disciples answered him, From whence can a man satisfy these men with bread here in the wilderness?	4 him, Whence shall one be able to fill these men with ¹bread here in a desert place?
5 And he asked them, How many loaves have ye? And they said, Seven.	5 And he asked them, How many loaves have
6 And he commanded the people to sit down on the ground: and he took the seven loaves, and gave thanks, and brake, and gave to his disciples to set before them; and they did set them before the people.	6 ye? And they said, Seven. And he commandeth the multitude to sit down on the ground: and he took the seven loaves, and having given thanks, he brake, and gave to his disciples, to set before them; and they set
7 And they had a few small fishes: and he blessed, and commanded to set them also before them.	7 them before the multitude. And they had a few small fishes; and having blessed them, he commanded to set these also before them.
8 So they did eat, and were filled: and they took up of the broken meat that was left seven baskets.	8 And they did eat, and were filled: and they took up, of broken pieces that remained over,

¹ Gr. *loaves*.

great. Upwards of four thousand persons, without counting women and children (Matt. xv, 38), gathered round him, and continued with him three days (Mark viii, 2). "In the East it is easy for the population, with their simple wants, and the mildness of the sky, which in the warm months invites sleeping in the open air by night, to camp out as they think fit."

2. *nothing to eat*] Either they had fasted for three days, or their supplies had given out; the latter is the more probable. The three days may be computed, however, according to Jewish methods, and may cover only one whole day and portions of two others.

4. *his disciples answered him*] The disciples did not see whence nor how bread for such a crowd could be had. They had forgotten the other miracle already. The sacred writers do not conceal their own shortcomings, or the fact that they had so soon forgotten so great a miracle.

whence can a man satisfy] Trench suggests that "it is evermore thus in times of difficulty and distress. All former deliverances are in danger of being forgotten; the mighty interpositions of God's hand in former passages of men's lives fall out of their memories. Each new difficulty appears insurmountable, as one from which there is no extrication; at each recurring necessity it seems as though the wonders of God's grace are exhausted and had come to an end." Comp. Ex. xvii, 1-7 and Ex. xvi, 13 with Num. xi, 21, 23. Farrar's excuse for the apostles' conduct is ingenious, but weak. He says: "Many and many a time had the apostles been with multitudes before, and yet on one occasion only had he fed them. Further, to suggest to him a repetition of the feeding of the five thousand would be a presumption which their ever-deepening reverence forbade, and forbade more than ever as they recalled how persistently he had refused to work a sign, such as this was, at the bidding of others."

6. *to sit down*] The Greek word signifies "reclining," after the usual Eastern custom, rather than sitting. *Where*, is not distinctly specified. It was on the eastern side of the lake, and in a *desert spot* (Matt. xv, 33). Trench places it on the same spot as the feeding of the five thousand; Ellicott, near Wâdy Semak; and others, near the south end of the lake.

7. *and he blessed*] i. e., "blessed God aloud." A different word from that in *v.* 6. This implies praise, that in *v.* 6 thanksgiving. The language suggests that the loaves and fishes were separately blessed and distributed.

8. *seven baskets*] The baskets were filled with fragments, indicating the

AUTHORIZED VERSION.	REVISED VERSION.
9 And they that had eaten were about four thousand: and he sent them away. 10 ¶ And straightway he entered into a ship with his disciples, and came into the parts of Dalmanutha.	9 seven baskets. And they were about four thousand: and he sent them away. And 10 straightway he entered into the boat with his disciples, and came into the parts of Dalmanutha.

abundance of God's provision, as also in nature. The basket was not the small wicker κόφινος of the former miracle, but large baskets of rope, such

as that in which Paul was lowered from the wall of Damascus (Acts ix, 25). The wicker baskets were used in travelling; the larger rope basket was used as a grain or provision basket, and was large enough to hold a man. The differences between this and the miracle of the five thousand are: (1) The people had been with the Lord upwards of three days; (2) seven loaves are now distributed and a few fishes, then five loaves and two fishes; (3) four thousand are fed now, then five thousand; (4) now seven large rope baskets are filled with fragments, then twelve small wicker baskets; (5) the inhabitants of the north would have made him a king (John vi, 15); the men of Decapolis permit him to leave them without any demonstration.

PRACTICAL LESSONS.—"They that have a full feast for their souls may be content with slender provisions for their bodies. It was an old saying among the Puritans. that 'Brown bread and the gospel are good fare.'"—*M. Henry*. "The bounty of Christ is inexhaustible. Those need not fear want who have Christ to live upon."

10–21. THE LEAVEN OF THE PHARISEES AND OF HEROD, A. D. 29.

10. *the parts of Dalmanutha*] or, as Matthew says, *into the borders of Magdala or Magadan* (xv, 39). Jesus recrossed the lake from the region of Decapolis. "Just before reaching Mejdel, we crossed a little open valley. the Ain-el-Barideh, with a few rich cornfields and gardens straggling among the ruins of a village. and some large and more ancient foundations by several copious fountains, and probably identical with the Dalmanutha of the New Testament."—*Tristram.* "If the reading *Magadan* in Matt. xv. 39 stands, we may conjecture either (a) that it and Dalmanutha were different names for the same place, or (b) that they denoted contiguous spots, either of which might give its name to the same region."—*Camb. Bible.* And Schaff remarks: "The two [Magadan or Magdala and Dalmanutha] were probably near each other and north of Tiberias...The theory that they were on the southeastern shore of the lake is altogether unsupported."

AUTHORIZED VERSION.	REVISED VERSION.
11 And the Pharisees came forth, and began to question him, seeking of him a sign from heaven, tempting him. 12 And he sighed deeply in his spirit, and saith, Why doth this generation seek after a sign? verily I say unto you, There shall no sign be given unto this generation. 13 And he left them, and entering into the ship again departed to the other side. 14 Now *the disciples* had forgotten to take bread, neither had they in the ship with them more than one loaf.	11 And the Pharisees came forth, and began to question with him, seeking of him a sign 12 from heaven, tempting him. And he sighed deeply in his spirit, and saith, Why doth this generation seek a sign? verily I say unto you, There shall no sign be given unto this 13 generation. And he left them, and again entering into *the boat*, departed to the other side. 14 And they forgot to take bread; and they had not in the boat with them more than one

11. *And the Pharisees*] Mark does not mention the coming of the Sadducees (Matt. xvi, 1), but does note the "sighing of Jesus," which Matthew omits. Jesus seems to have avoided Bethsaida or Capernaum, which had become the headquarters of the Pharisees; but they had apparently watched for his arrival, and now "*came forth*" to meet him, accompanied for the first time by the Sadducees (Matt. xvi, 1).

came forth, and began] This implies spying hostility. They had made their arrangements for a decisive contest, and began with a demand for a sign.

a sign from heaven] The same request had already been thrice made: (1) After the first cleansing of the Temple (John ii, 18); (2) after the feeding of the five thousand (John vi, 30); and (3) again shortly after the walking through the cornfields (Matt. xii, 38). By such a "sign" was meant some visible sign in the sky, the credentials of a prophet. The Jews believed that demons and false gods could give signs on earth, but only the true God could give a sign from heaven; *e. g.*, the manna of Moses from heaven; the sun and moon standing still for Joshua; hail and rain of Samuel; fire and rain of Elijah; sun on the dial of Hezekiah. The American revisers propose to read "trying him," or "making trial of him," in place of "tempting him." So also in x, 2 and xii. 15.

12. *he sighed deeply in his spirit*] "For the demand for a sign from heaven was a demand that he should, as the Messiah, accredit himself by a great over mastering miracle; thus it was fundamentally similar to the temptation in the wilderness, which he had repelled and overcome."—*Lange.*

There shall no sign be given] literally, *If a sign shall be given to this generation*, a Hebrew idiom, the form of a Hebrew oath. Comp. Heb. iii, 11, where see the margin; iv, 3, 5; Gen. xiv, 23; Num. xiv, 30. The sign of "Jonah the prophet" adds Matthew xvi, 4.

13. *he left them*] "Just severity."—*Bengel.* "It was his final rejection on the very spot where he had labored most, and he was leaving it, to return, indeed, for a passing visit, but never to appear again publicly, or to teach, or work miracles." "If the plough of grace cannot force its way through your ice-bound heart to-day, what likelihood is there that it will enter to morrow?"—*McCheyne.*

the other side] *i. e.*, back again to the eastern side of the Lake, or northern side; not the western side, as Canon Cook interprets it, for they had just left Dalmanutha, which was on the western shore. Those who hold to the existence of two Bethsaidas naturally fall into some confusion at this point. See v. 22.

14. *had forgotten*] or "forgot." In the hurry of their unexpected reembarkation they had altogether omitted to make provision for their own personal wants. See R. V.

AUTHORIZED VERSION.	REVISED VERSION.
15 And he charged them, saying, Take heed, beware of the leaven of the Pharisees, and *of* the leaven of Herod. 16 And they reasoned among themselves, saying, *It is* because we have no bread. 17 And when Jesus knew *it*, he saith unto them, Why reason ye, because ye have no bread? perceive ye not yet, neither understand? have ye your heart yet hardened? 18 Having eyes, see ye not? and having ears, hear ye not? and do ye not remember? 19 When I brake the five loaves among five thousand, how many baskets full of fragments took ye up? They say unto him, Twelve. 20 And when the seven among four thousand, how many baskets full of fragments took ye up? And they said, Seven. 21 And he said unto them, How is it that ye do not understand? 22 And he cometh to Bethsaida; and they bring a blind man unto him, and besought him to touch him.	15 loaf. And he charged them, saying, Take heed, beware of the leaven of the Pharisees, 16 and the leaven of Herod. And they reasoned one with another, ¹saying, ²We have no 17 bread. And Jesus perceiving it saith unto them, Why reason ye, because ye have no bread? do ye not yet perceive, neither understand? have ye your heart yet hardened? 18 Having eyes, see ye not? and having ears, hear ye not? and do ye not remember? 19 When I brake the five loaves among the five thousand, how many ³baskets full of broken pieces took ye up? They say unto him, 20 Twelve. And when the seven among the four thousand, how many ³basketfuls of broken pieces took ye up? And they say 21 unto him, Seven. And he said unto them, Do ye not yet understand? 22 And they come unto Bethsaida. And they bring to him a blind man, and beseech him

¹ Some ancient authorities read, *because they had no bread*. ² Or, It is *because we have no bread*.
³ *Basket*, in verses 19 and 20, represents different Greek words.

15. *charged them*] "The verb is in the imperfect tense, and implies that the command was more than once repeated."—*Ellicott*.

the leaven of the Pharisees] "Leaven in Scripture, with the single exception of the Parable (Matt. xiii. 33; Luke xiii. 20, 21), is always a symbol of evil, (comp. 1 Cor. v. 6, 7, 8; Gal. v. 9), especially insidious evil, as it is for the most part also in the Rabbinical writers. See Lightfoot on Matt. xvi. 6. The strict command to the children of Israel that they should carefully put away every particle of leaven out of their houses during the Passover week, rests on this view of it as evil."—*Maclear*. For varied rendering of the last clause of the verse, see R. V.

the leaven of Herod] "and." as it is in Matthew's Gospel, "*of the Sadducees*." The leaven of the Pharisees was *hypocrisy* (Luke xii. 1); of the Sadducees, *unbelief*; of Herod, *worldliness*. "The licentiousness admitted by the doctrine of the Sadducees was in other respects more suited to his palace and court, which bent religion into a mere species of political expediency."—*Bengel*.

17. *yet hardened*] not callous feeling, but dullness, as on the former occasion of the walking on the sea (Mark vi. 52).

19. *how many baskets*] The precise number and the precise kind of baskets taken up on each occasion are noted. See above, on vi. 43. Wyclif brings out this in his translation: "Whanne I brak fyue loones among fyve thousand, and hou many *coffyns* ful of brokene mete ye token up?...whanne also seuene looues among foure thousand, how many *leepis* of brokene mete ye token up?"

21. *ye do not understand*] or, "Do ye not yet understand?" They seem to have thought that he was warning them against buying leaven of the Pharisees and Sadducees.

PRACTICAL LESSONS.—What an absurdity for those who greedily swallow the traditions of elders to desire a sign. "Distrust of God makes Christ's disciples quarrel among themselves."—*M. Henry*. When we do not understand and remember God's mercies we are overwhelmed with care and trouble.

22-26. THE BLIND MAN OF BETHSAIDA, A. D. 29.

22. *Bethsaida*] which lay upon the north eastern coast of the sea of Ti-

AUTHORIZED VERSION.	REVISED VERSION.
23 And he took the blind man by the hand, and led him out of the town: and when he had spit on his eyes, and put his hands upon him, he asked him if he saw aught.	23 to touch him. And he took hold of the blind man by the hand, and brought him out of the village; and when he had spit on his eyes, and laid his hand upon him, he asked
24 And he looked up, and said, I see men as trees, walking.	24 him, Seest thou aught? And he looked up, and said, I see men; for I behold them as
25 After that he put his hands again upon his eyes, and made him look up: and he was restored, and saw every man clearly.	25 trees, walking. Then again he laid his hands upon his eyes; and he looked stedfastly, and
26 And he sent him away to his house, saying, Neither go into the town, nor tell it to any in the town.	26 was restored, and saw all things clearly. And he sent him away to his home, saying, Do not even enter into the village.

berias, near the Jordan. This would be on his way to Cæsarea Philippi, whither he soon went; see *v.* 27. Jesus led the man "out of town" to avoid publicity and hatred of enemies who were watching him, and to awaken faith in the man.

23. *he took the blind man*] Jesus led him out himself; "great humility," exclaims Bengel: "thus Jesus raised his hope and gained his confidence." See the case noted in Mark vii. 33. As then, so now, the cure was gradual and with external signs: (1) He leads the man out of the town; (2) anoints his eyes with the moisture of his mouth; (3) lays his hands upon him twice (Mark viii. 23, 25); (4) inquires of the progress of his restoration; (5) touched his eyes again and made him look up; "aught"= anything.

24. *as trees walking*] Comp. R. V. "I see men" was a joyful exclamation. Having once been able to see, he remembered the appearance of natural objects, and saw moving forms about him; "trees he should have accounted them from their height, but men from their motion."

BLIND IN SYRIA.

25. *look up*] or "looked stedfastly," as in R. V.; though several authorities read "and at once he saw plainly."

saw every man clearly] or *began to see all things clearly*. "So that he syz clerely alle thingis."—*Wyclif*. The word translated "clearly," literally = "far shining," "far-beaming." Comp. the R. V. The man meant that he could now see clearly *far and near*. This is one of the few instances of a strictly *progressive* cure recorded in the Gospels.

26. *to his house*] Bethsaida, therefore, was not the place of his residence; he was to go directly from the place to his own home. See *v.* 22.

AUTHORIZED VERSION.	REVISED VERSION.
27 And Jesus went out, and his disciples, in to the towns of Cæsarea Philippi: and by the way he asked his disciples, saying unto them, Whom do men say that I am? 28 And they answered, John the Baptist: but some say, Elias; and others, One of the prophets.	7 And Jesus went forth, and his disciples, into the villages of Cæsarea Philippi: and in the way he asked his disciples, saying unto 28 them, Who do men say that I am? And they told him, saying, John the Baptist: and others, Elijah; but others, One of the prophets.

PRACTICAL SUGGESTIONS.—Providence gains his ends by varied methods. The spiritually blind, when restored, often see things in a confused and imperfect manner. The blind man was not to tell it in Bethsaida, for its people had slighted his teaching. So "slighting Christ's favors is forfeiting them." The miracles of Christ were thus classified by Archbishop Thomson: I. *Miracles of Love*: (1) Raising the dead, three instances; (2) Curing mental diseases, six; (3) curing bodily infirmities, eighteen cases. II. *Miracles of Power*: (1) creating, two instances; (2) destroying (?), one; (3) setting aside ordinary laws of being, seven; (4) Over-awing the opposing will of men, three instances. "The time is coming when we shall see all 'clearly.'...Let us be content to wait and watch and work and pray."

27—IX. 1. CÆSAREA PHILIPPI. THE CONFESSION OF PETER, A. D. 29.

27. *And Jesus went out*] The course was in a northerly direction, some twenty five or thirty miles along the eastern banks of the Jordan and beyond the waters of Merom.

into the towns] or "villages," or the "*parts*" or "*regions*" (Matt xvi, 13) of the remote city of Cæsarea Philippi, near which it is possible he may have passed in his circuit from Sidon a very few weeks before (Mark vii, 24).—*Ellicott's Lectures.*

Cæsarea Philippi] It lay on the northeast of the reedy and marshy plain of *El Huleh*, and at the base of Mt. Hermon. (1) It was probably called Baal-gad (Josh. xi, 17; xii, 7; xiii, 5), or Baal-hermon (Judg. iii, 3; 1 Chron. v, 23), having a Phœnician or Canaanite sanctuary of Baal under the aspect of "Gad," or the god of good fortune. (2) It was also known as Panium or *Paneas*, from a cavern near the town, "abrupt, prodigiously deep, and full of still water," and associated with the worship of the sylvan *Pan.* Hence its modern appellation, *Baneas.* (3) Herod the Great built there a splendid temple, of the whitest marble, which he dedicated to Augustus Cæsar. (4) Afterwards the town became part of the territory of Herod Philip, tetrarch of Trachonitis, who enlarged it and called it *Cæsarea Philippi,* partly after his own name, and partly after that of the Emperor Tiberius (Jos. *Ant.* xv, 10, 3; *Bel. Jud.* i, 21, 3). It was also so called to distinguish it from Cæsarea *Palestinæ*, or Cæsarea "*on the sea.*" Dean Stanley calls it a Syrian Tivoli, and "certainly there is much in the rocks, caverns, cascades, and the natural beauty of the scenery, to recall the Roman Tiber. Behind the village, in front of a great natural cavern, a river bursts forth from the earth, the 'upper source' of the Jordan. Inscriptions and niches in the face of the cliffs tell of the old idol worship of Baal and of Pan."—*Tristram.* See Schaff's *Dict. of Bible.*

he asked his disciples] Hitherto he is not recorded to have asked the twelve any question respecting himself, and he would seem to have forborne to press his apostles for an avowal of faith in his divinity. He now wished to ascertain from them as the special witnesses of his life and daily words, the results of those labors.

28. *they answered*] In this answer we have the explanation which common rumor in his own days offered of his marvelous works. (1) Some, like the guilty Herod, said he was John the Baptist risen from the dead; (2) others,

CÆSAREA PHILIPPI. (From Photograph.)

MOUNT HERMON. (From Photograph.)

AUTHORIZED VERSION.	REVISED VERSION.
29 And he saith unto them, But whom say ye that I am? And Peter answereth and saith unto him, Thou art the Christ.	29 cts. And he asked them, But who say ye that I am? Peter answereth and saith unto him, Thou art the Christ. And he charged
30 And he charged them that they should tell no man of him.	them that they should tell no man of him.
31 And he began to teach them, that the Son of man must suffer many things, and be rejected of the elders, and of the chief priests, and scribes, and be killed, and after three days rise again.	31 And he began to teach them, that the Son of man must suffer many things, and be rejected by the elders, and the chief priests, and the scribes, and be killed, and after three days
32 And he spake tha' saying openly. And Peter took him, and began to rebuke him.	32 rise again. And he spake the saying openly. And Peter took him, and began to rebuke
33 But when he had turned about and looked on his disciples, he rebuked Peter, saying, Get	33 him. But he turning about, and seeing his disciples, rebuked Peter, and saith, Get thee

that he was Elijah, now returned, as Malachi predicted (iv, 5); (3) others, that he was Jeremiah (Matt. xvi, 14), who was expected to inaugurate the reign of the Messiah; (4) others, again, that he was one of the "old prophets" (Luke ix, 19). But they did not add that any regarded him as the Messiah.—*Camb. Bible.* Calvin shrewdly remarks: "As Satan could not rob the Jews of the conviction that Christ would come, he changed him into various shapes, and, as it were, cut him in pieces. His next scheme was to bring forward many pretended Christs...By similar contrivances he continued ever afterwards, either to tear Christ in pieces, or to exhibit him under a false character."

29. *Thou art the Christ*] "Thus, in the outskirts of the heathen town dedicated to the deified Augustus, Jesus was proclaimed...the king of the universal Israel...he assumed publicly the empire of all the world, as the Messiah."—*Geikie.* Peter, as the ready spokesman of the rest of the Apostles, made the memorable reply, *Thou art the Christ, the Messiah* (Matt. xvi, 16; Luke ix, 20), *the Son of the living God* (Matt. xvi, 16), but in this Gospel the promise of peculiar dignity in the Church the Lord was about to establish is not named.

30. *tell no man*] compare the similar charge in several cases of healing (i. 44; v, 43).

31. *he began to teach them*] The question and the answer were alike preparatory to strange and mournful tidings, which he now began to reveal distinctly to the apostles respecting himself; compare Dan. vi, 26; Matt. xvi, 21; Luke xxiv, 26.

32. *openly*] not publicly, but "*plainly*," and for the first time, "*without disguise.*" Comp. John xi,14. There had been intimations of his death, but then they had been dark and enigmatical. (1) The Baptist had twice pointed him out as *the Lamb of God destined to take away the sins of the world* (John i, 29). (2) At the first Passover he had spoken to the Jews *of a temple to be destroyed and rebuilt in three days* (John ii, 19), and to Nicodemus of a *lifting up of the Son of man, even as Moses had lifted up the serpent in the wilderness* (John iii, 12-16). (3) He had intimated that a day would come when *the bridegroom should be taken from them* (Matt. ix, 15), and (4) in the synagogue at Capernaum he had declared that he was about to give his *flesh for the life of the world* (John vi, 47-51).

And Peter] who a moment before had witnessed so noble and outspoken a confession; ardent, impulsive and capricious, was not prepared for this.

took him] *took him aside* (so Tyndale and Cranmer render it), by the hand, or by the robe, as if he would forcibly restrain Jesus from talking or thinking of suffering at the hands of the chief priests and scribes. The language here is against the view that Peter's act was one of friendly entreaty merely.

33. *turned about and looked on his disciples*] Observe the graphic touches of Mark. The evangelist does not suppress the record of mistaken zeal, nor of the terrible rebuke it called forth.

AUTHORIZED VERSION.	REVISED VERSION.
thee behind me, Satan: for thou savourest not the things that be of God, but the things that be of men.	behind me, Satan: for thou mindest not the 34 things of God, but the things of men. And he called unto him the multitude with his
34 ¶ And when he had called the people unto him with his disciples also, he said unto them, Whosoever will come after me, let him deny himself, and take up his cross, and follow me.	disciples, and said unto them, If any man would come after me, let him deny himself, 35 and take up his cross, and follow me. For whosoever would save his ¹ life shall lose it;
35 For whosoever will save his life shall lose it: but whosoever shall lose his life for my sake and the gospel's, the same shall save it.	and whosoever shall lose his ¹ life for my 36 sake and the gospel's shall save it. For what doth it profit a man, to gain the whole world,
36 For what shall it profit a man, if he shall gain the whole world, and lose his own soul?	37 and forfeit his ¹ life? For what should a 38 man give in exchange for his ¹ life? For
37 Or what shall a man give in exchange for his soul?	whosoever shall be ashamed of me and of my words in this adulterous and sinful genera-
38 Whosoever therefore shall be ashamed of me and of my words in this adulterous and sinful generation; of him also shall the Son of man be ashamed, when he cometh in the glory of his Father with the holy angels.	tion, the Son of man also shall be ashamed of him, when he cometh in the glory of his 9 Father with the holy angels. And he said unto them, Verily I say unto you, There be
CHAP. IX.—And he said unto them, Verily I say unto you, That there be some of.	

¹ Or, soul

Get thee behind me] The very words which he had used to the tempter in the wilderness (Matt. iv, 10), for in truth the apostle was adopting the very argument which the great enemy had adopted there. "As if he had said, 'What! adversary; is Satan come again to tempt me, as he did of old? Avaunt thou, get thee hence!' Then, addressing the astonished...Peter, in his own person, he describes the cause of the mistake he had just made "—*Alexander*.

thou savourest not] or "thou mindest not," as in R. V. "Thou dost not perceive God's purpose in the death of Messiah." Latimer, quoting 1 Cor. xiii, 11, writes "When I was a child I *savoured* as a child." "Thy words shew," our Lord would say to the apostle, "that in these things thou enterest not into the thoughts and plans of God, but considerest all things only from the ideas of men."

34. *he had called*] a crowd followed close upon him and his disciples. He had just been speaking to the disciples privately; now he calls and addresses to the multitude, as well as to his apostles, some of his deepest teaching, making them sharers in this part of his instruction. "Will" is used in the sense of "desires," or "is willing."

take up his cross] not so much an intimation of his own suffering upon *the cross*, as of the common custom of compelling a malefactor to bear his own cross to the place of his execution.

35. *shall lose it*] This solemn saying our Lord is found to have uttered on no less than *four* several occasions: (1) here, which corresponds with Matt. xvi, 25; Luke ix, 24; (2) Matt. x, 39; (3) Luke xvii, 33; (4) John xii, 25.

36. *soul*] or "life," for it is the same word ($\psi\nu\chi\eta\nu$) as in verse 35. See R. V. But it cannot mean simply the "life" of the body, for all must lose that at death; it must refer, therefore, to the eternal life of man. The word is, therefore, used in two senses. In v. 35 it must refer to the earthly life; in this verse, to the true, higher life, as also in v. 37.

37. *in exchange*] literally, "as a ransom price." The price which the earthly-minded man gives for the world is his soul. But, after having laid that down as the price, what has he for a "ransom-price," to purchase it again? The Greek word occurs in the Septuagint (Ruth iv, 7; Jer. xv, 13). Some read, "for what can be an exchange for his soul!"

38. *adulterous*] The generation is called "adulterous" because its heart was estranged from God. Compare Jer. xxxi, 32; Isa. liv, 5.

IX, 1. *And he said unto them*] This verse is closely connected with the

AUTHORIZED VERSION.	REVISED VERSION.
them that stand here, which shall not taste of death, till they have seen the kingdom of God come with power. 2 And after six days Jesus taketh *with him* Peter, and James, and John, and leadeth them up into a high mountain apart by themselves: and he was transfigured before them.	some here of them that stand *by*, which shall in no wise taste of death, till they see the kingdom of God come with power. 2 And after six days Jesus taketh with him Peter, and James, and John, and bringeth them up into a high mountain apart by themselves: and he was transfigured before

close of the eighth chapter. Ellicott says: "The present division may have been made with a view of connecting it with the transfiguration...but if so, it was based on what is at least a doubtful interpretation."

Verily I say unto you] "This well-known formula occurs thirteen times in Mark. thirty one times in Matthew, seven times in Luke, twenty-five times in John. It always introduces solemn and important announcements." —*Maclear*.

the kingdom of God] The meaning of this verse has been much disputed. Some refer it to the transfiguration only, some to the resurrection, some to the fall of Jerusalem, and others to the success of the Gospel in apostolic days. Its meaning cannot be fairly confined to any one of these, but probably includes all of them, as indicating the coming and first beginning of that kingdom in its power. Three of those then standing with the Lord beheld him transfigured six days afterward; all, save one, were witnesses of his resurrection and of the pentecostal scene: one at least, John, survived the capture of Jerusalem and the destruction of the temple, and on each of these occasions "the kingdom of God" was manifested "with power."

PRACTICAL SUGGESTIONS.—" Many praise Christ, yet rob him of his true honor."—*Beza*. "If Jesus Christ had come into the world as a mighty, opulent man, clothed with earthly glories and honors, he would have had a multitude of partisans, and most of them hypocrites."—*A. Clarke*. Satan conceals the worst and tells his followers only of pleasure. Christ deals fairly and is not afraid to tell his disciples the worst, for he knows that the advantages of his service overbalance the discouragements. Said Bishop Hooper, the night before his martyrdom, "True, life is sweet and death is bitter; but eternal death is more bitter, and eternal life is more sweet." "Christ's cross is the sweetest burden that ever I bore; it is such a burden as wings are to a bird, or sails to a ship, to carry me forward to my harbor." —*Rutherford*.

"No pain, no palm; no thorn, no throne;
No gall, no glory; no cross, no crown."—*Penn*.

"Of all unprofitable and foolish bargains that man can make, the worst is that of giving up his soul's salvation for the sake of the present world. It is a bargain of which thousands, like Esau...have repented, unhappily too late." —*Ryle*. "I find satisfaction in looking at nothing I have done. I have not fought. but Christ has fought for me; I have not run, but Christ has carried me; I have not worked, but Christ has wrought in me; Christ has done all." —*Payson*.

CH. IX. 2—13. THE TRANSFIGURATION, A. D. 29.

2. *after six days*] Luke's "*about an eight days after*" (ix. 28) includes the day at the beginning and at the end of the time reckoned, while Matthew and Mark exclude them.

Peter, and James, and John] the privileged three, who had witnessed the raising of Jairus' daughter.

into a high mountain] Tradition places this scene on Tabor. But Tabor is not a "high mountain," and besides, it was then occupied by a fortification. It was more probably on one of the spurs of the magnificent snow-

AUTHORIZED VERSION.	REVISED VERSION.
3 And his raiment became shining, exceeding white as snow; so as no fuller on earth can white them.	3 them: and his garments became glistering, exceeding white; so as no fuller on earth can whiten them.
4 And there appeared unto them Elias with Moses: and they were talking with Jesus.	4 And there appeared unto them Elijah with Moses: and they were talking

clad Hermon (10,000 feet high); also called Sion, "*sunny place*," and is now known as *Jebel-esh Sheikh*, "*the chief mountain*." Jesus was in the region of Hermon just before the transfiguration, and Mark, who never omits to notice our Lord's arrival at and departure from a place, makes no note of a change of place here. Thomson supposes the scene took place on mount Panium, a lower spur of Hermon. Canon Cook fixes it on one of the loftier peaks. " In whatever part of Palestine the Israelite turned his eye northward, Hermon was there terminating the view. From the plain along the coast, from the mountains of Samaria, from the Jordan valley, from the heights of Moab and Gi'ead, from the plateau of Bashan, that pale blue, snow capped cone forms the one feature on the northern horizon." See view of Mt. Hermon, on p. 101.

apart by themselves] Luke (ix. 28) tells us that Jesus withdrew that he might engage in *solitary prayer*. We may infer (comparing Luke ix. 37) that the transfiguration took place in the night, which must have added to the grandeur of the scene.

was transfigured] literally, "he was changed in form." Luke, writing primarily for Greek readers, avoids the word "transfigured," or " transformed" (" metamorphosed ") would be a still closer rendering), which Matthew and Mark employ. The associations of heathen mythology would almost inevitably attach themselves to it in the imagination of a Greek. In naming this great event " die Verklärung," or " the Glorification," German theology has seized this point, not the same as our " Transfiguration." " Mark borrows one image from the world of nature, another from that of man's art and device; by these he struggles to set forth and reproduce for his readers the transcendent brightness of that light which now arrayed, from head to foot, the person of the Lord, breaking forth from within, and overflowing the very garments which he wore; until in their eyes who beheld he seemed to clothe himself with light as with a garment. light being indeed the proper and peculiar garment of deity (Ps. civ, 2; Hab. iii, 4)."
—*Trench*.

3. *shining*] " A still more expressive term in the original, applied by Homer to the glistening of polished surfaces and to the glittering of arms; by Aristotle, to the twinkling of the stars; and by Euripides, to the flashing of lightning."—*Alexander*. Shining " as the light " is Matthew's expression.

fuller] one whose trade it was to cleanse linen and give it peculiar whiteness. The Romans had a white color, called *Candorem*, which was so " clear and deep as to glisten splendidly." The image is one which Dante might have used.

4. *there appeared unto them*] The three apostles had been weighed down with sleep, lying wrapped. like all Orientals, in their *abbas* on the ground, but awakened probably by the supernatural light, they thoroughly roused themselves (Luke ix, 32), and saw his glory and the two men standing with him. " No synod on earth was ever more gloriously attended than this. No assembly was ever more illustrious. Here is God the Father, God the Son. and God the Holy Ghost. Here are Moses and Elias, the chief of the prophets. Here are Peter, James, and John, the chief of the apostles."
—*Brentius*.

AUTHORIZED VERSION.	REVISED VERSION.
5 And Peter answered and said to Jesus, Master, it is good for us to be here: and let us make three tabernacles; one for thee, and one for Moses, and one for Elias.	5 with Jesus. And Peter answereth and saith to Jesus, Rabbi, it is good for us to be here: and let us make three ¹ tabernacles; one for thee, and one for Moses, and one for Elijah.
6 For he wist not what to say; for they were sore afraid.	6 For he wist not what to answer; for they became sore afraid.
7 And there was a cloud that overshadowed them: and a voice came out of the cloud, saying, This is my beloved Son: hear him.	7 And there came a cloud overshadowing them: and there came a voice out of the cloud, This is my beloved

¹ Or, *booths*

Elias with Moses] We are not told how the disciples knew Moses and Elijah. Jesus may have addressed them by name, or the conversation may have indicated in some other way who they were. Some suggest that the appearance of Moses and Elijah on the mount gives them a priority or prominence above all other O. T. prophets. These two were the acknowledged heads and representatives, the one of the law, the other of the prophets (comp. Matt. vii, 12).

they were talking] The subject of mysterious converse which the three were privileged to hear, was *the decease which Jesus was about to accomplish at Jerusalem* (Luke ix, 31). This exodus or departure of Jesus had been typified by the exodus of Israel under Moses, so Alexander thinks, and that of Elijah in a chariot of fire.

5. *And Peter*] The apostles were filled with a holy, spiritual ecstasy, and Peter sought to prolong the feeling, but under a mingled feeling of joy, confusion, and terror, he scarcely knew what he proposed (Luke ix, 33). It was too brief a converse, too transient a glimpse and foretaste of the heavenly glory, for him to recover his surprise.

it is good for us to be here] "Better, as no doubt he felt, than to be rejected of the Jews, better than to suffer many things of the elders and chief priests and scribes and be killed" (Matt. xvi, 21).—*Trench's Studies*.

three tabernacles] Three booths of wattled boughs, like those of the feast of tabernacles. It is vain to look for any specific motive or meaning in his proposition to build three booths, beyond that of wishing to prolong the heavenly manifestation and joy.

FORM OF TABERNACLE.

6. *he wist not*] The American revisers read "knew not" for "wist not." *Wist* is the past tense of A. S. *witan* = to know. Compare wit = *knowledge* (Ps. cvii, 27), and wit = *to know* (Gen. xxiv, 21). Filled with a religious awe at the scene, he tried to give some expression to his feelings, yet spoke half unconsciously.

sore afraid] Comp. Heb. xii, 21, " Moses said, I *exceedingly fear* and quake." Wyclif's rendering is very striking, "*agast by drede*."

7. *a cloud*] A bright cloud reminded them of the Shekinah, which was the usual symbol of the divine presence. "Light in its utmost intensity performs the effects of darkness, hides as effectually as the darkness would do." Comp. 1 Tim. vi, 16, and the words of Milton, "dark with excess of light," and of Wordsworth, "a glorious privacy of light."—*Trench*.

a voice came out of the cloud] Looking back afterwards on the scene, Peter speaks of himself and the two "sons of thunder" as "eyewitnesses of his majesty" (2 Peter i, 16), *i. e.*, literally, as men who had been *admitted and initiated into secret and holy mysteries*, and says that the voice "came from the excellent glory" (2 Peter i, 17), from him, that is, who dwelt in the cloud, which was the symbol and the vehicle of divine presence. John also clearly alludes to the scene, in John i, 14, and 1 John i, 1.—*Camb. Bible*.

AUTHORIZED VERSION.	REVISED VERSION.
8 And suddenly, when they had looked round about, they saw no man any more, save Jesus only with themselves.	8 Son: hear ye him. And suddenly looking round about, they saw no one any more, save Jesus only with themselves.
9 And as they came down from the mountain, he charged them that they should tell no man what things they had seen, till the Son of man were risen from the dead.	9 And as they were coming down from the mountain, he charged them that they should tell no man what things they had seen, save when the Son of man should have risen
10 And they kept that saying with themselves, questioning one with another what the rising from the dead should mean.	10 again from the dead. And they kept the saying, questioning among themselves what the rising again from the dead should mean.
11 And they asked him, saying, Why say the scribes that Elias must first come?	11 And they asked him, saying, [1] The scribes
12 And he answered and told them, Elias verily cometh first, and restoreth all things; and how it is written of the Son of man, that he must suffer many things, and be set at nought.	12 say that Elijah must first come. And he said unto them, Elijah indeed cometh first, and restoreth all things: and how is it written of the Son of man, that he should suffer

[1] Or, How is it *that the scribes say....come?*

The meaning of the voice, as of the transfiguration, was to assure the witnesses of the supernatural and spiritual character of Jesus and his mission.

This is my beloved Son] "In the words themselves of this majestic installation there is a remarkable honoring of the Old Testament, and of it in all its parts, which can scarcely be regarded as accidental; for the three several clauses of that salutation are drawn severally from the Psalms (Ps. ii, 7), the Prophets (Isa. xlii, 1), and the Law (Deut. xviii, 15): and together they proclaim him, concerning whom they are spoken, to be the king, the priest, and the prophet of the new covenant."—*Trench*. The same message was given at his baptism.

8. *suddenly...looked round*] as if startled by a touch of Jesus, they looked, but the celestial visitors had vanished. At first (1) they fell prostrate on their faces (Matt. xvii, 6; comp. Ex. iii, 6; 1 Kings xix, 13); then (2) recovering from the shock of the Voice from heaven (Matt. xvii, 6), they (3) suddenly gazed all around them, and *saw no man, save Jesus only*. "Hinc constat, hunc esse Filium, audiendum, non Mosen, non Eliam."...*Bengel.* "Quæ ex Verbo cœperunt, in Verbo desinunt."—*Ambrose.*

9. *they should tell no man*] This implies that they were forbidden to reveal the wonders of the night, and what they had seen, even to their fellow-Apostles till after the Resurrection. Why this silence was enjoined can only be conjectured. Some suppose the other disciples were not prepared for the information, or that these three, as leaders, needed this manifestation to strengthen them, or that publishing this might cause the people to make him king and interfere with his true mission.

10. *questioning one with another*] Mark alone mentions the perplexity which this language of their Lord occasioned to the Apostles. It was not the question of the resurrection generally, but of *his* death and resurrection which troubled them. This led to the question about Elijah. For, to their minds, Elijah had just come on the mount, while Jesus had already been recognized as the Messiah by the apostles.

11. *first come*] that is, before the Messiah (Mal. iv, 5). "It would be an infinite task," says Lightfoot, "to produce all the passages out of the Jewish writings which one might concerning the expected coming of Elijah." He was to restore to the Jews the pot of manna and the rod of Aaron, to cry to the mountains, "Peace and blessing come into the world, peace and blessing come into the world!" "Salvation cometh. Salvation cometh, to gather all the scattered sons of Jacob, and restore all things to Israel as in ancient times."

12. *and how*] It is true Elijah must first come, as the scribes say, but remember that the sufferings and rejection of the Messiah are also pre-

AUTHORIZED VERSION.	REVISED VERSION.
13 But I say unto you, That Elias is indeed come, and they have done unto him whatsoever they listed, as it is written of him. 14 And when he came to *his* disciples, he saw a great multitude about them, and the scribes questioning with them. 15 And straightway all the people, when they beheld him, were greatly amazed, and running to *him* saluted him. 16 And he asked the scribes, What question ye with them? 17 And one of the multitude answered and	13 many things and be set at naught? But I say unto you, that Elijah is come, and they have also done unto him whatsoever they listed, even as it is written of him. 14 And when they came to the disciples, they saw a great multitude about them, and scribes questioning with them. And straightway all the multitude, when they saw him, were greatly amazed, and running to him saluted him. And he asked them, What question ye with them? And one of the multitude an-

dicted. Or, "Elijah truly cometh first. But how or to what purpose is it written of the Son of Man that he cometh? *In order that he may suffer,* not conquer like a mighty prince." Some take the first clause as a question, "how is it written of the Son of Man?" and the last as the answer, "that he should suffer," etc. The R. V. takes the whole as one question.

13. *That Elias is indeed come*] Having shown them the relation between the work of Elijah and of himself, he now relieves their perplexity about the coming of Elijah, by showing them that not merely had Elijah just appeared on the mount, as they knew, but that John had come in the spirit of Elijah and had suffered death. It is difficult to understand how Romanists and a few Protestant writers can hold to the theory that Elijah is yet to come, in the face of this express declaration, "Elijah is come." Ryle, who inclines to the Romanist interpretation, concedes that the opposite view has been held by the great majority of Protestants since the Reformation. Matthew's account is explicit; the disciples understood that Jesus referred to John the Baptist as the Elijah foretold in prophecy (Matt. xvii, 13).

PRACTICAL TEACHINGS.—Calvin suggests that in the transfiguration Jesus meant to show that he had the power in himself to take his glory, had he willed it, and that hence he gave himself *willingly* to suffer. "God lets us have, even in this world, extraordinary glances and views, but they are only of short duration, because their longer duration would not be tolerable or profitable."—*Lange.* "What comfort and consolation a sight of glory can give a true believer!"—*Ryle.* In this appearance of Moses and Elias on the mount we have proof of the conscious existence of departed saints.

14—29. HEALING OF THE LUNATIC CHILD, A. D. 29.

14. *And when he came to his disciples*] Some MSS. read "when they came to the disciples." See R. V. All the evangelists place this miracle next after the transfiguration. Raphael, in his great picture, has enshrined forever the contrast between the scene on the mount of glorification and that which awaited the Saviour and the three apostles on the plain below; between the harmonies of heaven and the harsh discords of earth. "Hardly such another contrast can be found in the gospels as this," says Stier, "between the open heaven and sons of glory on the mount, and the valley of tears with its terrible forms of misery, pain and unbelief."

scribes] Jesus perceiving the disciples perplexed, and knowing the active hostility of the scribes, proposed to defend his followers.

15. *were greatly amazed*] "was astonied and much afraid."—*Rhemish Version.* His face, like that of Moses (Ex. xxxiv, 30), probably retained traces of the celestial glory, and filled the beholders with awe and wonder. So Bengel, De Wette, Meyer, Trench, Alford, and others, explain it. No wonder they ran and saluted him.

17. *my son*] "mine only child" (Luke ix, 38); "to thee"; he intended to bring him to Jesus.

AUTHORIZED VERSION.	REVISED VERSION.
said, Master, I have brought unto thee my son, which hath a dumb spirit;	swered him, ¹ Master, I brought unto thee 15 my son, which hath a dumb spirit; and
18 And wheresoever he taketh him, he teareth him; and he foameth, and gnasheth with his teeth, and pineth away: and I spake to thy disciples that they should cast him out; and they could not.	wheresoever it taketh him, it ² dasheth him down; and he foameth, and grindeth his teeth, and pineth away: and I spake to thy disciples that they should cast it out; and
19 He answereth him, and saith, O faithless generation, how long shall I be with you? how long shall I suffer you? bring him unto me.	19 they were not able. And he answereth them and saith, O faithless generation, how long shall I be with you? how long shall I bear
20 And they brought him unto him: and when he saw him, straightway the spirit tare him; and he fell on the ground, and wallowed foaming.	20 with you? bring him unto me. And they brought him unto him: and when he saw him, straightway the spirit ³ tare him grievously: and he fell on the ground, and wallowed foaming. And he asked his father,
21 And he asked his father, How long is it ago since this came unto him? And he said, Of a child.	How long time is it since this hath come unto 22 him? And he said, From a child. And oft-times it hath cast him both into the fire
22 And ofttimes it hath cast him into the fire, and into the waters, to destroy him: but if thou canst do any thing, have compassion on us, and help us.	and into the waters, to destroy him: but if thou canst do anything, have compassion on 23 us, and help us. And Jesus said unto him, If thou canst! All things are possible to him
23 Jesus said unto him, If thou canst believe, all things are possible to him that believeth.	24 that believeth. Straightway the father of the child cried out, and said ⁴, I believe;
24 And straightway the father of the child cried out, and said with tears, Lord, I believe; help thou mine unbelief.	

¹ Or, *Teacher*   ² Or, *rendeth him*   ³ Or, *convulsed*   ⁴ Many ancient authorities add *with tears*.

a dumb spirit] he could not utter articulate words, though he could *suddenly cry out* (Luke ix. 39).

18. *wheresoever*] According to Matthew, these attacks were supposed to have some connection with changes of the moon (Matt. xvii, 15).

he teareth him] indicating great pain, or violent convulsions, as St. Vitus' dance, or the like.

pineth away] "is parched," or "fainteth away." The effect is not permanent, but temporary and sudden, as in cases of epilepsy.

19. *how long shall I be with you*] This reply of Jesus has been variously interpreted: (1) Some, as Bengel, De Wette, and Meyer, understand it as applying only to the nine apostles; and this view seems to be favored by the reading, "them," in the R. V., but the term "generation" is too strong to apply to so small a company; (2) some apply it to the scribes only, to which Brown objects, but on the very insufficient ground that the context implies that it was want of faith which is rebuked, a fact which would favor the interpretation; (3) others, to the father of the child, as the reading of the A. V. suggests, but this is open to the same objection as the first view; (4) still others, as Alford Alexander, and Schaff, apply it to the generation living at the time of the Lord's ministry. In this would be included the father, the disciples, the scribes, and the multitude. The second view would satisfy the conditions of the narrative, while the fourth is sufficiently broad to include all the others.

22. *if thou canst*] more literally, *if at all thou canst*. This is a strong expression of an infirm faith, which at the beginning had been too weak, but had become more and more weak, owing to the failure of the disciples to aid him.

23. *If thou canst*] Compare R. V. "Thou hast said," replies our Lord, "*if I* can do anything. But as for thy *if thou canst*, the question is *if thou canst believe*; that is the hinge upon which all must turn." Then he pauses, and utters the further words. "*all things are possible to him that believeth*." Thus the Lord helps faith in the struggling soul.

24. *Lord, I believe*] The best authorities omit "with tears, Lord." See

AUTHORIZED VERSION.

25 When Jesus saw that the people came running together, he rebuked the foul spirit, saying unto him, *Thou* dumb and deaf spirit, I charge thee, come out of him, and enter no more into him.
26 And *the spirit* cried, and rent him sore, and came out of him: and he was as one dead; insomuch that many said, He is dead.
27 But Jesus took him by the hand, and lifted him up; and he arose.
28 And when he was come into the house, his disciples asked him privately, Why could not we cast him out?
29 And he said unto them, This kind can come forth by nothing, but by prayer and fasting.

REVISED VERSION.

25 help thou mine unbelief. And when Jesus saw that a multitude came running together, he rebuked the unclean spirit, saying unto him, Thou dumb and deaf spirit, I command thee, come out of him, and enter no more into him. And having cried out, and [1] torn him much, he came out: and *the child* became as one dead; insomuch that the more part
27 said, He is dead. But Jesus took him by the hand, and raised him up; and he arose. And when he was come into the house, his disciples asked him privately, [2] *saying*, We could
29 not cast it out. And he said unto them, This kind can come out by nothing, save by prayer.[3]

[1] Or, *convulsed* [2] Or, *How is it that we could not cast it out?* [3] Many ancient authorities add *and fasting.*

R. V. This does not affect the character or the object of the man's belief.

26. *and rent him sore*] "The kingdom of Satan, in small and great, is even stirred into a fiercer activity by the coming near of the kingdom of Christ. Satan has great wrath when his time is short."—*Trench*. The spirit acts, says the witty Fuller, "like an outgoing tenant, who cares not what mischief he does." "Nothing can be more touching and living than this whole most masterly and wonderful narration."—*Alford*. Trench quotes a curious passage from Lucian's Philopseudes, in which there is an ironical allusion to this miracle, and shows how widely a belief in Christ's miraculous power had spread, and is a good attestation of the early reception of the gospel, and of how skeptics explain away its character.

28. *Why could not we cast him out?*] He had given them "power and authority over all demons" (Luke ix, 1), and "against unclean spirits to cast them out" (Matt. x, 1); what was the reason of their failure now?

29. *This kind*] This order of beings, not this kind of demons; so Bloomfield and others understood it. The Lord impresses upon them a twofold lesson: (1) The power of a perfect faith (see Matt. xvii, 20, 21); (2) There are degrees of spiritual and moral wickedness so intense and malignant that they can be exorcised by nothing save by prayer. "Ministers would witness and be the instruments of more remarkable conversions if they were stronger in faith and more fervent in prayer."—*Scott*. "Two things are worthy of particular notice: (1) What is called the *spirit* or *grace* of prayer; (2) the *gift* of prayer. . . . Where there is a large measure of the *spirit* of prayer, there we are most apt to find a corresponding measure of the *gift* of prayer." . . . The happy union of the spirit and gift of prayer is the great object to be desired, and its attainment truly important to the usefulness of every minister of the Gospel."—*Samuel Miller*.

PRACTICAL SUGGESTIONS.—"Christ suffers in his honor by the difficulties and follies of his disciples."—*M. Henry*. "How deeply rooted must unbelief be in our hearts when we are surprised to find our prayers answered?"—*Hare*. "If thou canst grip Christ ever so weakly, he will not let thee perish."—*T. Adams*. "The little spark of faith which is kindled in his soul reveals to him the abysmal depths of unbelief which are there."—*Trench*. "God looks not at the oratory of your prayers, how urgent they may be; nor at the geometry of your prayers, how long they may be; nor at the arithmetic of your prayers, how many they may be; nor at the logic of your prayers, how methodical they may be; but the sincerity of them he looks at."—*T. Brooks*. "Unbelief is the greatest sin, hinders the greatest works of God, and plunges the soul in condemnation."—*Cramer*. Yet weak faith is faith; pray for its increase.

Authorized Version.	Revised Version.
30 And they departed thence, and passed through Galilee; and he would not that any man should know it.	30 And they went forth from thence, and passed through Galilee; and he would not that any man should know it. For he taught
31 For he taught his disciples, and said unto them, The Son of man is delivered into the hands of men, and they shall kill him; and after that he is killed, he shall rise the third day.	his disciples, and said unto them, The Son of man is delivered up into the hands of men, and they shall kill him; and when he is killed, after three days he shall rise again.
32 But they understood not that saying, and were afraid to ask him.	32 But they understood not the saying, and were afraid to ask him.
33 And he came to Capernaum: and being in the house he asked them, What was it that ye disputed among yourselves by the way?	33 And they came to Capernaum: and when he was in the house he asked them, What were ye reasoning in the way? But they
34 But they held their peace: for by the way they had disputed among themselves, who should be the greatest.	held their peace: for they had disputed one with another in the way, who was the ¹ greatest. And he sat down, and called the
35 And he sat down, and called the twelve, and saith unto them, If any man desire to be first, the same shall be last of all, and servant of all.	twelve; and he saith unto them, If any man would be first, he shall be last of all, and minister of all. And he took a little child,
36 And he took a child, and set him in the	and set him in the midst of them: and taking

¹ Gr. *greater*.

30-32. Second Prediction of the Passion, A.D. 29.

30. *And they departed thence*] From the regions of Hermon he now turned his steps once more toward Galilee. "It was the last time he was to visit the scene of so great a part of his public life, and he felt, as he journeyed on, that he would no more pass from village to village as openly as in days gone by, for the eyes of his enemies were everywhere upon him."

and passed] The word thus translated occurs five times in the N. T., Mark ii, 23; xi, 20; Matt. xxvii, 39; Mark xv, 29. Here it means going on by-ways or aside from the most frequented roads.

through Galilee] Some suppose that he left Cæsarea Philippi, crossed the upper Jordan by a bridge, just below Lake Huleh, and went on toward Capernaum. He went quietly, in order to have more opportunity to teach his disciples, as stated in the next verse.

31. *For he taught*] The tense in the original implies that the *constant* subject of his teaching in private now was his approaching suffering, death and resurrection; "the third day;" see R. V.

32. *were afraid*] Matthew adds that they were "exceeding sorry." His words concerning his violent death contradicted all their expectations, and they feared to question him: they had such forebodings of some terrible calamity, and shrank from asking, lest their worst apprehensions might be realized.

33-41. True Greatness in Christ's Kingdom, A.D. 29.

33. *he came*] or *they came to Capernaum*, as the R. V. reads. It was probably the house of Peter into which they entered. See i, 29. The next recorded event was the miraculous payment of the tribute money (Matt. xvii, 24-27), the half-shekel for the temple service. Their dispute shows how fully they recognized Jesus as Messiah, but how far they were from a true conception of the character and conditions required of the members of his kingdom.

34. *who should be the greatest*] or "who was the greatest" or "greater," as Meyer renders it.

35. *And he sat down*] "If, observes Beza, there was to be any *primacy* among the apostles (as of Peter), why was Christ here silent about it?" "Sit," or rather caused the child to stand, in the midst of them. Observe the many graphic and pathetic touches in this and the following verse. (1) He *sits* down ; (2) He *calls* the twelve to him ; (3) He *takes a little child*, and *places it in the midst* of them ; (4) He *takes it into his arms*, and then he *speaks* to them.

36. *took a child*] There is a tradition, not very trustworthy, that this

AUTHORIZED VERSION.

midst of them: and when he had taken him in his arms, he said unto them,

37 Whosoever shall receive one of such children in my name, receiveth me: and whosoever shall receive me, receiveth not me, but him that sent me.

38 And John answered him, saying, Master, we saw one casting out devils in thy name, and he followeth not us: and we forbade him, because he followeth not us.

39 But Jesus said, Forbid him not: for there is no man which shall do a miracle in my name, that can lightly speak evil of me.

40 For he that is not against us is on our part.

41 For whosoever shall give you a cup of water to drink in my name, because ye belong to Christ, verily I say unto you, he shall not lose his reward.

42 And whosoever shall offend one of these

REVISED VERSION.

37 him in his arms, he said unto them, Whosoever shall receive one of such little children in my name, receiveth me: and whosoever receiveth me, receiveth not me, but him that sent me.

38 John said unto him, ¹ Master, we saw one casting out ² devils in thy name: and we forbade him, because he followed not us. But Jesus said, Forbid him not: for there is no man which shall do a ³ mighty work in my name, and be able quickly to speak evil of me.

40 For he that is not against us is for us.

41 For whosoever shall give you a cup of water to drink, ⁴ because ye are Christ's, verily I say unto you, he shall in no wise lose his reward.

42 And whosoever shall cause one of

¹ Or, *Teacher* ² Gr. *demons.* ³ Gr. *power.* ⁴ Gr. *in name that ye are.*

child was Ignatius the Martyr, who was pastor at Antioch about A. D. 68 to 107. Others suggest that it was a child of one of the apostles, perhaps of Peter. "God has no children too weak, but a great many too strong, to make use of. God stands in no need of our strength or wisdom."—*Moody.*

38. *And John answered him*] The words *in my name*, of *v.* 37, seem to have reminded John of an incident in their recent journey, and he was probably anxious to divert discourse to a less humiliating subject, or to call attention to what he thought a proper act of his.

because he followeth not us] not "because he followeth not *thee.*" It is the utterance of excited party feeling. "There are men calling themselves Christians, who seem to look with doubt and suspicion on all that is done by those who do not walk with them. True likeness to the Saviour would lead us to rejoice...that the kingdom of Christ is advanced, whether by a Presbyterian, an Episcopalian, a Baptist, or a Methodist."—*Barnes.* "Some are so outrageously wedded to their own creed that they would rather let sinners perish than suffer those who differ from them to become the instruments of their salvation. This is vanity and an evil disease."—*A. Clarke.*

39. *Forbid him not*] Compare the words of Joshua and the reply of Moses in Num. xi, 28, 29. "O that all Christians would remember this." "A strong reproof to bigots who are ready to deny the Christian or churchly name to those who are not of their own organization."—*Whedon.* No one working in Christ's name in good faith is to be forbidden.

MILLSTONES.

40. *on our part*] Some, as Lachmann, read, "not against you is on your part."

41. *cup of water*] See R. V. and marginal reading of this verse. "Life affords few opportunities of doing great services for others, but there is scarcely an hour of the day that does not afford us the opportunity of performing some little, it may be, unnoticed kindness."—*Bowes.* "The disposition to give a cup of cold water to a disciple is a far nobler property than the finest intellect. Satan has a fine intellect, but not the image of God."—*Howels.*

42. *a millstone*] See R. V. Literally, *an ass millstone*, a millstone turned by an ass. These were much larger and heavier

AUTHORIZED VERSION.	REVISED VERSION.
little ones that believe in me, it is better for him that a millstone were hanged about his neck, and he were cast into the sea. 43 And if thy hand offend thee, cut it off: it is better for thee to enter into life maimed, than having two hands to go into hell, into the fire that never shall be quenched: 44 Where their worm dieth not, and the fire is not quenched. 45 And if thy foot offend thee, cut it off: it is better for thee to enter halt into life, than having two feet to be cast into hell, into the fire that never shall be quenched: 46 Where their worm dieth not, and the fire is not quenched. 47 And if thine eye offend thee, pluck it out: it is better for thee to enter into the kingdom of God with one eye, than having two eyes to be cast into hell fire: 48 Where their worm dieth not, and the fire is not quenched. 49 For every one shall be salted with fire, and every sacrifice shall be salted with salt.	these little ones that believe [1] on me to stumble, it were better for him if [2] a great millstone were hanged about his neck, and he 43 were cast into the sea. And if thy hand cause thee to stumble, cut it off: it is good for thee to enter into life maimed, rather than having thy two hands to go into [3] hell, 45 into the unquenchable fire.[4] And if thy foot cause thee to stumble, cut it off: it is good for thee to enter into life halt, rather than having thy two feet to be cast into [3] hell. 47 And if thine eye cause thee to stumble, cast it out: it is good for thee to enter into the kingdom of God with one eye, rather than 48 having two eyes to be cast into [3] hell; where their worm dieth not, and the fire is not 49 quenched. For every one shall be salted

[1] Many ancient authorities omit on me. [2] Gr. a millstone turned by an ass. [3] Gr. Gehenna.
[4] Ver. 44 and 46 (which are identical with ver. 48) are omitted by the best ancient authorities.

than the stones of hand-mills. Comp. Ov. *Fast.* vi, 318, and Sueton, *Oct.* lxvii. Such a mode of punishment by drowning is noted by Josephus (*Antiq.* xiv, 15, 10). Charity and unity of Christians are specially enforced here by our Lord.

43. *offend thee*] or, cause thee to stumble. See R. V. Our Lord makes special mention of the hand, the foot, the eye, those members whereby we *do* amiss, or *walk* astray, or *gaze on* what is sinful.

into hell] Literally, *the Gehenna*, or *the Gehenna of fire* (v. 47). Primarily, this phrase was applied to the "Ravine of Hinnom," also called "*Topheth*" (2 Kings xxiii, 10: Isa. xxx, 33; Josh. xviii, 16), on the south of Mount Zion. Its total length is a mile and a half. It is a deep, retired glen, shut in by rugged cliffs, with the bleak mountain sides rising over all. It became notorious in the times of Ahaz and Manasseh, as the scene of the barbarous rites of Molech and Chemosh, when the idolatrous inhabitants of Jerusalem cast their sons and daughters into the red-hot arms of a monster idol of brass placed at the opening of the ravine (2 Kings xvi, 3; 2 Chron. xxviii, 3; Jer. vii, 31). To put an end to these abominations the place was polluted by Josiah, who spread over it human bones and other corruptions (2 Kings xxiii, 10, 13, 14), from which time it seems to have become the common cesspool of the city. These inhuman rites and subsequent ceremonial defilement caused the later Jews to regard it with horror and detestation, and they also applied the name given to the valley, to *the place of torment*. Verses 44 and 46 are not found in many of the best MSS., but the same words are found in verse 48.

48. *fire is not quenched*] This phrase, though omitted by several authorities, in verses 44 and 46, is certainly genuine here. Endless punishment was a common doctrine in Christ's day, as now. The Pharisees held it, and Philo says, "The punishment of the wicked is to live forever dying, and to be for ever in pains and griefs that never cease."—*Quoted by M. Henry*. Whatever question there may be over the words in Matt. xviii, 8, there can be none here, respecting the endless duration of the punishment. Besides, the language implies that the sin will be endless as well as the punishment of it.

49. *every one shall be salted with fire*] The last clause is omitted in the

AUTHORIZED VERSION.	REVISED VERSION.
50 Salt is good: but if the salt have lost his saltness, wherewith will ye season it? Have salt in yourselves, and have peace one with another.	50 with fire[1]. Salt is good: but if the salt have lost its saltness, wherewith will ye season it? Have salt in yourselves, and be at peace one with another.

[1] Many ancient authorities add *and every sacrifice shall be salted with salt.* See Lev. ii. 13.

R. V. This is one of the most difficult passages in the Gospel, though the difficulty is greatly diminished by omitting the last clause of the verse, "every sacrifice," etc., as the revisionists, following the best authorities, have done. Those who accept the last clause as authentic, have various explanations: (1) Some, as Michaelis, Whitby, Alexander, Cook, apply the verse to the *lost*, as being preserved by and in this "salting of fire," in hell. This seems far-fetched. (2) Some refer it to the fiery trials of the righteous, who offer themselves a willing sacrifice to God. (3) Others, that the first clause of the verse refers to all members of the church, good and bad, whom the fire will try (1 Cor. iii, 13); and the second clause to the preserving effect of his grace on believers. Omitting the last clause as not authentic, and the verse may be explained: (1) All must enter the fire of God's purity, either willingly, as living sacrifices, like believers, or, unwillingly, into the fire of judgment, the eternal fire; or, (2) as referring to fire as a refiner, and limiting it to believers, their trials, sufferings, etc., which will cleanse and purify them. This view seems to be favored by the "these" of the context; as such persons were to cut off hand or foot, or pluck out the eye, if needful to purify themselves.

50. *Salt is good*] See Matt. v, 13, where it refers to believers; here, to the inward grace of the heart.

have lost] "It was the belief of the Jews that salt would, by exposure to the air, lose its virtue (Matt. v, 13) and become saltless. The same fact is implied in the expressions of Pliny, *sal iners, sal tabescere*, and Maundrell asserts that he found the surface of a salt rock in this condition."—*Camb. Bible.*

his saltness] Observe *his* here, where we should now use *its*. This is frequently the case in the Bible, and indeed the word *its* does not occur at all in the Version of 1611.

Have salt in yourselves] Among Orientals, salt was a sign of sacred covenant engagements and obligations (Lev. ii, 13; 2 Chron. xiii, 5). To eat salt together, meant to make peace, and enter into covenant with each other. Hence, in view of the contention between the disciples, the warning was timely to have salt in themselves and be at peace one with another.

PRACTICAL SUGGESTIONS.—"True greatness consists in perfect loveliness."—*Luther.* "In the kingdom of humility there is no contention. The more humble and simple we are, the nearer we are to the Saviour."—*Gossner.* "Give up anything that stands between us and the salvation of our souls. To an intolerant spirit we owe some of the blackest pages of church history. Better a thousand times that thy work should be done by other hands than not done at all."—*Ryle.*

Ch. X. 1–12. MARRIAGE LEGISLATION OF THE PHARISEES, A. D. 29 and 30.

As some help to the right study of this Gospel, notice that "the best harmonists place Matt. xviii, 15–35; Luke x, 1–xviii, 10 (except xv, 3–7); and John vii, 1–xi, 54, between the 9th and 10th chapters of Mark.—*Ellicott.*

According to Perowne and Maclear, the most important of the intervening events were:

1. *The visit of our Lord to Jerusalem at the feast of tabernacles* (John vii, 8–10); 2. *The rebuke of the "sons of thunder"* (Luke ix, 51–56); 3. *Discourses during the feast, and an attempt of the Sanhedrin to apprehend him*

AUTHORIZED VERSION.	REVISED VERSION.
CHAP. X.—And he arose from thence, and cometh into the coasts of Judea by the farther side of Jordan: and the people resort unto him again; and, as he was wont, he taught them again. 2 And the Pharisees came to him, and asked him, Is it lawful for a man to put away his wife? tempting him.	10 And he arose from thence, and cometh into the borders of Judæa and beyond Jordan: and multitudes come together unto him again; and, as he was wont, he taught them again. And there came unto him Pharisees, and asked him, Is it lawful for a man to put away his wife? tempting him. 3 And he answered and said unto them, What

(John vii. 11-51, viii, 12-59); 4. *The opening of the eyes of one born blind* (John ix, 1-41; *the good Shepherd* (John x, 1-18); 5. *Ministrations in Judea* (Luke x, etc.; 6. *Visit to Jerusalem at the feast of dedication* (John x, 22-39); 7. *Tour in Perœa* (Luke xiii, 22; xvii, 11); 8. *The raising of Lazarus* (John xi, 1-46); 9. *Resolve of the Sanhedrin to put him to death, and his retirement to Ephraim* (John xi, 47-54).

Robinson supposes that Jesus did not return to Galilee again, but went from Ephraim into Perœa, and this has been the commonly-accepted view. Clark dissents, and suggests that Jesus went from Ephraim on a tour into Samaria and Galilee; but his theory rests on a slender basis. Andrews follows Robinson, and fixes the departure of Jesus (verse 1) in November, A. D. 29, and the subsequent events (vs. 2—31), early in A. D. 30.

1. *he arose*] from Ephraim, according to Robinson, Geikie and others; or, according to some, this was his final departure from Galilee. The precise course of our Lord's journey is not clearly known. The place, whither he retired, has been identified with Ophrah, in the wide desert country northeast of Jerusalem, about five miles from Bethel, and on the confines of Samaria. So Eusebius and Jerome locate it, which has led to the identification of this Ophrah with the modern village of *et-Taiyibeh*. John's narrative shows that he visited Jerusalem twice in the interval, and hence this account (see R. V.) is literally correct. "He had already been in Perœa, or at least on the borders (John x, 40), after the feast of dedication, and before the raising of Lazarus."—*Schaff*. This appears to coincide with Robinson, though Schaff and Riddle interpret Mark x, 1, as referring to Christ's final departure from Capernaum and Galilee, and not from Ephraim or Perœa, as Robinson implies.

beyond Jordan] The R. V. clearly implies that he went *into Perœa*. The "again," also, seems to imply a previous visit to Perœa, and favors the view of Robinson and others, as Clark concedes.

he taught them again] Portions of his teaching are recorded by Luke, and include the parables of (1) *the unjust judge*, and (2) *the Pharisee and the publican* (Luke xviii, 1-14). In the region now traversed probably occurred the healing of the ten lepers (Luke xvii, 12-19), according to some scholars, but Robinson places it in Samaria, and during Christ's journey to the feast of tabernacles at Jerusalem.

2. *Is it lawful?*] "Nothing is lawful to any man who *doubts* its lawfulness.—*Farrar*.

for a man to put away his wife] "for every cause!" as Matthew adds (Matt. xix, 3). On this point the rival schools of Hillel and Schammai were divided, the former adopting the more loose, the latter the stricter view: the one holding that *any dislike* which he felt towards her would justify a man in putting away his wife, or even if she cooked his dinner badly; the other, that only notorious unchastity could be a sufficient reason. It has also been suggested that the object of the question may have been to offend the adulterous tetrarch, in whose territory he was. The American revisers read "trying," or "making trial of," in place of "tempting."

AUTHORIZED VERSION.	REVISED VERSION.
3 And he answered and said unto them, What did Moses command you?	4 did Moses command you? And they said, Moses suffered to write a bill of divorcement,
4 And they said, Moses suffered to write a bill of divorcement, and to put her away.	5 and to put her away. But Jesus said unto them, For your hardness of heart he wrote
5 And Jesus answered and said unto them, For the hardness of your heart he wrote you this precept.	6 you this commandment. But from the beginning of the creation. Male and female made
6 But from the beginning of the creation God made them male and female.	7 he them. For this cause shall a man leave his father and mother,[1] and shall cleave to his
7 For this cause shall a man leave his father and mother, and cleave to his wife;	8 wife; and the twain shall become one flesh: so that they are no more twain, but one flesh.
8 And they twain shall be one flesh: so then they are no more twain, but one flesh.	9 What therefore God hath joined together,
9 What therefore God hath joined together, let not man put asunder.	10 let not man put asunder. And in the house the disciples asked him again of this matter.
10 And in the house his disciples asked him again of the same matter.	11 And he saith unto them, Whosoever shall put away his wife, and marry another, com-
11 And he saith unto them, Whosoever shall put away his wife, and marry another, committeth adultery against her.	12 mitteth adultery against her: and if she herself shall put away her husband, and marry another, she committeth adultery.
12 And if a woman shall put away her husband, and be married to another, she committeth adultery.	

[1] Some ancient authorities omit *and shall cleave to his wife.*

3. *What did Moses*] By appealing to Moses, Jesus made an irresistible argument against easy divorces.

4. *Moses suffered*] They admit that Moses did not command, but only *suffered* this. Hovey suggests that "Moses merely presupposed the existence of this practice, and, by regulating, suffered it."

5. *this precept*] The depraved and low condition of society and of their hearts caused Moses to make this rule to regulate, not to introduce, easy divorces.

7. *For this cause*] He thus shows that God designed the marriage tie to be the closest and most indissoluble of all ties, and, according to Matthew (xix, 9), rebukes the adultery of Herod Antipas (though without naming him), in the severest terms.

8. *they twain*] the "two." "Twain" or "two" is not in the Hebrew, though it is fairly implied. The Septuagint and the Samaritan versions have it, however.

9. *What therefore God*] In Gen. ii, 24 these are the words of Adam; in Matthew xix, 4, the words of God; in Mark the words of Christ. They are words of Adam as uttering prophetically a divine ordinance; the words of God, as being eternally valid; the words of Christ, as rules for Christian life reëstablished by him.

10. *in the house*] Mark records several confidential household words of our Lord to his disciples; *e. g.*, concerning (1) the power of casting out demons (ix, 28, 29); (2) the great in the kingdom of heaven (ix, 33–37); and (3) here, the Christian law of marriage.

11. *marry another*] Some regard this as forbidding re-marriage after divorce under any circumstances; others as forbidding it only after divorce for other causes than adultery; but it implies where a divorce is granted because of infidelity to marriage vows, the innocent party thus divorced may marry again.

12. *if a woman shall put away*] This is the only instance in which Jesus states the nature of the guilt of a wife who leaves her husband and marries again. He also gives rules regarding the husband who divorces his wife, and the wife so divorced. "All three cases are dealt with on the same grounds: (1) that the marriage relationship ought to be indissoluble, and that one cause only (fornication) justifies or permits its dissolution; (2) that any further permission of divorce is but a concession to the hardness of men's hearts for the avoidance of greater evils."—*Ellicott.*

AUTHORIZED VERSION.	REVISED VERSION.
13 And they brought young children to him, that he should touch them: and *his* disciples rebuked those that brought them.	13 And they brought unto him little children, that he should touch them: and the disciples
14 But when Jesus saw *it*, he was much displeased, and said unto them, Suffer the little children to come unto me, and forbid them not: for of such is the kingdom of God.	14 rebuked them. But when Jesus saw it, he was moved with indignation, and said unto them, Suffer the little children to come unto me; forbid them not: for of such is the
15 Verily I say unto you, Whosoever shall not receive the kingdom of God as a little child, he shall not enter therein.	15 kingdom of God. Verily I say unto you, Whosoever shall not receive the kingdom of God as a little child, he shall in no wise enter
16 And he took them up in his arms, put *his* hands upon them, and blessed them.	16 therein. And he took them in his arms, and blessed them, laying his hands upon them.

ILLUSTRATION.—There is a fine allegorical representation of marriage on an antique gem belonging to the Duke of Marlborough. It presents the marriage of Cupid and Psyche. (1) Both are winged, to show the alacrity with which husband and wife should help each other; (2) both are veiled, to show the modesty attending this relation; (3) Hymen or marriage holds a lighted torch, leading them by a chain, to show they are unitedly led by pure love; (4) the chain is not of iron or brass, but of pearls, indicating that they are not slaves, but willing lovers; (5) they hold a dove, an emblem of innocence and fidelity; (6) a winged Cupid has gone before, to prepare a feast of love; (7) another comes behind with ripe fruits to place in their hands, a promise of happiness in children; (8) the genius of love follows them, with wings of feathers shrivelled, to intimate that love is never to fly away, but ever to abide with them.

13-16. JESUS RECEIVES LITTLE CHILDREN, A. D. 30.

13. *they brought*] The American revisers' rendering is better, "were bringing," and so in Luke xviii, 15. These probably were certain parents who honored him and valued his benediction. The "children" in Mark and Matthew are "infants" in Luke xviii, 15. The Greek word here is $παιδία$ the common one for a "child" of any age. The word "young" or "little" is added in the English version, though the R. V. lacks uniformity in its renderings. See Mark vii, 28; Luke vii, 32; xi, 7, where the same word is used. In Luke the Greek for "infants" is another word. Nicephorus says that Ignatius, afterward the bishop and martyr of Antioch, was one of these children.

that he should touch them] or, as Matthew adds, *that he should lay his hands upon them and pray* for them (xix, 13). Hebrew mothers were accustomed, in this manner, to seek a blessing for their children from rabbis of special holiness, who were wont to lay their hands upon them. "After the father of the child," says the Talmud, "had laid his hands on his child's head, he led him to the elders, one by one, and they also blessed him, and prayed that he might grow up famous in the law, faithful in marriage, and abundant in good works."

disciples rebuked those] "How chilling the rebuke of these disciples to fond parents, who had doubtless been greatly moved and drawn by the wise and tender words of Jesus?"—*Clark.*

14. *of such*] or "*to such belongs the kingdom of God*," as the American revisers render it. He says not *of these*, but *of such*, showing that it is not to children only, but also to such as have the like innocence and simplicity, the reward is promised. "Little children are not guileful or deceitful, but plain and simple; they are strangers to artful disguises; they are not obstinate; they rely on the instruction of their parents. . . . Here is, therefore, a fit and lively emblem of the followers of the Lamb."—*J. Edwards.* But President Edwards lived in another age; were he living now, might he not qualify somewhat his statement respecting children?

16. *took them up in his arms*] or "folded them in his arms." See

AUTHORIZED VERSION.	REVISED VERSION.
17 And when he was gone forth into the way, there came one running, and kneeled to him, and asked him, Good Master, what shall I do that I may inherit eternal life?	17 And as he was going forth [1] into the way there ran one to him, and kneeled to him and asked him, Good [2] Master, what shall I do that I may inherit eternal life? And
18 And Jesus said unto him, Why callest thou me good? there is none good but one, that is, God.	18 Jesus said unto him, Why callest thou me good? none is good save one, even God. Thou knowest the commandments, Do not kill, Do
19 Thou knowest the commandments, Do not commit adultery, Do not kill, Do not steal, Do	

[1] Or, on his way [2] Or, Teacher

chap. ix, 36 for the same Greek word. Twice we read of our Lord *taking persons into his arms*, and both times they were children, and both times the scenes are recorded only by Mark (ix, 36; x, 16).

blessed them] or, *He blesses them*, according to some MSS. The present tense is in keeping with the graphic style of Mark. Or, according to other MSS. and authorities (some of them the best), it reads, "fervently blessed them."

PRACTICAL SUGGESTIONS.—"Our children are given to us but for a little time. They are in a world of danger, sin and woe. They are exposed to temptation on every hand. If God be not their friend, they have no friend that can aid them in the day of adversity or keep them from the snares of the destroyer."—*Barnes.* "The children . . . were brought to Jesus by persons interested in them, in reliance on his power, in faith of the virtue which might proceed from him. When a like faith is shown in a like manner, the conduct of our Lord gives reason to suppose that he will not withhold his blessing."—*Bishop Sumner.*

17-31. THE RICH YOUNG RULER, A. D., 30.

17. *when he was gone forth*] See R. V. He was just starting, it would seem, on his last journey toward Jerusalem.

one] He was young (Matt. xix, 22), of great wealth, and a ruler of a local synagogue (Luke xviii, 18). All the Evangelists relate this incident in the same connection.

running] Ran up to him, apparently from behind, eager and breathless; then he knelt before him, as was usual before a venerated rabbi.

what shall I do] what work of merit? He had probably observed our Lord's gracious reception of children, and he desired to have part in the kingdom promised to them. His question betrays his serious deficiencies. Not by *doing*, but by *being*, was an entrance into it to be obtained. He also would "inherit," *i. e.*, have the kingdom by *right*, not by grace.

18. *Why callest thou me good?*[" As if he had said, 'Thou falsely callest me good Master unless thou acknowledgest that I have come from God.'"—*John Calvin.* The emphasis is on the "why." "Dost thou know what thou meanest when thou givest me this appellation?" If we combine the question and rejoinder as given by Matthew and Luke, it would seem to have run, *Why askest thou me about the good? and why callest thou me good? None is good save one, God; i. e.*, "good" in the absolute sense. Jesus repels it only in the superficial sense of the questioner, who regarded him merely as a good rabbi. Against the use of this by the Socinians, Stier puts these pointed syllogisms: " Either (1) there is none good but God—Christ is good, therefore Christ is God—or (2 there is none good but God—Christ is not God, therefore Christ is not good."

19. *Thou knowest the commandments*] The young man is referred to the commandments of the second table only, and they are cited generally from Ex. xx, 12-17. A striking instance of the free mode of quotation from the Old Testament, even in such a case as the ten commandments. Here the

AUTHORIZED VERSION.	REVISED VERSION.
not bear false witness, Defraud not, Honour thy father and mother. 20 And he answered and said unto him, Master, all these have I observed from my youth. 21 Then Jesus beholding him loved him, and said unto him, One thing thou lackest: go thy way, sell whatsoever thou hast, and give to the poor, and thou shalt have treasure in heaven and come, take up the cross, and follow me. 22 And he was sad at that saying, and went away grieved: for he had great possessions.	not commit adultery, Do not steal, Do not bear false witness, Do not defraud, Honour 20 thy father and mother. And he said unto him, ¹ Master, all these things have I observed 21 from my youth. And Jesus looking upon him loved him, and said unto him, One thing thou lackest: go, sell whatsoever thou hast, and give to the poor, and thou shalt have treasure in heaven: and come, follow 22 me. But his countenance fell at the saying, and he went away sorrowful: for he was one that had great possessions.

¹ Or, *Teacher*

seventh, then the sixth, eighth, ninth, tenth, and lastly fifth, are named. So in Luke. Matthew gives the sixth first, then the seventh, and then adds: "Thou shalt love thy neighbor as thyself."

Defraud not] The word thus rendered occurs in 1 Cor. vi, 7, 8; vii, 5; 1 Tim. vi, 5; James v, 4. It means *deprive none of what is theirs*, and has been thought to give the sum of the four commandments which precede, or most probably, of the tenth commandment.

Honor thy father and mother] Rendered by Wyclif "*worschippe* thi fadir and modir," which illustrates the meaning of the word as used in the Episcopal Marriage Service, "with my body I thee *worship*" = honor.

20. *all these have I observed*] adding, according to Matthew, *what lack I yet?* We are told that when the angel of death came to fetch R. Chamina, he said "Go and fetch me the book of the law, and *see whether there is anything in it that I have not kept.*"—*Farrar*. The ruler was a sincere, moral, but self-righteous and conceited young man.

21. *beholding him*] The same word, which occurs also in v. 27, in the original is applied (1) to the Baptist, when he "*looked upon Jesus*" (John i, 36), (2) to our Lord's *look* at Peter (3) when he named him Cephas (John i, 42), and (4) when he turned and *looked upon* him just before the cock crew for the second time (Luke xxii. 61).

loved him] or *was pleased with him*. Lightfoot remarks that the Jewish rabbis were wont to kiss the head of such pupils as answered well. Some gesture at least we may believe that our Lord used to show that the young man pleased him, both by his question and by his answer.

One thing thou lackest] Jesus does not concede that he had kept the law, but instead of stating his failure generally, he calls on the young man to give up what is his idol—a short, sharp test of his real condition. The young man fancied himself willing to do whatever could be required: he could now see if he were really willing. This test is applicable wherever the idol is the same, *i. e.*, wealth.

take up the cross and follow me] See ch. viii. 34; and R. V., which omits "take up the cross," as do the best MSS. Poor, friendless, outlawed, Jesus abated no jot of his awful claims, loftier than human monarch had ever dreamed of making, on all who sought citizenship in his kingdom.

22. *he was sad*] "*Sorrowful*," says Matthew (xix, 22); "*very sorrowful*," says Luke (xviii. 23); Mark says, "his countenance fell," R. V., or "he frowned," with a cloud upon his brow. The original word only occurs in one other place, Matt. xvi, 3, "for the sky is red and *lowering*." The test fell where least expected, but where most needed.

had great possessions] "great," or literally, "many" possessions may refer to *various kinds* of property, or a large amount of property. The former is the strict meaning of the Greek. His possessions he could not easily give up for possessions in heaven, and made, as Dante calls it, "the great refusal!"

AUTHORIZED VERSION.	REVISED VERSION.
23 And Jesus looked round about, and saith unto his disciples, How hardly shall they that have riches enter into the kingdom of God! 24 And the disciples were astonished at his words. But Jesus answereth again, and saith unto them, Children, how hard is it for them that trust in riches to enter into the kingdom of God! 25 It is easier for a camel to go through the eye of a needle, than for a rich man to enter into the kingdom of God. 26 And they were astonished out of measure, saying among themselves, Who then can be saved? 27 And Jesus looking upon them saith, With men it is impossible, but not with God: for with God all things are possible. 28 Then Peter began to say unto him, Lo, we have left all, and have followed thee. 29 And Jesus answered and said, Verily I say unto you, There is no man that hath left house, or brethren, or sisters, or father, or mother, or wife, or children, or lands, for my sake, and the gospel's,	23 And Jesus looked round about, and saith unto his disciples, How hardly shall they that have riches enter into the kingdom of God! 24 And the disciples were amazed at his words. But Jesus answereth again, and saith unto them, Children, how hard is it [1] for them that trust in riches to enter into 25 the kingdom of God! It is easier for a camel to go through a needle's eye, than for a rich 26 man to enter into the kingdom of God. And they were astonished exceedingly, saying 27 [2] unto him, Then who can be saved? Jesus looking upon them saith, With men it is impossible, but not with God: for all things are 28 possible with God. Peter began to say unto him, Lo, we have left all, and have followed 29 thee. Jesus said, Verily I say unto you, There is no man that hath left house, or brethren, or sisters, or mother, or father, or children, or lands, for my sake, and for the

[1] Some ancient authorities omit *for them that trust in riches.*   [2] Many ancient authorities read *among themselves.*

Concerning his later history and final decision the Scriptures are silent, and conjectures are worthless. "Yet within a few months," says Keble, "hundreds in Jerusalem remembered and obeyed this saying of our Lord, and brought their goods and laid them at the apostles' feet" (Acts iv, 34-37).

23. *looked round about*] Bengel observes that the countenance of Christ is often described as moved and affected by a deep and painful feeling for his hearers. Comp. Mark iii, 5, 34; viii, 33; Luke vi, 10; xxii, 61.

24. *Children*] a title intended to soften the sadness and sternness of his words.

for them that trust in riches] Some important MSS. omit these words, and read, "Children, how hard it is to enter into the kingdom of God." But the accepted reading harmonizes better with the context.

25. *It is easier for a camel*] This figure has been variously interpreted. (1) Some have rendered it an "anchor-rope," as though the word was "*kamilon,*" and not "*kamelon;*" but this is unsatisfactory. (2) Others think it refers to the side gate for foot passengers, close by the principal gate, called in the East the "eye of a needle"; or to the little gate within the larger; but (3) it is better to understand the words literally, as an Oriental proverb. Similar proverbs are common in the Talmud, *e. g.*, the same as this, except it uses an elephant instead of a camel, and this is quite in harmony with the modes of expression common in the East.

"NEEDLE'S EYE."

27. *impossible*] Their conclusion showed a lack of knowledge of God's wonderful works among his people in former ages, and a weak faith. "The character of the true philosopher is to hope all things not impossible, and to believe all things not unreasonable."—*John Herschel.*

28. *and have followed thee*] adding, as Matthew relates, "what shall *we* have therefore?" In reply to which our Lord uttered glorious words respecting the twelve thrones to be occupied by the apostles "in the regeneration," or "restoration of all things" (Matt. xix, 28).

AUTHORIZED VERSION.	REVISED VERSION.
30 But he shall receive a hundredfold now in this time, houses, and brethren, and sisters, and mothers, and children, and lands, with persecutions; and in the world to come eternal life.	30 gospel's sake, but he shall receive a hundredfold now in this time, houses, and brethren, and sisters, and mothers, and children, and lands, with persecutions; and in the world to come eternal life. But many that are first shall be last; and the last first.
31 But many *that are* first shall be last; and the last first.	31 ¹ world to come eternal life. But many that are first shall be last; and the last first.
32 And they were in the way going up to Jerusalem; and Jesus went before them; and they were amazed; and as they followed, they were afraid. And he took again the twelve, and began to tell them what things should happen unto him.	32 And they were in the way, going up to Jerusalem; and Jesus was going before them; and they were amazed; ² and they that followed were afraid. And he took again the twelve, and began to tell them the things

¹ Or, *age* ² Or, *but some as they followed were afraid*

30. *a hundredfold...houses*] "This cannot be taken literally, as promising a hundred times as many mothers, sisters, etc. It means, that the loss shall be a hundred times compensated or made up; or that in religion here we have a hundred times the *value* of all that we forsake."—*Barnes.*

with persecutions] an important limitation. See 2 Cor. xii, 10; 2 Thess. i, 4; 2 Tim. iii, 11.

31. *many that are first*] Very signally was the former part of this verse fulfilled *temporarily* in the case of Peter himself, *finally* in that of Judas; while the latter was wonderfully realized in the instance of Paul. To impress upon his hearers the important lesson that entrance into the kingdom of heaven is not a matter of mercenary calculation, our Lord delivered the parable of the *laborers in the vineyard* (Matt. xx, 1-16).

PRACTICAL SUGGESTIONS.—"A great fortune is great slavery."—*Seneca.* "He hath riches sufficient who hath enough to be charitable."—*Sir T. Browne.* "Great abundance of riches cannot of any man be both gathered and kept without sin."—*Erasmus.* "Riches, for the most part, are hurtful to them that possess them."—*Plutarch.* Of a rich man it was said, "Poor man! he toiled day and night, until he was forty, to gain wealth, and he has been watching it ever since for his victuals and clothes."

32—34. THIRD PREDICTION OF THE PASSION. A. D. 30.

32. *they were in the way*] Our Lord would seem to have now joined the caravans of the Galilean pilgrims going up to Jerusalem.

and Jesus went before them] Grotius and Trench suggest that, after the manner of some leader who heartens his soldiers by choosing the place of danger for himself, so Jesus led his disciples. And Cowper finely sings:

"The Saviour, what a noble flame
Was kindled in his breast,
When, hastening to Jerusalem,
He marched before the rest!"

and as they followed] or, "they that followed."—*R. V.* See also margin. The American revisers omit the marginal reading. The passage reads as though there were two bands of the apostles, of whom one went foremost, while the other had fallen behind. There are two explanations: (1) The whole body were amazed; *some* continued to follow, and these were afraid; (2) the twelve closest to him were amazed, and the larger company of followers farthest behind were afraid. This is the most satisfactory. "There are few pictures in the Gospel more striking than this of Jesus going forth to his death, and walking along the path into the deep valley, while behind him, in awful reverence and mingled anticipations of dread and hope—their eyes fixed on him, as with bowed head he preceded them in all the majesty of sorrow—the disciples walked behind and dared not disturb his meditations."—*Farrar.*

And he took again] for the third time he tells them privately of his coming

AUTHORIZED VERSION.	REVISED VERSION.
33 *Saying,* Behold, we go up to Jerusalem; and the Son of man shall be delivered unto the chief priests, and unto the scribes; and they shall condemn him to death, and shall deliver him to the Gentiles:	33 that were to happen unto him, *saying,* Behold, we go up to Jerusalem: and the Son of man shall be delivered unto the chief priests and the scribes; and they shall condemn him to death, and shall deliver him unto the Gentiles:
34 And they shall mock him, and shall scourge him, and shall spit upon him, and shall kill him: and the third day he shall rise again.	34 and they shall mock him, and shall spit upon him, and shall scourge him, and shall kill him; and after three days he shall rise again.
35 And James and John, the sons of Zebedee, come unto him, saying, Master, we would that thou shouldest do for us whatsoever we shall desire.	35 And there come near unto him James and John, the sons of Zebedee, saying unto him, ¹ Master, we would that thou shouldest do for us whatsoever we shall ask of thee. And
36 And he said unto them, What would ye that I should do for you?	36 he said unto them, What would ye that I should do for you? And they said unto him,
37 They said unto him, Grant unto us that we may sit, one on thy right hand, and the other on thy left hand, in thy glory.	37 Grant unto us that we may sit, one on thy right hand, and one on *thy* left hand, in thy glory.
38 But Jesus said unto them, Ye know not what ye ask: can ye drink of the cup that I drink of? and be baptized with the baptism that I am baptized with?	38 But Jesus said unto them, Ye know not what ye ask. Are ye able to drink the cup that I drink? or to be baptized with the baptism that I am baptized with? And they
39 And they said unto him, We can. And Jesus said unto them, Ye shall indeed drink of	39 said unto him, We are able. And Jesus said

¹ Or, *Teacher*

suffering. The two previous occasions are described in (1) Mark viii. 31, in the neighborhood of Cæsarea Philippi, just after Peter's confession, and (2) Mark ix, 30–32, shortly afterward, during the return to Capernaum. The particulars are now more full and more clear than ever before, and imply a judicial arrest and trial. Matthew (xx, 17) distinctly tells us that it was made *privately* to the apostles.

34. *and shall kill him*] or, as Matthew adds, "*crucify him*" (see Matt. xx, 19). Luke lays stress upon the fact that the disciples would not and could not understand his words (Luke xviii, 34). The terms seem plain enough to us, but they looked for him to reign as the Messiah, and, according to the prevailing view of their times, become a temporal king, a successor of David, to revive the splendors of his age. How could they understand his prediction to harmonize with such a view? The firmness with which this idea of a temporal reign had fixed itself in their minds is indicated by the request of James and John in the next verse.

35-45. THE AMBITIOUS APOSTLES, A. D. 30.

35. *James and John*] In this their mother, Salome joined, she falling on her knees (Matt. xx, 20). How ill-timed and circuitous the request! Indeed, the attempt to have Christ grant it before he heard what it was looks as if they were ashamed to ask, or were conscious that it might properly be refused.

37. *that we may sit*] Whether the mention of thrones (Matt. xix, 28), as in waiting for the twelve at the coming of their Master in glory, suggested the idea or not, is uncertain, unless Luke xix, 11 throws light on it. The two places on the right and left hand of a king or other person of dignity have ever been recognized, East and West, as the positions of honor. "*In thy glory*" refers to the earthly splendor of his kingdom.

38. *baptism I am baptized with*] Ryle calls attention to this expression as very remarkable, and thinks it implies "that there is such a thing as being baptized, in a certain sense, without the use of any outward form." And Clark and Olshausen regard the phrase as signifying not a literal baptism, but as a figurative description of the overwhelming sufferings of Jesus.

39. *And they said unto him, We can*] They knew not at the time what they said, but afterward they were enabled to drink of that cup, and to be baptized with that baptism of suffering. James was the first martyr of the

AUTHORIZED VERSION.	REVISED VERSION.
the cup that I drink of; and with the baptism that I am baptized withal shall ye be baptized: 40 But to sit on my right hand and on my left hand is not mine to give; but *it shall be given to them* for whom it is prepared. 41 And when the ten heard *it*, they began to be much displeased with James and John. 42 But Jesus called them *to him*, and saith unto them, Ye know that they which are accounted to rule over the Gentiles exercise lordship over them; and their great ones exercise authority upon them. 43 But so shall it not be among you: but whosoever will be great among you, shall be your minister: 44 And whosoever of you will be the chiefest, shall be servant of all. 45 For even the Son of man came not to be ministered unto, but to minister, and to give his life a ransom for many.	unto them, The cup that I drink ye shall drink; and with the baptism that I am baptized withal shall ye be baptized: but to sit 40 on my right hand or on *my* left hand is not mine to give: but *it is for them* for whom it hath been prepared. And when the ten 41 heard it, they began to be moved with indignation concerning James and John. And 42 Jesus called them to him, and saith unto them, Ye know that they which are accounted to rule over the Gentiles lord it over them; and their great ones exercise authority over them. But it is not so among you: 43 but whosoever would become great among you, shall be your ¹ minister: and whosoever 44 would be first among you, shall be ² servant of all. For verily the Son of man came not 45 to be ministered unto, but to minister, and to give his life a ransom for many.

¹ Or, *servant* ² Gr. *bond-servant*

apostolic band (Acts xii, 2): John (1) was bereaved, of his brother, then of the other apostles; (2) he became an exile in sea-girt Patmos (Rev. i, 9), and (3) died last of the apostles.

the cup] Comp. John xviii, 11, "*The cup* which my father hath given me, shall I not drink it?" and Mark xiv, 36, "Take away *this cup* from me." Their thoughts were fastened on thrones and high places: his on a cup of suffering and a baptism of blood. For this use of the word "baptism" here, compare Luke xii, 50. "I have *a baptism* to be *baptized* with."

DRINKING CUPS.

40. *but it shall be given*] "The throne," says Basil, "is the prize of toils, not a grace granted to ambition;" a reward of righteousness, not the concession of a reward." On the phrase, "it is not mine to give," see R. V. Alexander, D. Brown, Wordsworth and Canon Cook omit the words in italics and render "is not mine to give except," or "unless," "for whom it is prepared;" but this violates the general grammatical construction, as Alexander concedes. The R. V. is to be preferred.

41. *began to be much displeased*] "hadden endignacioun."—*Wyclif.* "Humanity is in self-conflict; the spirit is naturally competent to rein the animal into subjection, and yet it is often morally impotent to put on and pull up the curb."—*Hickok*. The sons of Zebedee had been in a better social position than most of their brethren, and this attempt to secure a preëminence of honor kindled a storm of jealousy, but it was soon allayed.

42. *which*] commonly used at the time our translation was made for the relative "*who*," and applied to persons. It is now obsolete in this sense, and it is to be regretted that the R. V. does not uniformly use "who" in such cases, as the American revisers desired.

are accounted] = those who are regarded and known to rule, those who have the reputation of being governors.

exercise lordship] The word is applied in Acts xix. 16, to the man possessed with an evil spirit *prevailing against* and *overcoming* the seven sons of Sceva. The idea is that superiority in worldly governments can only be sustained by force. Peter, in his first Epistle (v, 3), warns the elders of the church against "being lords over God's heritage." See also Matt. xx, 25.

45. *Verily...to give his life*] The American revisers prefer to read, "For

AUTHORIZED VERSION.	REVISED VERSION.
46 And they came to Jericho: and as he went out of Jericho with his disciples and a great number of people, blind Bartimeus, the son of Timeus, sat by the highway side begging.	46 And they come to Jericho: and as he went out from Jericho, with his disciples and a great multitude, the son of Timæus, Bartimæus, a blind beggar, was sitting by the

the Son of man also," etc. It is an announcement that the Redeemer was about to give his life as *a ransom for many* (1 Tim. ii, 6). The word translated "ransom" only occurs here, and in Matt. xx, 28. Wyclif renders it "and zyue his soule, *or lyf,* redempcioun, *or azen-biyng,* for manye." The three great circles of images which the Scriptures employ when they represent to us the purport of the death of Christ, are (*a*) *a sin-offering, or propitiation* (1 John ii, 2; iv, 10); (*b*) *reconciliation* (= *at-one-ment*) *with an offended friend* (Rom. v, 11; xi, 15; 2 Cor. v, 18, 19); (*c*), as here, *redemption from slavery* (Rom. iii, 24; Eph. i, 7; Col. i, 14). It here implies the great humility and condescension of Jesus.

PRACTICAL SUGGESTIONS.—"The tallest trees are most in the power of the winds, and ambitious men of the blasts of fortune."—*Penn.* "Fling away ambition; by that sin the angels fell; how can man then, the image of his Maker, hope to win by it?"—*Shakespeare.*

46–52. AT JERICHO. BLIND BARTIMEUS. A. D. 30.

46. *And they came*] either the evening of Thursday, Nisan 7, or the morning of Friday, Nisan 8, according to Farrar's conjecture. From Peræa they journeyed down to the sunken channel of the Jordan, and the luxuriant "district" of Jericho. Where he crossed the Jordan can only be conjectured. It was probably at one of the well-known fords above Jericho.

to Jericho] Jericho was the ancient stronghold of the Canaanites—taken by Joshua (ii, vi), founded for the second time under Hiel the Bethelite (1 Kings xvi, 34), visited by Elisha and Elijah before the latter "went up by a whirlwind into heaven" (2 Kings ii, 4–15)—was still, in the days of Christ, surrounded by towers and castles. Two of them lay in ruins since the time of Pompeius, but "Kypros, the last fortress built by Herod the Great, who had called it after his mother, rose, white, in the sun, on the south of the town. Jericho was on a plain about five miles west of the Jordan, and six miles north of the Dead Sea. Near the ancient city was "Elisha's Fountain." The Jericho of Christ's day was southeast of the ancient city, while the modern town, Er-Riha, is two miles further east. The city, when Jesus visited it, had been rebuilt, and perhaps exceeded the ancient town in its splendor. It has semi-tropical verdure, as the plain is nine hundred feet below the Mediterranean. "The great palace of Herod," says Geikie, "in the far-famed groves of palms, had been plundered and burnt down in the tumults that followed his death, but in its place a still grander structure, built by Archelaus, had arisen amidst still finer gardens and more copious and delightful streams. A grand theatre and spacious circus, built by Herod, scandalized the Jews, while a great stone aqueduct of eleven arches brought a copious supply of water to the city, and the Roman military road

ELISHA'S FOUNTAIN AT JERICHO.

AUTHORIZED VERSION.	REVISED VERSION.
47 And when he heard that it was Jesus of Nazareth, he began to cry out, and say, Jesus, *thou* Son of David, have mercy on me.	47 way side. And when he heard that it was Jesus of Nazareth, he began to cry out, and say, Jesus, thou son of David, have mercy on
48 And many charged him that he should hold his peace: but he cried the more a great deal, *Thou* Son of David, have mercy on me.	48 me. And many rebuked him, that he should hold his peace: but he cried out the more a great deal, Thou son of David, have mercy
49 And Jesus stood still, and commanded him to be called. And they call the blind man, saying unto him, Be of good comfort, rise; he calleth thee.	49 on me. And Jesus stood still, and said, Call ye him. And they call the blind man, saying unto him, Be of good cheer: rise, he 50 calleth thee. And he, casting away his gar-
50 And he, casting away his garment, rose, and came to Jesus.	

ran through it." The modern town consists of a group of miserable hovels, inhabited by about sixty families. See Schaff's *Dict. of Bible*.

as he went out] See *Special Note*.* (Comp. Luke xviii, 35; Matt. xx, 29, 30.)

a great number] of pilgrims from Perœa and Galilee, met at this central point to go up to the passover at Jerusalem.

Bartimeus] The better reading seems to be, *the son of Timæus, Bartimæus*. See R. V. "This account of him hints that he was a personage well known to Christians in Mark's time as a monument of the Lord's miracle, as was probably also Simon the leper; and the designation 'son of Timæus' would distinguish him, not merely from the father, but also from other sons."—*Lange*. "All the roads leading to Jerusalem, like the temple itself, were much frequented at the time of the feasts, by beggars, who reaped a special harvest from the charity of the pilgrims."

47. *Son of David*] This was the Jewish designation of the Messiah. His application of it to Jesus may be an indication of his faith. Perhaps he had heard of the recent resurrection of Lazarus, at Bethany, not far away.

48. *charged him*] "thretnyden hym that he schulde be stille."—*Wyclif*. They rebuked him and his companions, deeming their clamors ill-mannered towards a prophet, such as they held Jesus to be.

49. *good comfort*] given by Mark only, as the cheering words of bystanders, followed by the earnest act of the man, casting away (or aside) his garment (or outer mantle) and "leaping up" in his joy over the hope of having his sight restored.

50. *casting away his garment*] i.e. his *abba*, or upper garment.

---

* *Special Note on the healing of the blind men at Jericho.*—Harmonists find a difficulty in reconciling the gospel narratives of this healing. Compare Luke xviii, 35-43; Matt. xx, 29-34, and see R. V. Matthew mentions two blind men healed; Mark and Luke refer to only one; Matthew and Mark state that healing took place when Jesus left Jericho; Luke, as "Jesus drew nigh to the city." The difference as to the number healed is easily explained: Matthew speaks of *two*; Mark and Luke notice only *one*, probably the better known or more important case of the two. If there were two, there must have been one, and silence is no contradiction. The chief difficulty is on the other point, as to the time or place of healing: Several explanations have been proposed: (1) There were two Jerichos, an *old* and a *new* city; Jesus may have been *leaving* one and *approaching* the other, where the healing was performed, and so both statements be accurate; so McKnight; but this is weak. (2) That there were *three* or more blind men healed, one named by Luke (Luke xviii, 35), and *two* by the others (Matt. xx, 29); so Augustine, Kitto, Davidson; (3) Lightfoot, Tischendorf, Wieseler, Neander, Ebrard, and Greswell suppose that two distinct miracles were performed, and that Matthew blends both events in his account. This seems to remove one difficulty by making another; (4) Robinson, Owen, Grotius, and others, propose to render the Greek verb "to be nigh" or "near," instead of "come nigh"; hence Luke would state that the healing was performed while Jesus was still near the city, and so harmonize with the idea given by Matthew and Mark; (5) Many most reliable writers, as Calvin, Bengel, Stier, Trench, Ellicott, Lange, and John Hall, conclude that one blind man cried to him as he drew near to the city, and whom he cured not then, but on the morrow, at his going out of the city, together with the other, to whom he had in the meanwhile joined himself. On this theory Luke notes the first appeal, and relates the healing by anticipation. The first three explanations are the least satisfactory. But where there are so many reasonable solutions, the *apparent* discrepancy is not important.

AUTHORIZED VERSION.	REVISED VERSION.
51 And Jesus answered, and said unto him, What wilt thou that I should do unto thee? The blind man said unto him, Lord, that I might receive my sight.	51 ment, sprang up, and came to Jesus. And Jesus answered him, and said, What wilt thou that I should do unto thee? And the blind man said unto him, ¹ Rabboni, that I
52 And Jesus said unto him, Go thy way: thy faith hath made thee whole. And immediately he received his sight, and followed Jesus in the way.	52 may receive my sight. And Jesus said unto him, Go thy way; thy faith hath ² made thee whole. And straightway he received his sight, and followed him in the way.
CHAP. XI.—And when they came nigh to Jerusalem, unto Bethphage and Bethany,	11 And when they draw nigh unto Jerusalem, unto Bethphage and Bethany, at the mount

¹ See John xx, 16 ² Or, *saved thee*

51. *Lord*] = *my Master*. The blind man gives him the title of greatest reverence that he knew. The same form is used by Mary Magdalene to her risen Lord, John xx, 16. There were gradations of honor in the title, Rab = master was a title of respect, Rabbi = my master, of greater honor, and Rabbon or Rabboni = my great master, was the most honorable title of the three. Rabbi is simply the word for teacher, with the suffix meaning "my."

52. *and followed Jesus*] or "him" R. V.:, along the road, *glorifying God* as Luke adds (xviii, 43) and joining the festal company of his healer, and thus he obeyed the command "Go thy way," for it was going *his* way now, to follow Christ. Plumptre notices that in the apocryphal gospel of Nicodemus, Bartimeus appears as one of the witnesses for the defence of Jesus. After this the Lord accepted the hospitality of Zaccheus, a superintendent of customs or tribute at Jericho (Luke xix, 1—10); uttered the parable of "*the pounds*" in order to correct the idea that the kingdom of heaven was about to appear immediately (Luke xix, 11—27); and at length, six days before the passover, reached the mountain hamlet of Bethany (John xii, 1).

PRACTICAL LESSONS.—"Here is the history of many a soul. When a man is in earnest about his salvation, and begins to cry that his eyes may be opened * * * he will find infinite hindrances; and these not from professed enemies of the gospel, but from such as seem, like this multitude, to be on Jesus' side. Even they will try to stop his mouth."—*Trench.*

CH. XI. 1—11. THE TRIUMPHAL ENTRY.

(Sunday, day following Jewish Sabbath, 10th Nisan, 783, April 2d, A.D. 30.)

1. *And when*] The triumphal entry took place on Sunday the 10th of Nisan, according to the best authorities, though Robinson places it on Monday following. Readers will bear in mind that the Jewish mode of reckoning time differed from ours; their sabbath was on Saturday, and as their day was counted from sunset to sunset, their sabbath would begin on our Friday *after sunset* and end on Saturday at sunset. Our Sunday was their *first* day of the week, and therefore to them a secular day. The order of events were: (1) The Saviour apparently reached Bethany on the evening of Friday, Nisan 8. There (2) in quiet retirement he spent the sabbath before his crucifixion; and (3) in the evening (the Jewish sabbath ending at sunset), he sat down to a festal meal, attended by the sisters of Lazarus at the house of Simon, a leper (Matt. xxvi, 6); John xii, 1). (4) At this feast he was anointed by Mary (John xii, 3); and (5) during the night a council of the Jews consulted how to put, not him only, but Lazarus also to death (John xii, 10).

they came] See R. V. Mark passes by the events at Simon's house to relate the entry into Jerusalem From this triumphal entry made after the Jewish sabbath, and on the first day of the week, the day is celebrated as "Palm Sunday" by some churches. The narrative is written in the present tense.

unto Bethphage] On the first day of the week the Saviour left Bethany and

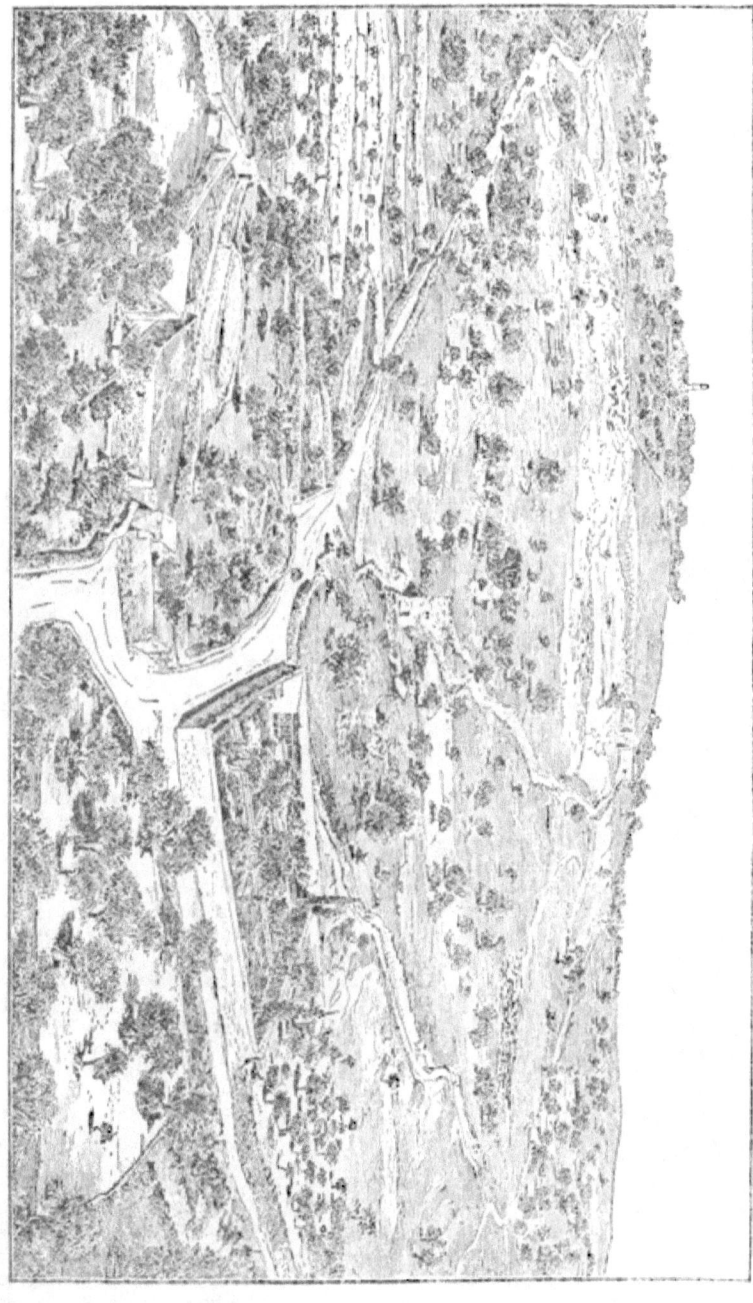

MOUNT OF OLIVES. (*After Photograph*).

AUTHORIZED VERSION.	REVISED VERSION.
at the mount of Olives, he sendeth forth two of his disciples, 2 And saith unto them, Go your way into the village over against you: and as soon as ye be entered into it, ye shall find a colt tied, whereon never man sat; loose him, and bring *him*. 3 And if any man say unto you, Why do ye this? say ye that the Lord hath need of him; and straightway he will send him hither. 4 And they went their way, and found the colt tied by the door without in a place where two ways met; and they loose him.	of Olives, he sendeth two of his disciples, and 2 saith unto them, Go your way into the village that is over against you: and straightway as ye enter into it, ye shall find a colt tied, whereon no man ever yet sat; loose 3 him, and bring him. And if any one say unto you, Why do ye this? say ye, The Lord hath need of him; and straightway he ¹ will 4 send him ² back hither. And they went away, and found a colt tied at the door without in the open street; and they loose him.

¹ Gr. *sendeth*.   ² Or, *again*.

proceeded toward Bethphage = *the house of unripe figs*, a little hamlet on the road between Jericho and Jerusalem. Some authorities omit Bethphage.

two of his disciples] Three Evangelists state the sending of "two disciples," but neither give the names of the two. Some conjecture that they were Peter and John, but this is only a guess.

2. *into the village over against you*] either Bethphage or an adjoining hamlet.

a colt tied] "In the East the ass is in high esteem. Statelier, livelier, swifter than with us, it vies with the horse in favor. Among the Jews it was equally valued as a beast of burden, for work in the field or at the mill, and for riding. In contrast to the horse, which had been introduced by Solomon from Egypt, and was used especially for war, it was the symbol of peace. To the Jew it was peculiarly national, for had not Moses led his wife, seated on an ass, to Egypt? Had not the judges ridden on white asses, and was not the ass of Abraham, the friend of God, noted in Scripture? Every Jew, moreover, expected, from the words of one of the prophets (Zech. ix, 9), that the Messiah would enter Jerusalem riding on an ass. No act could be more perfectly in keeping with the conception of a king of Israel, and no word could express more plainly that the king proclaimed himself the Messiah."—*Geikie*. Still, whether it was a mark of regal authority or of humiliation, is a question on which able writers widely differ. Tertullian (as cited by Gerhard) says the Gentiles, in ridicule, called Christians "*asinarii*," because they believed in Christ, who rode on an ass, and they even falsely charged his followers with worshiping an ass's head!

whereon never man sat] this agrees with Matthew's account of the she-ass (Matt. xxi, 2) and her colt with her. The colt would not have been used, so long as it was running with the mother. Animals that never yet had worked were put to sacred purposes. See Num. xix, 2; Deut. xxi, 3; 1 Sam. vi, 7.

3. *the Lord hath need of him*] Some suppose that the man may have been a secret disciple. "Secret disciples, such as the five hundred who afterwards gathered to one spot in Galilee, and the hundred and twenty who met after the resurrection (1 Cor. xv, 6; Acts i, 15), were scattered in many places." The reading of the R. V., "will send him back hither," or "send him hither again," is regarded as a promise "to return the colt soon."

4. *in a place where two ways met*] Wyclif, "in the meeting of tweye weyes," following the Vulgate *bivium*. The word in the original denotes (1) *any road that leads around a place, a street or a crooked lane*; (2) *around a block of houses*; (3) *the quarter of a town* = Lat. *vicus*. Here it means either *the passage round the house*, as Wordsworth understands, or *a lane or way around a block of houses*, as Alford and Trench suggest. They went and found the ass tied at the door (outside, not inside, the court-yard), and the colt with her, not in the highway, but in a back way or alley, which went round the house, and at *the* place

SYRIAN ASSES

AUTHORIZED VERSION.	REVISED VERSION.
5 And certain of them that stood there said unto them, What do ye, loosing the colt? 6 And they said unto them even as Jesus had commanded: and they let them go. 7 And they brought the colt to Jesus, and cast their garments on him; and he sat upon him. 8 And many spread their garments in the way: and others cut down branches off the trees, and strawed *them* in the way. 9 And they that went before, and they that	5 And certain of them that stood there said unto them, What do ye, loosing the colt? And they said unto them even as Jesus had said: and they let them go. 7 And they bring the colt unto Jesus, and cast on him their garments: 8 and he sat upon him. And many spread their garments upon the way; and others ¹ branches, which they had cut from the fields. And they that went before, and they

¹ Gr. *layers of leaves.*

where two roads met. The disciples were instructed what to answer, if questioned. All these points of the minute detail indicate that the account is from an eye-witness. The colt, untamed and tied at the back gate, as if ready for a rider, has been interpreted as a symbol of the Gentile world to be brought to Christ from the lanes and alleys of heathendom (Luke xiv, 21); the she-ass as symbolizing God's ancient people, who were familiar with the yoke of the law: but this is straining the simplicity of the narrative.

5. *What do ye*] This question was probably asked by the owners of the colt. The reply was in the words Jesus had foretold, and permission was granted.

7. *and cast their garments on him*] (Matt. xxi, 7), to do him regal honor, just as the captains "*took every man his garment, and put it under Jehu on the top of the stairs, and blew with trumpets, saying, Jehu is king*" (2 Kings ix, 13).

he sat upon] the unused colt; perhaps one of the apostles led it by the bridle, as some suppose.

8. *spread their garments*] *i. e.*, their "abbas" or "hykes," the loose blanket or cloak worn over the tunic or shirt. So myrtle-twigs and robes had been strewn by their ancestors before Mordecai (*Targ.* Esther viii, 15), so the Persian army had honored Xerxes when about to cross the Hellespont (Herod. vii, 54), and so Robinson says the inhabitants of Bethlehem threw their garments under the feet of the horses of the English consul at Damascus, whose aid they were imploring.

branches] not cut from the trees as they went along, as were the "branches" mentioned in Matt. xxi, 8, but *mattings* (*stoibades*) which they twisted out of the palm-branches as they passed. The original word denotes (1) *a bed of straw, rushes* or *leaves*; (2) *a mattress*, especially of soldiers; (3) the *nest* or *lair* of mice or fish.

off the trees] The reading of most ancient MSS. here is *from the fields*, see R.V., and the verse may be rendered: *And many strewed their garments in the way, and others twisted branches, cutting them from gardens or fields.* Eastern gardens are not flower gardens, but the orchards, vineyards and fig-enclosures round a town. The three separate roads from Bethany to Jerusalem passed by plantations of palm trees, and fruit and olive gardens. The best authorities omit, "and strewed them in the way." From Bethany to Jerusalem there are three roads leading over Olivet. It is generally supposed that Jesus made his triumphal entry by the middle road, but the southern one is usually taken by horsemen and caravans.

9. *they that went before*] From John xii, 12 it appears that a second stream of people issuing from the holy city came forth to meet the Saviour, and these joining the others coming from Bethany, turned round and swelled the long procession towards Jerusalem; compare Stanley's account in *Sinai and Palestine*.

AUTHORIZED VERSION.	REVISED VERSION.
followed, cried, saying, Hosanna; Blessed is he that cometh in the name of the Lord: 10 Blessed be the kingdom of our father David, that cometh in the name of the Lord: Hosanna in the highest. 11 And Jesus entered into Jerusalem, and into the temple: and when he had looked round about upon all things, and now the eventide was come, he went out unto Bethany with the twelve.	that followed, cried, Hosanna; Blessed is he 10 that cometh in the name of the Lord: Blessed is the kingdom that cometh, the kingdom of our father David: Hosanna in the highest. 11 And he entered into Jerusalem, into the temple; and when he had looked round about upon all things, it being now eventide, he went out unto Bethany with the twelve.

Hosanna] a Greek corruption of a Hebrew phrase used when persons applied to the king for help; it means "save now." This cry was not confined to children, as some infer.

10. *Blessed be the kingdom*] The shout of blessing for the kingdom and the coming king. See Ps. cxviii, 26: "What strange mingling of truth and error in the thoughts and hopes of the multitude that day! And the error was the more fatal because combined with the truth."—*Schaff*. "In the name of the Lord" is omitted in the best authorities.

11. *And Jesus entered*] At one point in the road the magnificent city burst into view. Then the procession may have paused, and our Lord wept over it (Luke xix, 41—44), and afterwards crossing the bridge over the Kedron, he passed through the gate, now St. Stephen's, into Bezetha, the new town, through narrow streets, "hung with flags and banners for the feast, and crowded on the raised sides, and on every roof, and at every window, with eager faces."

the temple] Jerusalem was crowded and stirred to to its very centre (Matt. xxi, 10). Who is this? His disciples answer: "*the prophet of Nazareth of Galilee*." They doubtless expected that he would, as he passed on towards the temple, display some unmistakeable "sign," and claim the sceptre, and ascend the throne of David. How sorely were they disappointed!

when he had looked round about upon all things] "The actual procession would not proceed further than the foot of Mount Moriah, beyond which they might not advance in travelling array, or with dusty feet." Before they reached the Shushan gate they dispersed, and Jesus entered the courts of the temple, examined the disorder and desecration still practiced, notwithstanding his former rebuke and cleansing. Some bring this visit on the 10th of Nisan, into connection with the selection of the paschal lamb, which was made on that day. Jesus was the true paschal lamb, giving a mystical significance to the fact. There is no discrepancy with Matthew or Luke here, as Meyer supposes; they connect the cleansing of the temple with the import of the entry, while Mark does not.

the eventide was come] or "it being now eventide" as in R.V.; an indefinite expression, including two or three hours before as well as after sunset. During it he returned to Bethany with the twelve.

PRACTICAL SUGGESTIONS.—"The Prince of Peace did not take a horse, a warlike animal; but he will ride on that by and by. Rev. xix, 11 ... Was it a mean attitude wherein our Lord then appeared? Mean even to contempt? I grant it; I glory in it; it is for the comfort of my soul, for the honor of his humility, and for the utter confusion of all worldly pomp and grandeur."—*Wesley*. "When Christians wake up, the people rejoice; while Christians slumber, the people will continue in the road to death. It is delightful to see people willing in the day of God's power. ... Not your garments he wants, but your hearts; not your willingness to rejoice in his light, but your fixed immovable purpose to be his forever."—*W. G. Schauffler*.

AUTHORIZED VERSION.	REVISED VERSION.
12 And on the morrow, when they were come from Bethany, he was hungry: 13 And seeing a fig tree afar off having leaves, he came, if haply he might find anything thereon: and when he came to it, he found nothing but leaves; for the time of figs was not yet. 14 And Jesus answered and said unto it, No	12 And on the morrow, when they were come out from Bethany, he hungered. And seeing a fig tree afar off having leaves, he came, if haply he might find anything thereon: and when he came to it, he found nothing but leaves; for it was not the season of figs. And he answered and said unto it, No man eat

12—26. THE FIG TREE AND THE CLEANSING OF THE TEMPLE, A. D. 30. (Monday, 11th Nisan, April 3d, A.D. 30.)

12. *he was hungry*] either after a night of fasting, or from rising very early and starting before the morning meal, he was hungry; shewing his humanity, as usual, when about to give a proof of his deity, that we may believe him to be both God and man."—*Bp. Wordsworth.*

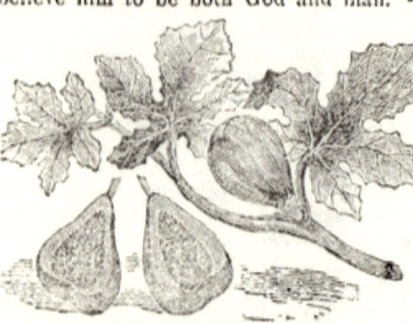

EASTERN FIGS.

13. *seeing a fig tree*] This was Monday, 11th Nisan, April 1st and 2d. The very name Bethany means "*the place for dates,*" while Bethphage, according to some, means "*the place for the green or winter fig.*"

having leaves] It stood alone, a single fig-tree, *by the wayside* (Matt. xxi, 19), having leaves was an indication of fruit, for the fig-tree puts forth its fruit first, and then its leaves, only when the fruit is about perfected.

if haply] or *if therefore, if as was reasonable to expect under such circumstances,* fruit was to be found. "Why should he who knows all, come if haply he might find (fruit) thereon" where there was none? It is not said he expected fruit; but he moved towards the tree as if fruit might be expected. The leaves were fitted to raise this expectation. He did this for the disciples' sake, exactly as in Luke xxiv, 28, "he made as though he would have gone further," not intending to go further, but to be constrained. He meant here to teach truth to the disciples, not to deceive (which is the essence of a lie), just as he did in his parables, where the form is fancy, but the substance is truth."—*John Hall, in Sunday School World.*

for the time of figs was not yet] that is the fig-season proper had not yet arrived. The rich verdure of this tree seemed to show that it was fruitful, and there was, as Farrar says, " every probability of finding upon it either the late violet-colored autumn figs, which often hung upon the trees all through the winter, and even until the new spring leaves had come, or the first-ripe figs (Isa. xxviii, 4; Jer. xxiv, 2; Hos. ix, 10; Nah. iii, 12), of which Orientals are particularly fond." But Prof. Post, of Beirut, advises me that fig-trees there have fruit formed as early as February, and which is fully ripe in April, about the time of the year when Jesus sought fruit on this tree near Jerusalem. This effectually disposes of the objections to this narrative, on the ground that figs could not be expected at this time of the year. The explanation proposed by Van Lennep and Heer are inconsistent with Mark's account, and are not required by what is now known of the growth of figs in Palestine. Yet this tree had nothing but leaves. It was the type of a fair profession without performance; a parable of the nation, which, with all its professions, brought forth no "fruit to perfection." Comp. Luke xix, 42.

14. *No man eat fruit*] "*And presently, i.e. immediately,*" writes Mat-

AUTHORIZED VERSION.	REVISED VERSION.
man eat fruit of thee hereafter for ever. And his disciples heard it.	fruit from thee henceforward forever. And his disciples heard it.
15 And they come to Jerusalem: and Jesus went into the temple, and began to cast out them that sold and bought in the temple, and overthrew the tables of the money changers, and the seats of them that sold doves;	15 And they come to Jerusalem; and he entered into the temple, and began to cast out them that sold and them that bought in the temple, and overthrew the tables of the money-changers, and the seats of them that sold the doves; and he would not suffer that any man should carry a vessel through the
16 And would not suffer that any man should carry any vessel through the temple.	16
17 And he taught, saying unto them, Is it not written, My house shall be called of all nations the house of prayer? but ye have made it a den of thieves.	17 temple. And he taught and said unto them, Is it not written, My house shall be called a house of prayer for all the nations? but ye

thew (xxi, 19), "the fig tree withered away," though the disciples did not notice it till the following morning. Thus our Lord exhibited at once a parable and a prophecy *in action*. This is the only miracle of judgment (or destruction) of Jesus on record; for the destruction of the swine was no miracle, but an incident following a miracle of mercy—the miracles of mercy were all in relief of suffering humanity; this one of judgment was upon a *tree*, to teach man a useful and important moral lesson.

15. *and Jesus went into the temple*] this was his second cleansing of the temple. The nefarious scene, which he had sternly rebuked at his first Passover, as noted by John (ii, 13—17), was still being enacted.

them that sold and bought] For the convenience of Jews and proselytes residing at a distance, a kind of market had been established in the outer court, and here sacrificial victims, incense, oil, wine and other things necessary for the service and sacrifices, were to be obtained. Jerome, regarding this cleansing of the temple as the most wonderful of miracles, supposes that a flame or starry ray darted from the eyes of the Saviour, but this is unwarranted by the narrative and unnecessary. The guilty feelings of the traders would make them cowards before an intrepid and wonderful rabbi, such as Jesus was held to be by the multitude.

the tables of the money changers] Money would be required (1) to purchase materials for offerings, (2) to present as free offerings to the temple treasury (Mark xii, 41; Luke xxi, 1), (3) to pay the yearly temple tax of half a shekel due from every Jew, however poor. All this must be paid in native coin called the temple shekel. Strangers, therefore, had to change their Roman, Greek, or Eastern, money into the coin required.

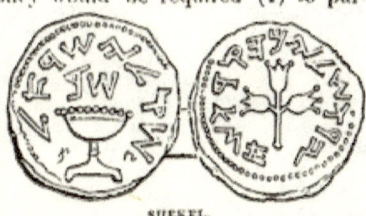

SHEKEL.

that sold doves[For the use of doves see Lev. xii. 6, 8; Luke ii, 24. The sale of doves appears to have been, in a great measure, in the hands of the priests themselves, and one of the high-priests especially is said to have gained great profits from his dovecots on Mount Olivet.

16. *any vessel*] *i. e.*, a pail or basket. Ellicott suggests that men were using the temple as a short cut from one part of the city to another. He would not allow laden porters and others to desecrate the honor due to his father's house by crossing the temple courts as though they were public streets.

17. *of all nations*] The words are cited from Isaiah lvi, 7.

a den of thieves] Literally, *a cave* or *den of robbers* or *bandits*. See Jer. vii, 11. The distinction is to be borne in mind between "the robber," brigand or violent spoiler (Matt. xxi, 13; xxvi, 55; Luke xxii, 52; John xviii,

AUTHORIZED VERSION.	REVISED VERSION.
18 And the scribes and chief priests heard *it*, and sought how they might destroy him: for they feared him, because all the people was astonished at his doctrine.	18 have made it a den of robbers. And the chief priests, and the scribes heard it, and sought how they might destroy him: for they feared him, for all the multitude was astonished at his teaching.
19 And when even was come, he went out of the city.	19 And ¹ every evening ² he went forth out of the city.
20 And in the morning, as they passed by, they saw the fig tree dried up from the roots.	20 And as they passed by in the morning, they saw the fig tree withered away from the roots.
21 And Peter calling to remembrance saith unto him, Master, behold, the fig tree which thou cursedst is withered away.	21 And Peter calling to remembrance saith unto him, Rabbi, behold, the fig tree which thou cursedst is withered away.
22 And Jesus answering saith unto them, Have faith in God.	22 And Jesus answering saith unto them, Have faith in God.
23 For verily I say unto you, That whosoever shall say unto this mountain, Be thou removed,	23 Verily I say unto you, Whosoever shall say unto this mountain, Be thou taken

¹ Gr. *whenever evening came.* ² Some ancient authorities read *they.*

40; 2 Cor. xi, 26; and the "thief" or secret purloiner (Matt. vi, 19; John xii, 6; 1 Thess. v, 2; Rev. iii, 3; xvi, 15).—*Trench.* What our Lord alludes to is one of "those foul caves which he had so often seen, where brigands wrangled over their ill-gotten gains."—*Farrar.* This cleansing was intended to point out to the Jews the corrupt and decayed character of their temple service, and that its fall, with that of the theocracy, had begun; that a spiritual reform was now at hand.

18. *chief priests*] This title was applied (1) to the high-priest properly so-called; (2) to all who had held the high-priesthood (the office under Roman sway no longer lasting for life, and becoming little more than annual); (3) the heads of the twenty-four courses (1 Chron. xxiv; Luke i, 9).

was astonished at his doctrine] Mark omits the healing of the lame man, and the children crying hosanna, as mentioned by Matthew, and which would tend to increase the fear of the officers and the astonishment of the people. Caution was therefore, essential.

19. *he went out*] or, *they went out,* of the city, as some MSS. read, and crossing Olivet, sought once more the retirement of Bethany.

20. *And in the morning*] the early morning of Tuesday, 12th Nisan, 783, or April 4th, A. D. 30.

as they passed by] on their return to the city.

dried up from the roots] in the original the word rendered "dried up" is the same as that rendered "withered away" in v. 21 of the A. V. From Matthew (xxi, 19) it would appear that "some beginnings of the threatened withering began to shew themselves, almost as soon as the word of the Lord was spoken; a shuddering fear may have run through all the leaves of the tree, which was thus stricken at its heart."—*Trench.*

21. *And Peter*] who, as some suppose, may have related the incident, with all its attendant circumstances, to Mark.

22. *Have faith in God*] as the personal source of miraculous power (Comp Matt. xvii, 20: Luke xvii, 6). "Faith is not sense, nor sight, nor reason, but a-taking God at his word."—*Evans.* "Faith makes invisible things visible, absent things present, things that are very far off to be very near the soul."—*Brooks.* Dr. Dwight defined *faith* as trust or confidence. A. Alexander says, "Faith is simply *a belief of the truth*, apprehended under the illumination of the Holy Spirit."

23. *verily I say unto you*] Jesus, by these words, would impress upon them that an unfaltering faith in God would overcome all difficulties, a truth they would be likely to recall when they began the work of spreading the gospel.

shall say unto this mountain] Language like this was familiar in the schools

AUTHORIZED VERSION.	REVISED VERSION.
and be thou cast into the sea; and shall not doubt in his heart, but shall believe that those things which he saith shall come to pass; he shall have whatsoever he saith. 24 Therefore I say unto you, What things soever ye desire, when ye pray, believe that ye receive *them*, and ye shall have *them*. 25 And when ye stand praying, forgive, if ye have aught against any: that your Father also which is in heaven may forgive you your trespasses. 26 But if ye do not forgive, neither will your Father which is in heaven forgive your trespasses.	up and cast into the sea; and shall not doubt in his heart, but shall believe that what he 24 saith cometh to pass; he shall have it. Therefore I say unto you, All things whatsoever ye pray and ask for, believe that ye have re- 25 ceived them, and ye shall have them. And whensoever ye stand praying, forgive, if ye have aught against any one; that your Father also which is in heaven may forgive you your trespasses.¹

¹ Many ancient authorities add ver. 26 *But if ye do not forgive, neither will your Father which is in heaven forgive your trespasses.*

of the Jews. They used to set out those teachers among them, that were more eminent for the profoundness of their learning or the splendor of their virtues, by such expressions as these: " He is a *rooter up* or *remover of mountains.*" " They called Rabbah Bar Nachmani, *a rooter up of mountains,* because he had a piercing judgment."—*Lightfoot.*

shall not doubt in his heart] The word here translated " doubt " means (1) *to discriminate, distinguish, discern,* as Matt. xvi, 3; Acts xv, 9; 1 Cor. xi, 29; (2) in the passive and middle voice, *to get a decision, go to law, to dispute,* as Acts xi, 2; James ii, 4. Poole observes: " It is not possible to pray with full persuasion that we shall receive, without being first satisfied that what we ask is according to the will of God. This we cannot know without a divine revelation."

24. *What things soever ye desire when ye pray*] " It is obvious that, as a rule, such words imply prayer for spiritual rather than temporal blessings." —*Ellicott.* Because *prayer* is the very language of *faith,* he passes on to speak concerning prayer. For " have received " the American revisers read " receive," with marginal reading " received."

25. *when ye stand praying*] The posture of prayer among the Jews seems to have been most often *standing:* comp. the instance of Hannah (1 Sam. i, 26), and of the Pharisee (Luke xviii, 11). When the prayer was offered with especial solemnity and humiliation, this was naturally expressed by (*a*) *kneeling*; comp. the instance of Solomon (1 Kings viii, 54), and Daniel (vi, 10); or (*b*) *prostration,* as Joshua (vii, 6), and Elijah (1Kings xviii, 42).

forgive] Faith in God would lead to godlikeness, one of the characteristics of it being forgiveness. We are not to forgive *to merit* forgiveness, but as a *condition* of receiving it. The *ground* of our forgiveness is in Christ's sacrifice for us; the condition required in us is the spirit which will forgive others; so we may receive forgiveness.

26. *your trespasses*] The original word thus translated denotes (1) *a falling beside, a falling from the right way.* This verse is not found in some of the best authorities. MSS. A. C. D. and Alford and Lachmann retain it in the text. The authorities do not seem to be strong enough against it to warrant its rejection, though the R. V. places it in the margin.

PRACTICAL LESSONS.—Fruitless; " so men and women join the church, promise to be faithful in every *good word* or work. When they are selfish, false, proud, greedy of gain or applause; when they cheat or deceive or *lie* in any way, when they are parse-proud or mean; when they shirk the burdens they ought to share; when they are fair outside and vile and hollow within; when they are smooth to the world and a torment at home, they have their symbol in this tree, " nothing but leaves!"—*John Hall, in S. S. W.* " No

AUTHORIZED VERSION.	REVISED VERSION.
27 And they come again to Jerusalem: and as he was walking in the temple, there come to him the chief priests, and the scribes, and the elders. 28 And say unto him, By what authority doest thou these things? and who gave thee this authority to do these things? 29 And Jesus answered and said unto them, I will also ask of you one question, and answer me, and I will tell you by what authority I do these things. 30 The baptism of John, was it from heaven, or of men? answer me. 31 And they reasoned with themselves, saying, If we shall say, From heaven; he will say, Why then did ye not believe him? 32 But if we shall say, Of men; they feared the people: for all men counted John, that he was a prophet indeed.	27 And they come again to Jerusalem: and as he was walking in the temple, there come to him the chief priests, and the scribes, and 28 the elders; and they said unto him, By what authority doest thou these things? or who gave thee this authority to do these things? 29 And Jesus said unto them, I will ask of you one [1] question, and answer me, and I will tell you by what authority I do these things. 30 The baptism of John, was it from heaven, or 31 from men? answer me. And they reasoned with themselves, saying, If we shall say, From heaven; he will say, Why then did ye 32 not believe him? [2] But should we say, From men—they feared the people: [3] for all verily

[1] Gr. *word*. [2] Or, *But shall we say, From men?* [3] Or, *for all held John to be a prophet indeed.*

physical barrier can resist the power of a divinely grounded and inspired faith. Mountains of sin, mountains of opposition, mountains of distress and misfortune, have often been removed by faith."—*Vincent.* What multitudes carry their business, their toils, their plans, their accounts, the implements of worldly toil, in thought into the sanctuary now, and, with all these distractions, attempt to worship God!

27-33. QUESTION RESPECTING JOHN THE BAPTIST.

27. *as he was walking*] (Tuesday, 12th Nisan). This is in keeping with Mark's vivid style of delineation. Again the scribes assail Christ's work.

elders] "eldere men."—*Wyclif.* The ancient representatives of the people. Elders acted in concert as a political body in the time of the Exodus (Ex. xix, 7; Deut. xxxi. 9). They exercised authority under (*a*) the judges (Judg. ii, 7; 1 Sam. iv, 3); under (*b*) the kings (1 Sam. xxx, 26; 1 Chron. xxi, 16; 2 Sam. xvii, 4); during (*c*) the captivity (Jer. xxix, 1; Ezek. viii, 1); (*d*) after the return (Ezra v, 5; vi, 7, 14; x, 8, 14); under (*e*) the Maccabees (1 Macc. xii, 6; 2 Macc. i, 10); (*f*) in the time of our Lord they were apparently *ex-officio* members of a local Sanhedrin, with other members. This is by no means certain, however, though some hold that they formed a distinct portion of the Sanhedrin by election.

28. *By what authority doest thou these things?*] From the reading of the R. V. two questions were asked: (1) Had he an inherent and general authority? or (2) did he claim some special authority? An answer to either might lay him open to a charge and trial, in which they could condemn him.

29. *And Jesus answered*] he answered their question by another, and so avoided the trap. " Before men we stand as opaque beehives. They can see the thoughts go in and out of us, but what work they do inside of a man, they cannot tell. Before God we are as *glass* beehives, and all that our thoughts are doing within us he perfectly sees and understands."—*Beecher.*

30. *The baptism of John*] The baptism evidently included his ministry also. John had distinctly testified to the Messianic authority of our Lord (John i, 29-34, 36): from whom did *he* receive *his* commission to baptize and to teach? Was it from heaven or a mere assumption of his own?

32. *if we shall say, Of men*] Observe the impressive hiatus (see R. V.), which is more significant than the full expression of Matthew (xxi. 26) and Luke (xx, 6). They dared not face the alternative, and were driven to a weak and evasive reply.

AUTHORIZED VERSION.	REVISED VERSION.
33 And they answered and said unto Jesus, We cannot tell. And Jesus answering saith unto them, Neither do I tell you by what authority I do these things. CHAP. XII.—And he began to speak unto them by parables. A *certain* man planted a vineyard, and set a hedge about *it*, and digged *a place for* the winefat, and built a tower, and	33 held John to be a prophet. And they answered Jesus and say, We know not. And Jesus saith unto them, Neither tell I you by what authority I do these things. 12 And he began to speak unto them in parables. A man planted a vineyard, and set a hedge about it, and digged a pit for the wine-

33. *Neither do I tell you*] The counter-question of Jesus was the consequence of the question of these men. "Him that inquires we are bound to instruct, but him that tempts we may defeat with a stroke of reasoning."

PRACTICAL SUGGESTIONS.—"Let us learn that every one should do his own duty or else yield up his place to another. Let us not be like the dog in the manger, who would neither eat the hay himself nor allow the ox to eat it."—*Brentius*. "The history of the church of Christ contains only too much of the dog in the manger. Ministers and teachers have often neglected the souls of their people shamefully, yet found fault with any who has tried to do good, and haughtily demanded his authority."—*Ryle*. Aug. Quesnel, a Roman Catholic writer, says: "There are no persons more forward to demand of others a reason for their actions than those who think they may do everything themselves without control."

CH. XII. 1—12. THE WICKED HUSBANDMEN.

(The discourses and events in this chapter are assigned to Tuesday, 12th Nisan, 783. April 4th. A. D., 30.)

1. *by parables*] He spoke three parables, (1) the two sons Matt. xxi, 28—32; (2) the husbandmen; (3) the marriage of the king's son, Matt. xxii, 1—14. Mark relates only the second of these three parables. The *began* implies an interruption since a former series of parables. This mode of teaching is now again resumed, and another series of parables is spoken.

A certain man planted a vineyard] This parable resembles the thought of the prophet Isaiah (v, 1—7). Comp. Deut. xxxii, 32; Ps. lxxx, 8—16; Ezek. xv, 1—6; Hos. x. 1. By the vineyard we understand the kingdom of God as successfully realized (1) by the Jew, and (2) by the Gentile. See *Trench*. In the parable of the two sons, Jesus had shown how he was received by the publicans, and rejected by the rulers: in this of the husbandmen, he shows how he is to be rejected by God's chosen people Israel, and put to death. (See illustration of Vineyard, p. 129).

planted] The householder possessed and "*planted*" the vineyard. So God *planted* his spiritual vineyard under Moses (Deut. xxxii, 12—14; Ex. xv. 17), and Joshua in the land of Canaan.

a hedge about it] not a hedge of thorns, but a stone wall to keep out wild boars (Ps. lxxx, 13), jackals and foxes (Num. xxii. 24; Cant. ii. 15; Neh. iv, 3). The word occurs (1) here, (2) in the parallel Matt. xxi.33, (3) in Luke xiv, 23, "go ye into the highways and *hedges*," and (4) Eph. ii. 14; "the middle *wall of partition*." "Enclosures of loose stone, like the walls of fields in Derbyshire or Westmoreland, in England, everywhere catch the eye on the bare slopes of Hebron, of Bethlehem, and of Olivet."—*Stanley*.

a place for the wine-fat] "dalf a lake." *Wyclif*. The original word only occurs here in the N. T., and is equivalent to the Latin *lacus*. The winepress, = *torcular* (Matt. xxi, 33), consisted of two parts; (1) the press (*gath*) or trough above, in which the grapes were placed, and there trodden by the feet of several persons amidst singing and other expressions of joy (Judg. ix, 27; Isaiah xvi. 10; Jer. xxv.30); (2) a smaller trough (*yekeb*),into which the expressed juice flowed through a hole or spout (Neh. xiii, 15; Isai.

AUTHORIZED VERSION.	REVISED VERSION.
let it out to husbandmen, and went into a far country. 2 And at the season he sent to the husbandmen a servant, that he might receive from the husbandmen of the fruit of the vineyard. 3 And they caught him, and beat him, and sent him away empty.	press, and built a tower, and let it out to husbandmen, and went into another country. 2 And at the season he sent to the husbandmen a ¹ servant, that he might receive from the husbandmen of the fruits of the vineyard. 3 And they took him, and beat him, and

¹ Gr. *bond-servant*

lxiii, 2; Lam. i, 15). Here the smaller trough, which was often hollowed ("digged") out of the earth or native rock and then lined with masonry, is put for the whole apparatus, and is called a *wine*-FAT, or wine-press; Robinson saw a wine-press at Hebleh, near ancient Antipatris, which had been hewn out of a rock. There were two parts to the press, an upper and shallow one, in which the grapes were put for pressing, and a lower and deeper place to receive the juice from the pressed grapes. *Fat* from A.S. fæt = a vessel, vat, according to the modern spelling. Comp. Shakespeare, *Ant. and Cleop.* ii, 7. 120:

> "Come thou monarch of the vine,
> Plumpie Bacchus, with pink eyne;
> In thy *fattes* our cares be drown'd."

and built a tower] *i.e.* a "tower of the watchman," rendered *cottage* in Isaiah i, 8, xxiv, 20. Here the watchers and vine-dressers lived (Isaiah v, 2), and frequently with slings, scared away wild animals and robbers. At the corner of each enclosure "rises its square gray towers, at first sight hardly distinguishable from the ruins of ancient churches or fortresses, which lie equally scattered over the hills of Judæa."—*Stanley.*

to husbandmen] by these, Trench understands the spiritual leaders and teachers of the Jewish nation (Mal. ii, 7; Ezek. xxxiv, 2) are intended. Their land, secluded and yet central, was hedged round on the east by the river Jordan, on the south by the desert of Idumæa, on the west by the sea, on the north by Libanus and Anti-Libanus, while they themselves were separated by the law from the Gentiles and idolatrous nations around." This would agree with Isaiah's figure, but not with Matt. xxi, 43, where the husbandman, as Dean Mansel observes, seems to refer to the Jewish nation, in contrast with the nation to which the vineyard would be given. Isaiah also speaks of a vineyard of 1000 vines, renting for 1000 silverlings, or shekels, equal to about $500. See Is. vii, 23.

went into a far country] This is too strong for the Greek; See R. V.; "*for a long while,*" adds Luke, or "*many times.*" "At Sinai, when the theocratic constitution was founded, and in the miracles which accompanied the deliverance from Egypt, the Lord may be said to have openly manifested himself to Israel; but then to have withdrawn himself again for awhile, not speaking to the people again face to face (Deut. xxxiv, 10—12), but waiting in patience to see what the law would effect, and what manner of works the people under the teaching of their spiritual guides, would bring forth."—*Trench.*

2. *at the season*] *i.e.* when the fruit season drew near.

a servant] so Luke xx, 10; *his servants,* Matt. xxi, 34; the prophets and other messengers of God.

of the fruit] the rent not being paid in money, a stipulated portion of the produce was to be given, according to the well-known *metayer* system once prevalent over great part of Europe. So prophets were sent to the people from time to time to require of them repentance and righteousness."

3. *they caught him*] the increased character of the outrages is clearly noted: (1) beating; (2) trying to kill; (3) killing—first one of their servants and then the son. Compare the confession of the Levites in Neh. ix, 26.

AUTHORIZED VERSION.

4 And again he sent unto them another servant; and at him they cast stones, and wounded *him* in the head, and sent *him* away shamefully handled.
5 And again he sent another, and him they killed, and many others; beating some and killing some.
6 Having yet therefore one son, his well-beloved, he sent him also last unto them, saying, They will reverence my son.
7 But those husbandmen said among themselves, This is the heir; come, let us kill him, and the inheritance shall be ours.
8 And they took him, and killed *him*, and cast *him* out of the vineyard.
9 What shall therefore the lord of the vineyard do? he will come and destroy the husbandmen, and will give the vineyard unto others.
10 And have ye not read this scripture; The

REVISED VERSION.

4 sent him away empty. And again he sent unto them another [1] servant; and him they wounded in the head, and handled shamefully.
5 fully. And he sent another; and him they killed: and many others; beating some, and
6 killing some. He had yet one, a beloved son; he sent him last unto them, saying,
7 They will reverence my son. But those husbandmen said among themselves, This is the heir; come, let us kill him, and the inheritance shall be ours. And they took him, and
8 killed him, and cast him forth out of the vineyard. What therefore will the lord of the
9 vineyard do? he will come and destroy the husbandmen, and will give the vineyard unto others. Have ye not read even this scripture;

[1] Gr. *bond-servant*

4. *wounded him in the head*] The original word, which generally denotes to *comprehend in one sum, or under one head,* is nowhere else used in this sense. Some MSS. omit "they cast stones" and after wounded him, read "handled shamefully." See R.V. The third servant is killed. The treatment of these three, was a fair specimen of the general treatment given to all the owner's messengers, and also a fair illustration of the manner in which Jehovah's messengers had been treated.

6. *Having yet therefore*] not only was he his son, but his *only one*, his *well-beloved*, "a sone most dereworth."—*Wyclif.* This marks as strongly as possible the difference of rank between Christ and the prophets.

7. *This is the heir*] "he for whom the inheritance is meant, and to whom it will in due course rightfully arrive, not as in earthly relations, by the death, but by the free appointment of the actual possessor." Christ is "heir of all things," not as he is the Son of God, but as he is the son of man. This is the main point in the parable, and intended to bring home to the Jewish rulers their sin in rejecting Christ.

come, let us kill him] Comp. Gen. xxxvii, 20; and especially John xi, 47–53, where "the servants" conspiring against "the heir of all things" actually assign as their motive that "if they let him alone," they "will lose both their place and nation."

8. *and killed him and cast him out of the vineyard*] The order is reversed in the first and third Gospels, which remind us of Naboth, whom they "carried forth *out of the city*, and stoned him with stones that he died" (1 Kings xxi, 13), and of him, who *suffered without the gate* (Heb. xiii, 12, 13; John xix, 17). Here they first kill the son, and then fling forth the body and deny it the ordinary rites of sepulture.

9. *he will come*] According to Matthew, this was the answer of the Pharisees themselves, either before they were aware, pronouncing sentence against themselves, or pretending, in the hardness of their hearts, not to see the drift of the parable. The answer was followed by "a deep God forbid" from several voices (Luke xx. 16). Some attempt to attach a spiritual meaning to every detail of the parable : *e. g.*, "the hedge" is "the middle wall of partition:" the "wine-press" is the services, ordinances, etc.; the tower, the office of the watchman, and so on. Such interpretations are fanciful and often misleading. These minor details are only incidental parts of the picture, to hold and exhibit the main teaching of the parable.

10. *have ye not read*] referring them to Psalm cxviii, 22, 23, a psalm

AUTHORIZED VERSION.	REVISED VERSION.
stone which the builders rejected is become the head of the corner: 11 This was the Lord's doing, and it is marvellous in our eyes? 12 And they sought to lay hold on him, but feared the people: for they knew that he had spoken the parable against them: and they left him, and went their way. 13 And they send unto him certain of the	The stone which the builders rejected, the same was made the head of the corner: 11 This was from the Lord, And it is marvellous in our eyes? 12 And they sought to lay hold on him; and they feared the multitude; for they perceived that he spake the parable against them: and they left him, and went away. 13 And they send unto him certain of the

which the Jews applied to the Messiah, and which is actually twice applied to him by Peter in Acts iv, 11 ; 1 Peter ii, 7.

the head of the corner] this does not refer to the top stone, but the main stone in the foundation, at the corner. The image of the vineyard is for a moment abandoned for that of a building. The "head of the corner" was a large and massive stone, so formed that when placed at a corner, it bound together the two outer walls of an edifice. There is no propriety in straining it to apply to the union of the Jews and Gentiles in the covenant of grace, though the corner-stone may have joined the two walls of a building. Comp. for the application of the expression to Christ, Eph. ii, 20, and consult Isaiah xxviii, 16 ; Dan. ii, 45. The penalties of rejecting him are more fully brought out in Matt. xxi, 43, 44 : Luke xx, 18.

12. *they sought*] The three evangelists supplement each other in this portion of the history. All note the purpose to seize Jesus ; Luke says the scribes sought to do it at once, but were afraid of the people (Luke xx, 19). Mark notes that they continued these efforts, and Matthew that they were thwarted because the multitude held him to be a prophet (xxi, 46). "Thus within a few hours of crucifixion, and conscious of the fact ; in the intervals of the mortal contest with the whole forces of the past and present, the wandering Galilean teacher, meek and lowly in spirit, so that the poorest and the youngest instinctively sought him ; full of divine pity, so that the most sunken and hopeless of penitents felt he was their friend ; indifferent to the supports of influence, wealth or numbers ; alone and poor, the very embodiment of weakness, as regards all visible help, he still bore himself with a serene dignity more than human. In the name of God he transfers the spiritual glory of Israel to his own followers ; throws down the barriers of caste and nationality ; extends the new dominion, of which he is head, to all races and through all ages, here and hereafter ; predicts the divine wrath on his enemies in this world, as the enemies of God, and announces the decision of the final judgment as turning on the attitude of men *toward himself and his message.*"—Condensed from *Geikie and Liddon.*

PRACTICAL LESSONS.—" Christ only means that, while God appoints pastors over his church, he does not convey his right to others, but acts in the same manner as if a proprietor were to let his vineyard to a husbandman, ... who would make annual return."—*Calvin.* The parable is a pictorial history of his dealing with Israel, and their treatment of his messengers and his Son. "If some from whom we expected well proved bad, it does not follow but that others will be better."—*Henry.* Ryle suggests that the man planting the vineyard refers to God ; the vineyard was the Jewish church ; the servants the prophets, and the son was Christ.

13—17. THE TRIBUTE MONEY, A. D. 30.

13. *And they send*] Mark does not notice the private council of the Pharisees and the spies (Matt. xxii, 15 ; Luke xx, 20), but mentions the two parties, Herodians and Pharisees. Having failed themselves, the Jewish authorities resolved to send some of the Pharisees, in company with the He-

AUTHORIZED VERSION.	REVISED VERSION.
Pharisees and of the Herodians, to catch him in his words. 14 And when they were come, they say unto him, Master, we know that thou art true, and carest for no man: for thou regardest not the person of men, but teachest the way of God in truth: Is it lawful to give tribute to Cæsar, or not? 15 Shall we give, or shall we not give? But he, knowing their hypocrisy, said unto them, Why tempt ye me? bring me a penny, that I may see it. 16 And they brought it. And he saith unto them, Whose is this image and superscription? And they said unto him, Cæsar's.	Pharisees and of the Herodians, that they might catch him in talk. 14 And when they were come, they say unto him, ¹ Master, we know that thou art true, and carest not for any one: for thou regardest not the person of men, but of a truth teachest the way of God: Is it lawful to give tribute unto Cæsar, or not? Shall we give, or shall we not give? But he, knowing their hypocrisy, said unto them, Why tempt ye me? bring 16 me a ² penny, that I may see it. And they brought it. And he saith unto them, Whose is this image and superscription? And they

¹ Or, *Teacher* ² See marginal note on Matt. xviii. 28, [quoted on page 82.]

rodians, to entrap him with their treacherous questions. Three distinct attacks were made: (1) by the Pharisees, on paying tribute to Cæsar; (2) by the Sadducees, on the resurrection; (3) by the scribes, on which was the greatest commandment, a question disputed then in the schools.

the Herodians] See note on ch. iii. 6. As before, so now, the Jewish royalists united themselves with the ultra-orthodox Pharisaic party. The Herodians came *in person*. The Pharisees sent *some of their younger scholars* (Matt. xxii. 16) to approach him with the pretended simplicity of a guileless spirit, and a desire to solve a perplexing question (Luke xx. 20).

to catch him] as a bird is caught in fowling.

14. *Master, we know*] This was said in a spirit of hypocritical flattery, as though they were ready to pay him honor as the Messiah. We find Nicodemus saying the same thing in a spirit of sincerity (John iii. 2).

and carest for no man] This was a cunning temptation to lift himself above all respect for the Roman authorities.

Is it lawful to give tribute?] Some Galilean Pharisees opposed this tax with special bitterness about this time. The snare was no longer laid in the sphere of ecclesiastical questions, but in the more dangerous area of political duty. The tribute-money alluded to was a capitation tax levied by the Roman government, and keenly resented by Judas of Galilee (Acts v. 37) and his followers. " If he said no, the Herodians might represent him an enemy to Cæsar; if he said yea, the Pharisees might represent him to the people as no friend to the nation."—*Whitby*. "Nothing is more likely to ensnare ministers," says the wise Matthew Henry, "than bringing them to meddle with controversies about civil rights, and to settle landmarks between prince and subjects."

15. *knowing their hypocrisy*] "It was with a *show* of truth they spoke." —*Bengel*. The American revisers read "try" or "make trial of me," in place of "tempt me."

bring me] "As if he had said, 'What! are you required to pay taxes to Romans? And in what coin? Let me see one.'"—*Alexander*. "They would not be likely to carry with them the hated Roman coinage, with its heathen symbols, though they might have been at once able to produce from their girdles the temple shekel. But they would only have to step outside the court of the Gentiles and borrow from the money-changer's tables a current Roman coin."—*Farrar*.

a penny] literally, *a denarius*, worth about 16 or 17 cents. The American revisers would transfer, not translate, the name of this coin, and read "a denarius" instead of "a penny."

16. *Whose is this image*] and superscription or other "inscription."

AUTHORIZED VERSION.	REVISED VERSION.
17 And Jesus answering said unto them, Render to Cæsar the things that are Cæsar's, and to God the things that are God's. And they marvelled at him.	17 said unto him, Cæsar's. And Jesus said unto them, Render unto Cæsar the things that are Cæsar's, and unto God the things that are God's. And there marvelled greatly at him.
18 Then come unto him the Sadducees, which say there is no resurrection; and they asked him, saying,	18 And there come unto him Sadducees, which say that there is no resurrection; and
19 Master, Moses wrote unto us, If a man's brother die, and leave his wife behind him, and leave no children, that his brother should take his wife, and raise up seed unto his brother.	19 they asked him, saying, ¹Master, Moses wrote unto us, If a man's brother die, and leave a wife behind him, and leave no child, that his brother should take his wife, and
20 Now there were seven brethren: and the first took a wife, and dying left no seed.	20 raise up seed unto his brother. There were seven brethren: and the first took a wife,
21 And the second took her, and died, neither left he any seed: and the third likewise.	21 and dying left no seed; and the second took her, and died, leaving no seed behind him;
22 And the seven had her, and left no seed: last of all the woman died also.	22 and the third likewise: and the seven left no seed. Last of all the woman also died.

¹ Or, Teacher

It was Tiberius Cæsar who was then reigning. Cæsar was a common name applied to many Roman emperors, beginning with Julius Cæsar. "The little silver coin, bearing on its surface the head encircled with a wreath of laurel, and bound round with the sacred fillet—the well known features, the most beautiful and the most wicked, even in outward expression, of all the Roman emperors, with the superscription running round, in the stately language of imperial Rome, '*Tiberius Cæsar, Divi Augusti filius Augustus Imperator.*' The image of the Emperor would be regarded by the stricter Jews as idolatrous, and to spare their feelings, the Romans had allowed a special coinage to be struck for Judea, without any likeness upon it, and only the name of the Emperor, and such Jewish emblems as palms, lilies, grapes, and censors." But it was the first and the hated coin which was handed to Jesus. See Geikie.

17. *Render*] literally, *Give back as being due.* "Therefore *zelde ze* to Cæsar."—*Wyclif.* It was not a question of a *voluntary gift*, but of a *legal due.* The head of the emperor on the coin, the legend round it, and its circulation in the country, were undeniable proofs of the right of the actually existing government to levy the tax.

and to God] "Render unto Cæsar all that he can lawfully demand, but render also to God what he requires of you as his spiritual subjects." "Give to God that which has the image and superscription of God, the soul."—*Erasmus.* "Man is the carriage" says Alford, "and bears the image of God. We owe *ourselves* to God."... The answer also gives them the real reason why they were now under subjection to Cæsar, namely: because they had fallen from their allegiance to God.

they marvelled at him] "No wonder; the answer of Christ is the wisest ever given to an entangling question, and contains in principle the solution of the great problem of church and state."—*Schaff.*

18–27. THE SADDUCEES AND THE RESURRECTION.

18. *Sadducees*] hitherto the Sadducees, "few, rich and dignified," had stood aloof, and affected to ignore the disciples of the despised "prophet of Nazareth." They were the materialists of their day.

19. *Moses wrote*] the law concerning the Levirate marriage is found in Deut. xxv, 5. It was ordained for the preservation of families, that if a man died without male issue, his brother should marry his widow, and that the first-born son should be held in the registers to be the son of the dead brother.

20. *there were seven brethren*] it was probably a fictitious case, but a probable one, even though the Jews were averse to fulfilling the enactment at all. They no doubt made the case as difficult as possible, though not ludicrous, as some suppose. It may have been founded on the case of Sara,

AUTHORIZED VERSION.	REVISED VERSION.
23 In the resurrection therefore, when they shall rise, whose wife shall she be of them? for the seven had her to wife. 24 And Jesus answering said unto them, Do ye not therefore err, because ye know not the scriptures, neither the power of God? 25 For when they shall rise from the dead, they neither marry, nor are given in marriage; but are as the angels which are in heaven. 26 And as touching the dead, that they rise; have ye not read, in the book of Moses, how in the bush God spake unto him, saying, I am the God of Abraham and the God of Isaac, and the God of Jacob?	23 In the resurrection whose wife shall she be 24 of them? for the seven had her to wife. Jesus said unto them, Is it not for this cause that ye err, that ye know not the scriptures, 25 nor the power of God? For when they shall rise from the dead, they neither marry, nor are given in marriage; but are as angels in 26 heaven. But as touching the dead, that they are raised; have ye not read in the book of Moses, *in the place concerning* the Bush, how God spake unto him, saying, I *am* the God of

recorded in the apocryphal book of Tobit (iii, 7, 8): "Sara, the daughter of Raguel, was also reproached by her father's maids, because she had been married to seven husbands."

23. *In the resurrection ...when they shall rise*] when the wife and her seven husbands shall rise. In v. 25 there is reference to *all* that arise. The Sadducees erroneously conjectured, that if there be a resurrection, the same relations must continue, as here. They did not ask the question to gain a solution, but to puzzle and entrap Jesus, and find ground for an accusation. Jesus solves their question, and, in doing it, condemns their creed, which denied a resurrection and a future life.

24. *ye know not*] our Lord traces their error to ignorance (1) of the Scriptures, and (2) of the power of God. He deals with the latter first.

25. *when they shall rise*] had they known the power of God they could not have imagined that it was limited by death, or that the life of "the children of the resurrection" was a mere repetition of man's present mortal existence. Compare the argument of Paul in 1 Cor. xv, 39-44.

as the angels] as the Sadducees denied the resurrection and the existence of angels and spirits (Acts xxiii, 8), the reply embraces the whole area of their unbelief. Jesus refers to the angels in heaven as persons whose personal existence was a fact. Moreover, in these words we have one of the few revelations which he was pleased to make as to the state after death. They imply that, as Paul teaches, at the resurrection "*we shall be changed*" (1 Cor. xv, 44), and the "*spiritual body*" will not be liable to the passions of the "*natural body*." This reply of the Lord made a deep impression on the Jewish mind. Keim and others claim that it has been substantially adopted in a Jewish treatise on the resurrection.

26. *in the book of Moses*] they had brought forward the name of *Moses* to perplex *him*. He now appeals to the same great name in order to confute *them*. Not that they rejected the authority of other portions of the O. T., as earlier and a few late critics have erroneously held; for he does not reprove the Sadducees for attaching a higher importance to the Pentateuch than to the prophets, but for not perceiving important teaching on the resurrection even *there*. The argument is an irresistible one.

in the bush] *i. e.*, in the section of the Book of Exodus (iii, 6) called "*the bush*." Similarly "*the lament of David over Saul and Jonathan*" in 2 Sam. i, 17-27 was called "*the bow;*" and Ezekiel i, 15-28, "*the chariot.*" Compare also Rom. xi, 2; "in Elias" = *the section concerning Elias*. In the Koran the chapters are named after the matter they contain, and Homer is often thus cited by ancient writers. Wyclif alone of our English translators gives the right meaning, "Han ze not rad in the book of Moyses *on the bousche*, how God seide to him."

God spake unto him, saying] God had revealed himself to Moses *as a personal God*, by the august and touching title of "*the God of Abraham, and*

AUTHORIZED VERSION.	REVISED VERSION.
27 He is not the God of the dead, but the God of the living: ye therefore do greatly err. 28 And one of the scribes came, and having heard them reasoning together, and perceiving that he had answered them well, asked him, Which is the first commandment of all?	Abraham, and the God of Isaac, and the God 27 of Jacob? He is not the God of the dead, but of the living: ye do greatly err. 28 And one of the scribes came, and heard them questioning together, and knowing that he had answered them well, asked him,

the God of Isaac, and the God of Jacob," and, therefore, as bearing a *personal relation* to these patriarchs. How unworthy would such a title be, if he, the Eternal and Unchangeable, had revealed himself only as the God of men who had long since crumbled into dust and passed away into annihilation!

27. *He is not the God of the dead*] *i. e.*, not the God of non-existent beings, as their theory would require. If the patriarchs were annihilated (dead), then it might be said, "God *was* their God," *i. e.*, when they were alive; but not "*is* their God," since they were not in existence any longer.

but the God of the living] the patriarchs, therefore, though their bodies were dead, must themselves have been still living in the separate state, and awaiting the resurrection when God made this declaration. Stier suggests that this passage is opposed to the "sleep of the soul" during or in an intermediate state. "It is absurd to think that God's relation to Abraham should be continued, and thus solemnly recognized, if Abraham was annihilated... Therefore you must conclude (1) that Abraham's soul exists separate from the body; (2) that, therefore, the body must rise again."—*M. Henry.*

PRACTICAL THOUGHTS.—On this question of the resurrection Hugh Miller observes: "Passing on to the revealed record, we learn that the dynasty of man in the mixed state and character is not a final one; but there is yet to be another creation or re-creation, known theologically as the resurrection, which shall be connected in its physical components, by bonds of mysterious paternity, with the dynasty that now reigns, and be bound to it mentally by a chain of identity, conscious and actual; but which, in all that constitutes superiority, shall be as vastly its superior as the dynasty of responsible man is superior to even the lowest of the preliminary dynasties [of brute creation]. We are further taught that at the commencement of this last of the dynasties there will be a re-creation of not only elevated, but also of degraded beings—a re-creation of the lost."

28—34. THE QUESTION OF THE SCRIBE.

28. *one of the scribes*] From Matt. xxii, 34, 35, it appears that he was a Pharisee and a master of the law. He seems to have heard the dispute and joined in it to aid in entrapping Christ. He was pleased to see the Sadducees overthrown, but he was ready to show his superior skill.

Which is the first commandment of all] that is, first in importance. On this question the schools of Hillel and Shammai were disagreed. The lawyer asked it, tempting our Lord (Matt. xxii, 35), hoping that he would commit himself as an enemy of tradition. The rabbinical schools taught that there were important distinctions between the commandments, some being great and others small, some hard and weighty, others easy and of less importance. Great commands were the observance of the sabbath, circumcision, minute rites of sacrifice and offering, the rules respecting fringes and phylacteries. They belittled the ceremonial and moral law, which they pretended to weigh and classify, concluding that there were "248 affirmative precepts, being as many as the members in the human body, and 365 negative precepts, being as many as the arteries and veins, or the days of the year; the total number being 613, which was also the number of the letters in the Decalogue."

AUTHORIZED VERSION.	REVISED VERSION.
29 And Jesus answered him, The first of all the commandments is, Hear, O Israel; The Lord our God is one Lord: 30 And thou shalt love the Lord thy God with all thy heart, and with all thy soul, and with all thy mind, and with all thy strength: this is the first commandment. 31 And the second is like, namely this, Thou shalt love thy neighbour as thyself. There is none other commandment greater than these. 32 And the scribe said unto him, Well, Master, thou hast said the truth: for there is one God; and there is none other but he: 33 And to love him with all the heart, and with all the understanding, and with all the soul, and with all the strength, and to love his neighbour as himself, is more than all whole burnt offerings and sacrifices. 34 And when Jesus saw that he answered discreetly, he said unto him, Thou art not far from	29 What commandment is the first of all? Jesus answered, The first is, Hear, O Israel; 30 ¹ The Lord our God, the Lord is one: and thou shalt love the Lord thy God ² with all thy heart, and ² with all thy soul, and ² with all thy mind, and ² with all thy strength. 31 The second is this, Thou shalt love thy neighbour as thyself. There is none other commandment greater than these. And the scribe said unto him, of a truth. ³ Master, thou hast well said that he is one; and there 33 is none other but he: and to love him with all the heart, and with all the understanding, and with all the strength, and to love his neighbour as himself, is much more than all 34 whole burnt, offerings and sacrifices. And when Jesus saw that he had answered discreetly, he said unto him, Thou art not far

¹ Or, *The Lord is our God; the Lord is one*   ² Gr. *from*.   ³ Or, *Teacher*

29. *Jesus answered him*] pointing, it may be, to the scribe's *tephillin*, the little leather box containing in one of its four divisions the *Shema* (Deut. vi. 4), which every pious Israelite repeated twice a day. For to say the *Shema* was a passport into paradise for any child of Abraham.

The first of all the commandments] or "first is," see R.V. The Saviour quotes the introduction to the ten commandments (Deut. vi. 4, 5) as the first command, not as forming one of the commandments, but as containing the *principle* of all. The scribe asks, which is the most *important* of all; for this was the thing disputed in his day.

31. *the second is,*] the Lord had named only one commandment as great to the rich young ruler (Luke x. 27). To the scribe he names two. The Jews and the Christian Fathers divided the ten commandments into two equal tables. See Josephus' *Antiq.*, iii, 6, 5. Parents were not regarded as *neighbors*, but as superiors, and representatives of divine authority on the earth. Hence the fifth commandment was placed on the first table, among those relating to our duties to God. Jesus gives the substance of each table according to this division current among the Jews.

33. *burnt offerings and sacrifices*] the phrase "with all the soul" is omitted in several of the best MSS.; and is rejected in the R.V. It is found in the Alexandrian, but not in the Sinaitic nor the Vatican MSS. The scribe gathers up in his reply some of the great utterances of the prophets, which prove the superiority of love to God and man over all mere ceremonial observances. See 1 Sam. xv. 22; Psalm li; Hosea vi, 6; Micah vi, 6-8. "The law which God delivered by Moses," says Bishop Hopkins, "was of three kinds: (1) ceremonial; (2) judicial; (3) moral." The ceremonial law related to the purification and worship of the Jews; the judicial to their civil government as a people; the moral law was a body of precepts embodying universal and natural equity. The ceremonial law is abrogated; the judicial is in suspense, because the Jews are scattered, and do not now form a nation; the moral law is of universal application, now in force, hence is not abrogated, except as to some of its circumstances, *e.g.* its condemning power over believers. See Gal. iii. 13; Rom. viii. 1.

34. *discreetly*] the original is stronger than "discreetly"—intelligently or "wisely," as Wyclif reads. It is not used elsewhere in the N. T.

Thou art not far] the perception of divine truth which his answer had shewed revealed that he wanted but little to become a disciple of Christ. "If thou art not far off, enter; better otherwise to have been far off."—*Bengel.*

AUTHORIZED VERSION.	REVISED VERSION.
the kingdom of God. And no man after that durst ask him any question. 35 And Jesus answered and said, while he taught in the temple, How say the scribes that Christ is the son of David? 36 For David himself said by the Holy Ghost, The Lord said to my Lord, Sit thou on my right hand, till I make thine enemies thy footstool. 37 David therefore himself calleth him Lord; and whence is he then his son? And the common people heard him gladly.	from the kingdom of God. And no man after that durst ask him any question. 35 And Jesus answered and said, as he taught in the temple, How say the scribes that the Christ is the son of David? David himself said in the Holy Spirit, The Lord said unto my Lord, Sit thou on my right hand, Till I make thine enemies [1] the footstool of thy feet.* 37 David himself calleth him Lord; and whence is he his son? And [2] the common people heard him gladly.

[1] Some ancient authorities read *underneath thy feet.* [2] Or, *the great multitude*

The scribe was not converted, but his spiritual perceptions were partially awakened. Even a blind man has some ideas of color. Dr. Sanderson, though blind from early infancy, "delivered an accurate course of lectures on light and color in the University of Oxford." So an unconverted man may talk correctly on theology and doctrine without having a glimpse of the beauty and glory of the truth. See A. Alexander, *Religious Experience*, p. 83.

no man...durst] none of the scribes or Pharisees dared try to entangle him with subtle questions; the disciples do not appear to have been kept from asking questions for information. Others alike kept aloof from one from whom chief priests and rabbis alike went away humbled. Though silenced, they did not desist from their wicked plans to destroy Jesus.

35--37. COUNTER QUESTION, "SON OF DAVID?"

35. *And Jesus answered and said*] he seemed to have turned to a number of Pharisees (Matt. xxii, 41) who had collected together, to converse probably over the day's discomfiture. Mark points out by the words "*Jesus answered*" that the statement contained a reply to some question already put. Jesus had already silenced their questioning; now, as Alford suggests, he silences their *answering*. His question now was not as if he had said "what think ye of me?" but "what think ye of Christ, the Messiah?"

36. *David himself said*] The Pharisees are referred to the 110th Psalm, which the rabbis regarded as distinctly Messianic. "*The Lord (Jehovah) said, unto my Lord, (Adonai) Sit thou on my right hand, till I make thy foes a footstool for thy feet.*" In this lofty and mysterious Psalm, David, speaking by the Holy Ghost, was carried out of and beyond himself, and saw in prophetic vision that his son would also be his Lord. The Psalm is more frequently cited by the New Testament writers than any other single portion of the ancient Scriptures (Acts ii, 34, 35; 1 Cor. xv, 25; Heb. i, 13; v, 6; vii, 17, 21). "In later Jewish writings nearly every verse of it is quoted as referring to the Messiah."—*Perowne.*

37. *whence is he then his son?*] There could be but one answer: Because that son would be David's son as regarding human birth, and so inferior to David in his human nature, but his Lord as regarding his divine nature, and hence, sovereign of a spiritual kingdom, in which even David must be a subject. This answer, however, the Pharisees declined to make, not through ignorance, but through unbelief. Skeptics like Renan do not know how to explain this passage any better than the Pharisees, but it is clear to all who hold that Jesus was the son of God, incarnate—and born of the seed of David according to the flesh.

the common people] *the great multitude.* "And *moche cumpany* gladli herde him."—*Wyclif.* "The rich and the mighty were too proud to listen to

AUTHORIZED VERSION.	REVISED VERSION.
38 And he said unto them in his doctrine, Beware of the scribes, which love to go in long clothing, and love salutations in the marketplaces, 39 And the chief seats in the synagogues, and the uppermost rooms at feasts: 40 Which devour widow's houses, and for a¹	38 And in his teaching he said, Beware of the scribes, which desire to walk in long robes, and to have salutations in the marketplaces, 39 and chief seats in the synagogues, and chief 40 places at feasts: they which devour widows' houses, ¹ and for a pretence make long pray-

¹ Or, *even while for a pretence they make*

his instructions. So it is still. The chief success of the gospel is there [among the poorer classes], and there it pours down its chief blessings. This is not the fault of the gospel."—*Barnes.*

38—40. BEWARE OF THE SCRIBES.

38. *And he said*] The terrible denunciations of the moral and religious shortcomings of the leaders of the nation are given more fully by Matthew, xxiii, 1-39. Only the Jewish Christians, for whom that evangelist wrote, could at once understand and enter into the defective nature of Pharisaic Judaism. To the Gentile Christians of Rome, for whom Mark wrote, " the great woe-speech" would be to a certain extent unintelligible. Hence the picture of the scribes is given in three principal features: (1) ambition, (2) avarice, and (3) hypocritical piety.

in long clothing] "that wolen wandre in stoolis."—*Wyclif. Stoolis* from Latin *stola* = robe. They came out to pray in long sweeping robes, wearing phylacteries of extra size, and exaggerated tassels, hung at the corners of their *abbas*. Many such were doubtless to be seen at Jerusalem at this very time, who had come up to celebrate the feast of the passover.

love salutations] the sounding title of " Rabbi," " Rabbi."

39. *chief seats*] the seats of honor for the elders of the synagogue were placed in front of the ark containing the law, in the uppermost part, where they sat with their faces to the people. In the synagogue at Alexandria there were seventy-one golden chairs, according to the number of the members of the Great Sanhedrin.

A JEWISH SCRIBE.

the uppermost rooms] or most honorable seats ; " places " is not an adequate translation of the Greek, as Alexander suggests, for it includes a "place to recline," " the first sitting places in soperis."—*Wyclif;* the highest place on the divan at the feast, as among the Greeks. Among the Romans, when a party consisted of more than three persons, it was the custom to arrange three of the couches on which they reclined round a table, so that the whole formed three sides of a square, leaving one side of the square open for the attendants. These couches were then respectfully designated *lectus medius, summus* and *imus.* The middle place in the *triclinium* was considered the most dignified. At a feast there would be many such *triclinia.* See Schaff's *Dict. of the Bible.*

40. *devour widows' houses*] as professed guardians and administrators of

AUTHORIZED VERSION.	REVISED VERSION.
pretence make long prayers: these shall receive greater damnation. 41 And Jesus sat over against the treasury, and beheld how the people cast money into the treasury; and many that were rich cast in much. 42 And there came a certain poor widow, and she threw in two mites, which make a farthing.	ers; these shall receive greater condemnation. 41 And he sat down over against the treasury, and beheld how the multitude cast ¹ money into the treasury: and many that were rich 42 cast in much. And there came ² a poor widow, and she cast in two mites, which 43 make a farthing. And he called unto him

¹ Gr. *brass*.   ² Gr. *one*.

their property. But compare the R.V., which makes these words begin a new sentence; the relative in the A.V. obscures the sense.

greater damnation] "thei taken longe dom."—*Wyclif*. The word denotes "judgment," "punishment." The verb from which it comes denotes "to judge," pass sentence, condemn. In 1 Cor. xi, 29, the words rendered *damnation*, *discerning*, *judged*, and *condemnation*, are all, in the original, parts or derivatives of the same word; and so Wyclif admirably rendered them into the language of his day by words connected with one and the same English verb; "He that etith and drinkith unworthili, etith and drinkith *doom* to him, not wisely, *demyng* the bodi of the Lord...and if we *demyden* wisely us silf we schulden not be *demyd*, but while we be *demyd* of the lord we be chastised, that we be not *dampnyd* with this world." Compare also Chaucer, *Monk's Tale*, 15091, "*Dampnyd* was he to deye in that prison."—*Bible Word Book*.

41—41. THE WIDOW'S MITE.

41. *And Jesus sat*] in perfect calmness and quietness of spirit after all the fierce opposition of this "day of questions."

the treasury] Lange suggests that the sacrifice fund is meant, which was distinguished from the proper temple treasury, though belonging to it. The treasury, according to the Rabbis, consisted of thirteen brazen chests, called "trumpets," because the mouths through which the money was cast into the chest were wide at the top and narrow below. They stood in the outer "Court of the Women." "Nine chests were for the appointed temple tribute, and for the sacrifice-tribute, that is money-gifts instead of the sacrifices; four chests for freewill-offerings, for wood, incense, temple decoration, and burnt-offerings."—*Lightfoot*. Alford suggests, that there was a building of that name, according to Josephus; but the former interpretation is generally accepted.

beheld] The imperfect tense in the original implies that he *continued watching and observing* the scene. "Christus in hodierno quoque cultu spectat omnes."—*Bengel*.

how the people] "Before the Passover, freewill-offerings in addition to the temple-tax were generally presented."—*Lange*.

42. *a certain poor widow*] One of the helpless class which he had just described as *devoured* by the extortion of the scribes and Pharisees. In three words Mark presents to us a picture of her desolation; she was alone, she was a widow, and she was poor.

two mites] The primary meaning of the word rendered mite is thin or tiny. The *Lepton*, or mite, here mentioned was the very smallest copper coin current among the Jews, and was equal to about one-fifth of a cent. "Ten lepta is a copper coin about as large as our [copper] cent, and we found it in common currency at Athens."—*Jacobus*. Two lepta made one Roman *quadrans*, which was one-fourth

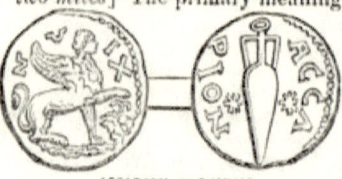

ASSARION, FARTHING.

AUTHORIZED VERSION.	REVISED VERSION.
43 And he called *unto him* his disciples, and saith unto them, Verily I say unto you, That this poor widow hath cast more in, than all they which have cast into the treasury: 44 For all *they* did cast in of their abundance; but she of her want did cast in all that she had, *even* all her living.	his disciples, and said unto them, Verily I say unto you, This poor widow cast in more than all they which are casting into the treasury: 44 for they all did cast in of their superfluity; but she of her want did cast in all that she had, *even* all her living. 13 And as he went forth out of the temple,

CHAP. XIII.—And as he went out of the

of an *as*. This poor widow gave two; Bengel incorrectly says, she might have kept one; but the law did not permit giving less than two, though the offering was voluntary. See Schottgen and Cook. She gave her "all." "If we have regard to the origin of the expression, it argues more of presumption than humility to call any gift, as many do, however liberal, unless it were our all, a 'mite,' while the frequent use of the term to excuse some shabby offering which costs the donor nothing, is a remarkable example of the serene unconsciousness with which persons will sometimes pass the most bitter sarcasms upon themselves."—*Davies*.

43. *more in, than all they*] it is not said that the gifts of the others were worthless. Many possessed, no doubt, no worth (Matt. vi, 1); others a greater or a less. "It is not so much for the rich to give thousands as for the poor to give tens."—*Jacobus*. "Thus Christ shows how he will as earnestly regard the smallest service of any of his people."—*Stier*. He discovers it amid the deepest corruption.

44. *of their*] or their abundance, "of that thing that was plenteous to them."—*Wyclif*.

she of her want] "of hir nyseste sente alle thingis that she hadde, al hir lyflode."—*Wyclif*. After this incident in the "court of the women," and apparently while the Saviour was still there, two of the apostles, Andrew and Philip, brought to him the inquiring Greeks, who had desired to see him (John xii, 20–22). No sooner did he behold these "inquirers from the west," than he broke into words of mysterious joy (John xii, 24-26), and presentiment of his coming passion (John xii, 27–28); after which was heard the last of the three heavenly voices, attesting the true dignity of his mission (John xii, 28). And so with the clear pre-vision that he was about to be "*lifted up*" he prepared to leave the temple, which he was never to enter again. His public work was over.

PRACTICAL LESSONS.—(1) "God is pleased with offerings made to him and his cause. (2) We are to give to his cause. (3) The proof of love is not merely the *amount*, but the amount compared with our ability. (4) It may be proper to give our all to God, and trust him for a supply of our wants. (5) God regards the humblest giver, and loves the cheerful giver. (6) Every giver may ask how much he gives, compared with what he has, and why he gives." A man "has contributed his mite" when he has given half his living, and his "two mites" when he gives "all his living."

CH. XIII. **1--23.** PROPHECIES OF THE DESTRUCTION OF JERUSALEM.
(Tuesday, 12th Nisan, 783, April 4th, A.D. 30.)

The following discourse on the mount of Olives is recorded by Matthew and Luke also. The prophecy in it refers to the fall of Jerusalem, and to the second coming of Christ. The disciples asked about the two events, and the answer relates to both. The difficulty of interpreting the prophecy is increased by this blending of two distinct things; as it requires great care and judgment to decide what relates to each of these two events.

1. *And as he went*] Jesus probably passed from the temple down the eastern steps toward the brook Kedron.

AUTHORIZED VERSION.	REVISED VERSION.
temple, one of his disciples saith unto him, Master, see what manner of stones and what buildings *are here!* 2 And Jesus answering said unto him, Seest thou these great buildings? there shall not be	one of his disciples saith unto him, [1] Master, behold, what manner of stones and what 2 manner of buildings! And Jesus said unto him, Seest thou these great buildings? there

[1] Or, *Teacher.*

the temple] the first temple built by Solomon, B. C. 1014–1007, was wonderful for richness, beauty, and splendor. Four centuries after, it was destroyed by Nebuzaradan, under Nebuchadnezzar, B. C. 586. The second and new Temple of Zerubbabel was built on the site of Solomon's Temple, by authority of Cyrus the Persian, and completed B. C. 517. A rival temple was built on Mount Gerizim, by the Samaritans, B. C. 409. The temple at Jerusalem was plundered B. C. 170, and again in B. C. 54. Herod the Great began to restore and enlarge the second temple, B. C. 17, and finished the main buildings in about eight years; but the work was only fully completed under Herod Agrippa II, in A. D. 64. It was destroyed at the siege of Jerusalem by Titus, A. D. 70.

manner of stones] the enormous size of the marble blocks of the temple, the grandeur of its buildings, awakened the admiration of one of the disciples, and he directed his Master's attention to them. "The buildings or structures included columns, chambers, porticoes, that were, as Luke tells us, the votive offerings of the faithful (Luke xxi, 5)."—*Ellicott*. Josephus tells us that while some of the stones were forty-five feet long, many were thirty-seven and a half feet long, twelve feet high, and eighteen broad.—Jos. *Bell. Jud.* v, 6, 6; *Ant.* xv, 11, 3.

2. *there shall not be left*] though now they seem immovably fixed in their places. Captain Wilson, of the Ordnance Survey, has shown that the present wall has been rebuilt, probably on the foundation of the older one, and that the same stones were re-used. These older stones can be recognized by their character and marks. The prophecy was fulfilled, but the stones are left, a witness to the accuracy of the narrative. In less than forty years after this prophecy, "Zion was *ploughed as a field*, and Jerusalem became heaps, and the mountain of the house as the high places of the forest" (Micah iii, 12), A. D. 70. The Emperor Titus was amazed at the massive buildings of Jerusalem, and traced in his triumph the hand of God (Jos. *Bell. Jud.* vi, 9, 1). After the capture of the city, the tenth legion, under the command of Terentius Rufus, completed the work of demolition, and Josephus tells us (*Bell. Jud.* vii, 1, 1) that the whole enclosing walls and precincts of the temple were "so thoroughly levelled and dug up that no one visiting the city would believe it had ever been inhabited." And Captain Wilson asserts that nothing is now *in situ* in the Haram wall, except perhaps the southwest corner, and a portion of the wall under the Mahkama; not any portion on which Jesus and his disciples were gazing; hence, it is literally fulfilled. Lange aptly suggests that the language of Jesus is intended to depict a *violent* rather than a regular breaking down of the temple. Ryle believes, however, that our Lord, in these prophecies, "had in view

THE WAILING PLACE OF THE JEWS.
(From photograph.)

AUTHORIZED VERSION.	REVISED VERSION.
left one stone upon another, that shall not be thrown down.	shall not be left here one stone upon another, which shall not be thrown down.
3 And as he sat upon the mount of Olives, over against the temple, Peter and James and John and Andrew asked him privately,	3 And as he sat on the mount of Olives over against the temple, Peter and James and 4 John and Andrew asked him privately, Tell
4 Tell us, when shall these things be? and what *shall be* the sign when all these things shall be fulfilled?	us, when shall these things be? and what *shall be* the sign when these things are all 5 about to be accomplished? And Jesus began
5 And Jesus answering them, began to say, Take heed lest any *man* deceive you:	to say unto them, Take heed that no man 6 lead you astray. Many shall come in my
6 For many shall come in my name, saying, I am *Christ;* and shall deceive many.	name, saying, I am *he;* and shall lead many 7 astray. And when ye shall hear of wars and
7 And when ye shall hear of wars and rumours of wars, be ye not troubled: *for such things* must needs be; but the end *shall* not be yet.	rumours of wars, be not troubled: *these things* must needs come to pass; but the end

a *second* siege of Jerusalem, and a *second* tribulation accompanying that siege, as well as the first siege and tribulation when the city was taken by Titus." He finds proof of this view in Zech. xiv. This interpretation of *two* sieges, and of Christ's coming following the *second* siege, he thinks, renders the chapter "plain and intelligible."

thrown down] the Greek is more closely rendered by Canon Cook, "shall be loosed," which is the precise impression made on the mind of an engineer exploring the wall now.

3. *the mount of Olives*] crossing the valley of the Kedron, the little company ascended one of the footpaths that lead over the mount of Olives in the direction of Bethany. When they had reached the summit, he sat down (Matt. xxiv, 3; Mark xiii, 3).

over against the temple] the summit of Olivet is directly opposite or facing the temple area, and from it there is a fine view of Jerusalem. The temple was really the *third* temple; the first temple was built by Solomon and destroyed by Nebuchadnezzar; the second was built by Ezra and Nehemiah; the *third* temple was an enlargement or rebuilding of the second, and was chiefly the work of Herod. It was not *completed* until after the death of Christ.

Peter and James and John and Andrew] These apostles probably now sat nearest to their Master. Andrew is added to the select company of three.

4. *what shall be the sign*] The question, as given more fully by Matthew (xxiv, 3) embraced three points: (1) the time of the destruction of the temple; the sign (2) of his Coming; and (3) of the end of the world.

5. *began to say*] which is something more than "said," as Alexander aptly suggests; (comp. also the R. V.) and seems here to imply that what he said was not restricted to a single topic; that he first spoke of one thing, and then proceeded to speak of another. This is the more probable because our Lord, instead of beginning with the signs or premonitions of his second coming, as many seem to think he does, and as the twelve may have expected, begins by telling what was not to be so reckoned, although apt to be mistaken for the signs in question.

Take heed] the disciples appear to have expected Jesus to assume the kingly power at once. "Having been convinced that as soon as the reign of Christ should commence, they would be in every respect happy, they leave warfare out of the account and fly all at once to a triumph."—*Abbott.* "The four moral key-notes of the discourse on the last things are '*Beware,*' '*Watch,*' '*Endure,*' '*Pray.*'"—*Farrar.*

6. *many shall come*] the "For" is omitted in R. V., as also in verses 7 and 9. Doddridge regards Josephus' history of the Jewish wars as the best commentary on this chapter. Five tokens are here given: (1) the rise of false prophets; (2) wars and rumors of wars; (3) the rising of nation against

AUTHORIZED VERSION.	REVISED VERSION.
8 For nation shall rise against nation, and kingdom against kingdom: and there shall be earthquakes in divers places, and there shall be famines and troubles: these *are* the beginnings of sorrows.	8 is not yet. For nation shall rise against nation, and kingdom against kingdom: there shall be earthquakes in divers places; there shall be famines: these things are the beginning of travail.
9 But take heed to yourselves: for they shall deliver you up to councils: and in the synagogues ye shall be beaten: and ye shall be	9 But take ye heed to yourselves: for they shall deliver you up to councils; and in synagogues shall ye be beaten; and before governors and kings shall ye stand for my sake,

nation; (4) earthquakes; (5) famines (some MSS. omit *troubles*, v. 8). The A. V. implies that there would be many false Messiahs, or false Christs, though that is not necessarily the meaning in the R. V. Since the fall of Jerusalem, upwards of fifty false Christs among the Jews are noticed by historical writers; it is not known that *many* appeared before that event.

8. *nation—against nation*] "There were serious disturbances, (1) which gave rise to the complaint against and deposition of Flaccus, and Philo's work against him, A. D. 38, in which the Jews as a nation were the especial objects of persecution; (2) At Sileucia, about the same time, in which more than fifty thousand Jews were killed; (3) at Jamnia, a city on the coast of Judæa, near Joppa. Many other such national tumults are recorded by Josephus."—*Alford*.

earthquakes] the following are some of the great earthquakes noted about that time: in Crete, about A. D. 51; in Phrygia, in 53; in Laodicea, in 60; in Campania, in 58; in Jerusalem, in 67; at Pompeii, in 63.

the beginnings of sorrows] The expression here is remarkable, and so the creation is said to be "groaning and *travailing*" (Rom. viii, 22), waiting for its *regeneration* (Matt. xix, 28) or new birth. For the fulfillment of these prophecies comp. Jos. *Ant.* xix, 1; Tac. *Ann.* xii, 38; xv, 22; xvi, 13; Sen. *Ep.* xci. Of these five classes of signs or tokens, the *first* was false prophets or Christs. There were, the Egyptian false prophet at the head of thirty thousand men, twelve years after Christ's resurrection; Theudas, Dositheus, and just after the fall of Jerusalem, Bar Cochba, Jonathan, and others. Hegesippus says many false Christs came. The *second* sign was wars: a long time of universal peace preceded the birth of Jesus; after his death, until Jerusalem was destroyed, there was little else but threatened or actual war among the Jews. The *third* and *fourth* signs were strikingly fulfilled, as secular history testifies. The *fifth* sign, as noted by Luke, "fearful sights," etc., according to Josephus, had several forms of fulfillment, as (1) a star like a sword hanging over the city; (2) a supernatural light in the temple; (3) the massive eastern gate of solid brass, requiring twenty men to open it, opened of its own accord; (4) armies fighting in the clouds; (5) a voice in the temple: "Let us depart"; (6) a countryman running through the streets, crying "A voice against Jerusalem and the temple. Woe, woe to Jerusalem," etc. See *Hist.* V *Josephus*. But Alexander thinks it difficult to find in contemporary history a state of things answerable to this description before the downfall of Jerusalem, the local wars and disturbances being, in his view, too insignificant to exhaust the terribly sublime description. These "signs" then preceded the destruction of Jerusalem, but realized on a larger scale they are to herald the end of all things; comp. 1 Thess. v, 3; 2 Thess. ii, 2.

9. *to councils*] not *the* council, *i. e.*, the Sanhedrin, but the lower courts. Some were brought before the great council, as in Acts iv, 3, we find all the apostles brought before the Sanhedrin; and again in Acts v, 18, 27. Similarly, Paul was brought before the same council, Acts xxiii, 1.

in the synagogues shall ye be beaten] "Of the Jews," says Paul (2 Cor. xi, 24), "five times received I forty *stripes* save one"; "thrice was I *beaten with*

AUTHORIZED VERSION.	REVISED VERSION.
brought before rulers and kings for my sake, for a testimony against them. 10 And the gospel must first be published among all nations. 11 But when they shall lead *you,* and deliver you up, take no thought beforehand what ye shall speak, neither do ye premeditate: but whatsoever shall be given you in that hour, that speak ye: for it is not ye that speak, but the Holy Ghost. 12 Now the brother shall betray the brother to death, and the father the son; and children shall rise up against *their* parents, and shall cause them to be put to death. 13 And ye shall be hated of all *men* for my name's sake: but he that shall endure unto the end, the same shall be saved.	10 for a testimony unto them. And the gospel must first be preached unto all the nations. 11 And when they lead you *to judgement,* and deliver you up, be not anxious beforehand what ye shall speak: but whatsoever shall be given you in that hour, that speak ye: for it is not ye that speak, but the Holy Ghost. 12 And brother shall deliver up brother to death, and the father his child; and children shall rise up against parents, and ¹ cause 13 them to be put to death. And ye shall be hated of all men for my name's sake: but he that endureth to the end, the same shall be saved.

¹ Or, *put them to death*

rods." It was part of the duties of the Chazzan, or minister in each synagogue, to maintain order and scourge the condemned.

before rulers and kings] The Roman tetrarchs are sometimes called kings. Paul stood before *Felix* (Acts xxiv, 10–22), *Festus* (Acts xxv, 1–11), *Agrippa* (Acts xxvi, 1–23), *Nero* (2 Tim. iv, 16). The general persecutions of Christians in later times, under Nero, in which Peter and Paul suffered martyrdom, may also be alluded to. Schaff doubts whether prophecy has such specific fulfillment as some commentators, like Alford, advocate, and Lange suggests that the wars referred to extend to the end of the world.

10. *the gospel must first be published*] or "proclaimed." The gospel was proclaimed throughout the Roman Empire, from Arabia to Damascus, from Jerusalem to Illyricum, in Italy and in Spain, during the lifetime of some of his hearers. Comp. Rom. xv, 19, 24, 28; Col. i, 6, 23. Alexander accepts the general spread of the church before the fall of Jerusalem, as a substantial fulfillment of this prediction. One point is clear, as Canon Cook suggests: tribulation must be the portion of the church whatever may be the duration of the interval during which the gospel is to be proclaimed in the world.

11. *take no thought beforehand*] See R. V. "Nyle the *thenke* what ye schulen speke."—*Wyclif.* "*Thought,*" in the time of King James, signified *undue care* or *anxiety*. Shakespeare, *Jul. Cæs.* II, i, 186, says,

"If he love Cæsar, all that he can do
Is to himself *take thought* and die for Cæsar."

but whatsoever shall be given you] the Greek word rendered premeditate is the common phrase for committing to memory a speech, as opposed to extempore speaking. It is omitted in several MSS. and in the R. V. If retained it gives no warrant to ministers who get up to preach unprepared every Sunday. Such a perverted "application of this passage is utterly unjustifiable." Comp. Matt. x, 19, 20, where the words occur as a portion of our Lord's charge to his twelve apostles. "These were very weighty words for the Roman Christians, at a time when the martyrdom of the apostles Peter and Paul, in Rome, was about to take place."—*Lange.* The apostles, according to Alexander's view, were simply to be the channels of the revelations which the Holy Spirit would make at such times.

13. *he that shall endure*] "he that shall *susteyne in* to the ende."—*Wyclif.* The endurance here spoken of is the *brave and persistent endurance* of the Christian in faith and love. In this noble word, the "queen of virtues," as Chrysostom does not fear to call it, "there always appears in the New Testament a background of *manliness;* it does not mark merely the *endurance,* the 'sustinentiam,' or even the 'patientiam,' but the '*perseverantiam,*' the 'brave patience' with which the Christian contends against the various hind-

AUTHORIZED VERSION.	REVISED VERSION.
14 But when ye shall see the abomination of desolation, spoken of by Daniel the prophet, standing where it ought not, (let him that readeth understand,) then let them that be in Judea flee to the mountains:	14 But when ye see the abomination of desolation standing where he ought not (let him that readeth understand), then let them that

rances, persecutions and temptations that befall him in his conflict with the inward and outward world." For further accounts of the fulfillment of these prophecies consult the Acts and Epistles; the writings of Josephus, and of Roman writers, as Seneca, *Epis.* xci, 9; Suetonius, *Claud.* xviii, Tacitus *Ann.* xv, 44, and Pliny, *Epis.* x, 97.

PRACTICAL TEACHING.—" Make it a rule that never a day shall pass without speaking for Christ. People won't like it. If you are a living witness for Christ it makes people against you. You will suffer persecution and be spoken against, and yet they will send for such a man first when they are in trouble, or on their death-bed. The man that is popular with the world is not a friend of Jesus."—*Moody.*

14. *But when ye shall see*] He had distinctly foretold the destruction of Jerusalem, now he notices some signs which would precede its fall, and tells them how they may secure their own safety.

the abomination of desolation] This expression comes from Dan. ix, 27, "and for the *overspreading of abominations* he shall make it *desolate*," or, as it is rendered in the margin, "and upon the battlements shall be the *idols of the desolator.*" The Septuagint renders it, "and upon the temple the abomination of desolations;" comp. 2 Macc. vi, 2. Hengstenberg would translate it, "and over the top of abomination comes the desolation." In the Apocrypha it is applied to the profanation of the altar by Antiochus, 1 Macc. i, 54. The key to the interpretation seems to be supplied by Luke xxi, 20, "And when ye shall see Jerusalem *compassed with armies*, then know that *the desolation* thereof is nigh." Hence, some would understand it to denote (1) any and all the abominations practiced by the Romans on the place where the temple stood. (2) Others, the eagles, the standards of the Roman army which were held in abomination by the Jews. The Roman eagles, therefore, rising over the site of the temple, "*where they ought not*," and "*compassing*" the city (Luke xxi, 20), was the sign that the Holy Place had fallen under the dominion of the idolators. Others (3) would refer the words not only to the Roman eagles, but to the outrages of lust and murder perpetrated by the "zealots," which drove every worshipper in horror from the sacred courts. See Jos. *Bell. Jud.* iv, 3, 7. The second explanation is ingeniously urged by Greswell, and is accepted by many; but the first view, that it applies to the pollution of the temple in any way, is preferable.

spoken of by Daniel] This phrase is omitted in many MSS. and is dropped in the R. V. It is found in Matthew, however. The reference is generally held to be to Dan. ix, 27, but Calvin stoutly disputes this, and thinks it refers to Dan. xii, 11.

flee to the mountains] Compare the flight of Lot from the "cities of the plain."

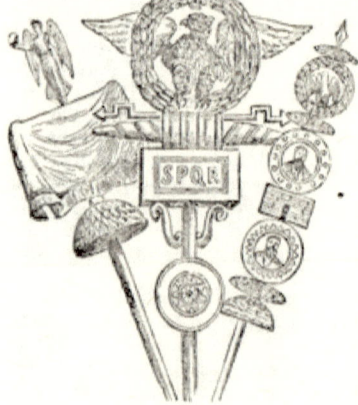

ROMAN STANDARDS.

Gen. xix, 17. Eusebius says the Christians were warned, by a revelation, to

AUTHORIZED VERSION.	REVISED VERSION.
15 And let him that is on the housetop not go down into the house, neither enter *therein*, to take anything out of his house:	15 are in Judæa flee unto the mountains: and let him that is on the housetop not go down, nor enter in, to take anything out of his
16 And let him that is in the field not turn back again for to take up his garment.	16 house; and let him that is in the field not 17 return back to take his cloke. But woe un'o
17 But woe to them that are with child, and to them that give suck in those days!	them that are with child and to them that 18 give suck in those days! And pray ye that
18 And pray ye that your flight be not in the winter.	19 it be not in the winter. For those days shall

flee to Pella. Hence, the Jewish Christians fled from Jerusalem to this Peræan town, a distance of about 100 miles. Hammond notices the providential and temporary raising of the siege by Gallus (who could have taken the city), thus affording an opportunity for escape to those heeding the warning of Jesus. So far as known, not a single *Christian* Jew perished in the fall of Jerusalem. "Somewhere on the slopes of Gilead, near the scene of Jacob's first view of the land of his descendants, and of the capital of the exiled David, was Pella (identified with *Tubakat Fah'l*), so called by the Macedonian Greeks from the springing fountain, which likened it to the birthplace of their own Alexander...From these heights Abner, in his flight from the Philistines, and David, in his flight from Absalom, and the Israelites, on their way to Babylon, and the Christian Jews of Pella caught the last glimpse of their familiar mountains."—*Stanley.*

15. *neither enter therein*] The houses of Palestine were furnished with a flight of steps outside, by which the housetops could be reached without actually entering the house. Comp. chap. ii, 3, 12. Roofs are used for sleep, retirement, prayer, or secretion. The Christians were thus warned by our Lord to flee by the outside staircase, or to run along the roofs to the city wall, and so make their escape.

16. *his garment*] *i.e.* his "outer garment."

18. *pray ye*] The fatalist and skeptic may smile at this exhortation, but it is based on the profoundest philosophy. The interposition of providence in answer to prayer may be made, not within a line seen by the suppliant, but in one which is to meet him on his path. "Herein," observes Isaac Taylor, "is especially manifested the perfection of divine wisdom, that the most surprising conjunctions of events are brought about by the simplest means, and in a manner that is perfectly in harmony with the ordinary course of human affairs. This is, in fact, the great miracle of providence; that no miracles are needed to accomplish its purposes." And J. McCosh calmly urges, "Read in the spirit of faith, striking coincidences will everywhere manifest themselves. What singular union of two streams at the proper place to help on the exertions of the great and good! What curious intersections of cords to catch the wicked as in a net, when they are prowling as wild beasts! By strange, but most opposite correspondences, human strength, when set against the will of God, is made to waste away, under God's burning indignation against it, as in heathen story Meleager wasted away as the stick burned which his mother held in the fire."—*Divine Government*, pp. 176, 203.

be not in the winter] with its rains and storms and swollen torrents, "*neither*;" Matthew adds (xxiv, 20), "*on the sabbath day.*" The reading "it" of the revised version, in place of "your flight," refers, rather to the siege, which took place in our October. But if Christ intended to refer to the flight of Christians, as in A.V., it is remarkable that immediately after the defeat and temporary raising of the siege by Gallus, their flight probably took place, which was in one of the mildest months in Syria. For (1) the compassing of the city by the Roman armies spoken of by Luke (xxi, 20) took place at the commencement of October, A.D. 66, when the weather was yet mild and

AUTHORIZED VERSION.	REVISED VERSION.
19 For in those days shall be affliction, such as was not from the beginning of the creation which God created unto this time, neither shall be.	be tribulation, such as there hath not been the like from the beginning of the creation which God created until now, and never
20 And except that the Lord had shortened those days, no flesh should be saved: but for the elect's sake, whom he hath chosen, he hath shortened the days.	20 shall be. And except the Lord had shortened the days, no flesh would have been saved: but for the elect's sake, whom he chose, he

favorable for travelling: (2) the final siege, if any Christian Jews lingered on till then, took place in the still more open months of April or May. See Lewin's *Fasti Sacri*, pp. 344 and 358. The Jewish custom, which forbade travelling on the sabbath beyond a distance of 2000 ells, would make the Christian Jews' travelling on that day infinitely more difficult, even though they might themselves be possibly free from any scruple. "They would, in addition to other embarrassments, expose themselves to the severest persecutions of fanaticisms."—*Lange*.

19. *such as...from the beginning of the creation*] Josephus declares of the calamities attending the fall of Jerusalem, in almost the words of this prophecy, "the misfortunes of all men. *from the beginning of the world*, if they be compared to those of the Jews, are not so terrible as theirs were," "nor did any age ever produce a generation more fruitful in wickedness, *from the beginning of the world*." The city was densely crowded by the multitudes which had come up to the Passover. Pestilence ensued, and famine followed. The commonest instincts of humanity were forgotten. Acts of violence and cruelty were perpetrated without compunction or remorse, and barbarities enacted which cannot be described. Mothers snatched the food from the mouths of their husbands and children, and one mother of rank actually killed, roasted, and devoured her infant son, and was discovered by some who sought to rob her of her food. (Comp. Lev. xxvi, 29; Deut. xxviii, 56, 57). Dead bodies filled the houses and streets of the city, while cruel assassins rifled and mangled with the exultation of fiends. The horrors of the war, famine and pestilence combined were indescribable. The besieged devoured even the filth of the streets, and so excessive was the stench that it was necessary to hurl 600,000 corpses over the wall, while 97,000 captives were taken during the war, and more than 1,100,000 perished in the siege, and nearly 500,000 more in various conflicts accompanying the fall of Israel, which occurred elsewhere in the land. See Josephus, *Bell. Jud.* vi, 9, 3; Tacitus, *Hist.* v, 13; Milman's *History of the Jews* ii, 16; Merivale's *History of the Romans*, vi, 59.

20. *except that the Lord had shortened*] If in God's pitying mercy the number of those awful days had not been shortened, no flesh could have been saved, referring, of course, to the Jewish people.

for the elect's sake] *i. e.* for the sake of the Christians. This was fulfilled literally, though the city was strong, and the provisions ample for many years' siege.

he hath shortened] They were shortened, (1) by the order of Claudius stopping Agrippa from completing the fortifications of Jerusalem; (2) by the division and factions among the Jews; (3) by the burning of the stores of provisions, which were sufficient for a siege of several years; (4) by the abandonment of the towers of the fortification by the Jews, on the arrival of Titus; (5) by the vigorous attacking and storming of the city, instead of sitting out a siege. Titus encircled the city with a wall, five miles in extent, and fortified it with thirteen strong garrisons, in the almost incredibly short space of three days, and Josephus makes special mention of his eagerness to bring the siege to an end. The city, which in the time of Zedekiah (2 Kings xxv, 1–6; Jer. xxxix, 1, 2) had resisted the forces of Nebuchadnez-

AUTHORIZED VERSION.	REVISED VERSION.
21 And then if any man shall say to you, Lo, here is Christ; or, lo, he is there; believe him not:	22 shortened the days. And then if any man shall say unto you, Lo, here is the Christ; 22 or, Lo, there; believe ¹ it not: for there shall
22 For false Christs and false prophets shall rise, and shall shew signs and wonders, to seduce, if it were possible, even the elect.	arise false Christs and false prophets, and shall shew signs and wonders, that they may
23 But take ye heed: behold, I have foretold you all things.	23 lead astray, it possible, the elect. But take ye heed: behold, I have told you all things beforehand.
24 But in those days, after that tribulation, the sun shall be darkened, and the moon shall not give her light,	24 But in those days, after that tribulation, the sun shall be darkened, and the moon 25 shall not give her light, and the stars shall
25 And the stars of heaven shall fall, and the powers that are in heaven shall be shaken.	be falling from heaven, and the powers that 26 are in the heavens shall be shaken. And
26 And then shall they see the Son of man coming in the clouds with great power and glory.	then shall they see the Son of man coming in

¹ Or, him

zar for sixteen months, was taken by the Romans in less than five. The strong language also seems to have reference to tribulations in the *last times*.

22. *false Christs and false prophets*] "Josephus tells us that false prophets and impostors prevailed on multitudes to follow them into the desert, promising there to display signs and wonders (comp. Acts xxi. 38); and even at the last, when the temple was in flames, numbers of all ages flocked thither from the city, upon the proclamation of a false prophet, and of six thousand assembled there on this occasion, not one escaped the fire or the sword. But such imposture is to be still more signally realized with '*signs and lying wonders*' before the final coming of Christ (2 Thess. ii, 1–10)."—*Maclear.*

23. *But take ye heed*] Do not ye be deluded; implying that these predictions would have a fulfillment in their day.

24–31. THE SECOND COMING OF THE LORD.
(Time same as last Section.)

24. *in those days*] This verse is explained in two ways; (1) *figuratively*; which limits "those days" to the fall of Jerusalem, and also "that tribulation" to the same event. Then the rest of the verse is understood to be figures, by which national and social revolutions are predicted, and that the coming of the Son of man, in v. 26, is an invisible coming as at the destruction of Jerusalem. (2) The other may be called *the literal view*; it explains "those days" to be the latter days, near the end of the world, and that a change in nations and in nature is implied, and a visible coming of the Son of man. In regard to the general description in this chapter, Abbott holds that there have been more remarkable wars, famines, pestilences, and earthquakes since, than before the fall of Jerusalem, and understands the language to apply to a long period of conflict and trial before the end will appear.

the sun shall be darkened] "The Jews expected that great calamities would precede the advent of the Messiah; yet at the time when these calamities should have reached their height, they hoped that he would unexpectedly appear."—*Kuinoel.*

26. *shall they see the Son of man*] either at the calamities attending the fall of Jerusalem, if the figurative view of v. 24 is accepted; or near the end of the world, if the literal view be taken. For the title Son of man, see note on ch. ii. 10, and compare John v. 22, 27. "the Father judgeth no man, but hath committed all judgment unto the son, and hath given him authority to execute judgment also, because *he is the Son of man.*"

in the clouds] so the Angels said to the Apostles at the ascension (Acts i,

AUTHORIZED VERSION.	REVISED VERSION.
27 And then shall he send his angels, and shall gather together his elect from the four winds, from the uttermost part of the earth to the uttermost part of heaven.	27 clouds with great power and glory. And then shall he send forth the angels, and shall gather together his elect from the four winds, from the uttermost part of the earth to the uttermost part of heaven.
28 Now learn a parable of the fig tree: When her branch is yet tender, and putteth forth leaves, ye know that summer is near:	28 Now from the fig tree learn her parable: when her branch is now become tender, and putteth forth its leaves, ye know that the
29 So ye in like manner, when ye shall see these things come to pass, know that it is nigh, even at the doors.	29 summer is nigh; even so ye also, when ye see these things coming to pass, know ye that
30 Verily I say unto you, that this generation shall not pass, till all these things be done.	30 ¹he is nigh, even at the doors. Verily I say unto you, This generation shall not pass away, until all these things be accomplished.
31 Heaven and earth shall pass away: but my words shall not pass away.	31 Heaven and earth shall pass away: but my

¹ Or, *it*

11); and Daniel foresaw him *coming with the clouds of heaven* (Dan. vii, 13 14).

27. *then shall he send his angels*] to him God hath delegated the universal and final judgment of mankind, that " as in our nature he performed all that was requisite to save us, as in our nature he was exalted to God's right hand, to rule and bless us, so he shall in our nature appear to judge us."—*Barrow's Sermons.*

28. *the fig tree*] They had already been taught one lesson from the withered fig tree. "Our Lord having spoken of the signs preceding the two grand events concerning which the apostles inquired (Comp. Matt. xxiv, 1-30), begins to speak of the time of them."—*Wesley.*

29. *it is nigh*] or "he" *i. e.* the judge spoken of in verse 26.
even at the doors] There is no "even" in the original. So James says, "Behold, the Judge standeth *before the door*" (James v, 9). "There is something solemn in the brevity of the phrase, without the nominative expressed."—*Wordsworth.*

30. *this generation shall not pass*] The word rendered generation denotes (1) *birth, age;* (2) *descent;* (3) *a generation* of men living at the same time; (4) in a wider sense, a nation, or race. The meaning of this passage is variously given: Some as Alexander hold that it refers to the Jews then living; others to the Jewish nation; and still others to the Jews as a people. The prophecy certainly cannot be said to have had a complete fulfillment during the lifetime of those living when it was uttered, nor indeed during the existence of the Jewish nation. The Jewish people still maintain their separateness though scattered widely, and have every prospect of long continuance. Geikie interprets the three accounts to mean that " this generation of living men shall not have passed away, before the beginning of the age of the Messiah, to be ushered in by the fall of Israel, and to be closed by all the signs, has come." Maclear and Perowne suggest "(1) *In reference to the destruction of Jerusalem,* he declares that the generation of the literal Israel then living would not pass away before the judgments here predicted would fall upon Jerusalem, just as God had made their forefathers wander in the wilderness "until *all the generation* was consumed" that had come out of Egypt "and done evil in the sight of the Lord" (Num. xxxii, 13); (2) *In reference to his second coming,* and the world at large, he affirms that the race of men, and especially *the generation* of them *that sought the Lord* (Ps. xxiv, 6), the faithful seed of Abraham, should not pass away until all these things should be fulfilled. This is substantially the same idea presented by Geikie.

31. *but my words shall not pass away*] Never did the speaker seem to stand more utterly alone than when he uttered this majestic utterance. Never

AUTHORIZED VERSION.	REVISED VERSION.
32 But of that day and that hour knoweth no man, no, not the angels which are in heaven, neither the Son, but the Father.	32 words shall not pass away. But of that day or that hour knoweth no one, not even the angels in heaven, neither the Son, but the Father.
33 Take ye heed, watch and pray: for ye know not when the time is.	33 Take ye heed, watch [1] and pray:
34 For the Son of man is as a man taking a far journey, who left his house, and gave authority	34 for ye know not when the time is. It is as when a man, sojourning in another country,

[1] Some ancient authorities omit *and pray*.

did it seem more improbable that it would be fulfilled. But as we look across the centuries we see how it has been realized. His words have passed into laws; they have passed into doctrines; they have passed into proverbs; they have passed into consolations; but they have never "passed away."— *Camb. Bible.*

32—37. FINAL EXHORTATION TO WATCHFULNESS.

32. *neither the Son*] Since the times of the early Fathers until now, critics have wrestled with this expression, to find a satisfactory solution, and relieve the seeming contradiction between this denial of knowledge and the omniscience of the Saviour. (1) Ambrose rejected the clause as an Arian interpolation, but this is proved to be unfounded; the clause is in all the ancient MSS. and versions, and it is unlikely the Arians could have tampered with them all. (2) Augustine said it meant that it was not a fact which Christ had received to tell, as it was not to be known by the disciples; so Luther, Melancthon, the older Lutherans, Porteus, Bengel, and Whitby, substantially held. (3) That the Son was not at the time in possession of the knowledge (similar to No. 2), as maintained by Lange, or did not know it in his Mediatorial office, as Alford suggests; but Schaff rejects these interpretations as "make-shifts." (4) That as the Son of man, in his human nature he did not know it; this is the view substantially of Athanasius, Cyril, Chrysostom, Calvin, Ryle, Alexander, Clarke, J. Pye Smith, Sumner, Da Costa, Schaff, and the great majority of later commentators. This last view does not *remove* the real difficulty, though it may be said to relieve it somewhat. For as Bishop Sumner aptly remarks, "it is hard to understand, how the Son coming in the flesh should divest himself of *knowledge* which he possessed as God, in the same way as, confessedly, he divested himself of *immortality*." How could he be ignorant of anything, when he asserts "I and my Father are one," and it is said by the apostle "In him are hid all the treasures of wisdom and knowledge" Col. ii, 3. It is inconsistent and unscholarly to attempt an escape from the difficulty by trying to explain away the force of the word "know," as Mimpriss and a few others do. It must be accepted in its ordinary and plain sense here, as elsewhere. Accepting the last as the most satisfactory interpretation, we must still confess it is a mystery we cannot comprehend; so Jesus is said to have "increased in wisdom" and in stature, Luke ii, 52; to have *prayed* to the Father, Matt. xiv. 23; xxvi, 39, 42-44, to have received a *commandment* from the Father, John xiv, 31; so here he asserts that a fact is hidden from him, and known only to the Father; all these statements reveal some of the mysteries of his incarnation which we cannot fully understand now, but may know when we see him face to face.

33. *Take ye heed, watch and pray*] "Se ye, wake ye, and preie ye."— Wyclif. The word rendered "watch" only occurs four times in the New Testament: (1) here; (2) in the parallel, Luke xxi, 36; (3) Eph. vi, 18, "Praying always...and *watching thereunto* with all perseverance;" (4) Heb. xiii, 17, "Obey them that have the rule over you,...for they *watch for* your souls." It denotes (1) *to be sleepless*, (2) *to be vigilant*.

34. *taking a far journey*] literally, one *who is absent from his people*,

AUTHORIZED VERSION.	REVISED VERSION.
to his servants, and to every man his work, and commanded the porter to watch. 35 Watch ye therefore: for ye know not when the master of the house cometh, at even, or at midnight, or at the cockcrowing, or in the morning: 36 Lest coming suddenly he find you sleeping. 37 And what I say unto you I say unto all, Watch. CHAP. XIV.—After two days was *the feast of*¹	having left his house, and given authority to his ¹ servants, to each one his work, commanded also the porter to watch. Watch therefore: for ye know not when the lord of the house cometh, whether at even, or at midnight, or at cockcrowing, or in the morning; lest coming suddenly he find you sleeping. And what I say unto you I say unto all, Watch. 14 Now after two days was *the feast of* the

¹ Gr. *bond-servants*.

who goes on foreign travel. "Which gon fer in pilgrimage."—*Wyclif.* "Be doing something, that the devil may always find you engaged."—*Jerome.* Even so our Lord left his Church, gave authority to his servants the apostles, and to those who should come after them, and to every man his work, and is now waiting for the consummation of all things.

the porter] Ellicott suggests that this refers primarily to Peter, and thinks it throws light on the porter of the sheepfold, John x, 3. Schaff, Riddle, and others suggest that apostles and all ministers and Christians are watchmen. This is true, but the parable is intended to teach the duty of watchfulness; the porter is a part of the "machinery" of the parable, not necessarily calling for any special application.

35. *at even, or at midnight*] On the night watches see ch. vi, 48. In the temple the priest, whose duty it was to superintend the night sentinels of the Levitical guard, might at any moment knock at the door and demand entrance. "He came suddenly and unexpectedly, no one knew when. The Rabbis use almost the very words in which Scripture describes the unexpected coming of the Master, when they say, Sometimes he came at the cockcrowing, sometimes a little earlier, sometimes a little later. He came and knocked, and they opened to him." Mishnah, *Tamid*, i, 1, 2, quoted in Edersheim's *The Temple and its Services*.

36. *Lest coming suddenly he find you sleeping*] "During the night the 'captain of the temple' made his rounds. On his approach the guards had to rise and salute him in a particular manner. Any guard found asleep when on duty was beaten, or his garments were set on fire—a punishment, as we know, actually awarded."—*Edersheim*.

37. *Watch*] Observe the emphasis given to Christ's exhortation, "*Watch!*" Peter, who had a strong influence on Mark, would seem to wish us to notice in spite of frequent warnings that he himself failed to watch, and fell. Matthew tells us how the Lord sought to impress these lessons of watchfulness and faithfulness still more deeply by the Parables of the "*ten virgins*" (Matt. xxv, 1-13), and the "*talents*" (Matt. xxv, 14-30). and closed all with a picture of the Awful Day, when the Son of man should separate all nations one from another as the shepherd divideth his sheep from the goats (Matt. xxv, 31-46).—*Camb. Bible.*

PRACTICAL SUGGESTIONS.—"I believe that heaven is real, hell is real, the devil is real, God is real. If God did not wish us to speak about heaven, he would not have put so much about it in the Bible."—*Moody.*

CH. XIV. **1, 2.**—THE SANHEDRIN IN COUNCIL.
Saturday April 1, and Tuesday April 4, A. D. 30.

1. *after two days*] There is much difference of opinion among harmonists in regard to the order of events, noted in this chapter. (1) Robinson places the conspiracy of the rulers on the evening following Wednesday, which he calls "Thursday *eve*" (not Thursday *night*), and fixes the anointing also on the same evening; Judas making his plan known to the priests

AUTHORIZED VERSION.	REVISED VERSION.
the passover, and of unleavened bread: and the chief priests and the scribes sought how	passover and the unleavened bread: and the chief priests and the scribes sought how they

in the course of the day, on Thursday; while the discourse on the fall of Jerusalem and the coming of Christ he places on the day before, *i. e.* on Wednesday, but this seems too late.

(2) Andrews holds to two consultations by the rulers, *one* on Saturday night, John xii, 10, 11, and the *second* on the following Tuesday night, noted here by Mark xiv, 1, 2, 10, 11, and in Matt. xxvi, 14, 16. The anointing at Bethany, he assigns to the previous Saturday night (April 1, A. D. 30), Mark xiv, 3-9; and places all the other events mentioned in Mark xii, 1, to xiv, 2 and xiv, 10, 11, on Tuesday April 4, A. D. 30. He explains this transposition of Mark xiv, 3-9, on the ground that Mark (and Matthew) bring in the account of the supper at Bethany parenthetically, and to explain the action of Judas, who was offended at the waste of so much money, and at the rebuke of his Master on that occasion. He identifies the supper in Matt. xxvi, 6-13, and Mark xiv, 3-9, with that in John xii, 1-9, as do Dean Mansel, Farrar, Ellicott, Canon Cook, Schaff and others, who likewise assign it to Saturday night, and the other events to the following Tuesday or possibly Wednesday, except Farrar, who assigns the proposal of Judas to the priests, to Saturday night after the anointing at Bethany, and the conclusion of the bargain with the council, to the following Tuesday night.

(3) Geikie assigns the utterance of the prophecy respecting the fall of Jerusalem and the coming of Christ to Tuesday afternoon, 12th of Nisan, and the anointing at Bethany, and the conspiracy against Jesus by the rulers, and their conference with Judas, to the same night. How Jesus spent Wednesday, Farrar and Geikie and Canon Cook think we are not informed.

A large number of commentators also assume that the anointing was on Tuesday night, some of them explaining the difficulty in John xii, 1, by supposing that to be another anointing, and some, that it was the same, and that there is a copyist's error in John, or that he refers to the arrival at Bethany only, and does not imply that the *anointing* took place "six days before the passover." But if the anointing noticed by John is not the same as this in Mark and Matthew, then there were two anointings at the same place, under much the same circumstances, only four days apart, which seems very improbable. If they were the same, and yet took place on Tuesday night, the *apparently* precise note of time by John must be explained. This is more difficult to do satisfactorily, than it is to explain the transposition in the narratives of Mark and Matthew. Hence the order given in No. 2 is the most satisfactory.

The *arrival* at Bethany from Jericho, is also variously assigned to Sunday, 10th Nisan, by Luthardt and Strong, to Saturday, 9th Nisan, by Greswell and Robinson, to Friday night by Wieseler, Tholuck, Andrews and the most critical commentators. Canon Cook observes that from this point to the resurrection there is almost a complete and minute argument in the synoptical narratives.

and of unleavened bread] The Passover was on the 14th of Nisan, and the " Feast of unleavened bread " commenced on the 15th and lasted for seven days, deriving its name from the *Mazzoth*, or unleavened cakes, the only bread allowed during that week (Exod. xii, 34, 39; Deut. xvi, 3). From their close connection they are generally treated as one, both in the Old and in the New Testament, and Josephus on one occasion, even describes it as "a feast for eight days." *Jos. Antiq.* ii, 15, 1.—*Edersheim.*

and the chief priests] While our Lord was in quiet retirement at Bethany

AUTHORIZED VERSION.	REVISED VERSION.
they might take him by craft, and put him to death.	might take him with subtilty, and kill him:
2 But they said, Not on the feast day, lest there be an uproar of the people.	2 for they said, Not during the feast, lest haply there shall be a tumult of the people.
3 And being in Bethany, in the house of Simon the leper, as he sat at meat, there came a	3 And while he was in Bethany in the house of Simon the leper, as he sat at meat, there

the rulers in the court of the palace of Caiaphas (Matt. xxvi, 3), consulted how they could put him to death. There was a great crowd at the passover at Jerusalem, and that would make it prudent for the rulers to avoid exciting a tumult.

by craft] by stratagem, deceit, or fraud; they dared not arrest him openly, because of the people.

2. *Not on the feast day*] See R.V. Their plan was to do it immediately after the feast, when the crowd would be gone, but Judas probably changed their plan.

3—9. SIMON'S FEAST AND THE ANOINTING BY MARY.

(Saturday eve following the Jewish Sabbath, April 1st, A. D. 30.)

3. *And being in Bethany*] This anointing is related by Matthew, Mark and John. The anointing narrated in Luke vii, 36-50, though held to be the same by the Romanists, was undoubtedly different, for it was at the house of "Simon" the Pharisee, probably at Capernaum, while this was at the house of Simon a leper, in Bethany. Some, as Theophylact and Lightfoot, suppose that the supper mentioned in John is a different one from that in Matthew and Mark, but without sufficient grounds, for as Robinson observes, the identity of circumstances is too great, and the alleged differences too few to support the conjecture. Matthew and Mark say the woman anointed his head; John, his feet, but neither excludes the other; and John speaks of Lazarus as one of those who reclined at the table, showing that he was a guest; hence, the supper may have been at the house of Simon, as the other gospels state. The conjecture that Simon owned the house, and that Lazarus was his tenant, the house being occupied by both, is more ingenious than probable. The anointing was on the evening following Saturday—the Jewish sabbath. It took place after sunset, at which time the sabbath ended. The evangelist Mark, on this view, goes back to narrate the anointing, and connect it with the offer of Judas to betray Jesus. Some conjecture that Judas made a similar offer to the rulers at an earlier date.

Simon the leper] and possibly one who had been cured by our Lord. He was probably a near friend or relation of Lazarus. Some conjecture that he was his brother, others that he was the husband of Mary.

as he sat at meat] We learn from John that Martha served at the feast while Lazarus reclined at the table as one of the guests. "Nothing can be more natural and easy," says Alexander, "than the introduction of this incident at this point, both by Mark and Matthew. The attempt to represent it as at variance with the chronology of John xii, 1, being altogether groundless, as the *six days* there relate to his arrival in the neighborhood of Jerusalem, and the *two days* here to his preparation for the paschal service. Equally groundless is the notion entertained by some, that the passages describe two different anointings."

there came a woman] John says her name was Mary, probably the sister of Martha, and of Lazarus. The name of the woman who was a sinner, and anointed Jesus at the house of Simon the Pharisee, is not given, so that the Romanist writers have no ground for identifying her with Mary of Bethany, or for regarding the anointing at Bethany as the same as the one described in Luke vii, 36—50.

AUTHORIZED VERSION.	REVISED VERSION.
woman having an alabaster box of ointment of spikenard very precious; and she brake the box, and poured *it* on his head.	came a woman having [1] an alabaster cruse of ointment of [2] spikenard very costly; *and* she brake the cruse and poured it over his head.
4 And there were some that had indignation within themselves, and said, Why was this waste of the ointment made?	4 But there were some that had indignation among themselves, *saying*, To what purpose hath this waste of the ointment been made?

[1] Or, *a flask*   [2] Gr. *pistic nard*, pistic being perhaps a local name. Others take it to mean *genuine*; others, *liquid*.

having an alabaster box] "box" is not expressed in the Greek. At Alabastron in Egypt there was a manufactory of small cruses or vases for holding perfumes, which were made from a stone found in the neighboring mountains. The Greeks called these vases after the city from which they came, *alabastrons*. This name was eventually extended to the stone of which they were formed, and at length the term *alabaster* was applied without distinction to all perfume vessels, of whatever materials they consisted.

ALABASTER VASES.

of ointment of spikenard] Or, *of pure (or pistic) nard or liquid nard*. See R.V. and margin for various renderings of this phrase. The American revisers prefer the reading "pure nard," and would omit the marginal readings; and so in John xii, 3. *Pure* or *genuine* seems to yield the best meaning, as opposed to the *psuedo-nardus*, for the spikenard was often adulterated. Pliny, *Nat. Hist.* xii, 26. It was drawn from an Indian plant, brought down in considerable quantities into the plains of India from such mountains as Shalma, Kedar Kanta, and others, at the foot of which flow the Ganges and Jumna rivers.

very precious] It was among the costliest anointing oils of antiquity, and was sold throughout the Roman Empire, where it fetched a price that put it beyond any but the wealthy. Mary had bought a vase or flask of it containing twelve ounces (John xii, 3). Of the costliness of the ointment we may form some idea by remembering that it was among the gifts sent by Cambyses to the Ethiopians (Herod iii, 20), and that Horace promises Virgil a whole *cadus* (= 36 quarts nearly) of wine, for a small onyx box of spikenard (*Carm.* IV, xii, 16, 17).=*Maclear*.

brake the box] "The Greek word implies not so much the breaking of the neck of the costly jar or flask, but the crushing it in its entirety with both her hands."—*Ellicott*. Others, however, regard it as meaning that she broke the seal (as Burder), or the small neck of the flask. See Schaff, Perowne and Bloomfield. "To anoint the feet of the greatest monarch was long unknown, and in all the pomps and greatnesses of the Roman prodigality, it was not used till Otho taught it to Nero."—Jeremy Taylor's *Life of Christ*, iii. 13.

4. *there were some*] The murmuring may have begun with Judas Iscariot, John xii, 4, and infected some of the others, or the feeling may have been a general one, and giving expression to it may have inflamed the feelings of

AUTHORIZED VERSION.	REVISED VERSION.
5 For it might have been sold for more than three hundred pence, and have been given to the poor. And they murmured against her.	5 For this ointment might have been sold for above three hundred ² pence, and given to the poor. And they murmured against her.
6 And Jesus said, Let her alone; why trouble ye her? she hath wrought a good work on me.	6 But Jesus said, Let her alone; why trouble ye her? she hath wrought a good work on me.
7 For ye have the poor with you always, and whensoever ye will ye may do them good: but me ye have not always.	7 For ye have the poor always with you, and whensoever ye will ye can do them good: but me ye have not always. She hath done what she could: she hath anointed my body
8 She hath done what she could: she is come aforehand to anoint my body to the burying.	8 but me ye have not always. She hath done what she could; she hath anointed my body aforehand for the burying. And verily I say
9 Verily I say unto you, Wheresoever this gospel shall be preached throughout the whole world, this also that she hath done shall be spoken of for a memorial of her.	9 aforehand for the burying. And verily I say unto you, Wheresoever the gospel shall be preached throughout the whole world, that also which this woman hath done shall be spoken of for a memorial of her.

¹ See marginal note on Matt. xviii, 28, [quoted on p. 82.]

others to a greater degree. So Mark's account implies. The objection may have been a hollow pretence on the part of Judas, while some others may have honestly felt that it was not a wise expenditure.

This waste] literally "loss" or "perdition." "But thou Judas, art the son of perdition."—*Bengel*. The objection was not that the use was luxurious and sinful, though this may possibly be implied, but that the value of the ointment might have been better spent in relieving the suffering poor.

5. *for more than three hundred pence*] *i. e.* for more than 300 *denarii*, equal to about $50. To Judas it was intolerable that there should be such an utter waste of money. It may have been his *office* to give to the poor, from their common fund. See the additional remark in John xii, 6.

they murmured] Wyclif renders it here "thei groyneden in to hir." De Wette, "they scolded her." The word "expresses a passionate feeling, which we strive to keep back in utterance." "Mark, without a doubt, presents here the most accurate historic picture; John defines most sharply the motive; Matthew gives the especially practical historic form."—*Lange*.

6. *wrought a good work*] any sacrifice and expense truly made for the Lord is not extravagance, but a "good work."

7. *poor with you always*] Those who *talk* much about the poor will have constant opportunities to *do* much for them. Let them *do*, as well as talk. Lightfoot conjectures that the Jews thought there would be no poor in the days of the Messiah

ye may do them good] To the papist argument (from this verse) in favor of the use of incense, tapers, and immoderate expense in a showy and pompous worship Calvin ingeniously if not forcibly answers, that Christ plainly makes this an exception and impliedly forbids its repetition as not agreeable to him, but rather desires us to bestow on the *poor* what superstition foolishly expends in the worship of God. The verse suggests, as Schaff observes, that under no reorganization of society will poverty be banished from the earth.

8. *she is come aforehand*] See R. V. The word thus rendered only occurs three times in the New Testament. (1) Here ; (2) 1 Cor. xi, 21 ; (3) Gal. vi, 1. It denotes (1) *to take beforehand;* (2) *to take before another;* (3) *to outstrip, get the start of, anticipate.*

what she could] "Blessed are they of whom the Saviour will say, They have done what they could!"—*Jacobus*. Literally it reads, "what she had, she did." Of how few could Jesus say this now!

9. *gospel shall be preached*] Christ and the world have widely different estimates of conduct. The world has utilitarian views. How useful the value of this ointment! It would do so much good for the poor! So the world raves about missions, when "all is needed at home." "What does it

AUTHORIZED VERSION.	REVISED VERSION.
10 And Judas Iscariot, one of the twelve, went unto the chief priests, to betray him unto them. 11 And when they heard it, they were glad, and promised to give him money. And he sought how he might conveniently betray him. 12 And the first day of unleavened bread, when	10 And Judas Iscariot, [1] he that was one of the twelve, went away unto the chief priests, that he might deliver him unto them. And 11 they, when they heard it, were glad, and promised to give him money. And he sought how he might conveniently deliver him unto them. 12 And on the first day of unleavened bread

[1] Gr. *the one of the twelve.*

give of love to the poor?" asks Dr. John Hall, "The supporters of foreign missions are almost the only helpers of the poor at home." And thus is this prophecy fulfilled by gospel missions the world over. From the omission of this incident by Luke, Alford draws an argument in favor of the independence of the gospel records.

10, 11. JUDAS WITH THE CHIEF PRIESTS.
Tuesday April 4, A. D. 30 (?).

10. *And Judas Iscariot*] Three causes, if we may conjecture anything on a subject so full of mystery, would seem to have brought about his present state of mind: (1) *avarice;* (2) *disappointment of his carnal hopes;* (3) *a withering of internal religion.* The reason for going at this time, is not as obvious from Mark's narrative alone, as from all the accounts combined. Judas was doubtless angered by the reproof of Jesus in the case of the ointment, and smarting under the reproach, carried into effect thoughts long brooding in his mind.

went unto the chief priests] he repaired from Bethany to Jerusalem, probably by night, and being admitted into the council of the chief priests proposes to betray his master into their hands.

11. *they were glad*] his proposal filled them with joy. Mark notices that they were glad, but does not give the price offered.

and promised] He had made his venture, and accepted what they offered. *Thirty pieces of silver* (Matt. xxvi, 15), the price of a slave (Exod. xxi, 32), were equivalent to 120 denarii, about $18 or $19 of our money. At this time the ordinary wages for a day's labor was one denarius; so that the whole sum amounted to about four months' wages of a day laborer.

conveniently] The arrest must be made quietly, therefore when he had but few of his friends about him; when he was alone with the twelve. Judas doubtless knew just when such an opportunity would occur.

12—31. PASSOVER AND THE LAST SUPPER.
Thursday eve, 16th Nisan, 783, April 6th, (?) A. D. 30.

12. *the first day of unleavened bread*] Wednesday would seem to have been spent by our Lord at Bethany. That night he slept at Bethany for the last time on earth. 'On the Thursday morning he awoke never to sleep again.'—*Farrar.**

* *Date of the Lord's Supper*] The two leading theories are: (1) that it was on the evening following the 14th of Nisan; the regular and legal time for eating the passover; (2) that it was on the eve following the 13th of Nisan, and therefore that the Friday on which Christ was crucified was the 14th; hence, the *legal* passover would be eaten upon the evening of the day of crucifixion. This view would place the last supper on the day previous to the legal time for the passover. Robinson maintains the first view. See *English Harmony*, pp. 200—205, and thinks that the term 'passover' sometimes means the whole paschal festival or feast, and to "eat the passover," may mean to keep the paschal festival. His view relieves the difficulty of John xiii, 1, 2, and xviii, 28, and is concurred in by many scholars, ac, Davidson, Fairbairn, Gardiner, Lange, Lewin, Lightfoot, Milligan, Norton, Olshausen, Stier, Tholuck, Wieseler, Bochart, Hengstenberg, Andrews, Geikie and Schaff. The latter theory that Jesus and his disciples partook of a substitute for the passover upon the day previous, that is, anticipated it by one day, is accepted, by Bleek, De Wette, Ebrard, Ellicott, Erasmus, Ewald, Grotius, Lücke, Meyer, Neander, Tischendorf, Westcott, Winer, Alford,

AUTHORIZED VERSION.	REVISED VERSION.
they killed the passover, his disciples said unto him, Where wilt thou that we go and prepare that thou mayest eat the passover? 13 And he sendeth forth two of his disciples, and saith unto them, Go ye into the city, and there shall meet you a man bearing a pitcher of water: follow him.	when they sacrificed the passover, his disciples say unto him, Where wilt thou that we go and make ready that thou mayest eat the passover? 13 And he sendeth two of his disciples, and saith unto them, Go into the city, and there shall meet you a man bearing a

when they killed the passover] i.e. the *Paschal victim.* Compare Luke xxii, 7; 1 Cor. v. 7. The name of the Passover, in Hebrew *Pesach*, and in Aramæan and Greek *Pascha*, is derived from a root which means to "step over," or to "*overleap*," and thus points back to the historical origin of the Festival. "And when I see the blood, I will *pass over* you and the plague shall not be upon you to destroy you, when I smite the land of Egypt" (Exodus xii, 13). This is the common view respecting the word "Passover," but is it the correct one? Compare the Hebrew of Isaiah xxxi, 5, with that of Exod. xii, 23. These passages imply, according to Lowth and Ryle, that there are two agents—the destroying angel passing through to smite, and Jehovah "springing forward" (not passing over) to defend the house marked with blood. In this interpretation Jehovah *opposes* himself to the destroyer as a protector, and saves the house.

Where wilt thou] Thursday morning the disciples came to our Lord for instructions as to the passover. "They may have expected that he would eat it at Bethany, for the village was reckoned, as regards religious purposes, part of Jerusalem by the Rabbis, and the lamb might be eaten there, though it must be killed at the Temple."—*Lightfoot. Hor. Heb.*

that we go and prepare] The lamb would have been bought on the 10th of Nisan, according to the rule of the Law (Exod. xii, 3), the very day on which he, the true paschal Lamb, entered Jerusalem in meek triumph. Of the method of killing the paschal lamb, Starke writes: "A crowd of Israelites were received into the court, the gates were shut, the trumpets sounded. The householders slew their lambs. The priests formed a row, which extended to the altar, received the blood in silver basins, which they passed on one from another, and those who stood nearest the altar poured it out at its feet, whence it flowed subterraneously into the brook Kedron. The householder lifted the slain lamb to a hook on the willow, took off its skin, and removed the fat. This last the priest burned on the altar. The householder uttered a prayer, and carried the lamb to his house, bound in its skin. The head of the house, where the feast was held, received the skin. When the first crowd departed another followed, and so on."

13. *he sendeth forth two of his disciples*] The apostles Peter and John, Luke xxii, 8. Alford finds in this verse a proof that Mark did *not* write his gospel under the superintendence of Peter, else he would have given the names of the two disciples, and not have omitted the other fact, that Jesus *first* gave the command to prepare the passover. But the first omission seems rather in harmony with the Petrine theory, as it might be due to Peter's desire not to make himself unnecessarily prominent.

a man] It was generally the task of women to carry water. Among the thousands at Jerusalem they would notice this *man* carrying an earthern jar

---

Mansel and Farrar. Either view is attended with difficulties, but the first has, on the whole, the less serious ones, and is in accord with the more natural meaning of the language in the various accounts. The first three gospels certainly give the impression that the supper was instituted during the passover feast at the regular time, and Christ who came to fulfill the law, would hardly have violated it in this case, nor would he probably have been permitted so to do, by having the lamb slain in the temple, as tradition says was the custom at that time. Hence, the chronology followed in these notes, assigns it to Thursday eve, 14th Nisan, 783, or April 6th, (?) A.D. 30.

AUTHORIZED VERSION.	REVISED VERSION.
14 And wheresoever he shall go in, say ye to the goodman of the house, The Master saith, Where is the guestchamber, where I shall eat the passover with my disciples?	14 pitcher of water: follow him; and wheresoever he shall enter in, say to the goodman of the house, The ¹ Master saith, Where is my guest-chamber, where I shall eat the passover with my disciples? And he will himself shew you a large upper room furnished and ready: and there make ready for us.
15 And he will shew you a large upper room furnished and prepared: there make ready for us.	15 over with my disciples? And he will himself shew you a large upper room furnished and ready: and there make ready for us.
16 And his disciples went forth, and came into the city, and found as he had said unto them: and they made ready the passover.	16 And the disciples went forth, and came into the city, and found as he had said unto them: and they made ready the passover.

¹ Or, *Teacher*

of water drawn from one of the fountains. We need not conclude, because it was a slave's employment to do this (Deut. xxix, 11; Josh. ix, 21), that he was a slave. The apostles were to follow him to whatever house he entered.

14. *say ye to the goodman of the house*] Some conjecture that the owner of the house was a disciple; see Bengel. "A disciple but not one of the twelve;" but the word rendered "guest-chamber" is also rendered "inn" in Luke ii, 7, and was apparently a generic term for hired lodging. Lightfoot says lodgings were free at Jerusalem during the passover, but Rosenmüller

EARTHEN WATER PITCHERS.

holds it to be certain that during the feast the Jerusalemites hired out rooms furnished for visitors to the passover. Hence there is no call for the ingenious guesses that he was Nicodemus, Joseph of Arimathæa, or John Mark; for the gospels and traditions alike are silent. "Universal hospitality prevailed in this matter, and the only recompense that could be given was the skin of the paschal lamb, and the earthen dishes used at the meal."—*Geikie*.

the guestchamber] curiously translated by Wyclif, "my fulfilling, or *etyng* place." Comp. R. V. It was common for those in Jerusalem to furnish or rent rooms, and make preparations for other Jews, not residents of the city, who came to keep the passover.

15. *a large upper room furnished and prepared*] "a greet souping place strewid."—Wyclif. *Furnished* implies that it was provided with couches, as the custom of reclining at meals required, and *prepared* implies special arrangements for the Passover, as searching for, and putting away every particle of leaven (1 Cor. v, 7), which was done with a lighted candle, and also getting ready the lamb, herbs, wine, bread, etc.

16. *they made ready the passover*] This preparation would include the provision of the unleavened cakes, of the bitter herbs, the four or five cups of red wine mixed with water, of everything, in short, necessary for the meal. The Passover was celebrated among the Jews in the time of our Lord: (1) By eating two or three flat cakes of unleavened bread (Exod. xii, 18), and by a succession of four cups of red wine always mixed with water (Ps. xvi, 5, xxiii, 5, cxvi, 13). These were placed before the master of the house where the paschal feast was celebrated, or before the most eminent guest, who was called the celebrant, the president, or proclaimer of the feast. (2) After those assembled had reclined, he took one of the four cups, known as the "cup of consecration," in his right hand, and pronounced the benediction over the wine and the feast, saying, "*Blessed be Thou, Jehovah, our God. Thou*

AUTHORIZED VERSION.	REVISED VERSION.
17 And in the evening he cometh with the twelve.	17 And when it was evening he cometh with the twelve. And as they ¹ sat and were eating, Jesus said, Verily I say unto you, One
18 And as they sat and did eat, Jesus said,	

¹ Gr. *reclined.*

King of the universe, Who hast created the fruit of the vine." He then tasted the cup and passed it round. (3) Water was then brought in, and he washed, followed by the rest, the hands being dipped in water. (4) The table was then set out with bitter herbs, such as lettuce, endive, succory, and horehound, the sauce called *charoseth*, and the passover lamb. (5) The celebrant then once more blessed God for the fruits of the earth, and taking a portion of the bitter herbs, dipped it in the *charoseth*, and ate a piece of it of "the size of an olive," and his example was followed by the rest. (6) The *Haggadah* or "shewing forth" (1 Cor. xi, 26) now commenced, and the celebrant declared the circumstances of the delivery from Egypt, as commanded by the Law (Exod. xii, 27, xiii. 8). (7) Then the second cup of wine was filled, and a child or proselyte inquired, "*What mean ye by this service?*" (Exod. xii, 26), to which reply was made according to a prescribed formula or liturgy. The first part of the "Hallel," Psalms cxiii, cxiv, was then sung, and the second cup was solemnly drunk. (8) The celebrant now washed his hands again, and taking two of the unleavened cakes, broke one of them, and pronounced the thanksgiving in these words, "*Blessed be Thou, O Lord our God, Thou King of the universe, Who bringest forth fruit out of the earth.*" Then he distributed a portion to each, and all wrapping some bitter herbs round their portion, dipped it in the *charoseth* and ate it. (9) The flesh of the lamb was now eaten, and the Master of the house, lifting up his hands, gave thanks over the third cup of wine, known as the "cup of blessing," and handed it round to each person. (10) After thanks for the food of which they had partaken, and for their redemption from Egypt, a fourth cup, known as the "cup of joy," was filled and drunk, and the remainder of the Hallel (Ps. cxv-cxviii,) was sung. See Buxtorf, *de Cœna Domini*; Lightfoot, *Temple Service*; *Edersheim.* The passover meal proper began with the second cup, and ended with the third.

17. *evening*] "It was probably while the sun was beginning to decline in the horizon, that Jesus and the disciples descended once more over the Mount of Olives into the Holy City. Before them lay Jerusalem in her festive attire. White tents dotted the sward, gay with the bright flowers of early spring, or peered out from the gardens and the darker foliage of the olive plantations. From the gorgeous Temple buildings, dazzling in their snow-white marble and gold, on which the slanting rays of the sun were reflected, rose the smoke of the altar of burnt offering....The streets must have been thronged with strangers, and the flat roofs covered with eager gazers, who either feasted their eyes with a first sight of the Sacred City, for which they had so often longed, or else once more rejoiced in view of the well-remembered localities. It was the last day-view which the Lord had of the Holy City—till His resurrection!"—*Edersheim.*

he cometh with the twelve] Judas must have stolen back to Bethany before daylight, and another day of hypocrisy had been spent under the penetrating glance of him who could read the hearts of men.—*Maclear.*

18. *And as they sat*] grouping together the four narratives, which, as they approach the Passion, expand into the fullness of a diary, we infer that (1) when the little company had taken their places on the *triclinia*, the Saviour, as celebrant or proclaimer of the feast, remarking that with desire he had desired to eat this passover before he suffered, took the first cup and divided it among them (Luke xxii, 15-18). (2) Then followed the un-

MODERN JERUSALEM. (*After Salons.*)

AUTHORIZED VERSION.	REVISED VERSION.
Verily I say unto you, one of you which eateth with me shall betray me. 19 And they began to be sorrowful, and to say unto him one by one, Is it I? and another *said*, *Is* it I? 20 And he answered and said unto them, *It is* one of the twelve, that dippeth with me in the dish. 21 The Son of man indeed goeth, as it is written of him: but woe to that man by whom the Son of man is betrayed! good were it for that man if he had never been born.	of you shall betray me, *even* he that eateth with me. They began to be sorrowful, and 20 to say unto him, one by one, Is it I? And he said unto them, *It is* one of the twelve, he 21 that dippeth with me in the dish. For the Son of man goeth, even as it is written of him: but woe unto that man through whom the Son of man is betrayed! good were it ¹ for that man if he had not been born.

¹ Gr. *for him if that man.*

seemly dispute touching priority (Luke xxii, 24-30), to correct which (3) he washed his disciples' feet (John xiii, 1-11). (4) Then the meal was resumed and he reclined once more at the table (John xiii, 12), the beloved disciple lying on his right.

one of you which eateth with me shall betray me] See R. V. He had already said, after washing their feet, "now ye are clean, but *not all*" (John xiii, 10), but at this moment the consciousness of the traitor's presence so wrought upon him (John xiii, 21), that he broke forth into words of yet plainer prediction. Now he declares it to be one of the twelve, for that is the plainest meaning of the phrase.

19. *they began to be sorrowful*] the very thought of treason was to their honest and faithful hearts insupportable, and excited great surprise and deepest sorrow.

Is it I?] "Surely it cannot be I," *Meyer*; or "It is not I, is it?" *Alexander*. None of them said "Is it *he?*" so utterly unconscious were they of the treachery that lurked in their midst. Notice that the repetition at the end of the verse found in the A. V. is omitted by many authorities, and also by the R. V.

20. *he answered and said unto them*] "*Answered*" is omitted in the best MSS. See R. V. The intimation was made privately to John, to whom Peter had made a sign that he should ask who could be so base as to betray their master (John xiii, 23-26).

one of the twelve] One of his own "familiar friends" (Ps. xli, 9).

that dippeth with me] "He who is just about to dip with me a piece of the unleavened cakes into the *charoseth*"—a sauce consisting of a mixture of vinegar, figs, dates, almonds, and spice, provided at the passover—"and to whom I shall give some of it presently" (John xiii, 26). "To this day, at the summit of Gerizim, the Samaritans, on the occasion of the Passover, hand to the stranger a little olive-shaped morsel of unleavened bread enclosing a green fragment of wild endive or some other bitter herb, which may resemble, except that it is not dipped in the dish, the very 'sop' which Judas received at the hands of Christ."—*Farrar.* Alford and others hold, however, that this is simply another form of stating that it was one of his nearest and most trusted friends, one who was eating with him (as in *v.* 18), who would betray him, but does not mean that the betrayer was at that moment dipping into the dish with him. This would satisfy the force of the Greek word. This act, on this view, would not *definitely* point out Judas as the traitor; it would lead the others however, to conclude who was meant.

21. *woe to that man*] The intimation just given was uttered privately, for the ear of John alone, and through him was possibly made known to Peter; but the incident was of so ordinary a character, that it would fail to attract any notice whatever, and could only be a sign to the apostle of love. Then aloud, as we may believe, Christ uttered his final warning to the

AUTHORIZED VERSION.	REVISED VERSION.
22 And as they did eat, Jesus took bread, and blessed, and brake it, and gave to them, and said, Take, eat: this is my body	22 And as they were eating, he took ¹ bread, and when he had blessed, he brake it, and gave to them, and said, Take ye: this is my

¹ Or, *a loaf*

traitor, and pronounced words of immeasurable woe on him by whom he was about to be betrayed. "*It were good for that man if he had never been born.*" But the last appeal had no effect upon him. "*Rabbi, is it I?*" he inquired. "*Thou hast said,*" replied the Saviour, and gave him "the sop," and Satan entered into him, as John tells us (xiii, 27). "*That thou doest, do quickly,*" the Saviour continued; and the traitor arose and went forth, and it *was night* (John xiii, 27-30). Whether Judas was present at the institution of the Lord's Supper is a disputed question. According to John xiii, 30, he retired immediately after the sop was given him, and was not present.*

22. *And as they did eat*] assuming that Judas left; after his departure, the Saviour, as though relieved of a heavy load, broke forth into words of mysterious triumph (John xiii, 31-35), and then, as the meat went on, proceeded to institute the Lord's Supper. Some accept the order of Luke, and in that case Judas was present at the supper.

Jesus took bread] that is, one of the unleavened cakes that had been placed before him as the proclaimer of the feast.

and blessed] giving thanks and pronouncing the consecration, probably in the usual words, see above, verse 16. "Eat" is omitted in R. V., in accord with the best authorities and MSS.

this is my body] Luke adds, "*which is being (or on the point of being) given for you;*" Paul (1 Cor. xi, 24) "*which is being (or on the point of being) broken for you,*" while both add, "*do this in remembrance of me.*" In the Greek, the pronoun for "this" is not of the same gender as "bread ;" hence, some infer that it cannot refer to bread. The words are interpreted (*a*) literally by (1) the Romanists, who claim that the substance of the bread in the Lord's Supper is changed to the real flesh of our Lord. This view is called transubstantiation. (2) The Lutheran, which declares that the body of Christ is present in, with, and under the bread. This view is called consubstantiation. (*b*) Others interpret the word in a figurative, or in a symbolical sense, as (1) the Zwinglian view, which holds that the Lord's Supper is a memorial service only; (2) The Calvanistic view, which affirms the *spiritual* presence of Christ in the supper, against the literal view of the Romanists, and in distinction from the real presence view of the Lutherans. The reformed churches hold (1) that the Lord's Supper is a commemorative ordinance and feast, wherein believers truly, though spiritually, receive Christ with all his benefits, and commune with one another as members of the body of Christ. The reformed churches also understand the

* *Judas not present.*—Was Judas present at the institution of the Lord's Supper, or not? This question has been much discussed, and commentators are divided in their answers. That he was present is favored by Jerome, Augustine, Chrysostom, the two Cyrils, Theodoret, Bellarmine, Maldonatus, Gerhard, Beza, Bucer, Lightfoot, Bengel, Stier, Alford, and most of the Lutherans. Among those holding that he was not present, are Meyer, Tischendorf, Robinson, Lichtenstein, Bucher, Ebrard, Lange, Wieseler, Regginbach, Ellicott, Schaff (though he regards it as possible that Judas was present at the distribution of the bread only), Geikie, and Andrews. Calvin and Farrar are undecided. If Judas was present, the institution of the supper in John's account must apparently be inserted between verses 20 and 21 of John xiii, and the order of Matthew and Mark must be explained. This is very awkward and difficult. The presence of Judas is inferred chiefly from Luke's account, but Luke's order is obviously not exact in other respects; for example, washing the disciples' feet. The statement in the A. V., "supper being ended," in John xiii, 2, is a mistranslation. See R. V., which reads, "during supper." If Judas left before the institution of the supper, the order of Matthew and Mark can be observed, and in John's account it would follow verse 32, which is much less awkward, and this arrangement accords with the order prescribed for the paschal supper in the Talmud.

AUTHORIZED VERSION.	REVISED VERSION.
23 And he took the cup, and when he had given thanks, he gave it to them: and they all drank of it. 24 And he said unto them, This is my blood of the new testament, which is shed for many. 25 Verily I say unto you, I will drink no more of the fruit of the vine, until that day that I drink it new in the kingdom of God. 26 And when they had sung a hymn, they went out into the mount of Olives.	23 body. And he took a cup; and when he had given thanks, he gave to them: and they all drank of it. 24 And he said unto them, This is my blood of ¹ the ² covenant which is shed for many. Verily I say unto you, I will no more drink of the fruit of the vine until that day when I drink it new in the kingdom of God. 26 And when they had sung a hymn, they went out unto the mount of Olives.

¹ Or, *the testament* ² Some ancient authorities insert *new*.

phrase to mean, "This represents my body." Similar usage is frequent in the Bible, and especially in the New Testament. "The seven good kine are seven years" (Gen. xli, 26); that is, they signified or represented seven years. "The good seed are the children," etc. (Matt. xiii, 38). "I am the door" (John x, 9). "I am the vine" (John xv, 1). "That rock was Christ" (1 Cor. x, 4). If, as Wordsworth suggests, "the bread was literally changed into Christ's human body, the disciples were to take and eat it, and that body was standing before them and gave them what they did eat, and remained with them visible and entire after they had eaten, and afterwards died on the cross." Again, if it be said that "Christ's body is now a spiritual body, and that, therefore, what could not be then, can be now;" this is to deny, as Howe remarks, "that the apostles at that time partook of the real sacrament; we must, therefore, admit a figure of speech, and this compels us to accept substantially the interpretation of the reformed churches."

23. *he took the cup*] possibly the third cup, and known as the "cup of blessing." See above, verse 16. But it is quite uncertain, and indeed unimportant, whether it was the third, or some other of the five cups used in the passover. There has been much discussion in regard to the "wine" used by our Lord, and the question is not settled. Some of those holding total abstinence views, insist that it was the unfermented juice of the grape. Other equally strong and sincere temperance advocates believe it was what is generally called wine, the fermented grape juice. The learned Arabic scholar, Dr. Van Dyck, after thirty years' residence in Syria, declares that he has never heard of wine preserved unfermented...they could not keep grape juice unfermented if they would; it would either become wine or vinegar in a few days. At the passover only fermented wine is used.. they have no idea of any other. Dr. Post, for twenty-five years a professor in Beirut, gives similar testimony. The "dibs" of grapes is a thick paste, not a drink.

24. *This is my blood of the new testament*] The R. V. reads "covenant," which is better than "testament," though neither word exhausts the meaning of the Greek. Some of the best MSS. here omit "new," as in the R. V. He reminds them of the old covenant also made in blood with their fathers in the wilderness (Exod. xxiv, 8).

which is shed for many] i. e., *which is being* (or *on the point of being*) *shed for many*. Matthew (xxvi, 28) adds, "*for the remission of sins;*" Paul adds (1 Cor. xi, 25), "*This do ye, as oft as ye drink it, in remembrance of me.*" Thus did our Lord ordain bread and wine to be the "outward part" or "sign" of the ordinance of our Redemption by his death. The order of events at this last passover is given by Robinson: (1) Jesus and the disciples taking their places at the table; (2) the contention; (3) and the first cup; (4) washing the disciples' feet and reproof; (5) pointing out the traitor; (6) foretelling Peter's denial; (7) institution of the supper. See also under verse 18.

26. *when they had sung an hymn*] that is, the concluding portion of the Hallel. See above, note on verse 16.

Authorized Version.	Revised Version.
27 And Jesus saith unto them, All ye shall be offended because of me this night: for it is written, I will smite the shepherd, and the sheep shall be scattered.	27 And Jesus saith unto them, All ye shall be ¹offended: for it is written, I will smite the shepherd, and the sheep shall be scattered
28 But after that I am risen, I will go before you into Galilee.	28 abroad. Howbeit, after I am raised up, I will 29 go before you into Galilee. But Peter said unto him, Although all shall be ¹offended,
29 But Peter said unto him, Although all shall be offended, yet *will* not I.	30 yet will not I. And Jesus saith unto him, Verily I say unto thee, that thou to-day, *even*
30 And Jesus saith unto him, Verily I say unto thee, That this day, *even* in this night, before the cock crow twice, thou shalt deny me thrice.	this night, before the cock crow twice, shalt 31 deny me thrice. But he spake exceeding vehemently, If I must die with thee, I will
31 But he spake the more vehemently, If I should die with thee, I will not deny thee in any wise. Likewise also said they all.	not deny thee. And in like manner also said they all.
32 And they came to a place which was named	32 And they come unto ²a place which was

¹ Gr. *caused to stumble.* ² Gr. *an enclosed piece of ground.*

27. *And Jesus saith unto them*] the prophecy of Jesus in verses 27-31, may have been spoken while they were at the table, and before the formal institution of the Lord's Supper. This is Robinson's view, followed by Maclear. Clark supposes that the prophecy was twice uttered, once at the table and again on the way to the garden, but this is hardly probable. Schaff, Alexander, Ellicott, and others think it was spoken only while on the way to Gethsemane, and hence the order given in Matthew and Mark is accepted. "*offended*"] = "*stumble*" or *made to fall* "Because of me this night" is not found in most of the best MSS. and is omitted in the R. V.

for it is written] The words are taken from Zech. xiii, 7. The good shepherd quotes the allusion to himself in his truest character (John x, 4).

28. *after that I am risen up*] The Angel afterwards referred to these very words at the open sepulchre on the resurrection morning (Mark xvi, 6, 7).

29. *But Peter said unto him*] "Stumble" or "offended" is same word as in verse 27, *i. e.* "make to fall." Ardent and impulsive as ever, the apostle could not endure the thought of such desertion. His protestations of fidelity are more fully given in Matt. xxvi, 33 and John xiii, 37.

30. *this night*] "Twice" is not found in a few MSS. but the majority have it. The *twice* crowing would be at two or three, and at five A. M. The midnight crowing would not be counted, as Canon Cook conjectures that the first trial before Caiaphas could not have taken place before one or two o'clock A.M. Before morning Peter would *thrice* deny that he had ever known his Lord. Mark, as usual, records two points which enhance the force of the warning and the guilt of Peter, viz. (*a*) that the cock should crow *twice*, and (*b*) that after such warning he repeated his protestation with greater vehemence.

31. *If I should*] literally, *If it be necessary for me to die with Thee;* as Wyclif renders it, "*if it bihoue* me to dye to gidere with thee." The Greek word for "more" or "exceeding vehemently" refers not so much to the *ardor* of his talk, as to the abundance of it; he kept on talking in this strain, etc. For what followed, see John xiv, to xvii; other discourses on his own approaching departure to the Father, and the coming of the comforter (John xiv, 1-31); (2) of himself as the true vine and his disciples as the branches (John xv, 1-5); (3) of the trials which the apostles must expect and the assured aid of the comforter (John xvi,); (4) lifting up his eyes to heaven, solemnly committing them to the care of the Father, (John xvii,); (5) then the concluding part of the Hallel (Ps. cxv-cxviii,) was sung, *i. e.* chanted, and the little company went forth to the garden.

32-42. THE AGONY IN THE GARDEN OF GETHSEMANE.
(Evening following Thursday 14th Nisan, April 6th, A. D. 30.)

32. *And they came*] they would pass through one of the city gates

AUTHORIZED VERSION.	REVISED VERSION.
Gethsemane: and he saith to his disciples, Sit ye here, while I shall pray. 33 And he taketh with him Peter and James and John, and began to be sore amazed, and to be very heavy; 34 And saith unto them, My soul is exceeding sorrowful unto death: tarry ye here, and watch.	named Gethsemane: and he saith unto his 33 disciples, Sit ye here, while I pray. And he taketh with him Peter and James and John, and began to be greatly amazed, and sore 34 troubled. And he saith unto them, My soul is exceeding sorrowful unto death:

"open that night, as it was passover," down the steep side of the Kedron (John xviii, 1), and coming by the bridge, they went onward towards

Gethsemane] Gethsemane means "oil-press." It was a *garden* (John xviii, 1) or olive orchard, on the slope of Olivet. Thither our Lord was wont to resort (John xviii, 2). Tradition places it at the foot of Olivet about 100 yards east of the bridge over the Kedron (black brook). It is a small irregular garden enclosed by a wall 12 feet high, 168 feet long on the north side, and 180 feet on the west side. The wall is modern, and was built in 1847. Within, there are 7 or 8 olive trees, the trunks cracked with age, and shored up with stones. One of the trees is 19 feet around at the base, and though of great age, cannot date back to Christ's time, for Titus cut down all the trees about Jerusalem. The Latin monks keep the place as a flower garden, presenting every traveller with a bouquet, for which he is expected to give at least one franc. The Greeks have set up another garden further up the Mount of Olives, but the one under the Latins is generally accepted as Gethsemane. See Schaff, *Dict. of the Bible.*

33. *he taketh with him*] the three most trusted and long-tried of the Apostolic body, who had been the privileged witnesses of the raising of the daughter of Jairus and of the transfiguration.

began to be sore amazed] "To drede"— *Wyclif*: "to be full of horror"— Meyer and DeWette. This word in ch. ix, 15 is applied to the *amazement* of the people when they saw the Lord after the transfiguration; in ch. xvi, 5, 6, it is applied to the holy women at the Sepulchre. Mark alone applies the word in connection with the agony in the garden.

to be very heavy] "to heuye"— *Wyclif*. The original word thus translated, only occurs (1) here, (2) in the parallel, Matt. xxvi, 37, and (3) in Phil. ii, 26, "for he [Epaphroditus] longed after you all, and was *full of heaviness.*" Buttmann suggests that the root idea is that of being "*away from home*" and so "confused," "beside one's self." Others consider the primary idea to be that of "loathing" and "discontent." It is used by Xenophon and Plato to express extreme anxiety and anguish.

34. *exceeding sorrowful*] A Greek compound used by Aristotle and Isocrates, and meaning grieved on every side; shut in by distress. Herod is said to have been "*exceeding sorry*" at the request for the Baptist's head Mark vi, 26. The young ruler was "*very sorrowful*" Luke xviii, 23. It points here to a depth of anguish and sorrow, and we may believe that he who at the first temptation had left the Saviour "*for a season*" (Luke iv, 13), had now returned, and whereas before he had brought to bear against the Lord, as Trench remarks, "all things pleasant and flattering, if so he might by aid of these entice or seduce him from his obedience, so now he thought with other engines to overcome his constancy, and to terrify, if it might be, from his allegiance to the truth, him whom manifestly he could not allure."

and watch] "*with me*" adds Matthew (xxvi, 38). Perfect man, "of a reasonable soul and human flesh subsisting." He yearned in this awful hour for human sympathy. It is almost the only personal request he is ever recorded to have made. It was but "a cup of cold water" that he craved.

AUTHORIZED VERSION.	REVISED VERSION.
35 And he went forward a little, and fell on the ground, and prayed that, if it were possible, the hour might pass from him.	35 abide ye here, and watch. And he went forward a little, and fell on the ground, and prayed that, if it were possible, the hour
36 And he said, Abba, Father, all things are possible unto thee; take away this cup from me: nevertheless, not what I will, but what thou wilt.	36 might pass away from him. And he said, Abba, Father, all things are possible unto thee; remove this cup from me: howbeit not
37 And he cometh, and findeth them sleeping, and saith unto Peter, Simon, sleepest thou? couldest not thou watch one hour?	37 what I will, but what thou wilt. And he cometh, and findeth them sleeping, and saith
38 Watch ye and pray, lest ye enter into temptation. The spirit truly is ready, but the flesh is weak.	38 unto Peter, Simon, sleepest thou? couldest thou not watch one hour? ¹Watch and pray, that ye enter not into temptation: the spirit indeed is willing, but the flesh is
39 And again he went away, and prayed, and spake the same words.	39 weak. And again he went away, and prayed,
40 And when he returned, he found them asleep again, (for their eyes were heavy,) neither wist they what to answer him.	40 saying the same words. And again he came, and found them sleeping, for their eyes were very heavy; and they wist not what to an-

¹ Or, *Watch ye, and pray that ye enter not*

But it was denied him! Very man, he leaned upon the men he loved, and they failed him! He *trod the winepress alone*; *and of the people there was none with him* (Isaiah lxiii. 3).

35. *might pass*] he went "*about a stone's throw*," Luke xxii, 41, for prayer, perhaps out of the moonlight into the shadow of the garden. "The whole feeling of suffering and judgment to be betrayed by the one-half of the world, and to be forsaken by the other half."—*Lange*. "The feeling cannot be entirely accounted for by the desertion of the creature merely; there was also to be the desertion of the Creator."—*Shedd*.

36. *Abba*] Mark alone has preserved for us this word. It is used only twice more in the New Testament, and both times by Paul, Rom. viii, 15, "ye have received the spirit of adoption, whereby we cry, *Abba, Father*," and Gal. iv, 6, "God hath sent forth the Spirit of his Son into your hearts, crying, *Abba, Father*." In Syriac it is said to have been pronounced with a double *b* when applied to a spiritual father, with a single *b* when used in its natural sense. With the double letter at all events it has passed into the European languages, as an ecclesiastical term, 'abbas,' 'abbot.' See Lightfoot on Gal. iv, 6.

not what I will] This is apt to give some difficulty, in respect to the character and nature of Christ. "I willingly submit my human will to thy divine will and pleasure."—*Bishop Hall*. Richard Baxter exclaimed "Lord, *when* thou wilt, *where* thou wilt, *as* thou wilt!" Some remarks of Petter, of 1692, may afford instruction and relief. "There are two distinct wills in Christ. ...Yet they are not contrary one to the other. The human will of Christ being always subject to his divine will." The Monotheists held there was but one kind of will in Christ, his divine will. This heresy first originated with Eutyches in the fourth century, and was fully developed 200 years later. It was sharply confuted by the early fathers, and condemned by councils, especially the Sixth of Constantinople.

37. *and saith unto Peter*] who had made so many impetuous promises.

38. *the flesh is weak*] It is not of course implied that his own "will" was at variance with that of his Father; but, very man, he had a *human will*, and knew the mystery of the opposition of the strongest, and at the same time the most innocent instincts of humanity. The fuller account of the "Agony" is found in Luke xxii, 43, 44.

40. *their eyes were heavy*] sothli her yzen were greuyd."—*Wyclif*. Even as had been the case on the mount of transfiguration. The original word, supported by the best MSS. only occurs here, and denotes that the apostles were utterly tired, and their eyes "*weighed down*."

what to answer him] A graphic touch peculiar to the second gospel

AUTHORIZED VERSION.	REVISED VERSION.
41 And he cometh the third time, and saith unto them, Sleep on now, and take your rest: it is enough, the hour is come; behold, the Son of man is betrayed into the hands of sinners. 42 Rise up, let us go; lo, he that betrayeth me is at hand. 43 And immediately, while he yet spake, com-	41 swer him. And he cometh the third time, and saith unto them, Sleep on now, and take your rest: it is enough; the hour is come; behold, the Son of man is betrayed into the hands of sinners. Arise, let us be going: behold, he that betrayeth me is at hand. 43 And straightway, while he yet spake,

gelist, just as the imperfect tense equally graphically implies that the eyes of the apostles were *constantly becoming weighed down*, in spite of any efforts they might *make to keep awake*. Comp. the scene at the transfiguration, Mark ix, 6. Dr. Rush suggests that profound sleep is a symptom of great grief. He often witnessed it in mothers just after the death of a child. Thus their "heaviness with sleep," as stated by the evangelists, is in entire accord with the natural results which might be expected from the sorrowful trials they were passing through, and is a proof of the genuineness and truthfulness of the sacred scene.

41. *the third time*] The temptation of the garden divides itself, like that of the wilderness, into three acts, following close on one another.

Sleep on now] The words are spoken in a kind of gentle irony, according to Calvin, but this is doubtful. See below. The golden hour for watching and praying was over.

it is enough] Some interpret this to mean: (1) enough of sleep, but that contradicts "sleep on now;" (2) others, as implying the conflict is over, or, still more naturally, (3) Stier adopts Neander's paraphrase, "sleep on now, I will no more awake you to watch with me, but ye will soon be roused out of your sleep, for behold ye, etc.;" (4) "It is enough of watching," which harmonizes best with the words that precede "sleep on now," with the charge to watch, and with the words which follow; (5) some see in the words "sleep on now" a sad irony, and take the words "it is enough" as earnest warning; (6) others make the first a question: "Do ye sleep on now?"

PRACTICAL SUGGESTIONS.—Some of the causes of Christ's agony may be reverently inferred from the gospels or surmised: (1) Jesus was in the prime of life, and conscious of rare abilities to do a great work; (2) into this hour were crowded the cruelty, shame, physical and spiritual torment coming on him; (3) he bore the griefs, sins, and sorrows of a world; (4) his friends forsook him, adding to his distress; Judas would betray him, his chosen people cry out for his blood; (5) he *might* escape all this; he suffered it for hard, stubborn hearts at enmity to him; (6) Satan doubtless oppressed him sorely, as hinted in John xiv, 30; (7) severest of all, the Father was to turn from him, and give him over to suffer the penalty of broken law, like a common malefactor. It was the burden of the sin of millions of souls, extending over thousands of years; it was an awful sense of the virulence of evil, and the frown of the Almighty, and the terrible judgment of righteous law, that brought this unutterable agony to the Son of God. See Alford, Farrar, Geikie, and Edwards on this theme. Be resigned to God's will. A minister prayed over a dying child, "If it be thy will spare —." The poor mother yearning over her loved one, exclaimed, "It *must* be his will, I cannot bear it." The child lived, to the surprise of many, and to the intolerable sorrow of the mother, who lived to see him hanged before he was two and twenty. "Oh, it is good to say not my will, but thine be done."—*Kilpin.*

43—52. THE BETRAYAL.
(Evening following Thursday, 14th Nisan, A. D., 30.)

43. *And immediately*] while he yet spake, the garden was filled with

GARDEN OF GETHSEMANE. (From a Photograph of the Palestine Fund.)

AUTHORIZED VERSION.

eth Judas, one of the twelve, and with him a great multitude with swords and staves, from the chief priests and the scribes and the elders.
44 And he that betrayed him had given them a token, saying, Whomsoever I shall kiss, that same is he; take him, and lead *him* away safely.
45 And as soon as he was come, he goeth straightway to him, and saith, Master, Master; and kissed him.
46 And they laid their hands on him, and took him.
47 And one of them that stood by drew a sword, and smote a servant of the high priest, and cut off his ear.

REVISED VERSION.

cometh Judas, one of the twelve, and with him a multitude with swords and staves, from the chief priests and the scribes and the
44 elders. Now he that betrayed him had given them a token, saying, Whomsoever I shall kiss, that is he; take him, and lead him
45 away safely. And when he was come, straightway he came to him, and saith, Rab-
46 bi; and ¹ kissed him. And they laid hands
47 on him, and took him. But a certain one of them that stood by drew his sword, and smote the ² servant of the high priest, and struck

¹ Gr. *kissed him much.* ² Gr. *bond-servant.*

armed men, and flashed with the light of numerous lanterns and torches, though the paschal moon was at the full, for "in the rocky ravine of the Kedron there would fall great deep shadows from the declivity of the mountains and projecting rocks, and there were caverns and grottoes in which a fugitive might retreat."—Lange, *Life of Christ,* iv, 292.

cometh Judas] during the two hours that had elapsed since he had gone forth from the upper room he had not been idle. He had reported to the ruling powers that the favorable moment had come, and had doubtless mentioned "the garden" whither his Master was wont to resort. He now returned, but not alone, for

with him a great multitude with swords and staves] "great" is omitted by the R. V. These consisted (1) of the regular guards of the temple, (2) of the detachment from the Roman cohort quartered in the tower of Antonia under the "chiliarch" or tribune in command of the garrison (John xviii, 3, 12). The high priest may have represented that the force was needed for the arrest of a false Messiah, dangerous to the Roman power.

44. *a token*] Judas had never imagined that our Lord would himself come forth to meet his enemies (John xviii, 2–5). He had anticipated the necessity of giving a signal whereby they might know him. The conjecture of some commentators (as Whitby), that Judas expected Jesus to escape from his enemies as he had formerly done, and because Christ did not escape, went and hanged himself, is unwarranted, if not absurd.

take him...safely] "take him," a strong word in Greek meaning to seize, overpower, secure him; "safely" means "securely," fearing possibly an attempt of the disciples to rescue him.

45. *and kissed him*] *kissed him fervently.* See R. V. The same word in the original, with its intensifying preposition, is used to express (1) the kissing of our Lord by the woman who was a sinner (Luke vii, 38, 45); (2) the kissing of the prodigal son by his father (Luke xv, 20); and (3) the kissing of Paul by the Christians at Miletus (Acts xx, 37).

47. *one of them that stood by*] this was Simon Peter (John xviii, 10), displaying his characteristic impetuosity. The omission here of Peter's name, lest it should bring him danger from the injured man, is without foundation, for Peter was recognized by a relative of Malchus soon after. John xviii, 26.

servant of the high priest] the servant's name was Malchus. John xviii, 10. John was an acquaintance of the high priest, hence he knew the name of his servant.

his ear] Both Mark and John use a diminutive—*little ear.* Luke alone (xxii, 50) tells us it was his *right ear.* Perhaps it was not completely severed, for Luke, who alone also records the healing, says that our Lord simply touched it and healed him.

AUTHORIZED VERSION.	REVISED VERSION.
48 And Jesus answered and said unto them, Are ye come out, as against a thief, with swords and with staves to take me?	48 off his ear. And Jesus answered and said unto them, Are ye come out, as against a robber, with swords and staves to seize me?
49 I was daily with you in the temple teaching, and ye took me not: but the scriptures must be fulfilled.	49 I was daily with you in the temple teaching, and ye took me not: but *this is done* that the
50 And they all forsook him, and fled.	50 scriptures might be fulfilled. And they all left him, and fled.
51 And there followed him a certain young man, having a linen cloth cast about *his* naked *body*; and the young men laid hold on him:	51 And a certain young man followed with him, having a linen cloth cast about him, over *his*
52 And he left the linen cloth, and fled from them naked.	52 naked *body*: and they lay hold on him; but he left the linen cloth, and fled naked.

48. *answered and said unto them*] those to whom he now spoke were some chief priests and elders and officers of the temple guard (Luke xxii. 52) who had been apparently watching his capture.

a thief] or robber. See R. V. and note on ch. xi. 17.

49. *the scriptures must be fulfilled*] or, *that the Scriptures might be fulfilled*. See R. V. This ought to have reminded the scribes of the Messianic predictions of the prophets, and how they were unconsciously fulfilling them.

50. *they all forsook him and fled*] even the impetuous Peter who had made so many promises; even the disciple whom He loved.

51. *a certain young man*] This forms an episode as characteristic of Mark as that of the two disciples journeying to Emmaus is of Luke. Some of the conjectures in respect to this young man are (1) that he was the owner of the garden; (2) as Plumptre, that he was Lazarus; (3) the apostle John; (see Smith's *Bible Dict.* and Ellicott's Commentary); (4) James, the brother of the Lord; (5) a youth of the family where Jesus had eaten the passover, and (6) that it was Mark himself, the son of Mary, the friend of Peter. There is little ground for these conjectures, beyond the minute narration of the event by Mark. The history is silent, and all guesses are of small value.

having a linen cloth] he had probably been roused from sleep, or just preparing to retire to rest in a house somewhere in the valley of Kedron, and he had nothing to cover him except the *sindôn* or upper garment, but in spite of this he ventured, in his excitement, to press on amongst the crowd. The word *sindôn* in Matt. xxvii. 59, Mark xv. 46 and Luke xxiii. 53 is applied to *fine linen*, which Joseph of Arimathæa bought for the body of Jesus. The LXX. use the word in Judges xiv. 12 and in Prov. xxxi. 24 for "*fine under garments.*"

the young men] this is omitted by Lachmann, Tischendorf and Tregelles. See R. V.

52. *naked*] it need not imply that he was absolutely naked. It may mean like the Latin *nudus*, "with only the *under* robe on." Comp. 1 Sam. xix. 24; John xxi. 7; Virg. *Georg.* 1, 299.

53—65. THE JEWISH TRIAL.
(Friday before day, 14th Nisan, A.D. 30.)

Jesus had two distinct trials: the first before the Jewish high priest and Council; the second before the Roman Procurator, Pilate. During the Jewish trial Jesus was arraigned three separate times: (1) Before Annas, related only in John xviii. 13—24. There is some difference of opinion about the details, compare A. V. with the R. V. in John xviii. 12. (2) Before Caiaphas, narrated in Matt. xxvi. 57—68; Mark xiv. 53—65; Luke xxii. 54—65. (3) Before the full Sanhedrin, early in the morning just before he was led to Pilate's court.*

* There has been much discussion on whether there were two or only one arraignment of Jesus before the high priest previous to his sentence by the full Sanhedrin. The answer depends largely, though not wholly, upon the interpretation of John xviii. 24. (1) The A. V. favors one

AUTHORIZED VERSION.	REVISED VERSION.
53 And they led Jesus away to the high priest: and with him were assembled all the chief priests and the elders and the scribes.	53 And they led Jesus away to the high priest: and there come together with him all the chief priests and the elders and the

Alexander holds that this last was only a private consultation respecting the next step, but his view rests on insufficient grounds. Of these three portions of the Jewish trial, the first was preliminary, perhaps resembling the examination now had in criminal cases before the committing magistrate; the second was the more formal trial, where witnesses were called and testimony brought before the court, the high priest presiding, and a decision of guilty was reached; the third was an apparent revision of the case by the full court, and a formal ratification of the decision, including a sentence and preparations to carry the case to the Roman civil court for approval. It must be borne in mind that the Jewish trial was ecclesiastical, not civil. The *charge* in both trials was in substance the same, namely: that of claiming to be a king or Messiah; the *crime*, however, religiously, was counted blasphemy, but politically and civilly, it was treason. See note on legality of trial, page 185, and also note on chap. xv, 1.

53. *And they led Jesus away*] they bound him first (John xviii. 12), and then conducted him across the Kedron and up the road leading into the city.

to the high priest] From the interference of the Roman power with the high priest's office, there were ex-high priests alive at this time. Antiochus, B. C. 160, had sold the office of high priest to the highest bidder. Annas was deposed by the Roman pro-consul, and Caiaphas appointed, but the Jews appear to have recognized Annas as high priest, according to the law of Moses, which made the office hereditary, not subject to arbitrary appointment. Accepting the reading of the R. V. in John xviii, 24, Jesus was first led to Annas the high priest, according to the Mosaic law, and given a brief examination, John xviii, 13, 19–24, and Annas sent him bound, for formal trial, to Caiaphas, the acting high priest under Roman appointment. The palace seems to have been jointly occupied by both as a common official residence, and thither, though it was midnight, the chief priests, elders and scribes repaired. The Jewish trial in its threefold arraignment must therefore, doubtless, have occurred in the same building, though it may have been in different rooms.

arraignment, and that before Caiaphas. It reads: "For Annas had sent him [Jesus] bound unto Caiaphas, the high priest," a fact, according to some, mentioned parenthetically, while the details in the preceding verses, John xviii, 19–23, are held to relate to his trial before Caiaphas. This interpretation is favored by Calvin, Beza, Grotius, Bengel, De Wette, Meyer, Robinson, Lücke, Tholuck, Andrews and Geikie. (2) The R. V. which reads, "Annas sent him bound, etc.," favors the other view of two arraignments before the sentence, to wit: (*a*) A preliminary examination before Annas, described in John xviii, 19–23, and (*b*) a second and formal trial before Caiaphas. This seems to be the more natural interpretation of the combined accounts, and has fewer difficulties than the first view, since it accords best with the force of the Greek text. For while the Greek aorist is sometimes used in the sense of the English past-perfect tense, it is not commonly so used. There was a good reason for taking Jesus before Annas, since he was the high priest according to Jewish law, and was, no doubt, so recognized by the strictest legalists. The age and influence of Annas also favor two hearings: first by Annas, second by Caiaphas, and this interpretation is supported by Chrysostom, Augustine, Olshausen, Schliermacher, Stier, Neander, Ebrard, Weiseler, Lange, Alford, Ellicott, Farrar, Dean Mansell, Schaff, David Brown and others.

A third arraignment was also had in the morning, before the full Sanhedrin, for a formal ratification of the decision. The decision had been already reached by the commission, or more probably by a smaller meeting of the Sanhedrin. At the full meeting in the morning, Jesus was arraigned for sentence. This view is held by Andrews, Farrar, Geikie and many others, though questioned by Alexander, who holds that it was not a formal, but an informal meeting. The Greek word, however, is used to designate a formal meeting, and the context in Mark xv, 1, and Matthew xxvii, 1, fairly implies an *official* meeting of the council or Sanhedrin. See R.V. This view is the most satisfactory. Naturally, the rulers would outwardly make a pretence of following legal forms, and therefore have the decision ratified, even though they did not delay a full day, as in strictness their rules, given in the Talmud, appear to have required.

AUTHORIZED VERSION.	REVISED VERSION.
54 And Peter followed him afar off, even into the palace of the high priest; and he sat with the servants, and warmed himself at the fire.	54 scribes. And Peter had followed him afar off, even within, into the court of the high priest; and he was sitting with the officers, and warming himself in the light *of the fire*.
55 And the chief priests and all the council sought for witness against Jesus to put him to death; and found none.	55 Now the chief priests and the whole council sought witness against Jesus to put him to death; and found it not. For many bare false witness against him, and their witness
56 For many bare false witness against him, but their witness agreed not together.	56
57 And there arose certain, and bare false witness against him, saying,	57 agreed not together. And there stood up certain, and bare false witness against him,

54. *And Peter...into the palace*] rather into the large open square court, in which public business was transacted. See R. V. Into it Peter and John ventured (John xviii. 15). The latter, as being acquainted with the high priest, easily obtained admittance; Peter, at first rejected by the porteress, was admitted at the request of John.

and warmed himself] in the centre of the court the servants of the high priest had made a fire of charcoal, probably on a brazier, and there Peter, now admitted, was warming himself.

55. *the chief priests*] Mark passes over the details of the examination before Annas, and the first commencement of insult and violence, recorded only by John (xviii. 19–24). He places us in the mansion of Caiaphas, whither our Lord was conducted across the courtyard, and where the council of the nation had met together.

sought for witness] By the law they were bound to secure the agreement of two witnesses on some specific charge. "As to be perfectly just is an attribute of the divine nature, to be so to the uttermost of our abilities, is the glory of man."—*Addison.* But they found no testimony against him. See R.V. It would not, probably, have been difficult to have secured witnesses against him, on a charge which would condemn him according to *Jewish* law. His claim to forgive sins, as in Mark ii. 7, or breaking the Sabbath, 3, 5, 6, would have sufficed for that. Geikie, following Keim, seems to question this view. But the Mosaic law is unmistakably clear and strong. Compare Exod. xxxi. 14, 15; xxxv. 2; Num. xv. 32–36; Lev. xxiv. 10–16; Jer. xvii. 27. The Jewish court could not execute a death penalty under Roman law. Hence, they wished to find and to prove a charge which would condemn him according to Roman law, in order to have ground of *appeal* to Roman authority, which must approve of any death sentence before it could be executed.

56. *their witness agreed not together*] "the witnessingis weren not couenable."—*Wyclif.* The law required that at least two witnesses must agree. See Deut. xvii. 6, xix. 15. The Greek literally reads "and equal their testimonies were not." The same phrase occurs in *v.* 59. Some interpret it to mean that the witnesses contradicted each other; others that it was insufficient, which is more probable, *i. e.* there were independent witnesses to a multitude of facts, but not two concurrent witnesses to one fact. In the Syriac, Persic, and Ethiopic versions the word "false" in the first clause of this verse is not expressed, but only that they bore witness against him.

57. *and there arose certain*] two at last came forward. Buxtorf cites the following Rabbinical testimony in regard to false witnesses against Jesus. "Against none of those guilty of death are snares to be laid, except against one who has endeavored to pervert another to idolatry and strange worship. And then it is done thus: they light a candle in an inner room, and place the witnesses in the outer, so that they may see him and hear his voice, without his seeing them. And so they did to the Son of Satda (Mary). They placed men privately in the next room, to witness against him in Jud (or Judea),

AUTHORIZED VERSION.	REVISED VERSION.
58 We heard him say, I will destroy this temple that is made with hands, and within three days I will build another made without hands. 59 But neither so did their witness agree together. 60 And the high priest stood up in the midst, and asked Jesus, saying, Answerest thou nothing? what *is it which* these witness against thee? 61 But he held his peace, and answered nothing. Again the high priest asked him, and said unto him, Art thou the Christ, the Son of the Blessed?	58 saying, We heard him say, I will destroy this [1] temple that is made with hands, and in three days I will build another made without hands. 59 And not even so did their witness agree together. 60 And the high priest stood up in the midst, and asked Jesus, saying, Answerest thou nothing? what is it which these witness against thee? 61 But he held his peace, and answered nothing. Again the high priest asked him, and saith unto him, Art thou the Christ, the Son of the

[1] Or, *sanctuary*

and hanged him upon a cross, on the evening of the passover."—*Hales' Chronology.*

58. *We heard him say*] The statements now made are given with more detail by Mark than any other of the evangelists. This was false testimony inasmuch as it was a perversion of Christ's words. It is probable, though not certain, that the witnesses were guilty of *willful* perversion, and therefore of perjury, in thus repeating the prophecy of Jesus concerning the destruction of the temple. The careless listener might have understood Jesus to say he would destroy the temple, instead of, "destroy this temple and in three days I will raise it up," (John ii, 19). This point is not important, however, for it was not on this that his condemnation was secured.

59. *neither...witness agree*] The statements of the witnesses did not tally, and their testimony was therefore worthless. Their memories had travelled over three years, to the occasion of the first passover at Jerusalem and the first cleansing of the temple. But they perverted the real facts of the case (John ii, 18–22). Mark alone notices the disagreement of their testimony. "The differences between the recorded words of our Lord and the reports of the witnesses are striking: '*I am able to destroy*' (Matt. xxvi, 61); '*I will destroy*' (Mark xiv. 58); as compared with '*Destroy...and I will raise*' (John ii, 19)."—*Wescott.* In the "Gospel of Nicodemus" and the so-called "Acts of Pilate" it is asserted that several witnesses voluntarily testified in favor of Jesus; among them were Nicodemus, Bartimeus, of Jericho, the lame man who was healed at the Pool of Bethesda, the woman who was cured of an issue of blood, and whose name is given as Veronica, and the centurion of Capernaum, whose servant was cured. These statements are founded on traditions, which, though very old, are not very trustworthy.

60. *And the high priest stood up*] The impressive silence which our Lord preserved, while false witnesses were being sought against him (Matt. xxvi, 62), was galling to the pride of Caiaphas. Comp. R. V. Standing up, therefore, *in the midst* (a graphic touch which we owe to Mark alone), he adjured him in the most solemn manner possible (Matt. xxvi. 63), to declare whether he was "the Malcha Meschicha"—the King Messiah, the son of the blessed. This was an attempt to make Jesus criminate himself; a procedure contrary to all our ideas of justice, though not uncommon to ancient courts, and modern ones in the East.

61. *held his peace*] "Euripides was wont to say, silence was an answer to a wise man; but we seem to have greater occasion for it in our dealing with fools and unreasonable persons, for men of breeding and sense will be satisfied with reason and fair words."—*Plutarch.* "What strange power there is in silence!...When some of those cutting, sharp, blighting words have been spoken, which send the hot indignant blood to the face and head, if those to whom they are addressed keep silence, look on with awe, for a mighty work

AUTHORIZED VERSION.	REVISED VERSION.
62 And Jesus said, I am: and ye shall see the Son of man sitting on the right hand of power, and coming in the clouds of heaven. 63 Then the high priest rent his clothes, and saith, What need we any further witnesses? 64 Ye have heard the blasphemy: what think ye? And they all condemned him to be guilty of death.	62 Blessed? And Jesus said, I am: and ye shall see the Son of man sitting at the right hand of power, and coming with the clouds of heaven. 63 And the high priest rent his clothes, and saith, What further need have we of witnesses? 64 Ye have heard the blasphemy: what think ye? And they all condemned him to

is going on within them. ...During that pause they have made a step toward heaven or toward hell, and an item has been scored in the book which the day of Judgment shall see opened. They are the strong ones of earth, the mighty food for good or evil."—*Emerson.*

62. *And Jesus said, I am*] Thus adjured, the Lord broke the silence and now replied, "I AM—*the Messiah, the Son of God, the Son of man—and hereafter ye shall see me sitting on the right hand of power, and coming in the clouds of heaven.*" Comp. Dan. vii, 13; Ps. viii, 4, cx, 1. Gerlach pronounces this the most clear and definite testimony in favor of the *divinity* of Christ. Caiaphas asked if in claiming to be Messiah he also claimed to be the Son of God. Jesus understood the question and affirmed his divine nature. If his testimony is not true, he must be called a deceiver, but he is pronounced a good man universally, hence his testimony is true.

63. *Then the high priest*] Caiaphas had now gained his end. The accused had criminated himself. This was blasphemy, according to their judgment, and it could be made constructive treason against the Roman government, for their ideas of Messiah as a temporal king would lead to rebellion against, and a dethroning of, Cæsar. All was uproar and confusion. The high priest rent, not his priestly robes (as some interpret), for these were only worn when officiating in the temple. Indeed it was not lawful for him to rend his clothes (Lev. x, 6, xxi, 10), though tradition, based on 2 Kings xviii, 37, held it allowable in cases of blasphemy. Yet, as Alford suggests, it is more probable that the high priest rent his *tunic*, as the Greek word implies. The tunics were of linen.

64. *what think ye?*] This was not a request for a colloquial opinion, but was most probably the customary legal form for gaining a decision of the court, as Alexander observes. The high priest did not illegally *assume* that all agreed with him, as some hold, and pronounce the condemnation in indecent haste, on his own opinion; he called for a formal judgment from the council, and "they all condemned him."

they all condemned him] "They all," *i. e.*, the majority; indeed we only know of one possible exception, see ch. xv, 43, unless the conjecture that Nicodemus was a member of the Sanhedrin and present at his trial, be accepted. Canon Cook infers that none had been summoned to this meeting who were suspected of being in favor of Jesus, though they may have been called to the more formal council in the morning, where alone legal sentence could be pronounced. Worse than false prophet, worse than seditious, he had declared himself to be the "*Son of God,*" and that in the presence of the high priest and the great Council. He had incurred the capital penalty. They could pass a sentence but only as an empty form, for it must be referred to the Roman governor, and be confirmed, to give it legal force. In regard to the confession that Jesus was the Son of God, as the Jews charged, Whately acutely remarks: "He must have *known* that they so understood him...they must have understood him *rightly.* For if he, condemned as he was on the evidence of his own words, had known that these words were understood differently from his real meaning, and yet had not corrected their mistake, he would himself have been bearing false witness against himself. If he were

AUTHORIZED VERSION.	REVISED VERSION.
65 And some began to spit on him, and to cover his face, and to buffet him, and to say unto him, Prophesy: and the servants did strike him with the palms of their hands.	65 be ¹worthy of death. And some began to spit on him, and to cover his face, and to buffet him, and to say unto him, Prophesy: and the officers received him with ²blows of their hands.

¹ Gr. *liable to*. ² Or, *strokes of rods*

not the Son of God in the sense the Jews meant, I am really at a loss to see on what ground we can find fault with the sentence they pronounced." This, then, is a very strong proof of his divine character.

guilty of death] We would say "guilty of blasphemy," but in ancient usage guilt is connected with the punishment fixed for the crime, not the crime itself, as in present usage.

65. *to spit on him*] In those rough ages a prisoner under sentence of death was ever delivered over to the mockery of the guards. It was so now with the holy one of God. Spitting was regarded by the Jews as an expression of the greatest contempt (Num. xii, 14; Deut. xxv, 9). Seneca records that it was inflicted at Athens on Aristides the Just, but it was only with the utmost difficulty that any one could be found willing to do it. But those who were excommunicated were specially liable to this expression of contempt. (Isaiah l, 6.) *Camb. Bible.*

did strike him with the palms of their hands] Notice the reading in the R. V. "The hands they bound had healed the sick, and raised the dead; the lips they smote had calmed the winds and waves. One word and his smiters might have been laid low in death. But as he had begun and continued, he would end—as self-restrained in the use of his awful powers on his own behalf as if he had been the most helpless of men—Divine patience and infinite love knew no wearying."*—

* *The Legality of the Trial.*—There has been much discussion on whether the trial of Jesus was conducted according to the prevailing forms of law. Jewish writers have generally maintained that it was. Salvador, a learned Jew, in his "History of the Institutions of Moses and of the Hebrew Prophets," defends the trial as a proper judicial procedure. Regarding Jesus as only a citizen, and briefly reciting his principal acts, especially his severe denunciations of cities and persons, his acts in the temple, and his claims to be the Son of God, Salvador holds that the high priest was compelled to notice and to repress by law such disturbers of the nation, who might bring the Roman power upon them. Hence the public order to arrest Jesus—an order of which he claims Jesus knew, and which was not given without warning; as he was asked for his authority; was arrested; the officers were resisted; one wounded; Jesus was brought before the grand council; the priests sustain the charge; the high priest appeals to Jesus in respect to the truth of the charge; he admits it; the council deliberate; Jesus claims to be God; he is condemned under Deut. xiii, and xviii, 20. The ill treatment following the sentence Salvador does not admit, but regards the account of the evangelists at this point as an exaggeration. The council met the next morning, as the law required, confirmed the sentence, and carried the case to Pilate, whose soldiers showed the barbarity common to them in those times. Pilate before signing the decree granted an appeal to the people, they chose another to be released, and so Jesus was condemned. Salvador holds that the priests did not mock him, but with dignity and sincerity demanded that he come down from the cross, as a miracle decisive of his claims. Another able Hebrew historian, however, concedes that there was undue precipitancy in the trial, which he excuses on the ground that Caiaphas and his colleagues belonged to the Sadducees, notorious for cruelty, and holds that it would not have occurred under the Pharisees. See Derenbourg. *Historie de la Palestine.* And Jewish writers generally maintain that whatever may be the real merits of the case, the trial was a regular judicial one, and "the sentence legally just."

Christian writers, on the other hand, have generally held that forms of law were grossly violated. But most Gentile Christians have been too ready to put a construction upon the N. T. history which would aid in casting increased obloquy upon the Jewish people. M. Dupin, in a reply to Salvador, maintains that the accused was deprived of rights belonging to him under the rules of Jewish law; was arrested in the night; bound as a malefactor; beaten before arraignment; struck in open court during trial; tried on a feast day, before sunrise; compelled to criminate himself, under a solemn judicial adjuration; was sentenced on the same day of conviction, and that in all these particulars the law was disregarded.

Salvador and Dupin represent extreme views, and the truth as to the observance of *legal* forms in the trial doubtless lies somewhere between these extremes. Eastern courts lack much of the regularity of procedure required and observed under our laws. Even the forms usually accepted

AUTHORIZED VERSION.	REVISED VERSION.
66 And as Peter was beneath in the palace, there cometh one of the maids of the high priest:	66 And as Peter was beneath in the court, there cometh one of the maids of the high

66—72. THE DENIAL BY PETER.

66. *And as Peter*] To the sad scene enacted in the hall of trial above, an almost sadder moral tragedy was added in the court (not "palace," as the A. V. reads) below. Calvin quaintly says, "Peter's fall is a bright mirror of

there are not infrequently put aside, by the caprice of the judge, or under strong pressure of any kind. Such instances are now too common there to excite remark, and under the semi-anarchy following the subjugation of the Jews under the Romans, we may well believe these irregularities no less frequent. Making due allowance for this general irregularity in following any forms of law and justice there, it must be conceded, by dispassionate minds, that the Jewish rulers *professed* to observe the *forms* of law in the trial about as closely as was customary in their times. Their fear of the populace, which had only a few days before heralded the coming of Jesus with such enthusiasm, would lead them to preserve the *outward* semblance of law, in his arrest and trial, that they might carry the people with them. This view receives further support from the fact that Peter, in his address in Solomon's porch, says that he knew the people rejected Christ and chose Barabbas through ignorance, as the Jews did also. See Acts iii, 17. And Paul also implies that Christ was condemned by the rulers of this world from lack of wisdom, 1 Cor. ii, 8. In Acts ii, 23, Peter says to his hearers that they "by wicked hands have crucified and slain" Jesus, *i. e.* by the hands of the Gentiles, or the Roman governor. The A. V. rendering "by wicked hands," is misleading. See Hackett, Alexander, Lange and David Brown *in loco*, and also the R. V. If in the successive steps of the trial they "honored the appearance of justice while mocking the reality," as Geikie asserts, still that is notoriously an oriental fashion, as ancient as it was common. On the other hand there can assuredly be no excuse for the guilt of the Jewish rulers in calling or accepting "false witnesses," or in refusing to accept the manifold proof of his real character which the life and miracles of Jesus afforded. They denied his divine character, and treated his Messianic claims as unfounded, and his further claim to work wonders by his own power and not in the name of God, was regarded as a sin, like unto that of Moses at Meribah, Num. xx, 12, and his acceptance of worship, as if divine, being, in their view, a sin which exposed him to death under Deut. xiii.

An able Christian jurist and professor of law, Simon Greenleaf, after reviewing the irregularities of the trial, calmly concludes, "If we regard Jesus simply as a Jewish citizen, and with no higher character, this conviction seems substantially right in point of law, though the trial were not legal in all its forms....It is not easy to perceive on what ground his conduct could have been defended before any tribunal, unless upon that of his superhuman character." The Jewish Sanhedrin were not convinced that Jesus was such a character, and would not for a moment admit his claim, and therefore could not do otherwise than condemn him. The appeal of the high priest to Jesus for an assent to or denial of the accusation brought against him, is not noted by Greenleaf as an example of illegal forms in the trial, nor is it likely that it would be so regarded in ordinary eastern courts. That the move was made of the confession, to change popular tide against the prisoner, was natural. It must not be forgotten that blasphemy was a crime regarded with peculiar horror among the Jews. Hence Jesus was regarded as a notorious and dangerous character. That they had resolved to put him to death was also natural. His offences against their laws and traditions were numerous, of galling publicity, and in their eyes of the very worst kind, calling for the severest penalties under *Mosaic* statutes. The false witnesses, the harshness, and whatever other irregularities of procedure they pursued, were illegal, as well as unjust, but how far there were other irregularities, cannot be fully determined.

The Talmudic rules for trials may not be identical with the accepted regulations of those times, since the accuracy of the Talmud in respect to rules on other matters has been sharply questioned. See Whiston's Josephus, vol. ii, p. 20. Gentile Christians who can now perceive the awful mistake of the Jews in respect to the true character of Jesus, had they lived in that day, amid the knowledge and prejudices then current, is it likely they would have failed to join in the popular clamor which rejected Jesus and accepted Barabbas?

Of the Roman proceedings it need only be added, two courses were open to the Jewish rulers: (1) To ask the Roman official to ratify their sentence without inquiry, or (2) to bring a charge which the civil court must recognize, and if true, condemn the accused. The Procurator in *imperial* provinces, in times of danger to the State, might become an unrestricted dictator, subject only to the pro-consul, or the Emperor. Pilate did not hesitate to exercise such powers. He did not at once accede to the first request of the Jews, as they hoped he would. He called for the grounds of their condemnation of Jesus. They exhibited petulance unbecoming a judicial tribunal, when called to give their accusation. And when Pilate pronounced the charge of treason unfounded, from the statements of Jesus that a *spiritual* kingdom was his aim, the Jewish rulers still persisted in their charge. When Pilate sought to escape condemning Jesus by an appeal to the populace, the rulers outwitted him, and Pilate finally delivered Jesus to be crucified, because he claimed to be the "King of the Jews." And he certified, by the title placed on the cross, that this was the charge upon which the accused was executed.

Authorized Version.	Revised Version.
67 And when she saw Peter warming himself, she looked upon him, and said, And thou also wast with Jesus of Nazareth. 68 But he denied, saying, I know not, neither understand I what thou sayest. And he went out into the porch; and the cock crew. 69 And a maid saw him again, and began to say to them that stood by, This is one of them. 70 And he denied it again. And a little after, they that stood by said again to Peter, Surely thou art one of them: for thou art a Galilean, and thy speech agreeth thereto.	67 priest: and seeing Peter warming himself, she looked upon him, and saith, Thou also wast with the Nazarene, even Jesus. But he denied, saying, [1] I neither know, nor understand what thou sayest: and he went out into the [2] porch; [3] and the cock crew. And the maid saw him, and began again to say to them that stood by, This is one of them. But he again denied it. And after a little while again they that stood by said to Peter, Of a truth thou art one of them; for thou art a

[1] Or, *I neither know, nor understand: thou, what sayest thou?* [2] Gr. *forecourt.* [3] Many ancient authorities omit *and the cock crew.*

our weakness. In his repentance also, a striking instance of the goodness and mercy of God is held out to us." The precise time and order of the three denials is left to conjecture. They here form one connected narrative, though they may have occurred at different periods during the trial.

67. *warming himself*] Probably shortly after his entrance. The maid or porteress who admitted him asked him the question in reproach. See form of her remark in R.V.

she looked upon him] with fixed and earnest gaze, as the original word used by Luke (xxii, 56) implies.

68. *But he denied*] thrown off his guard perhaps by the searching glances of the bystanders, Peter replied at first evasively, that he neither knew nor understood what she meant. See Lange, *Life*, IV. p. 316. Others think it means, "*I know him not, neither understand I what thou sayest.*" See R.V. He should have stopped at once. "A lie," says Carlyle, "should be trampled on and extinguished wherever found. I am for fumigating the atmosphere, when I suspect that falsehood like a pestilence breathes around me."

CHAFING DISH OF CHARCOAL.

into the porch] "The outer courtyard."—*Meyer.* "The fore court." R.V. margin. Anxious probably for a favorable opportunity of retiring altogether, the apostle now moved away from the centre of the court. Here the second denial took place (Matt. xxvi. 71, 72), and for the first time *a cock crew.* This cock crowing is omitted in some MSS. See R.V. margin.

69. *maid saw him again*] recognized at the porch, Peter seems to have returned once more towards the fire, and was conversing in his rough Galilean dialect with the soldiers and servants when, after the lapse of an hour, not another, but the same maid (see R. V.), again made the charge.

to them that stood by] on this occasion she addressed herself to the bystanders, amongst whom was a kinsman of Malchus (John xviii. 26).

70. *And he denied it again*] this denial was probably addressed to those round the fire. "Any man who is not supported by the hand of God," says Calvin, "will instantly fall by a slight gale, or the rustling of a falling leaf." Peter, "tempted by a woman's voice, immediately denies his master, and yet but lately thought himself a valiant soldier, even unto death."

a Galilean] Some authorities and the A. V. add, "and thy speech agrees thereto." But many omit these words, as the R. V. The thought is in Matt. xxvi. 73. The Galilean burr was rough, and they confounded the gutturals and the last two letters of the Hebrew alphabet in speech. Hence the

AUTHORIZED VERSION.	REVISED VERSION.
71 But he began to curse and to swear, *saying*, I know not this man of whom ye speak. 72 And the second time the cock crew. And Peter called to mind the word that Jesus said unto him, Before the cock crew twice, thou shalt deny me thrice. And when he thought thereon, he wept. CHAP. XV.—And straightway in the morning the chief priests held a consultation	71 Galilean. But he began to curse, and to swear, I know not this man of whom ye 72 speak. And straightway the second time the cock crew. And Peter called to mind the word, how that Jesus said unto him, Before the cock crew twice, thou shalt deny me thrice. ¹And when he thought thereon, he wept. 15 And straightway in the morning the chief priests with the elders and scribes, and the

⁷ Or, *And he began to weep.*

Galileans were not allowed to read aloud in the Jewish synagogues. Lightfoot gives examples of the confusion produced by their pronunciation, asking, Whose is *immar* (this lamb)? they pronounced it so that hearers did not know whether an ass, wine, wool or lamb was meant.

71. *he began to curse and to swear*] "We have reason to suspect the truth of that which is backed with oaths and rash imprecations. None but the devil's sayings need the devil's proofs."—*Henry.* But assailed by the bystanders just mentioned and by the kinsman of Malchus (John xviii, 26), the apostle now fell deeper still.

72. *And Peter called to mind*] all that his Lord had said, all his repeated warnings rushed back to his remembrance, and lit up the darkness of his soul.

when he thought thereon] there are various renderings and interpretations of this phrase, some of them strained and fanciful. Two, worthy of notice, are, (1) literally "casting on" it, *i.e.* his mind, is the rendering of the A.V. and R.V., and this usage accords with that of Plutarch, Galen and others. (2) "casting his eyes" on (him), as Jesus looked at Peter. This, if tenable, would give a happy antithesis between Luke and Mark, but the first is the better reading.

he wept] not with the remorse of Judas, but the godly sorrow of true repentance. Peter's fault is not lessened, for Mark states that the first crowing of the cock did not suffice to recall him to his duty, but a second was needed. Tradition says Peter could never hear a cock crow without tears, and it might well be true.

CH. XV. **1—15.** VERDICT OF THE SANHEDRIN AND TRIAL BEFORE PILATE.
(Friday, 15th Nisan, 783, April 7th, (?) A.D. 30.)

1. *And straightway*] See R.V., which implies that it was a full council, many important persons; as Ellicott notices, "the whole council is in apposition with" the chief priests. As the day dawned, a second meeting of the Sanhedrin was convened. "A legal Sanhedrin it could hardly be called, for there are scarcely any traces of such legal assemblies during the Roman period." The laws of this august court were humane, and the proceedings were, in theory, conducted with the greatest care. The axiom current was "the Sanhedrin was to save, not to destroy life." In trials before this court, the rules, according to the Talmud were: (1) the accused one to be held innocent until proved guilty. (2) No one could be tried or condemned in his absence. (3) Witnesses were to be warned of the value of life, and to omit nothing in the prisoner's favor. (4) He was to have counsel to defend him. (5) All evidence in his favor was to be admitted freely. (6) Any member of the court who had favored acquittal could not later vote for condemnation. (7) Votes of the youngest members were first taken that they might not be influenced by seniors. (8) In capital offences a majority of two, at least, was required to condemn. (9) A verdict of acquittal could be pronounced on the day of trial; of guilt, only on the day after trial. (10) No criminal trial could be carried through in the night. (11) The judges must fast for a day before the trial. (12) No one could be executed

AUTHORIZED VERSION.	REVISED VERSION.
with the elders and scribes and the whole council, and bound Jesus, and carried *him* away, and delivered *him* to Pilate.	whole council, held a consultation, and bound Jesus, and carried him away, and delivered

on the same day as the sentence. The trial before Caiaphas and the Sanhedrin was therefore, in violation of their rules, not preserving forms of justice, according to strict Jewish law. The rules were often pushed aside, as in Maccabean times. It is asserted that in the Talmud a new doctrine was invented, permitting one falsely claiming to be Messiah to be tried and condemned the same day, or in the night, to relieve the keenness of the feeling in the Jewish nation over the judicial murder of Jesus. A story was also coined, that a crier called aloud for forty days for witnesses to come forward in his defence. See Ginsburg, in *Kitto's Cyc.*, Keim, Edersheim and Geikie. Some, as Alexander, suppose the "consultation" in the morning was only an informal and private one; some, as Meyer and Ellicott, regard it as merely a continuation of the former meeting; others, as Greswell, Andrews, Farrar, Geikie, and most late writers, hold that it was an official meeting of the Sanhedrin to ratify the sentence, and order the case before the Roman procurator. This seems the most probable.

whole council] Lightfoot quotes from Maimonides a precept that it was not necessary for *all* members of the Sanhedrin to be present to transact business, but when all were specially summoned, then attendance was compulsory. Mark here implies such a compulsory meeting of the whole council.

carried him away] It is uncertain where the Prætorium was to which Jesus was taken. There are two prevailing views: (1) That it was in the tower or castle of Antonia, on the north side of the temple; formerly this was the prevailing opinion, and is maintained by some later critics, as Weiss, Tischendorf, Barclay, Lange and Weiseler. (2) That it was one of the two gorgeous palaces of Herod, on the western hill of Jerusalem, not far from the present Jaffa gate. This view is accepted by Winer, Lewin, Tobler, Farrar, Andrews, Geikie, Canon Cook, Schaff, and the majority of late critics. It renders the traditional journey to Golgotha, through the *via dolorosa*, improbable.

to Pilate] Early in the morning the Roman governor was called to preside in a case which has stigmatized his name through the centuries. (1) *His name*, Pontius, is thought by some to indicate that he was connected, either by descent or adoption, with the gens of the *Pontii*, conspicuous in Roman history; by others, that he came from Pontus, the kingdom of Mithridates. His surname, Pilatus, has been interpreted as (*a*) "armed with the *pilum* or javelin," or, = (*b*) from *pileus*, the cap or badge of manumitted slaves, or (*c*) that he was skilled in throwing the *pilum* or spear. (2) He was a native of Italy, or possibly of Gaul, and was appointed *procurator* under the governor (*pro-prætor*) of Syria, in A. D. 26 (or 29), succeeding Valerius Gratus. His wife was named Procla, or Procula. His proper residence was at Cæsarea (Acts xxiii, 23); he had assessors to assist him in council (xxv, 12); wore the military dress; was attended by a cohort as a body guard (Matt. xxvii, 27); and at the great festivals came up to Jerusalem to keep order. As judge he sat on a *Bema* or portable tribunal erected on a tesselated pavement, called in Hebrew *Gabbatha* (John xix, 13), and was invested with the power of life and death (Matt. xxvii, 26). (3) In *character* he was sharp, selfish and cunning, yet anxious at times to act justly, and even mercifully, but without moral courage to follow justice in the face of public clamor. As a ruler he had shown himself cruel and unscrupulous (Luke xiii, 1, 2), and in A.D. 36 the governor of Syria (for Pilate's title was not properly governor), accused him at Rome, for a cruel slaughter of Samaritans in consequence of which Pilate was banished to Gaul, where he is said to have committed suicide.

AUTHORIZED VERSION.	REVISED VERSION.
2 And Pilate asked him, Art thou the King of the Jews? And he answering, said unto him, Thou sayest it. 3 And the chief priests accused him of many things; but he answered nothing. 4 And Pilate asked him again, saying, Answerest thou nothing? behold how many things they witness against thee. 5 But Jesus yet answered nothing; so that Pilate marvelled.	2 him up to Pilate. And Pilate asked him, Art thou the King of the Jews? And he 3 answering, saith unto him, Thou sayest. And the chief priests accused him of many things. 4 And Pilate again asked him, saying, Answerest thou nothing? behold how many things they 5 accuse thee of. But Jesus no more answered anything; insomuch that Pilate marvelled.

Tacitus refers to him, as putting Christ to death. Near Vienne, on the Rhone, the modern traveler is shown a tower, from which, tradition says, Pilate threw himself. On lake Luzerne, in Switzerland, there is a noble peak of the Alps called "Pilatus," and a legend says he lived as a hermit on this mountain, and sought a grave beneath the waters of the lake. See M. J. Raphall's *Post-Biblical History of the Jews*. The so-called "Acts of Pilate" are now considered spurious. The power of life and death was taken from the Jewish rulers, when Archelaus was removed, A.D. 6; though the Talmud says it was done forty years before the fall of Jerusalem.

2. *And Pilate asked him*] some conjecture that this was a private investigation within the *prætorium*. At any rate the Jews carefully suppressed *the religious grounds* on which they had charged and condemned our Lord, and changed the form (not the substance), of their accusation, so as to make it a *political* offence; he opposed giving tribute to Cæsar, because he himself was Messiah, a king. See Luke xiii, 2. This claim to be Messiah, and hence king, was substantially the same charge on which they had condemned him in the Jewish court, only in their court the religious crime was called *blasphemy*, while in the civil court it would be *treason*. That the accusation was substantially the same as the charge on which he had already been condemned, will appear more clearly by comparing Luke xxiii, 2, 3, and John xviii, 33–37. When this charge broke down, as not proven, then they resorted to various other accusations, and to the general clamor against Pilate as Cæsar's enemy, if he "let this man go." This clamor derived its greatest force from the fact that Jesus was charged with being a king, and hence opposed to Cæsar, John xix, 22; and the Jewish rulers, also tauntingly reminded the Roman Governor that they had convicted Jesus of sedition and of a capital crime, under their law, and that this conviction only needed the customary and formal Roman approval; compare Luke xxiii, 2, 5; John xix, 7. Calvin long ago observed: "he [Jesus] was accused on various grounds; but it is evident, from the whole of the narrative, this [of claiming to be a king] was the chief ground of accusation." Having no *quæstor* to conduct the examination, Pilate was obliged to hear the case in person.

Thou sayest] John tells us (1) of Christ's counter question to Pilate; (2) why he asked the question; his explanation of the real nature of his kingdom (John xviii, 37, 38). This relieved Jesus of any treason, since his kingdom was only spiritual. The Jews, however, persisted in the charge, as they held Messiah's kingdom was temporal and therefore opposed to Cæsar.

3. *And the chief priests accused him*] Pilate declared his conviction of the innocence of the accused (John xviii, 38 Luke xxiii, 4). This was the signal for a furious clamor of the chief priests and members of the Sanhedrin, and they accused our Lord of many things (Luke xxiii, 5). The last clause of the verse is omitted in the R. V., the only important MSS. containing it being the Alexandrian.

4. *And Pilate asked*] The renewed accusations led to further questions from Pilate, but Jesus was silent and Pilate amazed, and confident of his innocence, proposed to release him, as it was his custom to release one at the

AUTHORIZED VERSION.	REVISED VERSION.
6 Now at *that* feast he released unto them one prisoner, whomsoever they desired.	6 Now at [1] the feast he used to release unto them one prisoner, whom they asked of him.
7 And there was *one* named Barabbas, *which* lay bound with them that had made insurrection with him, who had committed murder in the insurrection.	7 And there was one called Barabbas, *lying* bound with them that had made insurrection, men who in the insurrection had committed
8 And the multitude crying aloud began to desire *him to do* as he had ever done unto them.	8 murder. And the multitude went up and began to ask him *to do* as he **was wont to do**
9 But Pilate answered them, saying, Will ye that I release unto you the King of the Jews?	9 unto them. And Pilate answered **them,** saying, Will ye that I release unto **you the King**
10 For he knew that **the** chief priests had delivered him for envy.	10 of the Jews? For he perceived **that for envy**

[1] Or, *a feast*

feast. Mark omits the examination before Herod. It was not "many things" stated by the witnesses, as the A. V. implies, but the many accusations of the priests, as the R. V. reads, that Pilate referred to in his question.

6. *Now at that feast*] "every feast." See R. V. The limitation of the custom to the feast of the passover in the A. V. is not required by the original words, nor by the parallel in John xviii, 39. The original for "released" implies not a single act only, but a custom. The origin of the custom is unknown. It may have been of Jewish origin, and continued by the Roman governors from motives of policy. Even the Romans were accustomed, at the *Lectisternia* and *Bacchanalia*, occasionally to allow an amnesty for criminals.

7. *one named Barabbas*] He was a celebrated robber, a rebel and murderer. See Luke xxiii, 19; John xviii, 40. The description indicates that he was a Zealot, and as an insurgent against the Romans, he was esteemed by the Jewish rulers as a patriot and a hero; in three MSS of Matt. xxvii, 16, his name is given as "*Jesus Bar-abbas*," and this reading is supported by the Armenian and Syriac Versions and is cited by Origen. Some regard this fact of two criminals of the same name—Jesus—hinted at in John xviii, 40.

them that had made insurrection] Barabbas had led one of the numerous and bloody insurrections against the Roman power.

8. *crying aloud*] The R. V. has "went up," which is after the best text. The evangelist notes that at this point the multitude came to make request for the usual release of some prisoner; the Jewish rulers were prepared for this exigency, and finally persuaded the people to ask for Barabbas instead of Jesus.

9. *Pilate answered them*] Pilate may have wished, but could hardly have expected that the rulers would accept his proposal to release Jesus. He might have expected that there would be a large popular faction in favor of it. The form of the question implies only a half hope of a favorable answer.

10. *for envy*] Knowing, or perceiving the envy of the rulers and chief priests, Pilate may have thought that he could procure the release of Jesus by appealing direct to the multitude. If so, he was disappointed, for the chief priests held the multitude under their influence, by using very energetic measures to stir up public feeling, as Matthew implies.

Pilate made three distinct attempts to secure the consent of the Jewish rulers to a release of Jesus after he had required them to state the charge on which they asked his condemnation, though the " order " of the efforts is not the same in all the evangelists. The attempts may be arranged as follows: (1) After examining the charge that Jesus is a King, and finding the kingdom is a spiritual one, Pilate declared him innocent of a civil offence (Luke xxiii, 4). (2) After the return from Herod, Pilate proposes, after chastising him, to release Jesus, in accordance with custom, at the feast (Luke xxiii, 13–16; Mark xv, 6–10; Matt. xxvii, 15–17; John xviii, 39). (3) After the choice of Barabbas, and the message from Pilate's wife (Matt. xxvii, 20–26; Mark

AUTHORIZED VERSION.	REVISED VERSION.
11 But the chief priests moved the people, that he should rather release Barabbas unto them. 12 And Pilate answered and said again unto them, What will ye then that I shall do unto *him* whom ye call the King of the Jews? 13 And they cried out again, Crucify him. 14 Then Pilate said unto them, Why, what evil hath he done? And they cried out the more exceedingly, Crucify him. 15 And so Pilate, willing to content the people, released Barabbas unto them, and delivered Je-	11 the chief priests had delivered him up. But the chief priests stirred up the multitude, that he should rather release Barabbas unto 12 them. And Pilate again answered and said unto them, What then shall I do unto him 13 whom ye call the King of the Jews? And 14 they cried out again, Crucify him. And Pilate said unto them, Why, what evil hath he done? But they cried out exceedingly, Cru- 15 cify him. And Pilate, wishing to content the multitude, released unto them Barabbas, and

xv, 11-15; Luke xxiii, 18-23; John xviii, 40), when the Jews threatened to impeach him at Rome, for not being Cæsar's friend if he released Jesus (John xix, 12); Pilate at last yielded. He was baffled by the superior shrewdness of the Jewish rulers.

11. *the chief priests moved*] Pilate received a message from his wife imploring him to have nothing to do with "*that just person*" (Matt. xxvii, 19). He resolved to effect a release. But the chief priests stirred up the people, and urged them to choose Barabbas, the patriot leader, the zealot for their country, the champion against oppression. The word translated "moved" denotes (1) *to shake to and fro, to brandish*; (2) *to make threatening gestures*; (3) *to stir up* or *instigate*. The people did not regard Barabbas as a common murderer, but a patriot; hence, there was nothing low or infamous in the motives of the *multitude* in accepting Barabbas. Their patriotism was appealed to by the proposition of the rulers; but the *rulers* were actuated by bad motives in prompting the people to this choice.

12. *What will ye*] Some think this question put in disdain and anger at their fickleness, and at the failure of his efforts to stem the torrent.

whom ye call the King of the Jews] Lachmann and Tregelles omit "him whom ye call." Their reading is a strong incidental proof of the real charge Pilate understood the priests to bring against Jesus.

13. *Crucify him*] Crucifixion was a Roman, not a Jewish mode of punishment. Why, then, did the Jewish multitude fix on such a mode? Some answer, because the punishment for Barabbas would have been crucifixion, and they put Jesus in his place.

14. *And they cried out the more*] See R. V. The cry was kept up, unbroken, *Away with this man, Crucify Him! Crucify Him!* In vain Pilate expostulated. In vain he washed his hands openly before them all (Matt. xxvii, 24) in token of his conviction of the perfect innocence of the accused. The mob, under artful leaders, carried the point against the vacillating procurator.

15. *Pilate...to content the people*] or *satisfy*. This shows that Pilate did not accede to the justice of the sentence, but yielded to popular clamor. The "willing" or "wishing" implies more than simple yielding, and includes an earnest wish to satisfy the popular demand. Felix and Festus also tried to please the Jews, by their treatment of Paul, Acts xxiv, 27; xxv, 9. "Would to God" exclaims Calvin, "that the world were not now filled with many Pilates!" Time-serving rulers are the curse of any nation, and among the greatest enemies to the cause of truth. Irresolution had gone too far, and he could not retrace his steps. He released Barabbas to content the people. There is little ground for supposing, as some do, that Pilate still hoped to compromise and satisfy the populace and the rulers by simply scourging Jesus. The scourging was the common prelude to crucifixion, and in doing it, Pilate shows that he had given up Jesus to death, as the whole narrative also implies.

AUTHORIZED VERSION.	REVISED VERSION.
sus, when he had scourged *him*, to be crucified. 16 And the soldiers led him away into the hall, called Prætorium; and they call together the whole band. 17 And they clothed him with purple, and	delivered Jesus, when he had scourged him, to be crucified. 16 And the soldiers led him away within the court, which is the ¹ Prætorium; and they 17 call together the whole ² band. And they

¹ Or, *palace* ² Or, *cohort*

when he had scourged him] usually the scourging before crucifixion was inflicted by lictors (Livy, xxxiii, 36; Jos. *Bell. Jud.* ii, 14, 9; v. ii. 1). The criminal was bound firmly to a post, or column, his hands tied, his back laid bare, and the scourge made of three thongs of leather or small cords; and sometimes iron points or bits of lead were at the end of the thongs, to make the punishment more severe. Nineteen strokes of this scourge were equal to thirty nine lashes, and under the Mosaic law, not more than forty could be given. (Deut. xxv. 1-3). Paul received thirty-nine. (2 Cor. xi, 24). Many died under this terrible punishment. Pilate had no lictors and therefore the punishment was inflicted by soldiers. He had once proposed this punishment, and then the release of Jesus (Luke xxiii. 16). The soldiers added mockery to the scourging, and hence probably fulfilled their duty in all the usual severity. They would seize the opportunity to repay a grudge against the Jews, for insurrectionary and dangerous acts.

to be crucified] "If thou let this man go," they cried, "thou art not Cæsar's friend: whosoever maketh himself a king speaketh against Cæsar" (John xix, 12). This crafty, well-chosen cry roused all Pilate's fears. He could only too well divine the consequences if they accused him of sparing a prisoner who had been accused of treason before the gloomy, suspicious Tiberius. He gave the word, "Ibis ad crucem," which was the customary form, "*Let him be crucified*" (John xix, 16); so the struggle was over. John, it is to be observed, mentions the scourging as one of Pilate's final attempts to release Jesus. Mark, like Matthew, looks upon it as the first act in the awful tragedy of the crucifixion. Both views are equally true. The scourging should have moved the people: it only led them to greater obduracy: it proved, as Mark brings out, the opening scene in the crucifixion. See Andrews and Farrar.

16—24. MOCKERY OF THE SOLDIERS. WAY TO THE CROSS.
(Friday, 15th Nisan, 783, April 7 (?) A. D. 30.)

16. *the hall called Prætorium*] "into the *floor of the moot hall."—Wyclif.* The building here alluded to is called by three of the evangelists the *Prætorium*. In the King James Version the Greek word is variously rendered: as "common hall" (Matt. xxvii, 27); margin, "governor's house," "hall of judgment," and "judgment hall," (Acts xxiii, 35; John xviii, 28, 33, and xix, 9), margin, "Pilate's house" and "palace" (Phil. i, 13). It is a marked example of the unwarrantable differences introduced by King James' translators. The R. V. reads "palace" uniformly, except in Phil. i, 13; with the Greek "prætorium" in the margin. There is some question, however, whether the word in Mark means the palace or the court, though the weight of authority inclines to "palace."

the whole band] the word translated "*band*" is applied to the detachment brought by Judas (John xviii. 3), and occurs again, Acts x, 1; xxi, 31; xxvii, 1. It signifies a whole Roman cohort of soldiers, but the number of soldiers in a cohort often varied.

17. *clothed him with purple*] instead of the white robe, with which Herod had mocked him, they threw around him a scarlet *sagum*, or soldier's cloak. Matthew (xxvii. 28) calls it "*a scarlet robe;*" John (xix, 2) "*a purple robe.*" It was a war-cloak, such as princes, generals, and soldiers wore: "probably

AUTHORIZED VERSION.	REVISED VERSION.
platted a crown of thorns, and put it about his head.	clothe him with purple, and plaiting a crown
18 And began to salute him, Hail, King of the Jews!	18 of thorns, they put it on him; and they began to salute him, Hail, King of the Jews!
19 And they smote him on the head with a reed, and did spit upon him, and bowing *their* knees worshipped him.	19 And they smote his head with a reed, and did spit upon him, and bowing their knees
20 And when they had mocked him, they took off the purple from him, and put his own clothes on him, and led him out to crucify him.	20 worshipped him. And when they had mocked him, they took off from him the purple, and put on him his garments. And they lead him out to crucify him.
21 And they compel one Simon a Cyrenian, who passed by, coming out of the country, the	21 And they [1] compel one passing by, Simon

[1] Gr. *impress.*

a cast-off robe of state out of the prætorian wardrobe," a burlesque of the long and fine purple robe worn only by the Emperor.—*Lange.*

a crown of thorns] formed probably of the thorny *nâbk*, which yet "grows on dwarf bushes outside the walls of Jerusalem;" it was placed about his head in mimicry of the laurel and myrtle wreaths worn by victors at games, or by royal persons. The Jews derided Jesus for his prophetic reputation, and the Romans for his regal claims.

19. *smote him*] *began to smite* or *kept smiting him.*
with a reed] The same which they had already put into his hands as a sceptre. All this was harsh and cruel mockery.

20. *and led him out*] The place of execution was without the gates of the city, as was customary in such cases. See Lev. xxiv, 14; Naboth, 1 Kings xxi, 13; and Stephen, Acts vii, 58. An old tradition says he was led along the Via Dolorosa; but if the trial was at Herod's palace, which is very probable, he could not have gone by that street. In what direction they led him, or where Pilate held his court, or where Golgotha was situated, is unsettled. Those who believe that Pilate's court was in the castle of Antonia, and that Golgotha was where the present Church of the Holy Sepulchre stands, also believe he was led along the Via Dolorosa, according to tradition. Those who hold that Pilate held his court in Herod's palace (as most recent critics), and that the true site of Calvary is not at the Church of the Holy Sepulchre, but without the city, probably near the Grotto of Jeremiah (as Bishop Gobat, Schick, Schaff, Howe, and Conder), hold that Jesus was led out northward instead of westward, but do not attempt to fix the precise route.

21. *they compel*] The condemned were usually obliged to carry either the entire cross, or the cross-beams fastened together like the letter V, with their arms bound to the projecting ends. Hence the term furcifer = "*cross-bearer.*" The original word translated "*compel*" is a Persian word adopted by the Greeks, and signified the compulsory employment of men and beasts by the royal couriers, and thus any forced assistance.

Simon a Cyrenian] Cyrene was a city in northern Africa, where there dwelt many Hellenistic Jews, who had a synagogue in Jerusalem (Acts ii, 10; vi, 9. Some conjecture that he was a merchant. As he was passing from the country (literally, the field) to the city, he appears to have been taken at random. John says Jesus bore his cross; and both statements may be explained as true, by supposing that Jesus bore the cross part of the way, perhaps to the gate, and then sinking down, from exhaustion, they compel Simon to bear it. Or, as Alexander suggests, Simon may have borne one end of it with Jesus. The former seems the most likely (Luke xxiii, 26).

the father of Alexander and Rufus] Mark alone adds this. The mention of his two sons implies that they were well known at the time Mark wrote. Paul speaks of Rufus and his mother (Rom. xvi, 13), possibly the same person; Polycarp also names a Rufus, who was a noted martyr.

AUTHORIZED VERSION.	REVISED VERSION.
father of Alexander and Rufus, to bear his cross. 22 And they bring him unto the place Golgotha, which is, being interpreted, The place of a skull. 23 And they gave him to drink wine mingled with myrrh: but he received it not.	of Cyrene, coming from the country, the father of Alexander and Rufus, to go *with them*, that he might bear his cross. And they 22 bring him unto the place Golgotha, which is, 23 being interpreted, The place of a skull. And

to bear his cross] On a white tablet, called in Latin *titulus*, the reason for the punishment was declared (Sueton. *Calig.* 32). It was borne either suspended from the neck, or carried before the sufferer. Simon may have borne both title and cross. The traditional story about the finding of the cross by Helena, mother of Constantine the Great, in A. D. 326, under the temple of Venus, said to have been built over Golgotha by the hatred of the heathen, and to blot out the traces of Christ's death, is as untrustworthy as the story that on finding three crosses the true one was distinguished by bringing a sick person, who was cured when she touched one of the three, and this was declared to be the cross on which Christ was crucified. There is wood enough in existence, claimed to be parts of the true cross, to make a hundred real crosses!

22. *bring him*] literally "they bear him," or it may be rendered "lead him." In other passages it generally implies an infirmity or weakness in the person brought, and hence some understand that Jesus, from the awful scourging, had become too weak to walk, and sinking down, was *borne* to the place. If the trial was at Herod's palace on Mount Zion, he could not have passed along the Via Doloroso, as tradition, reaching to the 14th century only, declares.

the place Golgotha] Mark interprets the Hebrew word "Golgotha." Luke omits it altogether. It was (1) apparently a well-known spot; (2) outside the gate (comp. Heb. xiii, 12); but (3) near the city (John xix, 20); (4) near a thoroughfare (Luke xxiii, 26); and (5) a "garden" or "orchard" (John xix, 41). From the Vulgate rendering of Luke xxiii, 33, "qui vocatur *Calvariæ*" (= *a bare skull*, "the place of *Caluarie*," *Wyclif*), the word *Calvary* has been introduced into the English Version (Luke xxiii, 33), obscuring the meaning of the Evangelist.* The name probably refers to the rounded or skull-shaped form of the spot; it is not likely to come from skulls of malefactors scattered about, for the Jews always buried them. There is no Scriptural ground for calling it "Mount" Calvary.

23. *wine mingled with myrrh*] Lightfoot says (*Hor. Heb.* ii, 366), it was a special task of wealthy ladies at Jerusalem to provide this portion. The custom was founded on a Rabbinic gloss on Proverbs xxxi, 6, "Give *strong drink* unto him that is ready to perish, and *wine* unto those that be of heavy hearts." It was a sour wine or vinegar (Matt. xxvii, 34). The drink was a strong narcotic, intended to stupefy, and so lessen the suffering. They *offered* it, see R. V. and Matt. xxvii, 34, and unconsciously fulfilled prophecy. (Ps. lxix, 21).

MYRRH.

* J. A. Alexander makes a remarkable mis-statement under this verse, to wit: "Calvary, a word familiar to us by tradition, although not used in the English Bible. It is used not only in

AUTHORIZED VERSION.	REVISED VERSION.
24 And when they had crucified him, they parted his garments, casting lots upon them, what every man should take. 25 And it was the third hour, and they crucified him.	they offered him wine mingled with myrrh: 24 but he received it not. And they crucify him, and part his garments among them, casting 25 lots upon them, what each should take. And it was the third hour, and they crucified him.

but he received it not] the two malefactors, who were led forth with him, probably partook of it, but he would take nothing to cloud his faculties.— Maclear.

THREE FORMS OF THE CROSS.

24. *when they had crucified him*] or *they crucify him and part his garments among them*. See R.V. There were four kinds of crosses, (1) the *crux simplex*, a single stake driven through the chest or longitudinally through the body; (2) the *crux decussata* (×); (3) the *crux immissa* (†); and (4) the *crux commissa* (T). From the mention of the title placed over the Saviour's head, it is probable that his cross was of the third kind, and that he was laid upon it either while it was on the ground, or lifted and fastened to it as it stood upright, his arms stretched out along the two cross-beams, and his body resting on a little projection, *sedile*, a foot or two above the earth. That his feet were nailed as well as his hands is apparent from Luke xxiv. 39, 40. The cross was not such a high pole as most pictures represent it to be. The body of the crucified was raised only a little above the ground, as already noted. See Andrews' *Life of Our Lord*.

they parted] *i.e.* the soldiers, a party of four with a centurion (Acts xii. 4), for each sufferer, detailed, according to the Roman custom, *ad excubias*, to mount guard, and see that the bodies were not taken away.

casting lots] the garments of the crucified belonged to them by law or by custom. The soldiers took only their rights and their usual method of deciding how the distribution should be made. It fulfilled prophecy, Ps. xxii. 18.

what every man should take] the clothes fell to the soldiers as part of their perquisites. The inner garment, like the robes of the priests, *was without seam, woven from the top throughout* (John xix. 23). It would have been destroyed by rending, hence they cast lots for it, unconsciously fulfilling the words of the Psalmist, *They parted my raiment among them, and for my vesture did they cast lots* (Ps. xxii. 18).

25–38. THE DEATH.
(Friday, 15th Nisan, 783, April 7th, (?) A.D. 30.

25. *it was the third hour*] or nine o'clock; John says "sixth hour." There are three leading explanations of this apparent discrepancy. (1) that John refers to a different incident, *i.e.* the preparation or the close of a period of time roughly noted and called the "sixth hour," while Mark notes the beginning; so Calvin and Ewald. (2) That John writing in Asia Minor used the Roman official mode of reckoning from midnight to midnight instead of the Jewish from sunset to sunset; so Ebrard, Hug, Olshausen, Tholuck,

---

the King James Version of 1611, but also in Wyclif's, Tyndale's, and several other English versions, of Luke xxiii. 33. On a supposed site of Calvary, the Empress Helena caused a church to be erected, about A. D. 326, displacing (it is said), a temple of Venus built under Adrian. Whether this was the *true* site of Calvary is disputed; the weight of evidence is against the view that the Holy Sepulchre now covers the true Calvary.

AUTHORIZED VERSION.	REVISED VERSION.
26 And the superscription of his accusation was written over, THE KING OF THE JEWS. 27 And with him they crucify two thieves; the one on his right hand, and the other on his left. 28 And the scripture was fulfilled, which saith, And he was numbered with the transgressors. 29 And they that passed by railed on him, wagging their heads, and saying, Ah, thou that destroyest the temple, and buildest it in three days, 30 Save thyself, and come down from the cross. 31 Likewise also the chief priests mocking	26 And the superscription of his accusation was written over, THE KING OF THE JEWS. 27 And with him they crucify two robbers; one on his right hand, and one on his left.[1] And they that passed by railed on him, wagging their heads, and saying, Ha! thou that destroyest the ² temple, and buildest it in three 30 days, save thyself, and come down from the 31 cross. In like manner also the chief priests mocking him among themselves with the

[1] Many ancient authorities insert ver. 28, *And the scripture was fulfilled, which saith, And he was reckoned with transgressors.* See Luke xxii, 37. ² Or, *sanctuary*

Wordsworth and others. (3) That it is a copyist's mistake of the Greek sign for 6, instead of a 3. The two signs somewhat resemble each other. So Bengel, Beza, Eusebius and Robinson. None of these are entirely satisfactory; the second is, on the whole, to be preferred.

26. *And the superscription*] "and the title of his cause was written".— *Wyclif.* The cause of execution was generally inscribed on a white tablet, *titulus*, smeared with *gypsum*.

The King of the Jews] written in three languages, Latin, Greek and Hebrew or Aramaic. The official Latin would naturally come first—" The King of the Jews;" the Greek, as read by Hellenists next.—

ישוע הנצרי מלך היהודים

Οὗτός ἐστιν Ἰησοῦς ὁ Βασιλεὺς τῶν Ἰουδαίων.

Rex Judæorum.

"This is Jesus, the King of the Jews;" and the Aramaic last,—"Jesus the Nazarene, King of the Jews." The three are given, the Hebrew by John, the Greek by Matthew, and the Latin by Mark. This may account for the slight variations in the form. For the endeavor of the Jewish high priest to get the title altered, see John xix, 21, 22.

27. *two thieves*] or *malefactors* as Luke calls them (xxiii, 33). Some conjecture that they belonged to the band of Barabbas and had been engaged in one of those fierce and fanatical outbreaks against the Romans which, on a large scale or a small, so quickly succeeded one another in the latter days of the Jewish commonwealth. This explains the fact that we read of no mockery of *them*. They were the popular heroes. They realized to some degree the popular idea of the Messiah. See Trench's *Studies*. An old tradition gives the names of the thieves as Dimas and Gestas, Dimas being the one who was penitent. This tradition is preserved in the apocryphal gospel of Nicodemus.

V. 28 is omitted in the best MSS. The reference in it is to Isaiah liii, 12.

29. *railed on him*] "wagging" or shaking their heads, signifying their assent to his punishment as just, and also implying that they rejoiced or gloated over it. The natural feelings of pity were quenched in the fierceness of malignant hatred and religious bigotry.

Ah] "Fyz."—*Wyclif.* an exclamation of derision = the Latin *Vah*.

that destroyest the temple] This remark of our Lord at his cleansing of the temple was never forgotten, though its meaning was misrepresented or misunderstood.

31. *mocking said*] "scornynge him, ech to other, with scribis, seiden." —*Wyclif.* The ordinary bystanders, *blaspheme* (v. 29), the members of the Sanhedrin *mock*, but with a peculiar venom and sting to their sarcasm.

AUTHORIZED VERSION.	REVISED VERSION.
said among themselves with the scribes, He saved others; himself he cannot save. 32 Let Christ the King of Israel descend now from the cross, that we may see and believe. And they that were crucified with him reviled him. 33 And when the sixth hour was come, there was darkness over the whole land until the ninth hour. 34 And at the ninth hour Jesus cried with a loud voice, saying, Eloi, Eloi, lama sabachthani? which is, being interpreted, My God, my God, why hast thou forsaken me?	scribes said, He saved others; [1] himself he 32 cannot save. Let the Christ, the King of Israel, now come down from the cross, that we may see and believe. And they that were crucified with him reproached him. 33 And when the sixth hour was come, there was darkness over the whole [2] land until the 34 ninth hour. And at the ninth hour Jesus cried with a loud voice, Eloi, Eloi, lama sabachthani? which is, being interpreted, My God, my God, [3] why hast thou forsaken me?

[1] Or, *can he not save himself?* [2] Or, *earth* [3] Or, *why didst thou forsake me?*

He saved others] They admit his miracles. His bitterest enemies would not have admitted this had the fact not been established beyond question. It is also worth noting, as an incidental proof of the accuracy of the gospel narratives, that all this jeering took place before the miraculous darkness; after that, all mocking, even by enemies, is subdued by a general feeling of awe. The priests did not consider if he was the Messiah, as he claimed to be, that his death, according to prophecy, would be a far stronger proof of his claim than his miraculous descent from the cross. Some authorities read this as an interrogation, "He saved others, can he not save himself?"

32. *they that were crucified with him*] At first both the robbers joined in reproaching him. One of them was guilty of blaspheming him (Luke xxiii, 39), the other, beholding the meekness and forgiving spirit of Jesus, turned in penitence and faith to him (Luke xxiii, 42). When the Eastern Empire became Christian, the cross became a symbol of honor. It was engraven on shields, woven into banners, worn as a badge; was the national emblem of nearly all European countries during the crusades.

33. *And when the sixth hour was come*] *i.e.* 12 o'clock. The clearness of the Syrian noontide was obscured, and darkness settled over the "whole land." This may refer to Jerusalem and the surrounding country of Judea. So Calvin understands the phrase, and aptly suggests that if the darkness covered Judea only, while the sun was shining elsewhere, the miracle would be more striking than universal darkness over the whole world. It is impossible to explain away the origin of this darkness. The passover moon was then at the full, so that it could not have been an eclipse. The Pharisees had often asked for a "sign from heaven." Now one was granted them, calculated to strike terror and awe into the stoutest heart.

until the ninth hour] *i. e.* till 3 o'clock. A veil hides from us the incidents of these three hours, and all the details of what our Lord, shrouded in the supernatural gloom, underwent "for us men and for our salvation."

34. *And at the ninth hour*] the hour of the offering of the evening sacrifice.

Eloi! Eloi!] Mark gives the Aramaic form, and this is the only one of the "seven words" or utterances from the cross which Mark records. The Sinaitic MSS. reads, "lema" for "lama;" the sense is the same. This expression *apparently* of despair, is variously explained. Some, as Calvin, suggest that it was the weakness of the flesh crying out under the awful sense of the load of sin, coming upon the Saviour, *as if* God had forsaken him, and yet implying that he still relied on God, as David, "though he slay me, yet will I trust in him." The cry cannot be regarded as arising from physical causes alone, but must have some mysterious significance from the sin of, and spiritual death due to, the whole race, which came upon him in this terrible hour.

Of the "seven words" from the cross, the first three referred to others,

AUTHORIZED VERSION.	REVISED VERSION.
35 And some of them that stood by, when they heard it, said, Behold, he calleth Elias.	35 And some of them that stood by, when they heard it, said, Behold, he calleth Elijah. And
36 And one ran and filled a sponge full of vinegar, and put it on a reed, and gave him to drink, saying, Let alone; let us see whether Elias will come to take him down.	36 one ran, and filling a sponge full of vinegar, put it on a reed, and gave him to drink, saying, Let be; let us see whether Elijah cometh 37 to take him down. And Jesus uttered a loud
37 And Jesus cried with a loud voice, and gave up the ghost.	38 voice, and gave up the ghost. And the vail of the ¹ temple was rent in twain from the
38 And the vail of the temple was rent in twain from the top to the bottom.	

¹ Or, *sanctuary*

(1) his murderers, (2) the penitent malefactor, (3) his earthly mother; the next three referred to his own mysterious and awful conflict. (1) his loneliness, (2) his sense of thirst, (3) his work now all but ended; the seventh commends his soul into his Father's hands.

35. *Behold, he calleth Elias*] Some regard this as a real misapprehension of his words. Buchanan in his *Researches* supposes that the exclamation was mistaken for "*Hil*" or "*Hila*" which he says was old Syriac for vinegar. Others conjecture that it was mistaken for Elias; but most interpreters hold that it was an ironical and sarcastic remark, arising from an affected misapprehension.

36. *full of vinegar*] Burning thirst is the most painful aggravation of death by crucifixion, and it was as he uttered the words, "*I thirst*," that the soldiers ran and filled a sponge with vinegar, or the sour wine-and-water called *posca*, the ordinary drink of the Roman soldiers.

and put it on a reed] i. e. on the short stem of a hyssop-plant (John xix, 29).

Let alone] This was a wicked and cruel jest, if the interpretation of the previous verse as irony, is accepted. According to Mark, the man himself cries "Let be;" according to Matthew, the others cry out thus to him as he offers the drink; according to John, several filled the sponge with the sour wine. Combining the statements together, we have a natural and accurate picture of an excitement under such circumstances, every one calling out with advice or direction.

37. *And Jesus cried with a loud voice*] saying, "It is finished." The three evangelists all dwell upon the loudness of the cry. Some think it implied the triumphant note of a conqueror.

and gave up the ghost] "There may be something intentional in the fact that in describing the death of Christ the evangelists do not use the neuter verb, '$\theta\alpha\nu\epsilon\nu$,' but the phrases, '*He gave up the ghost*' (Mark xv, 37; Luke xxiii, 46; John xix, 30); '*He yielded up the ghost*' (Matt. xxvii, 50); as though they would imply, with Augustine, that he gave up his life, '*quia voluit, quando voluit, quomodo voluit.*' Comp. John x, 18."
—*Farrar.* This phrase, "gave up the ghost," is not a *strict* rendering of the one Greek word representing it. It is an English idiomatic paraphrase, for the Greek "breathed out," or expired.

the ghost] *ghost*, from the A. S. *gást*, G. *geist*, = spirit, breath, opposed to body. "The word has now acquired a kind of hallowed use, and is applied to one Spirit only, but was once common."—*Bible Word-Book.*

38. *And the vail of the temple*] the beautiful, thick, costly veil of purple and gold, inwrought with figures of Cherubim, and twenty feet long and thirty broad, which separated the Holy Place from the Most Holy.

was rent in twain] for the full symbolism of this see Heb. ix, 3: x, 19. For the earthquake which now shook the city, see Matt. xxvii, 51. Such an event must have made a profound impression, and perhaps was the first step

AUTHORIZED VERSION.	REVISED VERSION.
39 And when the centurion, which stood over against him, saw that he so cried out, and gave up the ghost, he said, Truly this man was the Son of God. 40 There were also women looking on afar off: among whom was Mary Magdalene, and Mary the mother of James the less and of Joses, and Salome;	39 top to the bottom. And when the centurion, which stood over against him, saw that he ¹so gave up the ghost, he said, Truly this man was ² the son of God. And there were also women beholding from afar: among whom were both Mary Magdalene, and Mary the mother of James the ³ less and of Joses,

¹ Many ancient authorities read *so cried out, and gave up the ghost.* ² Or, *a son of God* ³ Gr. *little.*

towards the change of feeling which afterwards led a great number of "*the priests to become obedient to the faith*" (Acts vi, 7).

39—41. THE CONFESSION OF THE CENTURION.

39. *when the centurion*] he usually commanded a hundred men, but the term was applied somewhat widely to subordinate officers of a Roman legion. This centurion had in charge the execution, and with him a quaternion of soldiers.

ROMAN CENTURION.

that he so cried out] The words "cried out and" are omitted in the R. V. The spirit and conduct of Jesus, the darkness, and the manner of his death, convinced the stern Roman. Death he must have often witnessed, on the battle-field, in the amphitheatre at Cæsarea, in tumultuous insurrections in Palestine, but never before had he been confronted with the majesty of a death undergone for the salvation of the world.

the Son of God] or "a son of God;" but whether he said "the" or "a" cannot be determined, for the Latin, in which he doubtless spoke, has no definite article. In an ecstacy of awe and wonder "*he glorified God.*" "*Certainly this was a righteous man,*" (Luke xxiii, 47); nay, he went further and declared, "*This man was a* (or *the*) *Son of God.*" The centurion may have heard the mysterious declaration of the Jews, that by their Law the Holy One ought to die, because he *made himself the Son of God* (John xix, 7). "Together with the centurion at Capernaum (Matt. viii), and Cornelius at Cæsarea (Acts x), he forms in the Gospel and Apostolic histories," says Maclear, "a triumvirate of believing Gentile soldiers." But others, as Calvin, do not think the centurion became a believer, but only was struck with awe at the extraordinary display of God's power, a feeling which soon ends in indifference, when the cause of the fear passes away.

40. *Mary Magdalene*] out of whom had gone forth seven demons (Luke viii, 2). This is the first time she is mentioned by Mark. She is not to be confounded with the nameless sinner in Luke vii, 37. The popular use of "Magdalen" to describe harlots is a gratuitous assumption, founded on an unwarrantable mis-interpretation of Scripture.

Mary the mother of James the less] Some, as Schaff, hold that this Mary was *not* the sister of our Lord's mother, but that Salome was; others think that this Mary, the mother of James, was the sister of our Lord, and the same as Mary of Clopas. Comp. John xix, 25; Matt. xxvii, 56. The first view seems most probable, and also that James, son of Alpheus, was not identical with James the brother of our Lord.

James the less] Those who regard this James as the same who presided at

AUTHORIZED VERSION.	REVISED VERSION.
41 Who also, when he was in Galilee, followed him, and ministered unto him; and many other women which came up with him unto Jerusalem.	41 and Salome; who, when he was in Galilee, followed him, and ministered unto him; and many other women which came up with him unto Jerusalem.
42 And now when the even was come, because it was the preparation, that is, the day before the sabbath,	42 And when even was now come, because it was the Preparation, that is, the day before
43 Joseph of Arimathea, an honourable counsellor, which also waited for the kingdom of God, came, and went in boldly unto Pilate, and craved the body of Jesus.	43 the sabbath, there came Joseph of Arimathæa, a councillor of honourable estate, who also himself was looking for the kingdom of God: and he boldly went in unto Pilate, and
44 And Pilate marvelled if he were already dead: and calling *unto him* the centurion, he	44 asked for the body of Jesus. And Pilate marvelled if he were already dead: and call-

the council in Jerusalem (Acts xv, 13), think he may have assumed the title in humility, and out of deference to the martyred James. The evidence that he was the same James is altogether insufficient. James the son of Zebedee had been put to death long before Mark wrote his gospel, and this title, "James the less," or the little, was used to distinguish him from "James the Just," the brother of our Lord. So Schaff and others understand the phrase.

PRACTICAL LESSONS.—"Look at the serpent," says Augustine, "that the serpent may not harm you. Look at death, that death may not hurt you. But at whose death? At the death of him who is the life. Christ, our life, died on the cross, and in his death, death died: Life, by dying, destroyed death; Life, by dying, swallowed up death: death died in Christ." The following was found written in Dr. Bethune's Greek Testament:

"O God, pardon what I have been,
Sanctify what I am,
Order what I shall be,
And thine shall be the glory,
And mine the eternal salvation,
Through Jesus Christ my Lord. Amen."

42—47. THE BURIAL.

42. *the preparation*] *i. e.,* for the Sabbath, which Mark, writing for other readers than Jews, explains as "*the day before the Sabbath.*"

43. *Joseph of Arimathæa*] The place is called in the LXX "Armathaim," and by Josephus "Armathia." Joseph was a man of wealth (Matt. xxvii, 57), and from being called "honorable counsellor," it is inferred that he was a member of the Sanhedrin (Luke xxiii, 50), and a secret disciple of Jesus (John xix, 38), who had not consented to the death of Jesus (Luke xxiii, 51).

waited for the kingdom] like Simeon (Luke ii, 25), and Anna (Luke ii, 36).

went in boldly] No longer a secret disciple, he casts away all fear. The cross transfigures cowards into heroes. "It was no light matter Joseph had undertaken: for to take part in a burial, at any time, would defile him for seven days, and make everything unclean which he touched (Num. xix, 11; Hag. ii. 13); and to do so now involved his seclusion through the whole Passover week—with all its holy observances and rejoicings."—*Geikie.* In the so-called "Acts of Pilate," it is said the Sanhedrin caused Joseph to be imprisoned for this act of love.

craved the body of Jesus] The Roman custom was to let the bodies of criminals moulder and rot on the cross.—Cic. *Tusc. Quæst.* 1, 43; or be devoured by wild beasts, Hor. *Epist.* xvi, 48. Jewish law, however, did not allow such barbarities, and the Roman rulers had made an express exception in their favor.

44. *And Pilate marvelled*] death by crucifixion did not generally come

AUTHORIZED VERSION.	REVISED VERSION.
asked him whether he had been any while dead. 45 And when he knew *it* of the centurion, he gave the body to Joseph. 46 And he bought fine linen, and took him down, and wrapped him in the linen, and laid him in a sepulchre which was hewn out of a rock, and rolled a stone unto the door of the sepulchre. 47 And Mary Magdalene and Mary *the mother* of Joses beheld where he was laid.	ing unto him the centurion, he asked him 45 whether he ¹ had been any while dead. And when he learned it of the centurion, he 46 granted the corpse to Joseph. And he bought a linen cloth, and taking him down, wound him in the linen cloth, and laid him in a tomb which had been hewn out of a rock; and he rolled a stone against the door of the 47 tomb. And Mary Magdalene and Mary the *mother* of Joses beheld where he was laid.

¹ Many ancient authorities read *were already dead.*

even for three days, and thirty-six hours is said to be the earliest period when it would be thus brought about. Pilate, therefore, marvelled at the request of Joseph, and called for the evidence of the centurion to assure himself.

45. *he gave the body to Joseph*] The word translated "gave" only occurs in the New Testament here and in 2 Peter i, 3, 4. It appears to be used designedly by Mark, implying that Pilate, who from his character might have expected a bribe from the wealthy "counsellor," *freely gave up* the body, an unusual act for him.

46. *And he bought fine linen*] having secured the body, and the linen, with Nicodemus, formerly a secret disciple like himself, and who brought *a mixture of myrrh and aloes, about an hundred pound weight* (John xix, 39), he proposed to remove the body to the tomb.

wrapped him in the linen] Thus assisted, Joseph took down the body, laid it in the fine linen, and sprinkled the myrrh and aloes among the folds.

a sepulchre] a new one which he had hewn out of the limestone rock in a garden he possessed hard by Golgotha (John xix, 41). The precise location of the sepulchre, like the site of Calvary, is sharply disputed. The topographical arguments are strongly against the *traditional* site, under the church of the Holy Sepulchre; but the historical arguments are certainly less decided against it, indeed, they are the chief arguments in its favor. The testimony of Eusebius is regarded as strongly favoring the traditional view. But consult Schaff's *Dict. of the Bible* for a summary of the arguments on both sides.

rolled a stone] of large size (Matt. xxvii, 60) to the horizontal entrance, and this stone was sealed with an official seal, and a military guard set before it, to prevent any removal of the body, and ground for a *false* report of his resurrection. Lewin infers from the narratives that the stone was circular, rolling in a groove cut in the rock in front of the cave tomb, such as may now be seen at the "Tombs of the Kings" near Jerusalem.

47. *Mary Magdalene*] and Mary the mother of Joses, the same as in *v.* 40, and the other women (Luke xxiii, 55), "beheld," *i. e. observed carefully*, the place where he was laid.

PRACTICAL SUGGESTIONS.—"For this very reason *we believe;* because Christ did not come down from the cross."—*Bengel.* "He had come into the world to save others, regardless of himself."—*Ellicott.* "Such was the honorable nature of the title, saith Baur, that in the midst of death Christ began to triumph by it. The cross began to change its own nature: and, instead of an engine of torture, it became a throne of majesty."—*Flavel.* "The cross is always ready and waits for thee in every place; run where thou wilt thou canst not avoid it. Turn where thou wilt, either to things above, or things below; to that which is within, or that which is without thee; thou wilt in all certainty find the cross; and if thou wouldst enjoy peace, and obtain an unfading crown of glory, it is necessary that in every

AUTHORIZED VERSION.

CHAP. XVI.—And when the sabbath was past, Mary Magdalene, and Mary the mother of James, and Salome, had bought sweet spices, that they might come and anoint him.

2 And very early in the morning, the first *day* of the week, they came unto the sepulchre at the rising of the sun.

3 And they said among themselves, Who shall roll us away the stone from the door of the sepulchre?

4 And when they looked, they saw that the

REVISED VERSION.

16 And when the sabbath was past, Mary Magdalene, and Mary the *mother* of James, and Salome, bought spices, that they might

2 come and anoint him. And very early on the first day of the week, they come to the tomb

3 when the sun was risen. And they were saying among themselves, Who shall roll us away the stone from the door of the tomb?

4 and looking up, they see that the stone is rolled

place, and in all events, thou shouldst bear it willingly, and in patience possess thy soul."—*Thomas à Kempis.*

CH.-XVI. 1—8. THE RESURRECTION.
(Sunday, 17th Nisan, April 9th, A. D. 30.)

1. *And when the sabbath was past*] Friday night, Saturday, and Saturday night passed away, three days according to the Jewish reckoning (comp. (*a*) 1 Sam. xxx, 12, 13; 2 Chron. x, 5, 12; (*b*) Matt. xii, 40; John ii, 19; Matt. xxvii, 63.

bought sweet spices] Meanwhile the women having observed the spot on the evening of his burial, had returned, but not to complete the embalming of the body, as some infer, for that was the work of physicians, or of specialists, not of women. They brought the spices as a mark of affection, and to apply externally, as Mary had done while Jesus was alive. The spices were probably "bought" on the previous evening, but after the close of the sabbath, *i.e.* after sunset.

2. *And very early*] while "*it was yet dark*" (John xx, 1), on the morning following the Jewish sabbath. Joseph and Nicodemus had bought an hundred weight of myrrh and aloes to use in preparing the body for burial. They would bring more. As Hackett observes, "cordial love thinks all is not done that should be, unless itself be at the doing."

the first day of the week] the *Lord's day* (Rev. i, 10), and our Sunday.

they came] (Observe again the graphic present tense of the evangelist), *draw near* to the tomb. The R. V. endeavors to preserve the distinction of the Greek by using "tomb" and "sepulchre" for two similar Greek words.

3. *And they said among themselves*] Unaware of the deputation of the Jewish rulers, which had gone to Pilate, and secured the sealing of the stone and the setting of the watch over the tomb (Matt. xxvii, 62-66), their only anxiety was, *who shall roll away the stone from the door of the sepulchre.* Tombs belonging to rich families were often large structures, generally with a vestibule or open corridor in front of the opening leading to the place where the body was deposited. This inner opening would be closed by the large stone. In the "Holy Sepulchre" at Jerusalem, the ante-chamber is seventeen feet in length; through this is the entrance to the reputed tomb of Joseph, in which Jesus was laid.

ROLLING STONE AT THE MOUTH OF AN EASTERN TOMB.

4. *And when they looked*] or *looking up* they saw that all cause of anxiety was removed, for the stone was already rolled away. In their sorrow,

AUTHORIZED VERSION.	REVISED VERSION.
stone was rolled away: for it was very great. 5 And entering into the sepulchre, they saw a young man sitting on the right side, clothed in a long white garment; and they were affrighted. 6 And he saith unto them, Be not affrighted: ye seek Jesus of Nazareth, which was crucified: he is risen; he is not here: behold the place where they laid him. 7 But go your way, tell his disciples and Peter that he goeth before you into Galilee: there shall ye see him, as he said unto you.	5 back: for it was exceeding great. And entering into the tomb, they saw a young man sitting on the right side, arrayed in a white 6 robe; and they were amazed. And he saith unto them, Be not amazed: ye seek Jesus, the Nazarene, which hath been crucified: he is risen; he is not here: behold, the place 7 where they laid him! But go, tell his disciples and Peter, He goeth before you into Galilee: there shall ye see him, as he said

they would naturally go with *downcast* countenances, and absorbed in thought. Whether the tomb was above them, or on a level with the ground, cannot be determined by this expression: "an accurate and graphic detail."

for it was very great] Maclear and Perowne infer from this verse that the mouth of the tomb was up a height, but this is hardly warranted by the narration. The stones were usually large, to prevent any access to the bodies by wild beasts—and being very large they would see the stone even in the faint light of the early morning. Mark seems to hear some skeptic say, the stone could not be seen in the twilight, so he answers it could, for it was exceeding great.

5. *And entering into the sepulchre*] It is conjectured by some that all entered except Mary of Magdala, who, seeing in the rolling away of the stone the confirmation of her worst fears, fled away to find Peter and John. On her return to weep at the tomb she met the risen Lord. See v. 9. Others suppose that she remained behind when the other women departed from the sepulchre, and had a second vision, and met Christ himself.

a young man] In Luke xxiv, 4, it is said there were *two* sitting on the right hand. (Comp. Luke i, 11.) They had the appearance of angels.

clothed in a long white garment] white or "*glistering*" (Luke xxiv, 4); "hilid with a whit stoole."—*Wyclif.* The white refers not to the color alone, but the brightness of their covering.

and they were affrighted] see above, ch. ix, 15. It is not mere fright, but awe, arising from the appearance of some angelic being.

6. *he is risen*] Precisely when he had risen the "keepers" well knew, for the lightning-like appearance of the angel made them quail with awe (Matt. xxviii, 4). There were no traces of violence. All was order and calm. The linen bandages lay carefully unrolled by themselves. The cloth that had covered the face lay not with them. It was folded up in a place by itself. There had been no haste or confusion in his departure from the tomb. He had risen, even as he had said.

ye seek] The seeking was right, though directed to the wrong place. The motives were approved by the celestial visitant, and the women directed to the place where they would see the Lord.

behold the place] which did not contain him now. It was a call to notice the evidence of a quiet and actual resurrection, not a hasty snatching away of the body by deceivers.

7. *go your way*] action now in place of vague astonishment. There was a message to be borne.

and Peter] No wonder that in the Gospel of Mark we find this wonderful touch. Who afterwards would have been so likely as the Apostle himself to treasure up this word, the pledge of possible forgiveness, after the dreadful hours he must have spent during Friday night, Saturday, and Saturday night? What story would he have so often told to his son in the faith, either in eastern Babylon or the capital of the West?

he goeth before you] It is the same word (*a*) He himself used on the even-

AUTHORIZED VERSION.	REVISED VERSION.
8 And they went out quickly, and fled from the sepulchre; for they trembled and were amazed: neither said they anything to any man; for they were afraid.	8 unto you. And they went out, and fled from the tomb; for trembling and astonishment had come upon them; and they said nothing to any one; for they were afraid.
9 Now when *Jesus* was risen early the first day of the week, he appeared first to Mary Mag-	9 ¹ Now when he was risen early on the first day of the week, he appeared first to Mary

¹ The two oldest Greek manuscripts, and some other authorities, omit from ver. 9 to the end. Some other authorities have a different ending to the Gospel.

ing of the betrayal, "After I am risen again, I will *go before you* into Galilee" (Matt. xxvi. 32; Mark xiv. 28); (*b*) applied to the star *going before* the Magi at his nativity; (*c*) to his own *going before* his apostles on the road towards Jerusalem.

8. *they went out quickly*] overwhelmed with alarm at the sight they had witnessed and the words they had heard; "quickly" is implied, but not expressed in the original. See R. V.

they trembled] or as Wyclif renders it, "forsothe drede and quakynge hadde assaylid hem." They fled, not merely walked, or ran away; implying the terror attending the escape. There was speed and silence in their movements.

"For in some dignified similitude, alike, yet different in glory,
This body shall be shaped anew, fit dwelling for the soul:
The hovel hath grown to a palace, the bulb hath burst into flower,
Matter hath put on incorruption, and is at peace with spirit."—*M. F. Tupper.*

for they were afraid] in a tumult of rapture and alarm they fled back from the tomb towards the city. Those who would throw doubt on the rest of this chapter, have offered no satisfactory explanation of the evangelist's motives for omitting the appearance of the Lord after the resurrection, nor of the abrupt ending of the gospel at this verse with "$\gamma\alpha\rho$" = "for." Even the skeptical Renan objects to ending the gospel in this way.

9—11. THE APPEARANCE TO MARY MAGDALEN.
(Sunday, April 9th, A. D. 30.)

The genuineness of this section, vs. 9-20 has been much discussed among critical scholars. The great majority of those who have entertained doubts in regard to the authorship of this passage, have nevertheless granted that it was an authentic portion of scripture. After admitting the full force of all that has been urged against it, as a production of Mark, there are two solutions of the difficulty; (1) That he was interrupted from completing the work at first; but afterwards, in another land and in more peaceful circumstances, added the closing section, or that an incomplete copy may have got into circulation. So Ellicott, Lange and others. (2) That the last leaf was accidentally lost, and reproduced by some later transcriber, and hence the omission in some of our older MSS. For additional facts see INTRODUCTION, page 19.

9. *he appeared first*] The first person to whom the Saviour shewed himself after his resurrection was Mary of Magdala. A discussion on the nature of the risen body of the Lord does not come within the scope of this work. It will be sufficient to notice that while the body was in many respects like the other; *e.g.* in appearance, in the marks upon it, in its power to take food; it was also in many remarkable features quite unlike his former body. "He came and went, appeared and disappeared in a most mysterious and inscrutable manner." He comes suddenly into a room, the doors being shut, he talks and walks with familiar disciples unrecognized; he vanishes as mysteriously as he appears; all these facts place his appearances after resurrec-

AUTHORIZED VERSION.	REVISED VERSION.
dalene, out of whom he had cast seven devils.	Magdalene, from whom he had cast out seven
10 *And* she went and told them that had been with him, as they mourned and wept.	10 ¹ devils. She went and told them that had been with him, as they mourned and wept.
11 And they, when they had heard that he was alive, and had been seen of her, believed not.	11 And they, when they heard he was alive, and had been seen of her, disbelieved.

¹ Gr. *demons.*

tion in the sphere of the supernatural. Alford suggests that the normal condition of his body before the resurrection was to be visible to mortal eyes, the normal condition of it after the resurrection to be invisible; Ellicott thinks that the glorification which was perfected at the ascension had already begun after the resurrection.

whom he had cast seven devils] That Jesus was seen first after his resurrection not by the whole apostolic company, but by a woman, and that woman not his earthly mother, but Mary of Magdala, made a strong impression on the early church.

10. *she went and told*] the first to see the risen Lord, she was the first to tell the sorrowing disciples.

as they mourned and wept] or literally "mourning and weeping." "Weylinge and wepynge" is Wyclif's rendering.

11. *had been seen of her*] The original word here translated "had been seen" occurs nowhere else in Mark except here in this section and in verse 14.

believed not] or "disbelieved" a positive belief on the opposite side; so incredible to them did the whole story appear, though Jesus had told them he would arise the third day.

PRACTICAL SUGGESTIONS.—"Jesus was, even upon our journeyings, with us."—*Quesnel.* Woman last at the cross, first at the sepulchre. The stone was rolled away. "A large proportion of the saints' anxieties arise from things which never really happen." "The friends of Christ have no cause to be afraid of angels." "The very doubts of the eleven apostles are the confirmation of our faith in these latter days."—*Ryle.* "The historical problem is as hard to solve as the pictorial, not more so...a key is afforded by the simple suggestion that in this account of the Saviour's resurrection and subsequent appearances, a specific purpose of the writer is to point out the successive steps by which the incredulity of the apostles was at length subdued."—*Alexander.* "They doubted, that we might never doubt."—*Birney.* "A singular and significant testimony to the truth of the resurrection is afforded by the change in the Sabbath day. It was changed not by any express command in the N. T., but by the almost universal consent of the church."—*Abbott.* "Those first saw Jesus who most loved him, and most zealously sought him."—*Cyprian.* The Jews call their synagogues *Beth chayim*—the house of the living, showing that they believe in the resurrection—"I see no greater difficulty in believing the resurrection of the dead or the conception of the virgin, than the creation of the world. Is it not less easy to reproduce the human body than it was to produce it at first."—*Pascal.* "When we pluck down a house with intent to rebuild or repair it, we warn the inhabitants out of it, lest they be soiled with the dust and rubbish, or offended with the noise, and so for a time provide another place for them; but when we have now trimmed and dressed up the house, then we bring them back to a better habitation; thus God when he overturneth this rotten room of our flesh, calleth out the soul for a little time, and lodgeth it with himself in some corner of his kingdom, repaireth the imperfections of our bodies against the resurrection; and then having made them beautiful, yea, glorious and incorruptible, he doth put our souls again into their acquainted mansions."—*Chrysostom.*

AUTHORIZED VERSION.	REVISED VERSION.
12 After that he appeared in another form un-	12 And after these things he was manifested

12–18. APPEARANCE TO TWO AND TO THE ELEVEN.
(Sunday, April 9, A. D. 30).

12. *After*] The risen Saviour manifested himself first to Mary Magdalene. The Evangelist notices the appearance to the two disciples journeying towards Emmaus, which is more fully described by Luke (xxiv, 13-35).

he appeared] "*he is schewid.*"—*Wyclif.* In regard to the *number* of recorded appearances of the Lord after his resurrection, commentators are not agreed. Some hold that there are *four* different ones described as occurring on the day of resurrection, others say *five*; some regard the appearance to the disciples by the sea of Galilee, and to the five hundred as the same, others hold that they are two different appearances. Robinson gives five on the first day and ten before the ascension, as follows: (1) to the women, (Matt. xxviii, 9); (2) to Mary Magdalene; (3) to Peter; (4) to the two going to Emmaus; (5) to the eleven (Thomas absent); (6) to the eleven (Thomas present); (7) to the seven by the sea; (8) to the eleven and five hundred on a mountain in Galilee; (9) to James; (10) to the eleven at Jerusalem just before the resurrection. Farrar and Schaff agree also with Robinson, except that they place the appearance to Mary Magdalene first, as Mark fairly implies, then to the other women. Ellicott's view is similar, except that he holds to a second appearance to Mary, when she joined the other women. Many hold only four recorded appearances on the first day, regarding Nos. 1 and 2 in the above list as the same. The order of appearances, would then be: (1) to Mary Magdalene and the other women (John xx, 14-18; Mark xvi, 9; Matt. xxviii, 9); (2) to Peter, (Luke xxiv, 34; 1 Cor. xv, 5); (3) to the two on the way to Emmaus, (Luke xxiv, 13-35; Mark xvi, 12); (4) to the "eleven" in the evening, Thomas not present, (John xx, 19-24); (5) to the eleven, Thomas present, (one week later than the former appearance) (John xx, 25-29; Mark xvi, 14-18) (?); (6) to seven apostles by the sea of Galilee, (John xxi, 1-24); (7) to the disciples and five hundred brethren in a mountain of Galilee, (Matt. xxviii, 16-20; 1 Cor. xv, 6); (8) to James, (1 Cor. xv, 7); (9) to the apostles at Jerusalem, (Acts i, 3-5; 1 Cor. xv, 7); (10) near Bethany at the ascension, (Acts i, 6-11; Mark xvi, 19; Luke xxiv, 50, 51). He was also seen of Paul, but after, not before the ascension, as Godwin assumes, (1 Cor. xv, 8), compare Acts ix, 17. Among those who favor the order last named substantially are: Lightfoot, Krafft, Lichtenstein, Wieseler, Da Costa, Canon Cook, Geikie. Andrews, Canon Cook, and some others hold that of the company of women going to the sepulchre early on the first day, only Mary Magdalene saw Jesus. This view is not absolutely required by the narratives, and gives much difficulty in harmonizing the accounts in Matt. xxviii, 1-9 and John xx, 9-18. Their explanations of Matthew's account are plausible but unsatisfactory. If there was an appearance to "the women," one of whom was Mary Magdalene, as Matthew states, this does not contradict, but confirms the appearance reported by Mark and by John, who name only Mary Magdalene, but omit to name the other women as seeing Jesus. An *omission* is not a *contradiction*. Those who maintain that the appearances at the sea, and on the mountain in Galilee are the same, do so on altogether insufficient grounds. There were no doubt many other unrecorded appearances of the Lord during the forty days, as Luke's language implies, (Acts i, 3). These are recorded that we might believe, and have good grounds for the faith that is in us.

in another form] This implies that he was not at first recognized, as stated more fully in Luke xxiv, 16.

AUTHORIZED VERSION.	REVISED VERSION.
to two of them, as they walked, and went into the country. 13 And they went and told *it* unto the residue: neither believed they them. 14 Afterward he appeared unto the eleven as they sat at meat, and upbraided them with their unbelief and hardness of heart, because they believed not them which had seen him after he was risen. 15 And he said unto them, Go ye into all the world, and preach the gospel to every creature. 16 He that believeth and is baptized shall be	in another form unto two of them, as they 13 walked, on their way into the country. And they went away and told it unto the rest: neither believed they them. 14 And afterward he was manifested unto the eleven themselves as they sat at meat; and he upbraideth them with their unbelief and hardness of heart, because they believed not them which had seen him after he was risen. 15 And he said unto them, Go ye into all the world, and preach the gospel to the whole 16 creation. He that believeth and is baptized

unto two of them] The name of one was Cleopas = Cleopatros, not the Clopas of John xix. 25, and another whose name is not known. Some have conjectured it was Nathanael, others the Evangelist Luke.

as they walked] into the country from Jerusalem to the village of Emmaus. Luke says it was *sixty stadia* (A. V. "threescore furlongs"), or about seven-and-a half miles from Jerusalem.

13. *they went and told it unto the residue*] They recognize the Lord in the breaking of bread (Luke xxiv. 35), and returned in haste to Jerusalem, found ten of the apostles met together (Luke xxiv. 33), and the apostles greeted them with the joyful tidings, "The Lord is risen indeed and appeared to Simon" (Luke xxiv. 34 ; 1 Cor. xv. 5).

neither believed they them] They had refused to believe Mary Magdalene (Mark xvi. 11), and even now they could not credit the testimony of the two disciples. The evangelists multiply proofs of the slowness of the apostles to accept the fact of their Lord's resurrection. The resurrection, it is to be remembered, was unlike any of the recorded miracles of raising from the dead, or any of the legends of Greece or Rome. It was "not a restoration to the old life, to its wants, to its inevitable ending, but the revelation of a new life, foreshadowing new powers of action and a new mode of being." See Westcott's *Gospel of the Resurrection*.

14. *as they sat at meat*] The Greek suggests a suddenness to this appearance, causing them to be terrified (Luke xxiv. 37). To assure them that his appearance was real, he spake to them, reproving their unbelief. If this was on the evening of the day of the resurrection, as seems most probable, then Thomas was absent, and only ten of the apostles were present.

upbraided them] "reproached" them; they were full of mingled feelings of joy and fear; joy at the glimmer of hope that it was all true, fear lest it would prove delusive

hardness of heart] So he had spoken after the feeding of the five thousand and the four thousand.

them which had seen him] Alford holds that Mark here joins in one at least *four* appearances of the Lord. (1) That to the eleven, Luke xxiv. 36-49. (2) On the mountain, Matt. xxviii. 16-20. (3) An unrecorded appearance vs. 16-18, though these words may have been spoken on the mountain in Galilee. (4) The appearance at the ascension.

15. *And he said unto them*] A final commission to them and to all disciples.

16. *He that believeth and is baptized*] Faith and baptism were required by the Lord. Compare the words of Philip the deacon, to the Ethiopian eunuch, Acts viii, 37. Baptism was a well-known religious rite before Jesus began his ministry. John's baptism of repentance was accepted by the Jewish people as a familiar religious act. Christ adopted and formally appointed baptism as a Christian ordinance, and as such it is clearly distinguished in the New Testament from the baptism of John. See Acts xix, 3-5. Christian baptism is an ordinance of Christ, by which water administered, " in the name of the

AUTHORIZED VERSION.	REVISED VERSION.
saved; but he that believeth not shall be damned.	shall be saved; but he that disbelieveth shall be condemned. And these signs shall follow them that believe: in my name shall they cast out ¹ devils; they shall speak with ² new
17 And these signs shall follow them that believe; in my name shall they cast out devils; they shall speak with new tongues;	17

¹ Gr. *demons*. ² Some ancient authorities omit *new*.

Father, and of the Son, and of the Holy Ghost" Matt. xxviii, 19, is a sign and a seal of the covenant of grace; an inward cleansing from sin, and renewal of the heart by the Holy Spirit; and of a believer's spiritual union with Christ, his membership in the visible church, and his professed engagement to be wholly and only the Lord's. The declaration in this verse is clear: "He that believeth and is baptized shall be saved, but he that disbelieveth shall be condemned." It cannot fairly be inferred from this, however, that salvation is impossible without baptism, for it does not read "he that is not baptized shall be condemned." The penitent thief on the cross was not baptized, and Cornelius received the Holy Ghost before baptism. Many martyrs had no opportunity to be baptized; multitudes of unbaptized children have died in infancy. "It is not the want of baptism, but the contempt of it that condemns." Nor does it imply that baptism of itself will regenerate the soul. Simon the sorcerer was baptized, but was still " in the gall of bitterness " Acts viii, 13, 23; so also, without doubt, Ananias and Sapphira had received baptism.

In respect to the *mode* and the *subjects* of baptism, there have been many warm disputes among Christians. Water is regarded as essential to baptism, but as to the *quantity* (sprinkling, pouring or immersion), and the *quality* (warm or cold, rain, spring or river water) required, Christians are not agreed. Baptists believe in immersion as the only scriptural *mode* of baptism, and that it should be administered only to professed believers, and they reject infant baptism. The Greek church and some small bodies of Protestants practice trine immersion. Other Protestant churches do not insist on immersion, but accept sprinkling or pouring as also valid *modes* of baptism; and in common with the Greek and Latin Churches, hold to infant baptism. In the Protestant, Episcopal, Lutheran, and German Reformed Churches there is a course of catechetical instruction followed by confirmation, which admits the baptized children into full communion with the church. In other Protestant churches holding to infant baptism the baptized children are not received into *full* communion until they give evidence of conversion, or regeneration by the Holy Spirit. Some do not accept water or any outward or ritual baptism; though they hold to baptism by the Holy Spirit, in common with all orthodox Christians.

he that believeth not] or "disbelieveth," it is more than want of belief because of insufficient evidence: it implies a positive refusal to believe on proper evidence; so there is nothing said of baptism here, for he who refuses to believe will refuse to be baptized.

shall be damned] or "condemned." He who wilfully rejects the gospel when offered him, shall have no share in its saving mercies, but be left to the condemnation due to his sins.

17. *And these signs*] As Meyer observes, "Jesus does not mean that each of these signs should manifest itself with each believer, but this miracle with one, and that with another." It does not necessarily mean that *every* believer would perform miracles. There are some variations in this verse as it appears in the Arabic and Persic versions.

shall follow] Literally, *proceed along with*.

In my name shall they cast out devils] so did Philip the deacon in Samaria (Acts viii, 7), and Paul at Philippi and Ephesus (Acts xvi, 18; xix, 15, 16).

they shall speak with new tongues] as on the day of Pentecost, the friends

AUTHORIZED VERSION.	REVISED VERSION.
18 They shall take up serpents; and if they drink any deadly thing, it shall not hurt them; they shall lay hands on the sick, and they shall recover.	18 tongues; they shall take up serpents, and if they drink any deadly thing, it shall in no wise hurt them; they shall lay hands on the sick, and they shall recover.
19 So then, after the Lord had spoken unto them, he was received up into heaven, and sat on the right hand of God.	19 So then the Lord Jesus, after he had spoken unto them, was received up into heaven, and sat down at the right hand of God.

of Cornelius (Acts x, 46), the disciples at Ephesus (Acts xix, 6), and many afterwards in the Church of Corinth (1 Cor. xii, 10).

18. *they shall take up serpents*] Paul shook off the viper at Malta (Acts xxviii, 5). Comp. Luke x. 19.

and if they drink] Tradition says that John and Justus Barsabas drank the cup of hemlock which was intended to cause death, and suffered no harm from it. See Eusebius, *Eccl. Hist.* III. 39. The manner in which Eusebius treats this tradition, as Canon Cook justly observes, shows how completely the memory of these signs had died out, even in the fourth century, and may account in part for the suspicion he throws on this section. In the "Epistle of Ignatius to the Romans," there is a reference to the persecutions of the early Christians, and their fighting with wild beasts, and the writer of the Epistle says: "May I enjoy the wild beasts that are prepared for me...and whom for that end I will encourage that they may be sure to devour me, and not serve me as they have some, whom out of fear *they have not touched.*" This indicates a fulfilment of the Lord's prophecy or promise.

they shall lay hands on the sick] this Peter did on the lame man, at the beautiful gate of the temple (Acts iii, 7), and Paul on Publius, in the island of Malta (Acts xxviii, 8). "Gifts of healing" are mentioned in 1 Cor. xii, 9, and James v, 14, 15.

19—20. THE ASCENSION.
Thursday, May 18th, (?) 783. A. D. 30.

19. *So then after the Lord*] The Latin and Syriac versions add "Jesus;" the Ethiopic reads, "our Lord, the Lord Jesus;" the Syriac and Persic, "our Lord." These versions show that the ending to this gospel, substantially as we now have it, was in existence before these early versions were made.

spoken unto them] The original word here rendered "*had spoken unto them,*" signifies *to teach, to instruct by preaching and other oral communication*. Compare its use in Mark xiii, 11; John ix, 29. Irenæus twice quotes this final clause in Mark, showing that it was accepted as a part of the gospel in his day.

into heaven] Luke gives a more full account of the final scene. See Luke xxiv, 50, 51; Acts i, 7. The precise spot from which the ascension took place is unknown. The place pointed out by tradition since the seventh century is on one of the four summits of Olivet, now covered by the village and chapel *Jebel-et-Tur*. The chapel is of comparatively recent date, and is too far from Bethany and too near to Jerusalem to meet the requirements of the gospel narratives. Stanley fixes the scene "on the wild uplands which immediately overhang the village" of Bethany, and Barclay also suggests a hill about five hundred yards above the village. The ascension must have taken place on some one of the heights near Bethany, on the eastern slope and just below the summit of Olivet.

and sat on the right hand of God] The session at the right hand of God, recorded only by Mark, forms a striking and appropriate conclusion to his gospel, and "conveys to the mind a comprehensive idea of Christ's majesty and rule." Our Lord was "taken up" and bore our redeemed humanity into

AUTHORIZED VERSION.	REVISED VERSION.
20 And they went forth, and preached everywhere, the Lord working with *them*, and confirming the word with signs following. Amen.	20 God. And they went forth, and preached everywhere, the Lord working with them, and confirming the word by the signs that followed. Amen.

the very presence of God, into " the place, of all places in the universe of things, in situation most eminent, in quality most holy, in dignity most excellent, in glory most illustrious, the inmost sanctuary of God's Temple above."
—Barrow's *Sermon on the ascension.*

20. *and they*] the apostles.

went forth] This word is a usual one in Mark's gospel. They went forth but not immediately. They were commanded not to "depart from Jerusalem," but to "tarry" there until at Pentecost they should be endued with power from on high (Luke xxiv. 49; Acts i. 4).

and preached everywhere] Mark himself when he wrote his gospel, had witnessed the spread of the church from Babylon in the distant East to Rome in the West. Augustine's prayer is a fitting one now: "Lord, give us strength to do what thou dost command; and then command whatsoever pleaseth thee."

the Lord working with them] The word translated "*working with them*" only occurs here in the gospels, but is used by Paul, Rom. viii, 28, "all things *work together* for good to them that love God;" 1 Cor. xvi, 16; 2 Cor. vi, 1. "The laws of nature," observes Whewell, "are the laws which God in his wisdom prescribes to his own acts: his universal presence is the necessary condition of any course of events; his univeral agency the only origin of any efficient force." Sir Isaac Newton declares that the various parts of the world, organic and inorganic, " can be the effect of nothing else than the wisdom and skill of a powerful and ever-living agent, who, being in all places is more able by his will to move the bodies within his boundless uniform *sensorium*, thereby to form and reform the parts of the universe, than we are by our will to move parts of our own body." And here it is declared that he used these powers for the upbuilding of his spiritual kingdom on the earth.

> "In God's great field of labor
> All work is not the same;
> He hath a service for each one
> Who loves his holy name."—HAVERGAL.

confirming] strengthening the cause of truth. The Syriac and Persic versions render it, "with signs following which they did." Tertullian declared, in regard to the increase of Christians in the Roman Empire, "Though but of yesterday, yet have we filled your cities, islands, castles, corporations, councils, your armies themselves, your tribes, companies, the palace, the senate, and courts of justice; only your temples have we left you free." The apostolic period of the Christian Church is usually regarded as beginning about A. D. 30, and ending with A. D. 100. The three stages of growth were: (1) founding the church among the Jews; (2) among the Gentiles; (3) blending of the Jewish and Gentile Christians in unity. The local centres were Jerusalem, Antioch, and Ephesus, and lastly, Rome, the capital and mistress of the world.

Amen] This word closes each of the four gospels, according to the A. V., but the R. V. omits it in all the gospels except Mark's. At the end of a prayer and of a writing, as here, "Amen" is a devout wish or prayer that what is asked or written may be fulfilled. The word comes from the Hebrew, meaning "true," or "let it be so," and was used as a solemn affirmative response to an oath. It was also used by our Saviour, at the beginning of an important utterance, to gain attention and give solemnity to the truth. Mark having witnessed the dark shadows of coming persecutions at Rome, and perhaps writing from that city, must have earnestly prayed and anxiously looked for the fulfillment of the Lord's promises respecting the spread of the gospel. The "Amen" gives expression to these desires, and it is also a solemn seal to testify his and every devout believer's assurance that these things are true, and that the Lord's kingdom will be established gloriously over all the earth.

PRACTICAL SUGGESTIONS.—"The words of Christ are words of majesty, for that may well be termed majesty, by virtue of which these poor beggars are commanded to go forth and preach this new truth, not in one city or country, but in all the world...no injunction of earth has surpassed it."—*Luther.* "God will exclude no one from eternal blessedness who does not exclude himself through unbelief."—*Osiander.* "All miracles which accompany the proclamation of the divine word are signs; they point to that internal wonder of salvation and the new birth which the word effects, and only in so far have they value."—*Gerlach.* "To disbelieve is very different from not knowing the gospel; unbelief and ignorance are two essentially distinct ideas."—*Heubner.*

The spread of the gospel at the present time may be partially shown by the following late estimate of those embracing the various religions in the world:

Jews	6,000,000	Protestant	97,139,000
Mohammedans	160,823,000	Roman Catholic	195,000,000
Pagans	766,342,000	Greek Church	69,692,700
		Oriental Christians	6,500,000
Total Non-Christian	933,165,000	Total Christians	368,331,700

or about one-third of the total population of the world now accept the Christian religion.

The numerical progress of the gospel since the time of Christ may be indicated by the following approximate statement of the number accepting Christianity at successive periods, according to Sharon Turner (except the nineteenth century), given in round numbers:

First century	500,000	Tenth century	50,000,000
Second "	2,000,000	Eleventh "	70,000,000
Third "	5,000,000	Twelfth "	80,000,000
Fourth "	10,000,000	Thirteenth century	75,000,000
Fifth "	15,000,000	Fourteenth "	80,000,000
Sixth "	20,000,000	Fifteenth "	100,000,000
Seventh "	24,000,000	Sixteenth "	125,000,000
Eighth "	30,000,000	Seventeenth "	155,000,000
Ninth "	40,000,000	Eighteenth "	200,000,000

Nineteenth century, 400,000,000.

"The portals of grace stand open to all; oh! let us enter and not delay!"—*Nova Bibl. Sub.* "The ascension of Jesus is our after-ascension. Where the Head is there are the members...The heavens stand open, we are certain of our salvation...The presence of Christ in the earth has not ceased with his ascension; it is rather established, being combined with his session at the right hand of God."—*Starke.* "Where the spiritually blind are enlightened," says Hedinger, "the spiritually dead quickened, the spiritually deaf and dumb made to hear devoutly and speak piously, the spiritually lame made to be industriously active, and the spiritually leprous are cleansed from sins, these are greater signs and wonders than physical changes." "The age of spiritual miracles is not past," says Ryle; "The renewal of every saint is as great a marvel as the casting out of a devil...The conversion and perseverance in grace of every member of the church is a sign and wonder as great as the raising of Lazarus from the dead." These signs still follow them that believe. Happy are they who can humbly and truly exclaim: "I was blind, but now I see." "I was dead, but am alive again." "I am a miracle of grace!"

INDEX.

Abba, 175.
Abiathar, 46.
Abimelech, 46.
Abomination of desolation, 154.
Agony in the garden, 175.
Ahimelech, 46.
Alabaster box, 163.
Alexander the Great, 69.
Alphæus, 42, 52, 74.
Amazement of disciples, 65, 85, 108, 121.
" of others, 94, 134, 142.
" of Jesus, 75, 174.
Andrew, 51, 52, 84, 151.
Angels, ministry of, 29, 158, 201.
Anger of Jesus, 47.
Anointing with oil, 77.
Annas, account of, 180.
Ambitious apostles, 122.
Anointing at Bethany, the, 161, 162.
Antipas, 48, 50, 77, 81.
Appearance of Jesus to Mary Magdalene, 205.
" " to the eleven, 207.
Apostles, calling of, 30, 42, 50.
" mission of, 75.
" return of, 81.
Ascension of Jesus, 210.
Attempt to seize Jesus, 140.
Aramaic expressions, 52, 73, 94, 198.
Aretas, 78, 79.
Aristobulus, 79.
Arrest of Jesus, 165.
Ass, the, 128, 129.

B

Baal, 100.
Baneas, 100.
Baptism, 29, 122, 208.
" of John, 25, 136.
" of repentance, 26, 136.
Barabbas, 191.
Bartholomew, 51, 52.
Bartimeus cured, 124, 125, 126.
Baskets, 83, 96, 135.
Bed, 41, 86.
Beelzebub, 54.
Belief, 30, 109.
Beginning, the, 25.
" of Christ's ministry, 30.
Benches, 42, 87.
Bethany, 126, 130, 132, 161, 165.
Bethphage, 126, 132.
Bethsaida, 84, 93, 98.
Betrayal, intimation of, 170
" the, 176.
" foretold, 170.
" Beware of the scribes," 147.
Bigotry reproved, 112.
Birthday observance, 79.
Blasphemy, warning against, 55.
Blessing little children, 117.
Blood of Jesus, why shed, 172.
Blind man at Jericho, 125, 126.
" cure of, 99.

Boanerges, 52.
Boat, 32, 64, 84.
" Body, this is my," 171.
Book of Moses, 143.
Bottles, 44, 167.
Brethren of Jesus, 56, 74.
Burnt offerings and sacrifices, 145, 148.
Burial of Jesus, 203.
Bush, the Lord's appearance to Moses, 143.
Bushel, a, 60.

C

Cæsar, 142.
Cæsarea Philippi, 100, 101.
Caiaphas, 162.
Calling the disciples, 30, 50.
Camel, the, 120.
Candle, a, 60.
Capernaum, 30, 33, 93, 111.
Carpenter, the, 74.
Casting lots for the garments of Jesus, 196.
Centurion, the, acknowledges Christ the Son of God, 200.
Chains, 67.
Charger, a, 80.
Christians, flight of, 155.
Chief priests, 134, 161, 165, 192.
" stir up the people, 192.
Children received by Jesus, 117.
Christ's kingdom, 111.
" second coming, 157.
Church and State, 142.
Cities of Decapolis, 69.
Cleansing of a leper, 37.
" the temple, 133.
Clopas, 74.
Cock crowing, 173.
Colt, a, 128.
Coming of Christ, second, 157.
Commandments, the, 118, 144.
Condemnation, 148.
" of Jesus, 184.
Confession of Peter, 100, 122.
" of sin, 26.
Conspiracy of the Jews, 140.
Corban, 88.
Corner stone, 140.
Corn plucking on the Sabbath, 45.
" yield of, 58.
Courts of Jews, 70, 136, 152, 188.
Covetousness, 89.
Crown of thorns, 194.
Cross, bearing the, 103, 104, 119.
Crosses, kinds of, 196.
Cup, the, 123, 172.
Custom, receipt of, 42, 141, 142.

D

Dalmanutha, 96.
Dance, the Oriental, 79.
Danger of riches, 120.
Daughter of Herodias, 79.
Dead raised, 70, 142, 144.
Deaf and Dumb, healing of, 93
Death of Jesus, intimations of, 102, 106, 111, 121.

INDEX.

Decapolis, 69, 93, 94.
Demoniacs cured, 33, 66.
" in Lebanon, 69.
Demosthenes, 59.
Denarius, 82, 141, 165.
Denial of Peter, 187.
Destruction of Jerusalem, 149, 154, 158.
Devils' recognition of Jesus, 34, 67.
Desert places, 36, 39, 81, 82.
Didymus, 52.
Disciples, call of, 30, 42, 50.
" secret, 128.
" ordained, 51.
Divorce, 115.
Dogs, 92.
Doubt, 135.
Dove, a, 28, 133.
Duty to magistrates, 142.

E

Æschylus, 59.
Eagles, Roman, 154.
Eating, traditions as to, 86.
Edom, 48.
Entry, triumphal, 126, 131.
Elders, the, 70, 87, 136.
Eleusis, 59.
Elisha's Fountain at Jericho, 124.
Elijah, 73, 102, 105, 107, 108.
Eloi, the cry of Jesus, 198.
Ephraim, 115.
Euripides, 72.
Evil, its depth and extent, 66.
Executioner sent to behead John, 80.

F

Fall of Jerusalem, 149, 154, 158.
False Christs, 157.
" witnesses, 182.
Faith, 30, 65, 109, 134.
Farthing, 148.
Fasts, 43.
Feast of unleavened bread, 161.
Fear of disciples, 65.
Fertility of Palestine, 59.
Figs, 132.
Fig tree withered, 133, 134, 158.
Final judgment, 158.
Fishes, 83.
Five thousand fed, 82.
Flight of Christians, 155.
Following Jesus, 37, 119, 126.
Forgiving sins, 39, 40.
Forgiveness, 135.
Four thousand fed, 94.

G

Gadara, 66.
Galilee, 30.
" Sea of, 30, 64, 84.
Gardens, Eastern, 130.
Garments, 44, 71, 76, 86, 125, 130, 147.
Gateway, Eastern, 120.
Gehenna, 113.
Gennesaret, 86.
Generation, 158.
Gergesa, 66.
Gersa, 68.
Gethsemane, 174.
God (Jehovah), 25, 143.
" (the Father), 28, 107, 175.
" of the Living, the, 143.
Golgotha, 195.
Gospel, beginning of, 25.

Gospel, meaning of, 25.
" preaching of, 153, 164.
Growth of the kingdom, 63, 111, 212.
Grain, yield of, 58.
Guest chamber, the, 167.

H

Hands, 87.
Hardness of heart, 47.
Hattin, Horns of, 51.
Healing the daughter of the Syrophœnician woman, 91.
Healing demoniacs, 33, 66.
" withered hand, 46.
Hedge, a, 137.
Hell, 113.
Hermon, Mount, 100, 101, 105.
Herod Antipas, 48, 50, 77, 81.
Herodians, the, 48, 98, 140, 141.
Herodias, 78.
High mountain, a, 104.
" Priest, the, 180.
Hinnom, 113.
Holy Ghost, 28.
Holy One of God, 34, 50.
Hospitality, 76.
Hospitals, 67.
Hosanna, 131.
Hunger of Jesus, 132.
Husbandmen, wicked, 137.
Housetop, 39, 40, 155.
Hymn sung after Lord's Supper, 168, 172.

I

Idumea, 48, 50.
Ignatius, the martyr, 112.

J

Jairus' daughter, cure of, 70.
James and John, request of, 122.
" 32, 51, 72, 104, 122, 151.
" the Less, 42, 51, 52, 200.
" and Joses, 74.
Jericho, 124.
Jerusalem, destruction of, 149, 150, 154, 158.
" its strength, 150.
" modern, 169.
Jesus—
Baptism of, 27.
Temptation of, 29.
Begins his ministry and calls four disciples, 30.
Boldness of, 53.
Cures demoniac at Capernaum, 33.
Cures Peter's wife's mother, 35.
Cures sick in Capernaum, 36.
Retires for solitary prayer, 36.
Cleanses a leper, 37.
Acknowledges the law, 38.
Heals the paralytic and forgives sins, 39.
Call of Matthew, 42.
At feast in his house, 42.
Answers John's disciples about fasting, 44.
Defends his disciples for plucking corn on Sabbath, 45.
Cures the withered hand, 47.
Calls the twelve, 50.
Mother and brothers, 56, 74.
Parable of the sower, 57.
" " seed, etc., 61.
Stilling the storm, 64.
The legion cast out, 66.
Restoration of Jairus' daughter, 70.
Cure of woman with issue of blood, 71.

INDEX. 217

Jesus—
  Rejection at Nazareth, 73.
  Feeds the five thousand, 81.
  Walks on the water, 84.
  Reproves Pharisees for their ceremonial cleanliness only, 87.
  Cures the daughter of the Syrophœnician woman, 90.
  Heals a deaf and dumb man, 93.
  Feeds four thousand, 94.
  Cures the blind man of Bethsaida, 99.
  Confession of Peter, 100, 122.
  His Transfiguration, 104.
  Heals the lunatic child, 108.
  Rebukes ambitious Apostles, 122.
  Answers the Pharisees on marriage and divorce, 115.
  Receives little children, 117.
  Tests the rich young ruler, 118.
  Teaches the danger of riches, 120.
  Heals Bartimeus, 124, 125, 126.
  Triumphal entry into Jerusalem, 126.
  Curses the fig tree, 132.
  Cleanses the temple, 133.
  His authority questioned, 136.
  The wicked husbandmen, 137.
  Answers Pharisees about tribute, 141.
  Answers Sadducees about the resurrection, 143.
  The question of the scribe, 144.
  Denounces the scribes, 147.
  The widow's mite, 148.
  Foretells destruction of Jerusalem, 149.
  Foretells his second coming, 157.
  His command to watch, 159.
  Anointed by Mary, 162.
  Judas conspires to betray him, 165.
  The Passover, 168.
  Foretells his betrayal, 170.
  Agony in the garden, 173.
  Betrayed and taken, 178.
  His trial before the high priests, 179.
  False witnesses accuse him, 183.
  His denial by Peter, 186.
  Before Pilate, 189.
  Clamor against, 192.
  Clothed with purple, 193.
  Crucified, 196.
  His words on the cross, 198.
  His burial, 202.
  His resurrection, 203.
  His appearances, 205, 207, 208.
  His ascension, 210.

J

Jewish mode of reckoning time, 126.
Jewish trial, the, 179.
John, 32, 51, 52, 72, 104, 122, 128, 151, 166.
John the Baptist, 26, 77.
  His clothing, etc., 26.
  The messenger, 25.
  His preaching, 26.
  Teaching respecting, 136.
  Imprisoned, 30.
  Death of, 78.
  Tomb of, 81.
Jordan, 27.
Joseph of Arimathæa secures Jesus' body, 202.
Judas Iscariot, 51, 53, 163.
  Conspires to betray Christ, 165.
  Betrays Christ, 178.
  Was he at the Lord's Supper?, 171.
Judas of Galilee, 141.
Judgment, final, 158.

K

Kedron, 149.
Kerza, 68.
Kind acts, 112, 164.
Kingdom of God, 30, 59, 104, 117, 131.
  "   growth of, 63, 111.

L

Lamb, the passover, 166.
Lamp, a, 60, 61.
Latchet, 27.
Lazarus, 72, 126.
Leaven of Pharisees, etc., 98.
Legality of the trial of Jesus, 185.
Legion, the, 67.
Leper, cleansing the, 37.
Leprosy, 37.
Long clothing, 147.
Loaves, 83.
Lord, 126.
Lord's Supper, the, 165.
Lunatic child, cure of, 108.

M

Machærus, 78, 79.
Magadan, 96.
Magdala, 96.
Maniac in Lebanon, 69.
Mariamne, 79.
Marriage legislation of Pharisees, 114.
Mary (Virgin Mary), 74.
  Sister of, 74.
  Of Bethany, 126, 162.
Mary Magdalene, 68, 126, 200.
  Appearance of Jesus to, 205.
Master, 72, 126, 141.
Matthew, 42, 51, 52.
Measures, 60, 87.
Merchandise in temple, 133.
Millstone, 112.
Miracles of Jesus—
  Bartimeus cured, 124, 125, 12
  Blind man cured, 99.
  Classified, 100.
  Extent of belief in Christ's miracles, 110.
  Deaf and dumb healed, 93.
  Demon cast out, 33.
  Five thousand fed, 82.
  Four thousand fed, 94.
  Differences between these two miracles, 96.
  Fig tree withered, 133, 134.
  Jairus' daughter restored, 70.
  Gennesaret, in, 86.
  Legion, the, cast out, 66.
  Leper cured, 37.
  Lunatic child cured, 108.
  Paralytic cured, 39.
  Peter's wife's mother cured, 35.
  Stilling the storm, 64.
  Syrophœnician woman's daughter cured, 91.
  Walking on the sea, 85.
  Withered hand cured, 47.
  Woman with issue of blood cured, 71.
Mission of the twelve, 75.
  Return from, 81.
Mites, 148.
Money, 76, 82, 133, 148, 164, 165.
Money changers, 133.
Mount Moriah, 131.
Molech, rites of, 113.
Moses, 43, 105, 116, 142
Mode of working in the East, 42.
Mother of Jesus, 50, 74.
Mount Sinai, Moses in, 43.

INDEX.

Mustard seed, 62.
" tree, 62.
Multitude, a, 48, 50, 94, 178.
Murder of John the Baptist, 77.
Mystery, 59.

N

Net, 32.
Naboth, 139.
Nazareth, 73.

O

Offering of a cleansed leper, 38.
Oil, anointing with, 77.
Ointment of spikenard, 163.
Olives, Mount of, 127, 130, 151.
Old Testament, citations from, 25, 88, 140, 143, 146, 154.
Ophrah, 115.
Origin of the Gospels, 7.

P

Palm Sunday, 126.
Parables, 57, 59, 61, 115, 137.
Parables of Jesus—
  Of the sower, 57.
  Seed and mustard seed, 61.
  Sower and tares, 62.
  Pounds, 126.
  The wicked husbandmen, 137.
Paralytic, the, cure of, 39.
Passion of Jesus, 102, 106, 111, 121.
Passover, the, 161, 166.
" mode of eating, 171.
" preparations for, 166, 167.
Patience, 153.
Paul, 77, 96.
Penny, 82, 141, 164.
Persons raised from dead, 70.
Persecution of disciples foretold, 152.
Peter, Simon, 30, 35, 39, 51, 72, 84, 86, 100, 104, 128, 134, 151, 166, 173.
Peter's denial foretold, 173.
Peter's wife's mother, cure of, 35.
Pharisees, the, 43, 47, 86, 97, 98, 114, 140.
" conspire against Jesus, 47.
Philip (the apostle), 51, 52, 82, 84.
Philip (the tetrarch), 78, 79.
Phœnicia, cities of, 48, 90.
Pilate, 189.
" yields to people's clamor, 192.
" scourges Jesus, 193.
Pillow, 64.
Pindar, 67.
Pitcher, water, 197.
Plucking ears of corn, 45.
Poor, the, 164.
Posture in prayer, 135.
Pots, 87.
Powers, 74.
Prayer, 36, 84, 94, 105, 110, 135, 155, 159, 174.
Preparations for the Passover, 167.
Prætorium, the, 193.
Priests, 134, 161, 165, 192.
Prince of Peace, the, 131.
Prophets, citations from, 25, 88, 154.
Psalms, citations from, 140, 146.
Publicans and sinners, 42.
Punishment of wicked, 113.

R

Receipt of custom, 42, 141, 142.
Rejected at Nazareth, 73.
" Capernaum, 97.
Remission of sins, 26, 172.
Repentance, 26, 30.

Resurrection, 142, 144.
Return of the twelve, 81.
Rich young ruler, the, 118.
Riches, 120.
Roof, 39, 40, 155.
Rooms, uppermost, 147, 167.
Roman legion, 67.
" triclinium, 42, 87, 147.
Rulers' consultations, 161.

S

Sabbath day, charged with breaking the, 45.
" the, 36, 45, 46, 156.
Sacrifices, burnt offering and, 145.
Sadducean belief, 77, 143.
Sadducees, the, 97, 98, 142.
" and the resurrection, 143.
Salome, 32, 51, 122.
" daughter of Herodias, 79.
Salted with fire, 113.
Sandals, 76.
Satan, 29, 37, 55, 69, 102.
Sanhedrin, the, 70, 136, 152, 160, 188.
Scribe, 33, 144, 147.
Scrip, 76.
Sea of Galilee, 30, 31, 84.
Seats, chief, 147.
Second coming of Jesus, 157.
Seed, the, 61.
Selection of Peter, James, and John, 72, 104.
Servants, 33.
" God's, their work, 63.
Shekel, 133.
Shekinah, the, 106.
Showbread, eaten by David, 45.
" table of, 45.
Ship, 32, 64, 84.
Sidon, 91, 93.
Sickle, the, 62.
Siege of Jerusalem, 155, 156.
Signs, 74, 97.
" of Christ's coming, 151.
Simon of Cyrene compelled to bear the cross, 194.
" the leper, 126, 162.
" feast of, 162.
" the Canaanean, 51, 53.
Sin, remission of, 55, 72, 90.
Sorrow, beginning of, 152.
Son of David, 125, 146.
" God, 25, 35, 50, 85, 105, 159.
" Man, 41, 46, 157.
Sorrow of Jesus, 174.
Soul, 103.
Sower, parable of the, 57.
" (*frontispiece*).
Spirit, The Holy, 28.
Spikenard ointment, 163.
Spread of the Gospel, 212.
Staff, 75.
Standards, Roman, 154.
Stilling the storm, 64.
Stone rolled away, 203.
Stony ground, 58.
Storm, stilling the, 64.
Supper, the institution of, 171.
Supremacy of Peter, 111.
Superscription, the, on the cross, 197.
Swine, 68.
Syria, division of, 91.
Synagogue, the, 31, 33, 70, 73.
Syrophœnician woman, 90.

T

Tables, 42, 87.

Tabor, Mount, 104.
Taxes, Roman, 42, 141, 142.
Tabernacles, 106.
Tax gatherers, 42.
Temple, the, 133, 150, **151**.
Temptation, the, 29.
Tetrarchs, 153.
Thaddeus, 51, 53.
Thieves crucified with **Jesus mock Him**, 198.
Thirty pieces of silver, 165.
Thomas, 51, 52.
Thorns of Palestine, 58.
Tiberius Cæsar, 142.
Time, 36, 45, 85, 126, **131**, 160, **161**, **168**, **173**.
Titus, 150, 156.
Tombs, 66.
Tophet, 113.
Tower, 138.
Traditions, 87, 88.
Transfiguration of Jesus, 104, 105.
Treasury, the, 148.
Trespasses, 135.
Trial before Pilate, 188, 190.
Tribunes, 79.
Tribute money, the, 140.
Triclinium, Roman, 42, 87, **147**, **168**.
Tr'umphant entry, 129, 131.
Troubles, 151, 152, 156.
True greatness, 111.
Types of Christ's death, 124.
Tyre, 48, 49, 91.

U
Upper room for passover, **167**.
Uppermost rooms, 147.

V
Vineyard, 129, 137.
Voice from heaven, 28, 106.

W
Wailing place of Jews, 150.
Walking on the sea, 84.
Washing hands, 87.
Watch (time), 85, 131, 168.
Watch, 160, 174.
Watchfulness enjoined, 159.
Weakness of disciples, 109.
Weariness of Jesus, 65.
Wickedness, 90.
Widow's mite, the, 148.
Wilderness, 25, 36, 39.
Will of God, 56.
Wind rebuked, 64.
Wine mingled with myrrh given to Christ, 195.
Wine press, 137.
" skins, 44.
Withered hand, healing the, 46.
Women at the sepulchre, 204.
Wonders, 74.
Works, mighty, 74.
Worship of Jesus, 67.

X
Xenophon, 37, 72.
Xerxes, 130.

Z
Zaccheus, 126.
Zealot, Simon, the, 51.
Zebedee, 32, 51.

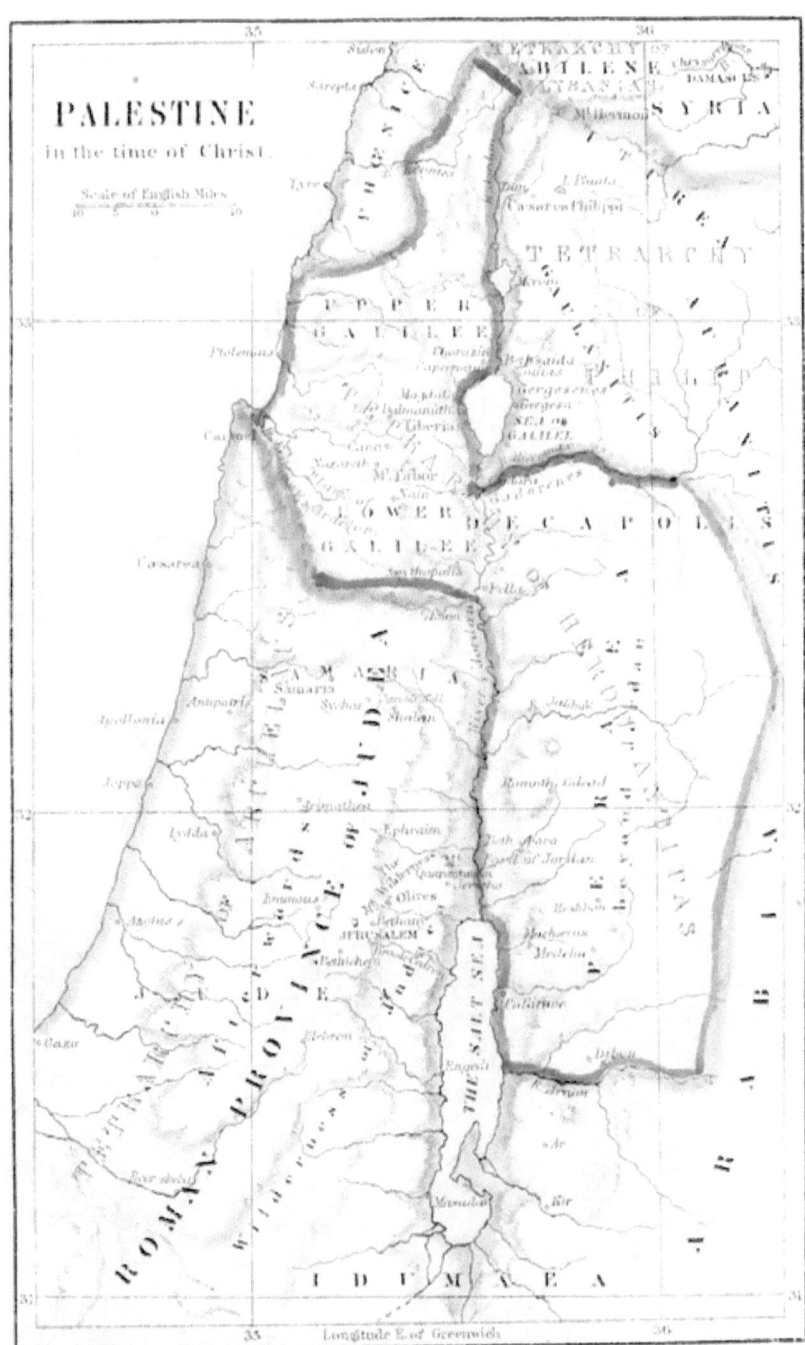

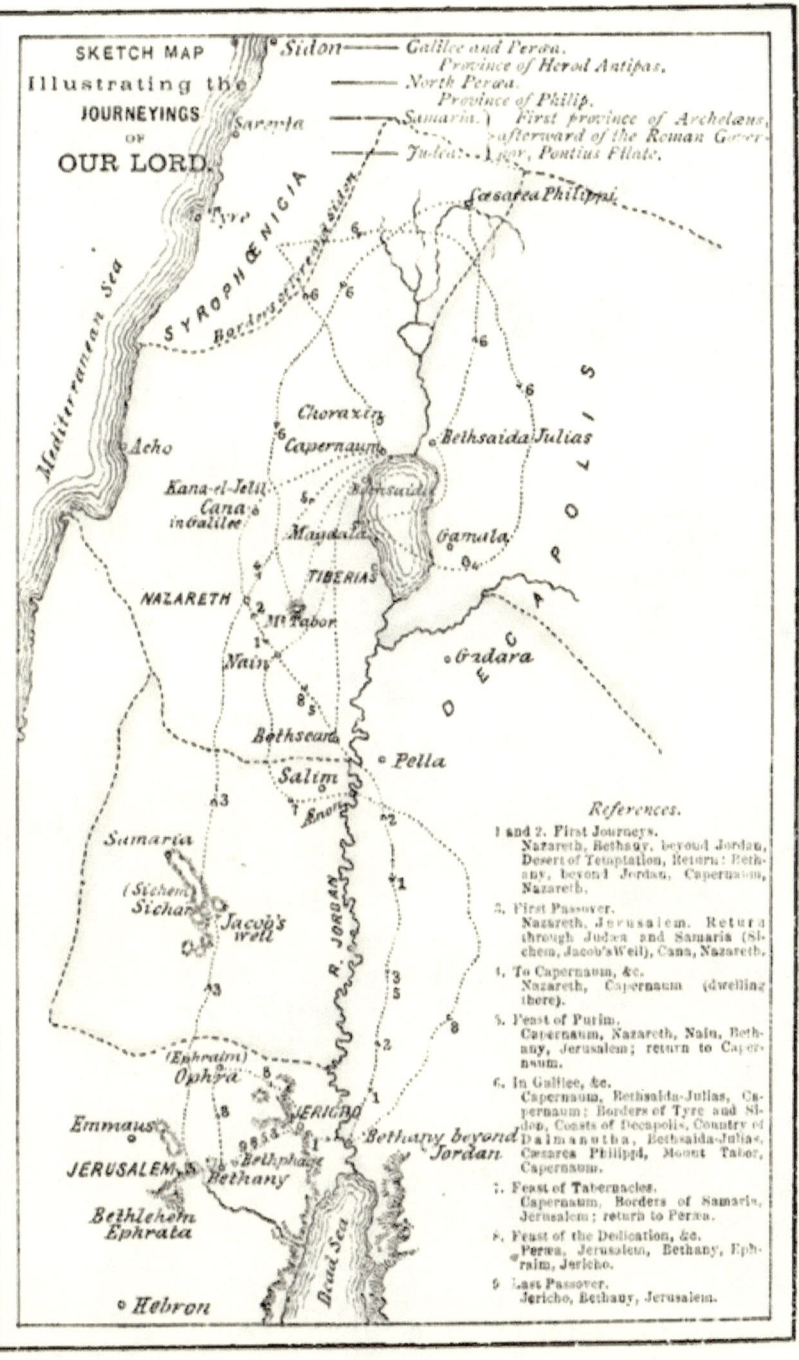

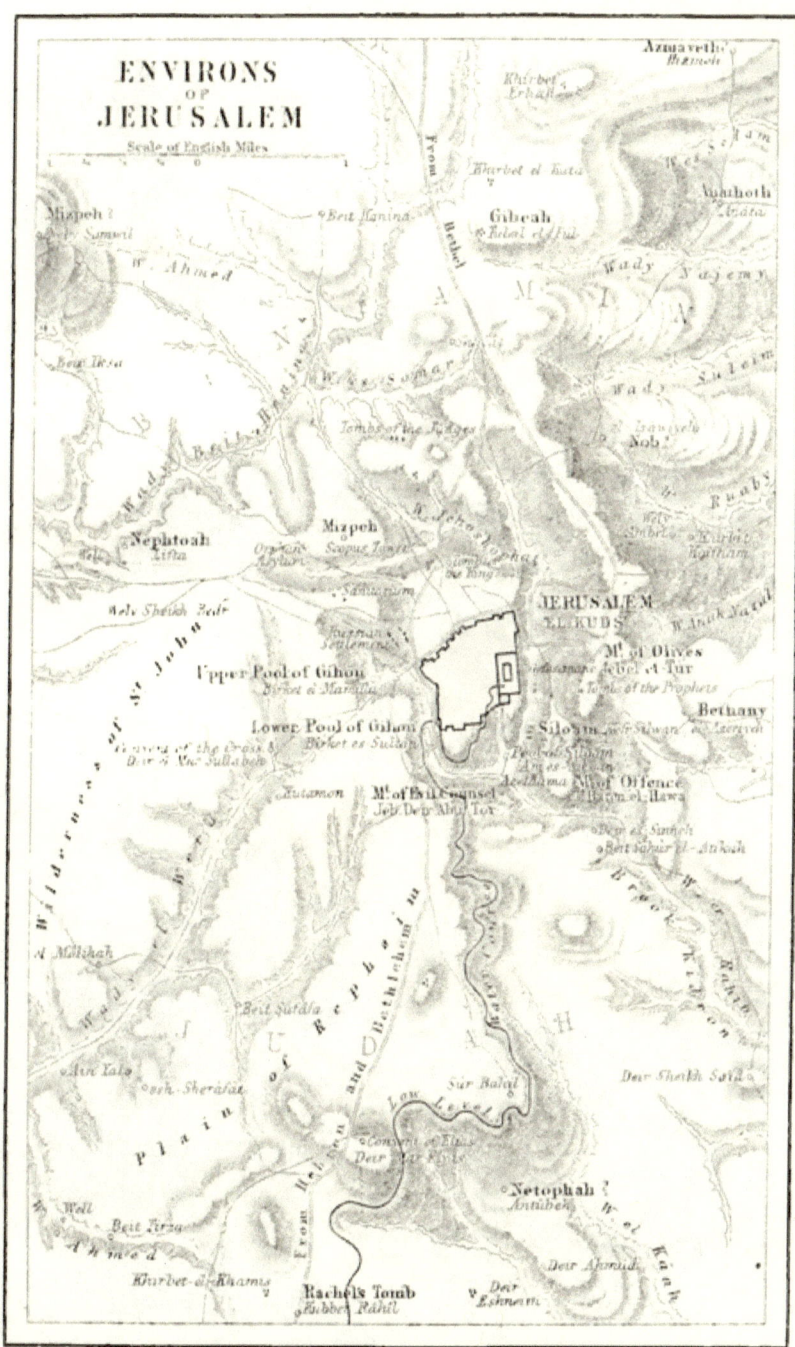

www.ingramcontent.com/pod-product-compliance
Lightning Source LLC
Chambersburg PA
CBHW021828230426
43669CB00008B/896